Believers Church
Bible Commentary

Douglas B. Miller and Loren L. Johns, Editors

BELIEVERS CHURCH BIBLE COMMENTARY

Old Testament
Genesis, by Eugene F. Roop, 1987
Exodus, by Waldemar Janzen, 2000
Judges, by Terry L. Brensinger, 1999
Ruth, Jonah, Esther, by Eugene F. Roop, 2002
Psalms, by James H. Waltner, 2006
Proverbs, by John W. Miller, 2004
Ecclesiastes, by Douglas B. Miller, 2010
Isaiah, by Ivan D. Friesen, 2009
Jeremiah, by Elmer A. Martens, 1986
Ezekiel, by Millard C. Lind, 1996
Daniel, by Paul M. Lederach, 1994
Hosea, Amos, by Allen R. Guenther, 1998

New Testament
Matthew, by Richard B. Gardner, 1991
Mark, by Timothy J. Geddert, 2001
Acts, by Chalmer E. Faw, 1993
Romans, by John E. Toews, 2004
2 Corinthians, by V. George Shillington, 1998
Ephesians, by Thomas R. Yoder Neufeld, 2002
Colossians, Philemon, by Ernest D. Martin, 1993
1-2 Thessalonians, by Jacob W. Elias, 1995
1-2 Timothy, Titus, by Paul M. Zehr, 2010
1-2 Peter, Jude, by Erland Waltner and J. Daryl Charles, 1999
1, 2, 3 John, by J. E. McDermond, 2011
Revelation, by John R. Yeatts, 2003

Old Testament Editors
Elmer A. Martens, Mennonite Brethren Biblical Seminary, Fresno, California
Douglas B. Miller, Tabor College, Hillsboro, Kansas

New Testament Editors
Willard M. Swartley, Associated Mennonite Biblical Seminary, Elkhart, Indiana
Loren L. Johns, Associated Mennonite Biblical Seminary, Elkhart, Indiana

Editorial Council
David W. Baker, Brethren Church
Derek Suderman, Mennonite Church Canada
Christina A. Bucher, Church of the Brethren
Eric A. Seibert, Brethren in Christ Church
Gordon H. Matties, Mennonite Brethren Church
Paul M. Zehr (chair), Mennonite Church USA

**Believers Church
Bible Commentary**

Epistles of
1, 2, 3 John

J. E. McDermond

HERALD PRESS
Harrisonburg, Virginia
Waterloo, Ontario

Library of Congress Cataloging-in-Publication Data
McDermond, J. E. (Jay E.), 1953-
  Epistles of 1, 2, 3 John / J.E. McDermond.
    p. cm. — (Believers church Bible commentary)
  Includes index.
  ISBN 978-0-8361-9555-2 (pbk. : alk. paper)
  1. Bible. N.T. Epistles of John—Commentaries. I. Title. II. Title: Epistles of
First, Second, Third John.
  BS2805.53.M39 2010
  227'.94077—dc22
                              2010054378

BELIEVERS CHURCH BIBLE COMMENTARY: 1, 2, 3 JOHN
Copyright © 2011 by Herald Press, Harrisonburg, VA 22802
     Released simultaneously in Canada by Herald Press,
        Waterloo, ON N2L 6H7. All rights reserved
Library of Congress Control Number: 2010054378
International Standard Book Number: 978-0-8361-9555-2
Printed in the United States of America
Cover by Merrill R. Miller

19 18 17 16 15 14 13 12 11   10 9 8 7 6 5 4 3 2 1

To order or request information, please call 1-800-245-7894 or visit
www.heraldpress.com.

To my family—Wanda, Malcolm and Duncan

Abbreviations

//	parallel reference
*	*see* TBC
+	*see* TLC
AD	*anno Domini*, in the year of the Lord, in the Christian era
AT	author's translation = literally
BC	before Christ, before the Christian era
c.	century
ca.	*circa,* approximately
CD	Cairo Genizah copy of the *Damascus Document*
cf.	*confer,* compare
d.	died
Did.	*Didache*
Ed.	Edited
Ed(s)	Editor(s)
e.g.	*exempli gratia*, for example
esp.	especially
hb	hardback
GNB	Good News Bible = Today's English Version
KJV	King James Version of the Bible
LXX	Septuagint, ancient Greek translation of the OT
mg.	a reading in margin or footnote
NASB	New American Standard Bible, 1995
NEB	New English Bible
NIV	New International Version of the Bible
NRSV	New Revised Standard Version of the Bible
NT	New Testament
OT	Old Testament
pb	paperback
1QH	*Hodayot*, or *Thanksgiving Hymns*, from Qumran Cave 1
1QpHab	*Pesher Habakkuk*, from Qumran Cave 1
1QS	*Serek Hayaḥad*, or *Rule of the Community*, from Qumran Cave 1
REB	Revised English Bible
RSV	Revised Standard Version of the Bible
TBC	Text in Biblical Context, in the commentary
TLC	Text in the Life of the Church, in the commentary
TNIV	Today's New International Version of the Bible
v./vv.	verse/verses
Weymouth	*The New Testament in Modern Speech*, R. F. Weymouth
x	times, such as a term appearing 2x (two times)

Pronunciation Guide for Certain Transliterated Hebrew Consonants

ʾ	(not pronounced)
ʿ	(not pronounced)
ḥ	ch (Scottish *loch*)
ṣ	ts
ś	s
š	sh
ṭ	t

Contents

Abbreviations and Pronunciation Guide 6
Series Foreword 13
Author's Preface 15

Introduction: 1–3 John 19
Relevance 19
Main Themes 21
    Christology 21
    Love 21
    Duality 22
Coherence and Rhetoric 23
Literary Form and Content 26
Historical Context and Date 28
Nature of the Secessionists' Christology (Bearing on Date) 31
Authorship 32

1 John

Introduction, 1:1-4
The Content of Our Proclamation, 1:1a-d 38
The Content of Our Writing, 1:1e-2 43
The Reason We Proclaim, 1:3 45
The Reason We Write, 1:4 46
* Connection to the Gospel of John 47
* Incarnation 48
* Fellowship 50
+ Incarnation as Foundation 51
+ Incarnation and Worldliness 52
+ Fellowship through Incarnation 54

Section 1: Knowing *and* Doing, 1:5–2:17 Overview 56

Our Claims and Reality, 1:5–2:2........................... 58
Theological Introduction, 1:5................................. 60
Claiming Fellowship, Walking in Darkness, 1:6-7 61
Claiming Sinlessness, Deceiving Ourselves, 1:8-9 65
Claiming Not to Have Sinned, Making Him a Liar, 1:10–2:2 69
* Sin 74
* Confession 79
+ A Balanced View of Sin 79

To Know Is to Obey, 2:3-11 82
Introduction of a General Principle, 2:3 83
A General Test of the Principle, 2:4-6 88
A Parenthetical Clarification on the Principle's Origin, 2:7-8 94
A Specific Test of the Principle, 2:9-11 96
* Knowing God 100
* Obedience 102
+ Christian Behavior 104

Why I Write to You, 2:12-14 108
Triplet One, 2:12-13 110
Triplet Two, 2:14 118
* Assurance 119
+ Confidence Before God 123

Do Not Love the World, 2:15-17........................... 126
An Exhortation and First Reason, 2:15 128
Behavior Revealing One's Orientation to the World, 2:16 130
A Second Reason for the Exhortation, 2:17 132
* The World 134
* Desire or Lust 136
+ The World and Desires: Materialism 138

Section 2: The Present Situation: Confidence Amid Conflict and Confusion, 2:18–3:24 Overview 141

The Last Hour and Confusion, 2:18-27 143
The Last Hour: Confusion and Schism, 2:18-20 144
Who Is the Liar? 2:21-25 149
Do Not Be Deceived: Be Confident, 2:26-27 153
* The "Last Hour" and Deception 155
* The Uniqueness of Jesus 158
+ Schism and Doctrinal Truth 160

Abiding and Doing Right, 2:28–3:10 165
General Comments 168
Little Children (Part One), 2:28–3:6 169
Little Children (Part Two), 3:7-10 172
* Two Forces at Work and Our Choice 174
* We Shall See God and Be Like God 176
+ Holiness 177

Illustration, Encouragement, and Transition, 3:11-24 180
General Comments 182
Introduction, 3:11 183
Illustrations of Hate and Love, 3:12-18 185
A Pastoral Parenthesis, 3:19-22 190
Summary and Transition, 3:23-24 193
* The Role of "Religion" 195
* Having and Helping 197
+ Imitating Christ 198

Section 3: The Work of the Spirit, 4:1–5:12 Overview 202

Belief and the Spirit, 4:1-6 203
Testing Spirits, 4:1-3 205
Words of Encouragement, 4:4-6 211
* Spiritual Influences 214
+ Christology 217
+ Discerning Spiritual Claims 219

Love and the Spirit, 4:7–5:4a 223
The Source and Purpose of Love, 4:7-11 225
Further Exploration and Implications of This Love, 4:12-19 227
Polemic Against the Separatists in Light of Love, 4:20–5:4a 231
* Theology, Experience, and Daily Living 234
+ The New Birth and Believers Churches 237

Testimony of the Spirit, 5:4b-12 241
A Rhetorical Question, Answer, and Testimonial Support,
   5:4b-8 243
The Result of Accepting or Rejecting the Testimony, 5:9-12 246
* Jesus' Victory on the Cross 248
+ *Christus Victor* in the Early Church 250

Concluding Words, 5:13-21 253
Believing in the Name, Having Eternal Life, 5:13 255

Confidence in Prayer in the Face of Sin, 5:14-17 256
Foundational Knowledge 5:18-20 258
Final Admonition, 5:21 261
* The Complexity of Sin 261
* Intercessory Prayer 264
+ Sin and Church Life 265

2 John

Greetings, 1-3 271
Body, 4-11 273
Rejoicing and Encouragement, 4-6 273
Directions Regarding Deceivers, 7-11 275
Closing, 12-13 277
* Hospitality 278
+ Hospitality and Divergent Views 280

3 John

Prescript, 1 287
Prayer and Author's Joy, 2-4 288
Body of the Letter, 5-12 288
Affirming Gaius's Support for Missionaries, 5-8 288
Criticizing Diotrephes' Refusal to Support Missionaries, 9-10 . . .290
Another Opportunity for Hospitality, 11-12 291
Closing, 13-15 292
* Imitation 292
+ Supporting Missionaries 293
+ Church Conflicts 294

Outline of 1, 2, 3 John 297
Essays 300
    "Abiding" in the Johannine Letters 300
    Apocalypticism 301
    Children of God / Born of God 302
    Docetism 304
    Duality in the Epistles 304
    Eschatology 306
    Gnosticism 308
    The Johannine Comma 309
    John's Cross Chronology 309
    Letters in the Ancient World 310
    Sin and Perfectionism 311

Map of the New Testament World 313
Bibliography 314
Selected Resources 323
Index of Ancient Sources 326
The Author 341

Series Foreword

The Believers Church Bible Commentary Series makes available a new tool for basic Bible study. It is published for all who seek more fully to understand the original message of Scripture and its meaning for today—Sunday school teachers, members of Bible study groups, students, pastors, and others. The series is based on the conviction that God is still speaking to all who will listen, and that the Holy Spirit makes the Word a living and authoritative guide for all who want to know and do God's will.

The desire to help as wide a range of readers as possible has determined the approach of the writers. Since no blocks of biblical text are provided, readers may continue to use the translation with which they are most familiar. The writers of the series use the *New Revised Standard Version* and the *New International Version* on a comparative basis. They indicate which text they follow most closely and where they make their own translations. The writers have not worked alone, but in consultation with select counselors, the series' editors, and the Editorial Council.

Every volume illuminates the Scriptures; provides necessary theological, sociological, and ethical meanings; and in general makes "the rough places plain." Critical issues are not avoided, but neither are they moved into the foreground as debates among scholars. Each section offers explanatory notes, followed by focused articles, "The Text in Biblical Context" and "The Text in the Life of the Church." This commentary aids the interpretive process but does not try to supersede the authority of the Word and Spirit as discerned in the gathered church.

The term *believers church* has often been used in the history of the church. Since the sixteenth century, it has frequently been applied to the Anabaptists and later the Mennonites, as well as to

13

the Church of the Brethren and similar groups. As a descriptive term, it includes more than Mennonites and Brethren. *Believers church* now represents specific theological understandings, such as believers baptism, commitment to the Rule of Christ in Matthew 18:15-20 as crucial for church membership, belief in the power of love in all relationships, and willingness to follow Christ in the way of the cross. The writers chosen for the series stand in this tradition.

Believers church people have always been known for their emphasis on obedience to the simple meaning of Scripture. Because of this, they do not have a long history of deep historical-critical biblical scholarship. This series attempts to be faithful to the Scriptures while also taking archaeology and current biblical studies seriously. Doing this means that at many points the writers will not differ greatly from interpretations that can be found in many other good commentaries. Yet these writers share basic convictions about Christ, the church and its mission, God and history, human nature, the Christian life, and other doctrines. These presuppositions do shape a writer's interpretation of Scripture. Thus this series, like all other commentaries, stands within a specific historical church tradition.

Many in this stream of the church have expressed a need for help in Bible study. This is justification enough to produce the Believers Church Bible Commentary. Nevertheless, the Holy Spirit is not bound to any tradition. May this series be an instrument in breaking down walls between Christians in North America and around the world, bringing new joy in obedience through a fuller understanding of the Word.

—*The Editorial Council*

Author's Preface

These Three Enigmatic Little Letters

For a number of years I taught a course titled "Johannine Literature" (a colleague teaches Revelation; see Yeatts, BCBC, 2003) in which we were to study the Gospel of John and 1–3 John. Now that I have tenure, I will admit we rarely covered 1 John and we ignored 2 and 3 John completely. I argued the Gospel is so rich and deep that it deserves an entire semester itself. My unstated assumption was the letters lacked depth. In fact, they were confusing, especially 1 John with its nonlinear argument and repeating themes. Second John seemed to be a boiled-down version of 1 John. As a child I had been caught reading a neighbor's erroneously delivered postcard, and I still recall my mother's strong rebuke: "Never read another person's mail." Third John is clearly another person's mail.

Having spent the past decade with John's epistles, my attitude has shifted significantly. First John makes it clear that what we think of Jesus impacts the way we live or how we are supposed to live. That way of living is to have love as its core. Basic theology and ethics are related. More than that, they are inextricably intertwined. Although my theological convictions are Anabaptist and Pietist, I worship well in a liturgical setting. Every Sunday our liturgical brothers and sisters take seriously the encouragement to confess their sins and accept the assurance of forgiveness found in 1 John 1:8-9. My main ministry at my home congregation is to lock up the building five nights a week. Each night I am reminded of 1 John's value as I enter the kindergarten classroom to check the external door. Plastered there on the wall beside the door, in foot-high colorful letters, are the words "God is love" (1 John 4:8, 16). That is an excellent foundational theological statement. We do well to remember it. Finally, after reading and rereading these three documents, I am amazed at the pressure the author and his readers faced. The existence of their community is at risk. In this context the author responds intensely, sometimes a little too intensely, but always keeping in mind the church's teaching about the marvelous work of God in Jesus Christ. I now realize I had shortchanged these enigmatic little letters.

I am convinced that no one achieves goals alone. This volume certainly stands as supporting evidence for this conviction. My employer, Messiah College, contributed to the completion of the text by granting me a sabbatical leave for the 2001–2002 academic year. This sabbatical was followed by a teaching load reduction in 2007–2009, when I held the Hostetter Chair of Religious Studies. During the sabbatical year my family and I lived in Clydebank, Scotland. We were blessed beyond words by the members of the Clydebank Central Church, where I served as the part-time pastor and worked on the commentary.

In addition to the very helpful comments made by the members of the Editorial Council, five individuals kindly agreed to take time from their busy schedules to read the draft. David Rensberger, professor of New Testament at the Interdenominational Theological Center, scrutinized the text with a keen academic eye. Emmanuel Bellon, vice chancellor at Nairobi International School of Theology, offered an international perspective on the content. Jay Forth, my former work-study assistant and colleague during the 2009–2010 academic year, raised important questions and offered new leads. Richard Morrison, close friend, lawyer, and college English major, did what lawyers and English majors do, and the text is better for it. Pauline Allison Peifer, associate pastor at the Grantham Church, my home congregation, read the volume with a pastoral eye. Thanks also to Jamie Gardner for the good mug shot heading my bio on page 341. All these individuals made this commentary a better work; but a very special thank you goes to Willard M. Swartley, the editor. Willard patiently encouraged me as I slowly balanced teaching, writing, and family life. He offered excellent feedback and provided new sources I had not considered. I suppose that is what editors do, but Willard did it extremely well, and I am thankful we worked together on this project.

Finally, I will stumble toward expressing my love for the people to whom this volume is dedicated: my family. I want to thank Malcolm and Duncan for simply being who they are. They are sources of both joy and pride. In terms of people I know and love, they are tied for second, and a sign of my deep affection for them is the fact that no swim meets were missed for this commentary. The harsh reality, however, is they are runners up because their mom, Wanda, has them beat by miles. She has been and continues to be both a blessing and a gentle prod, encouraging me, mostly by her example, to be a better human being and disciple of Jesus Christ. She may not understand the Greek behind the Johannine epistles or the complexities of the author's thinking, but she certainly embodies the Johannine tradition's witness to the Gospel. And that is crucial.

A Special Tribute

In the fall of 1973 no one would have described me as a serious student. It was my third semester of college, and I was closer to the registrar's academic probation list than the Dean's List. At that time Messiah College offered creative and engaging courses during the three-week January term. A course titled "The Nature of the Holy Life" caught my attention, mainly because it was a road trip to three different seminaries. I did not expect an academic course to be a life-altering event.

Nevertheless, the week we spent at Associated Mennonite Biblical Seminaries (Elkhart, Indiana) had a profound impact upon my unfocused life. As I reflect on that week, one person in particular stands out: Gertrude Roten. We spent the afternoons with her as she lectured on 1 John's theology and ethics. She clearly loved the biblical text and what she was doing. I was a religion major at the time, but I had never had a course taught by someone like Gertrude. She was a biblical scholar. I found her mesmerizing.

By the end of the week I knew I was going to seminary, and AMBS was the seminary. My work was cut out for me because the average grade required for admission was a "B." Upon returning to Messiah, I changed my major to Bible and started to take my studies seriously. In a real sense Gertrude Roten was a positive influence on my college career even though we spent only one week together.

Over the next five semesters my GPA steadily improved, and in August 1976 I officially registered as an AMBS student. I have a fairly clear recollection of that first semester, but my first January term is what stands out. I cannot recall the course options from which I had to choose because there was only one class I wanted to take. It was a Greek Readings course based on 1 John taught by Gertrude Roten. My reasoning was simple: If her one-week class was so engaging three years before, this three-week course would be three times as enthralling. Gertrude did not disappoint. Her workload was heavy, and I worked hard because I wanted to learn as much as I could. Moreover, I did not want to disappoint Gertrude. Her knowledge of the Greek, her insights on the letter's theology, and her gracious handling of students and their ideas made me want to give her my best. I can honestly say it was a highlight of my seminary career.

As I began working on this commentary, the Editorial Council gave me an early draft of Gertrude's work on 1–3 John. I was encouraged to make good use of it. Although she is not extensively cited, her thoughts and ideas on these letters appear regularly in the text. How could they not? After all, *we* studied it "together" for years.

The text you are about to read owes much to Gertrude Roten, as do I.

Introduction to 1–3 John

Relevance

Although not formally trained as a historian, I thoroughly enjoy history. My family will tell you that I have invested more time in the History Channel than is perhaps warranted. Often I find myself asking such questions as these: "What were civilians doing and experiencing during World War II? What was it like to be poor and living in Victorian London? Why did John Wesley and the early Methodists face such opposition from the English in general and the Church of England leadership in particular?"

I admit that the further back my attention attempts to focus, the more difficult the task. Thus, when I or anyone else thinks about the first century AD, I am keenly aware of a significant gap between my world and that world. The problem is that the first-century Christians' lives, thoughts, and experiences are important for believers today. After all, they too were human beings attempting to live faithfully in their own complex and pluralistic societies. Then as now, it is not always easy to know exactly how to live faithfully. Among other things, those early Christians can be our role models.

Readers of this volume who are heirs of the sixteenth-century Anabaptist movement may have inherited an idealized view of the NT church. As John H. Yoder and Alan Kreider have observed, our spiritual ancestors "were not interested in simply reforming the church; they were committed to restoring it to the vigor and faithfulness of its earliest centuries" (via Dowley: 401). Some of us may confuse "vigor" and "faithfulness" with "perfection" and thus assume a flawless period when the people of God perfectly submitted to the lordship of Christ. Yet a close reading of the NT reveals a different picture. The Galatians vacillated on the issue of salvation (Gal 1:6-10; 3:1-5;

4:8-20). The Philippians, although loved by Paul, did not always seem to love each other (Phil 1:27–2:18). And the Corinthians had both internal conflicts and moral failures (1 Cor 1:10-17; 3:1-23; 5:1-13; 6:1-20). From the beginning, the Christian church has wrestled with human frailty despite its vigor and laudable attempts at faithfulness. In this respect the letters of John also reflect a church in turmoil. There are doctrinal disputes about the inherited tradition. These disputes are so intense that the church has experienced a schism. Sometimes love as the way of interacting with other believers has been abandoned, leaders are ignored and even opposed, and there is confusion regarding who and what is "correct."

Sadly for some contemporary readers, their congregations may have "restored" the negative elements of the earliest church. Too many people have either experienced or heard horror stories of congregations in the midst of serious conflict. Some of these conflicts have resulted in church splits. I further suspect that the inherited tradition was the focus of many of these conflicts. Many congregations and denominations are asking important questions about social relevance on the one hand and faithfulness to the traditions on the other. For example, many good congregations in North America have been harmed or even divided over issues relating to musical styles in their worship services. Other congregations cannot agree on what facilities to have as they seek to minister faithfully. And what is a church to do and think in the midst of shifting moral convictions?

Change is difficult. When facing significant change, there is a real possibility that our behavior will change before our thinking does. By this I mean that we may be tempted to forget to love those with whom we disagree. We may gossip and snipe about those on the other side. In these situations it is not easy to be a congregational or denominational leader.

The letters of 1–3 John are valuable to the contemporary church. The author reminds us of the nonnegotiable centrality of following Jesus' commandment to love one another, even if he may not have embodied that love perfectly. In this respect, he reminds us to avoid the temptation to resort to name-calling in tense situations, even if his behavior as writer is a negative reminder. At the same time, he knows there are theological issues and times when a church must draw a line in the sand and not go beyond it. In these situations he reminds us of the importance of discernment and relying on the leading of the Holy Spirit. He humbles us when he reminds us we cannot deny the power of sin in our lives, and he reassures us we are still children of God when sin is evident. Ultimately he sets out the fundamentals of the faith for us when he writes, *And this is his commandment, that we should believe in the name of his Son Jesus Christ and love one another* (1 John 3:23).

Main Themes

Although these three documents are relatively brief, their theological breadth is significant. Perhaps what impresses readers most is 1 John's meandering approach: scholars identify at least a dozen theological themes touched upon in these letters. These include discernment, images of God, sin and salvation, ecclesiology, assurance, eschatology, the relationship between tradition and the Spirit, eternal life, the world, abiding, truth, and hospitality. A number of these "secondary" topics will be addressed in the sections titled The Text in Biblical Context (TBC, marked in Contents as *) and The Text in the Life of the Church (TLC, marked in Contents as +). In this introduction we will explore three fundamental themes: Christology, love, and duality.

Christology

Rensenberger (36) writes, "The confession of Jesus as the divine Christ and Son of God who has come in the flesh is central to the epistles (1 John 2:22-23; 3:23–4:3; 5:1, 5-13; 2 John 3, 7, 9)." Given the particular context John faces, he asserts that Jesus is God's messianic agent (1 John 4:15; 5:1) and this role fully involved the "human Jesus" (5:6; 4:2; 2 John 7), a theme John passes on from the tradition going back to *the beginning* (1 John 1:1-4). As God's divine agent, Jesus Christ reveals God's basic nature as love (4:7-10, 14-16) and shows who is the true God and source of eternal life (5:20). Specifically, this divine revelation through Jesus of Nazareth enables a divine/human relationship, especially through his death on the cross (1:7, 9; 2:1-2; cf. 5:6-8), which is an *atoning sacrifice for our sins* (2:2). Additionally, Jesus is our *advocate* or intercessor before God (2:1). Anyone who places her or his faith and trust in him lives through him (4:9; 5:10-13, 20). Moreover, they pass from the realm of death to that of life (3:14) through faith (2:23-25; 4:9, 13-14; cf. 5:5, 9-12).

Love

Inextricably intertwined with John's christological agenda is his emphasis on love. These two themes are bound together at key places in John's first letter: 3:23 and 4:7-18. Because the human Jesus revealed God as essentially a loving being (4:9-10), John logically concludes that we *also ought to love one another* (4:11). In fact, John's first agenda in 1 John is to explore human sinfulness (1:5–2:2) and then explain how the teachings of Jesus, especially the love commandment, reorder our lives with a love for God and not the world (2:3-11; 2:12-14; 2:15-17). While correct christological confession and practiced love (3:18) are *the* two sound tests for identifying God's children (5:1), love is a vital test for various aspects of the Christian life (Rensberger: 37). It is a test of whether one knows God (2:3-6; 4:7-8, 12, 16). To paraphrase John's view: "Love for one another is evidence we *walk in the light* (1 John 2:9-11). We know we are God's children if we love (1 John 3:10; 4:7)." A person whose life has been reordered by love in the present will have confidence on the day of judgment (4:17-18). Our author refuses to accept the notion that a person can love God while at the same time refusing to love a brother or sister in the faith (4:20). In fact, anyone claiming the former while refusing to do the later is a liar (2:3-11).

Duality

While the author of these documents does not directly say so, there is little doubt that his basic worldview is dualist in an apocalyptic and ethical sense. Scholars like Judith Lieu note that John's perspective is fundamentally "characterized by a dualism between light and darkness, truth and falsehood, life and death, love and hatred, . . . the (or this) world against that which is "not of the 'world' " (2008: 18). John's world and experience are easily and simply divided into two distinct camps. There is God, Jesus (God's agent), the Spirit, and the children of God—and there is the camp that opposes God. Those opponents include the devil and his children (1 John 3:8), the antichrist(s) (2:18, 22; 4:3; 2 John 7), the spirit of the antichrist (1 John 4:3), and the world that has come under the evil one's influence. In John's mind it is easy to determine where a person's allegiances lie. One's actions speak volumes, as 1 John 3:10 shows: *The children of God and the children of the devil are revealed in this way: all who do not do what is right are not from God, nor are those who do not love their brothers and sisters.*

Although it is common for scholars expounding John's Gospel and epistles to use the word "dualism," in this commentary I will use "duality" since John's theology is not ontologically and cosmologically dualist: it does not claim that God and the devil have equal power (instead, God will win! [1 John 3:2, 5, 8]), or that the spirit world is good and the material world is evil (Platonic dualism; instead, *Christ has come in the flesh* [4:2]). However, John's duality is more pervasive than simply an assumed worldview. John makes his argument by giving his readers two crucial options: they can either love or not love, and they can either adhere to a "right" or "wrong" view of Christ. I try to provide visual clues to this thematic approach in the commentary by setting out the biblical text in "competing" columns at those points where duality is present. This duality is established in the very first argumentative unit, 1 John 1:5–2:2. There John makes a case for believers to be living in a way consistent with their words and actions. Verse 6 begins with *If we say . . .* and this is then countered by *but if we . . .* in verse 7. The opening words in verse 8 are *If we say . . .* and they are countered by *If we . . .* in verse 9. Finally, verse 10 begins with *If we say . . .* and this idea is countered in 2:1b with *But if anyone. . . .* For a fuller depiction of this duality, see Preview for 1 John 1:5–2:2. Further exploration of this theme is in the essay "Duality in the Epistles."

Coherence and Rhetoric

One apparent issue is 1 John's structure and writing style, both of which are often confusing. This is particularly true of the structure. David Rensberger (31) speaks for many: "The structure of 1 John is every bit as hard to specify as its genre. . . . Some parts of it seem carefully designed, for example 1:5–2:11, and the way that 3:23-24 introduces 4:1-18. Yet there is no obvious overall outline, and efforts to find a tight structure generally prove artificial and unconvincing." Some scholars fall back on the image of a spiral to explain the structure (Houlden: 22-24; Jackman: 18). Others, following an initial suggestion by von Dobschütz (1-8), have tried to explain the lack of structure by speculating about the author's use of existing texts and sources. For example, Bultmann (1927: 138-58) argues that the author cobbled together pre-Christian Gnostic documents, and J. C. O'Neill (6) points to Jewish sectarian poetic admonitions reworked by our author. Not many scholars accept Bultmann's suggestions, and even fewer find O'Neill convincing.

While we may never get a firm grip on the first letter's structure, Colin Kruse, relying on Duane Watson's initial idea (1993: 100-118), puts forth an interesting explanation that the document is an example of epideictic rhetoric. This type of rhetoric is primarily designed "to increase their [the readers'] adherence to the traditional truths of the community" (Kruse: 29; see 29-31 for Kruse's entire explanation). There are five elements of ancient epideictic rhetoric: (1) attempts to increase already-held convictions regarding honorable values, (2) the main stress on the present time and actions, (3) blame and praise employed to increase the readers' convictions, (4) prescription of the best course of action, and (5) use of amplification rather than logical proof. This final point would explain the author's tendency to repeat his points because amplification essentially consists of repetition instead of a linear and logical argumentation. Kruse's closing thoughts are instructive: "The upshot of all this is that we should read 1 John, not trying to discern the flow of the argument as we would in a Pauline letter. . . . It does not seek to prove anything; on the contrary, it seeks to increase the readers' adherence to traditional truths of the Christian community in the face of the threat posed by the secessionists' doctrine and ethics" (31).

When we change our focus to the letter's writing style, we move from one baffling matter to another. Even eminent scholars like Raymond Brown, in his comments on "walking in truth" (3 John 4), takes this puzzling Greek phrase to be a sign of common authorship of the three letters. Not hiding his frustration with the letters' often confusing writing style, Brown comments: "If the authors are not thought to be the same, at least one must admit that they have similar pastoral roles vis-à-vis their addressees. And as becomes apparent in vv. 5-6, they have much the same vocabulary and lack of concern about syntax" (1982: 683n11). It is not uncommon for scholars to admit that the wording of the Johannine letters is obscure at places. Often a range of possible meanings are offered, and their relative merits are weighed.

How do we account for a conclusion such as "his style is far removed from that usual in Greek or Hellenistic literature" (Schnackenburg 1992: 8) and bordering on the "deficient and somewhat simplistic" (9)? Schnackenburg sees evidence of "Semitisms," with the author using Greek but having underlying thought patterns that are more Hebraic in nature. For example, John uses the Greek word for *and* (*kai*) as Hebrew speakers use the more versatile Hebrew word *wĕ* to express a variety of conjunctions. Participles become substantives and personal pronouns are often placed beside verbs. Additionally, he uses expressions known to be used by rabbis, such as *do the truth* (1 John 1:6, cf. KJV), *believe in the name* (3:23), and *shut up his bowels* (3:17, cf. KJV; *refuses help*, NRSV). Schnackenburg attributes the problematic syntax to "an author of Jewish birth, with Aramaic as his mother tongue, who has acquired flawless Koine Greek but has otherwise retained a Semitic feel for language" (1992: 9). While Schnackenburg may be overconfident with regard to details, we can at least conclude that our author's first language was probably Hebrew or Aramaic and not Greek, which he used to write these letters.

Although some of John's wording may be obscure, his views on love and who is to be the object of that love are crystal clear. They are also challenging for many contemporary readers. On the one hand, we are reading documents that strike us as both simple and profound, as in 1 John 4:8: *Whoever does not love does not know God, for God is love.* We appreciate the author's view that genuine Christian love is more than emotion. It involves tangible actions in the real world, as seen in 3:18: *Little children, let us love, not in word or speech, but in truth and action* (cf. 3:10, 16-17; 4:20-21; 2 John 5-6). People in believers church traditions are inspired by and resonate with John's conviction that God and Jesus' love are models to be imitated (1 John 3:1-3, 16; 4:10-12).

Yet when we read the letters closely, we realize there is another, less appealing side to John's love. This love is primarily, if not exclusively, to be expressed to those who "belong" to the community of faith that faithfully holds to the tradition passed down as expressed in the opening four verses. Believers are repeatedly encouraged to *love one another* (1 John 3:14, 23; 4:7, 12, 19; 5:2). The *world*, however, is beyond the community of faith and is not to receive love from the faithful (2:15). Even harsher words are reserved for the secessionists who have left the church and gone out into the world (2:19; 2 John 7). They deceive themselves regarding sin (1 John 2:8) and make Jesus a liar in their denials that they have sinned (2:10). In fact, John says they are (the) liars (2:4, 22). They are blind and in darkness, as is evidenced by their refusal to love fellow community members (2:11). Additionally, they are described as deceivers (2 John 7) and antichrists (1 John 2:18, 22; 2 John 7; cf. 1 John 4:3). Finally, they are nothing more than *children of the devil* (3:8, 10). While the content of the letters clearly contains theological reflection and conviction, we need to keep in mind that John also employs widely accepted ancient rhetorical forms in his attempt to delineate the two sides in this conflict. These forms were often harsh (see the "antitheses" in 1:6–2:1 and 2:4-11) and relied on generalizations (see 2:23, 29; 3:3-10 and 15; cf. Rensberger: 31).

Many, including myself, believe it is essentially unwise to depict anyone and everyone outside the church in such a strident fashion. At this level, the author's views thus differ from our contemporary convictions. We must, however, seek to understand a key factor that contributed to his attitude: persecution. There is reliable evidence that from near the church's beginning, the followers of the Johannine tradition faced conflict and persecution. The Gospel of John is, in one respect, a dialogue with Judaism regarding the "true" nature of Judaism. Obviously John advocated a form of messianic Judaism where Jesus is central to Jewish self-understanding. His viewpoint, however, was not accepted by most Jews, as is evidenced by John 9:22; 12:42; and 16:2. In fact, many scholars view John 9 as a story reflecting the intense struggles between the early Jewish Christians and Pharisaical Judaism for control of Judaism after the fall of Jerusalem in AD 70. Ultimately the "Christian" minority within Judaism was searched out and expelled from the synagogues.

Having experienced that initial conflict and loss, the bearers of the Johannine tradition face a second theological conflict from within. It is possible, or perhaps probable, that those who remained faithful to the tradition were in the minority. One can certainly read 1 John in such a way as to conclude that those who left were less than gracious and loving in their interactions with the followers of the traditional view. While the author's strident polemic may not be advisable for the modern readers' approach to those outside the faith or those claiming to be "inside" while holding to ideas that depart from the mainstream, the modern reader is well advised to be understanding of John's context.

Literary Form and Content

Most scholars see these documents as forming a distinctive group within the NT letters. They share a similar form, and this is especially true of 2 and 3 John. As David Rensberger (17) argues, they have overlapping features, such as literary style and vocabulary. These features are also shared with the Gospel of John. That is not to say they are identical; they are not, and even a cursory reading reveals this. The most notable difference is the form; 1 John differs from 2 and 3 John. Since it is significantly easier to identify the literary form of 2 and 3 John, we begin there.

Third John is clearly a private letter written by an anonymous sender, the elder, to the recipient, Gaius. It generally conforms to the model of letters in the ancient world. The opening salutation identifies the sender and is followed by positive affirming words and a "health wish" for the receiver. After the letter's body, it closes with a fairly traditional final greeting. The one exception is peace to you (v. 15), which is often found at the beginning of an ancient letter. The content both affirms Gaius for the hospitality he has extended to strangers, probably traveling missionaries, and criticizes Diotrephes, who refuses to welcome strangers, challenges the writer's authority, and engages in self-promotion. The letter also serves as an introduction and voucher for Demetrius, who probably was the bearer of the letter and may have been a traveling missionary.

Second John is also an ancient letter, but it is not a private document. *The elder* has sent what might be described as an "open letter" to *the elect lady and her children*. The second Johannine epistle is designed to be read to a corporate body, probably a congregation or group of "house churches" in a given area. Like many other NT letters, the opening is followed by a section affirming basic Christian theological points that replace the "health wish" of secular ancient letters. The body begins with an affirmation and then touches upon a number of themes addressed in 1 John. These topics include the love commandment, walking according to the commandments, the deceivers who refuse to confess Jesus Christ as having come in the flesh, encouragement to be on one's guard against these people, and the importance of *abiding* in Christ. The thematic overlap between this letter and 1 John is so clear that some scholars view it as a summary of 1 John. Finally, the readers are firmly directed not to receive anyone who does not follow the accepted teachings. The letter closes in a way similar to 3 John.

First John, on the other hand, clearly is not a letter; at least it does not follow the ancient letter form as do 2 and 3 John. There is no formulaic opening or closing. There is no "health wish," either secular or Christianized. The document begins and ends abruptly. Some scholars, such as Robert Kysar, believe 1 John "lack[s] clear order and structure" (1986a: 16). Thus, he concludes, 1 John is an "anthology of bits of sermons patched together" (16). Others have labeled 1 John a homily, tract, or essay. One clear fact is the document's pastoral tone, which it shares with 2 and 3 John. Equally unmistakable is the polemical nature of the writing. Thus Rensberger (31) rightly notes the "letter" incorporates elements of epideictic rhetoric. As accurate as that observation is, one should point out that Kysar's observation regarding order and structure is equally valid. Therefore, we should not conclude the author was formally trained in rhetoric; yet he was trying to make a rhetorical impact upon his readers' lives. First John is probably best viewed as a rhetorical document that repeatedly addresses a few key themes.

In addition to the shared themes noted in 2 John, we see 1 John begins with a strong affirmation of the reliable tradition that has been handed down from the beginning (1:1-4). This is immediately followed by an argument about believers, sin, and forgiveness (1:5–2:2) and an extended pastoral purpose statement (2:12-14). The readers are warned to not love the world, and to be alert to the *last hour* (2:18) and the coming of *antichrists* who have left the church, but apparently once were fellow believers (2:18-27). These secessionists are evidently disseminating teachings that run counter to the Johannine tradition, and John seeks to encourage his readers that they, not the secessionists, are the genuine children of God because they do what is right and abide in him (2:28–3:10). More specifically, they embody the message that was from the beginning: love one another (3:11-24). In the midst of conflicting doctrine and ethics, John encourages his readers to rely on the Spirit as they *test the spirits* (4:1-6). The closing sections of the document reemphasize the importance of both love (4:7–5:4a) and sound Christology (5:4b-12). However, the alternating address of ethical (love) and theological (Christology) concerns is not limited to the end of the letter. Charles Talbert (7) suggests the following outline:

THE PROCLAMATION (1:1-5)
THE EXPOSITION (1:6–5:13)
A Ethical (1:6–2:17)
B Christological (2:18-28)
A' Ethical (2:29–3:24a)
    B' Christological (3:24b–4:6)
A" Ethical (4:7-12)
    B" Christological (4:13-16a)
A''' Ethical (4:16b–5:4a)
    B''' Christological (5:4b-12)
THE STATEMENT OF PURPOSE (5:13)
POSTSCRIPT (5:14-21)

Historical Context and Date

There is near unanimous agreement on the historical context giving rise to at least 1 and 2 John. The congregations under the writer's pastoral care have been badly shaken by a schism, as evidenced by 1 John 2:19; 4:1; and 2 John 7. These repeated references to *going out from us* are widely regarded as evidence that some members have left the Johannine community. Though we cannot be 100 percent certain as to the nature of the disagreement that resulted in the division, we do know it was intense and acrimonious. Why else would the author label his opponents as antichrists, liars, false prophets, and link them to the devil (1 John 2:18, 22; 3:7-8; 4:1, 3; 2 John 7)?

We cannot be absolutely certain about the points of contention, but we do have enough evidence to identify probable issues. The bottom line is the secessionists' refusal to accept the traditional Johannine community's teachings. This is why the first letter both imitates elements of the Gospel of John, such as the opening and closing as well as the stress on the love commandment, and begins by stressing the reliability of the tradition (1:1-4). The separatists may have also viewed themselves as valuing the tradition but interpreted it in such a fashion as to make it more relevant to their peers, who were probably Gentiles and no longer primarily Jews, as was the case when the Gospel of John was being formed. At some level the Johannine tradition opens the door for this in light of John 14:15-31 and 16:4-15, which promise that the Holy Spirit who "will teach you everything" (14:26) and "will guide you into all the truth" (16:13). Urban von Wahlde offers a tempting theory regarding the role of the tradition and the Spirit in this divided community. He argues that the separatists were influenced by "the wisdom-oriented conviction that, in accord with their Jewish traditions, . . . in the last days Yahweh would send his Spirit upon the people in a new and complete way" (114-15). Thus the Johannine traditions became irrelevant to John's opponents because "this eschatological outpouring of the Spirit would be enough for the community. It would teach them everything they needed to know and they would have no need to be rooted in a 'tradition' since they now possessed the Spirit of Yahweh who had also guided Jesus" (115). John also wants to rely on the Spirit (1 John 4:1-6), but he is confident the Spirit will make clear the separatists' errors regarding the Johannine tradition.

What might those errors be? First John 2:18-27; 4:1-6 and 2 John 7-11 are crucial for sketching the picture. Perhaps it is wise to work backward from what seems obvious. One of the secessionists' errors is the fact that they left the church and its tradition(s) (1 John 2:19; 4:1; 2 John 7). By separating themselves from John's community, they have gone out into *the world* and show themselves to be of the world (1 John 4:1, 5-6; cf. 2:19; 2 John 7). Having left the Johannine church, the secessionists have also abandoned the tradition, in John's mind, but how so exactly? Second John 9 reads, *Everyone who does not abide in the teaching of Christ, but goes beyond it, does not have God.* This is an important hint coupled with John's other charges. The separatists have probably formulated a new Christology and understanding of Christian ethics, especially regarding the love commandment.

Repeatedly our author argues that his opponents possess a flawed view of Jesus. In particular, they refuse to acknowledge that

Jesus Christ *has come in the flesh* (1 John 4:2; 2 John 7; cf. 1 John 5:1-12). The author's later argument clarifies this charge for us. In 1 John 5:5-6 John asserts that Jesus is God's Son and came *with the water and the blood* (cf. John 19:34). Many writers, including myself, see these verses as an accusation against the secessionists. In particular, John rejects their belief that the "spiritual Christ" descended upon the human Jesus at his baptism, hence the *water* reference, but departed from him prior to his death on the cross, thus the *blood* reference. John insists Jesus was the Christ both at his baptism and his death. By doing this he is firmly within the Johannine community, for the Gospel of John repeatedly points to the cross as Jesus' hour of glory. The human Jesus was God's Christ or agent for our salvation and deliverance from sin, as 1 John 1:5–2:2 argues, in both his life and his death.

John levels at least one other crucial charge against his opponents: they do not exercise love and might even be described as ignoring Jesus' commandment that is firmly engrained in the early thinking of the Johannine community (cf. John 13:34-35; 15:12-14). First John repeatedly addresses the importance of embodying Jesus' commandment to love, and he does so in three separate detailed arguments (2:3-11; 3:11-24; 4:7–5:4). The only way to resolutely know if a person knows God is if they *obey his commandments* (2:3), which is specifically understood as loving *a brother or sister* (2:10). This is the message believers have heard from the beginning (3:11; cf. 2:7). John offers Cain as a negative role model in the first epistle's addressing the love theme. Simply and characteristically put, John believes a failure to love is evidence that one is still spiritually dead and therefore does not have eternal life (3:14-15). The believers' positive role model is Jesus Christ, who *laid down his life for us* and thus revealed true love (3:16). Real love is embodied love in daily living (3:18). We can only speculate as to what triggered this aspect of John's polemic.

It would not be unreasonable, however, to assume that the trigger was connected to the secessionists' nontraditional Christology. The author concludes his second exploration of the importance of love thus: *And this is his commandment, that we should believe in the name of his Son Jesus Christ and love one another, just as he has commanded us. All who obey his commandments abide in him, and he abides in them* (1 John 3:23-24a). It may be that the secessionists' high and innovative Christology resulted in a downplaying of Jesus' teaching on love, while they elevated a new "teaching" of the Spirit that did not take seriously a lived-out faith. Whatever the details of the historical reasons for the split, John personally highlights nontraditional Christology and an abandonment of the love commandment as the bone of contention between himself and his opponents.

The Gospel of John was written likely between AD 80 and 90, and the Johannine epistles' author knew of it. If so, the earliest that the letters could have been written is 90. If the epistles' depiction of the opponents' Christology as a type of early Docetism is accurate, then he may well be addressing a situation from around the turn of the century or a little later (see below).

While the vast majority of scholars view the Gospel of John as written before the letters, there are notable exceptions. Charles Talbert argues, "The Fourth Gospel was written alongside or after the period of the epistles' composition" (56; on the priority of the letters, see also Kenneth Grayston: 12-14). Talbert believes that the Gospel was penned in an attempt to resolve the christological and ethical issues documented in the letters. Talbert correctly observes "that most of the controversial issues of the epistles are echoed in the Fourth Gospel at one place or another" (56-57). His argument is damaged, however, when he further concedes, "The Gospel's scope is not reduced to matters of the controversy of the epistles" (57). Such an admission makes it difficult to explain why the Gospel added material if the goal was to resolve the controversies. It is more plausible that the epistles simply use the larger, earlier, and tradition-laden Gospel to resolve the specific controversies around Christology and ethics that developed since the Gospel was written and the Johannine community incorporated more and more Gentiles.

Nature of the Secessionists' Christology (Bearing on Date)

We can only guess at the exact nature of the secessionists' Christology, but those guesses can be described as "educated" and certainly plausible. A second-century tradition reported by Irenaeus (*Against Heresies* 1.26.1) says that church leaders opposed a man named Cerinthus, who argued for a sharp distinction between the human Jesus and the spiritual Christ. Cerinthus believed Jesus was an excellent and wise teacher, but nothing more than that. The Christ, on the other hand, was a spiritual being who descended upon the human Jesus at his baptism and departed from him before his death on the cross. In several letters, another second-century Christian named Ignatius warned believers about "docetic" Christology (*To the Trallians* 9-10; *To the Smyrnaeans* 1-7). The term *Docetism* comes from the Greek word *dokeō*, which means "to seem." Docetists taught that Jesus only "appeared" or "seemed" to be human and only "seemed" to suffer and die. Finally, we are well aware of another later theological movement challenging Christianity: Gnosticism.

As Marianne Meye Thompson (17) reports, "Cerinthus' views were of gnostic orientation, and some Gnostics were also Docetists." Well-defined Gnosticism, however, appears later than both Cerinthus and Ignatius, and even then it is a complex movement. Both the Johannine community and Gnostics are dualist, but they held to differing types of duality. John accepts a kind of behavioral or moral duality: light/dark, love/hate, and so forth. The Gnostics' entire worldview is driven by a cosmic dualism: things are assigned to either the spiritual (good) or physical (evil) realms. Since God is spiritual, God is good; but since humans are physical, they are entrapped in evil. They need to be "redeemed" from physical matter (*hylē*). Therefore the human Jesus had serious limitations in the Gnostic worldview. For many Gnostics, salvation comes not from the human Jesus' death on the cross, but from a special revealed knowledge, or *gnōsis*, the Greek word for "knowledge." [*Gnosticism, p. 308*; see also articles on Gnosticism in other BCBC volumes: Martin: 289-90; Yoder Neufeld: 346-47; Yeatts: 454.]

The overlapping thought between John's depiction of his opponents and the three parties above might tempt us to conclude that the secessionists were Cerinthians, Docetists, or Gnostics, or a combination of all three. However, in 1 John an early manifestation of the diverse Christologies emerges that will develop in the middle to late second century and beyond. At best, we should conclude that John's opponents were the embodiment of a prototype of docetic Gnosticism. This conclusion, however, helps us establish a broad time period for the letters' writing. For this reason the hypothesis above on dating is valid: the Gospel of John was written during the decade of AD 80-90; the Johannine epistles' author knew of it; and these letters were written later than AD 90. The epistles depict the opponents' Christology as a type of early Docetism, and they address a situation from around the turn of the century or a little later.

Authorship

Although the documents are traditionally associated with someone named John, we have no internal documentary evidence confirming this tradition. In fact, all three writings are anonymous. First John jumps directly into the argument; 2 and 3 John follow the ancient letter form and simply identify the sender as *the elder* without giving a personal name.

Where does this traditional association with *John* come from, and which *John* is it? As early as the late second century, some early church voices associated these writings with the apostle John. However, the early church historian Eusebius refers to another early second-century view that may differ from this. In *Ecclesiastical History* (3.39.3-4) he refers to a list of early leaders given by a bishop named Papias. The bishop's list is both tantalizing and confusing because it cites two men named John: the apostle and the elder. Thus some people have believed the letters are not from the apostle John, but from the elder John.

Given the lack of internal evidence as well as confusing and conflicting traditional views, some scholars put forward a reasonable alternative. Raymond Brown (1982) and R. Alan Culpepper (1975) refer to the "Johannine School" when working with the Gospel of John and the Johannine letters. There is certainly commonality between the Gospel and 1 John. For example, both stress the importance of the love commandment given by Jesus (1 John 2:7-11; John 13:34); the letter's opening and closing seem to resemble those in the Gospel (1 John 1:1-4 and 5:13; John 1:1-18 and 20:31); and both stress the importance of keeping Christian traditions. There are differences as well, but these differences can be explained without concluding that the two documents are unrelated. For example, the length and genre of each differ, and the situations being addressed are unique. As David Rensberger (18) suggests, the Gospel and these letters come from "the same circle within early Christianity."

Hence the letters were written by someone who accepted and valued the Gospel traditions associated with the Gospel of John. As 1 John 1:1-4 shows, he was trying to remain faithful to that tradition while making it relevant to a new situation. In this sense, these letters are "Johannine," and I will refer to the author as John despite not knowing who he was. Furthermore, I am inclined to conclude that all three letters were written by the same anonymous writer from "the Johannine school" or "the Johannine community"—the more current term—as will become evident in the explanatory notes. While the shortness of 2 and 3 John limit the amount of thematic and linguistic internal evidence, I believe there is enough evidence to see common authorship.

One final enigma, related to authorship, is a famous textual variant in 1 John. With more than five thousand complete or partial hand-copied manuscript texts of the NT, it should not be surprising that every NT book has textual variants. Words are omitted or misspelled or added. Corrections and notes have been made in the margins of these ancient texts. First John contains a famous textual variant known as the Johannine Comma (comma in the sense of "interval"). Modern translations of 1 John 5:7-8 read something like this: *For there are three that testify: the Spirit, the water and the blood; and the three are in agreement* (NIV). Yet as anyone who has memorized the KJV as a child knows, there is a longer version of these verses: *For there are three that bear record <u>in heaven, the Father, the Word, and the Holy Ghost; and these three are one. And there are three that bear witness in earth,</u> the Spirit, and the water, and the blood: and these three agree in one.* The underlined words are the Johannine Comma. This portion is not found in any early Greek or more reliable later Greek manuscripts: thus it does not come from the author. Much debate and many fascinating details surround the history of how the Comma became part of the text [*The Johannine Comma, p. 309*].

1 John 1:1-4

Introduction

PREVIEW

Benefiting from two thousand years of Christian theology, we realize the complexity of any attempts to explain the central Christian concept of God taking on human form. A divine being in physical form is one of the numerous paradoxes found in Christianity. It is usually only the gifted who can hold together both aspects of the issue without falling to one side or the other.

That is the situation facing John and his community. As recognized in the commentary's introduction, it appears that his Christian community was divided over this issue. As 1 John 2:19 indicates, a schism has occurred, and elsewhere in these letters we learn that the divisive issue was Christology. Yet this is not the author or the community's only concern. This flawed Christology has resulted in a flawed ethic as well, as is evident in the next section (1:5–2:2) and elsewhere. Before John can address the ethical issue, however, he sees a need to establish a firm foundation upon which a Christian ethic can stand. And that foundation is the life of Jesus, which the community has held to in the past. Indeed, for the author, orthopraxy, or "right behavior," grows out of orthodoxy, or "right theology," especially the Johannine community's tradition about Jesus Christ and his ministry.

The opening four verses are an unapologetic defense of the Johannine tradition, which proclaims that God's good news was fully disclosed in the historical person of Jesus of Nazareth. The author and others who hold to the tradition accept a "high Christology," as verses 2 and 3 suggest: the Father and Son are bound closely together. The relationship is so intimate that later the author will assert that no one who denies the Son *has* the Father, and anyone who confesses the Son has the Father also (1 John 2:23; cf. John 14:7). In fact, the Johannine Christology is so "high" that near the end of the first letter the author affirms that Jesus is both the Christ and the Son of God (1 John 5:1-13; cf. 2 John 3, 7).

The human Jesus, however, is unmistakably and repeatedly presented as well. He was heard, seen, and touched (v. 1); he was not a spectral apparition, but a flesh-and-blood being. As evident in this letter, the believers in the Johannine community were aware of a heterodox Christology that denies the fullness of God's revelation in Jesus of Nazareth. Perhaps they were tempted by a Christology influenced by an early form of docetic Gnosticism [*Gnosticism, p. 308*]. In part, John's introduction reminds his readers of their tradition's balance between a high and low Christology, but the "low Christology" receives the bulk of the attention because it is the aspect of the tradition that is under attack by the secessionists.

This early passage emphasizes the *fellowship*, or *koinōnia*, that the recipients and writer share with one another. Just as *koinōnia* was a trait of the early Jerusalem church (Acts 2:42), and as Paul and Titus shared a common, or *koinē*, faith (Titus 1:4), so also the Johannine congregation(s) holding to a proper Christology experience *koinōnia*, both with other humans and with God (see Swartley 1998: 214-29).

Using speech-act theory, Dietmar Neufeld, however, minimizes the polemical element of the sensory words in verses 1 and 2. According to Neufeld, the "witness to what has been heard, seen and touched concerning the word of life does not represent the abstract theological propositions of an author reflecting on the error of his opponents" (80). Rather, "Setting aside proper rules of grammar, the author of 1 John writes an impressive introduction with dramatic sensitivity which in its overall impact captures the essence of the author's theological thought" (80). John's goal, Neufeld argues, is "to establish the credibility of his message before an audience unknown to him" (71). The author of 1 John wants to establish his personal "integrity," which "is dependent upon the soundness of his message" (75). Much of what Neufeld describes as John's attempt to connect with his readers in these opening verses is reasonable; yet I believe that Neufeld underestimates the extreme tension created by the schism and the thoroughness of John's polemic, which begins subtly in the opening four verses, becomes obvious in the next section's emphasis on sin, and intensifies as the letter develops. Additionally, the author employs far too many terms of affection—such as *children* (1 John 2:14, 18), *little children* (2:1, 12, 14, 28;

3:7, 18; 4:4; 5:2, 21), and *beloved* (3:2, 21; 4:1, 7, 11; 3 John 2, 5, and 11)—to be writing to an unknown group before which he needs to establish his credibility.

The reader of 1 John immediately confronts an enigma: the "letter" of 1 John, unlike 2 and 3 John, does not contain any of the characteristics of a true letter *[Letters in the Ancient World, p. 310]*. This raises the question of the book's genre. It has been described as a homily, a teaching document, or a handbook. Given the fact that 1 John does not neatly fit into any readily identifiable genre, we follow Brown's suggestion that we seek no specific literary genre, but rather endeavor to observe what 1 John attempts to do (1982: 90).

Additionally, the reader faces one of the most challenging sentences in the New Testament in these opening verses. This sentence has been variously described as incoherent, unclear, and complex. Such comments initially seem justified. The sentence begins with four clauses (most of v. 1) that are followed by a parenthetical digression (the remainder of v. 1 and all of v. 2). Further, the sentence's main verb, *declare*, finally appears in verse 3. Moreover, verse 4 seemingly introduces a new thought.

While we must concede the uneven quality of the Greek in these verses, we need not conclude that the author's thoughts are nothing more than incoherent ramblings. Rather, his thoughts focus on the content of the Johannine tradition, which he defends, as well as the spoken and written word. He begins by identifying the content of the Christian proclamation (1:1a-d), which is the life and death of Jesus Christ, and this is followed immediately by the content of his writing (1:1e-2), which again is the Christian message centered upon God's work in Jesus Christ. He then shifts focus to identify his motivation for both proclamation (1:3) and writing (1:4).

Thus the writer begins the text by writing about *the word of life*, identifying what is, in short, his major theme: the life and death of Jesus Christ. He calls upon sound, sight, and touch, all elements of the Christian community's experience of Jesus and proclamation of the gospel message, in an attempt to express the depth of meaning he seeks to communicate. This *word of life*, says the author, is the basis for fellowship between believers; and furthermore, this message brings with it the joy of mutual fellowship that is characterized by being *with the Father and with his Son Jesus Christ*. For the author and his community, their theology about Jesus informs and molds their relationships with each other.

The thoughts of this text are so dense and tightly compacted that they merit a visual diagram:

The Content of Our Proclamation 1:1a-d
We declare to you
>*what was from the beginning,*
>*what we have heard,*
>*what we have seen with our eyes,*
>*what we have looked at and touched with our hands,*

The Content of Our Writing 1:1e-2
concerning the word of life—this life was revealed,
>*and we have seen it,*
>*and testify to it,*
>*and declare to you the eternal life that was with the Father*
>>*and was revealed to us—*

The Reason We Proclaim 1:3
we declare to you what we have seen and heard
>*so that you also may have fellowship with us;*
>*and truly our fellowship is with the Father*
>*and with his Son Jesus Christ.*

The Reason We Write 1:4
We are writing these things
>*so that our joy may be complete.*

OUTLINE
The Content of Our Proclamation, 1:1a-d
The Content of Our Writing, 1:1e-2
The Reason We Proclaim, 1:3
The Reason We Write, 1:4

EXPLANATORY NOTES

The Content of Our Proclamation 1:1a-d
How does one respond to innovative ideas? It often depends upon the standards and values by which one measures innovation. Americans, who tend to value efficiency, are generally open to new technologies that make life more efficient. Therefore, cell phones that take pictures, connect to the Internet, and contain global positioning capabilities are popular: one device with three functions in addition to making telephone calls. We enjoy devices that make life easier. What if, however, the innovation has great potential for destruction? That

is John's concern as he begins writing this document. A group has begun teaching an innovative christological doctrine that has split the Johannine community. John counters it by appealing to tradition.

This unit begins with four clauses, all starting with the word *what*. The latter three uses of *what* are associated with three of the five human senses: hearing, sight, and touch. The meaning of the first use of *what* is the most unclear: *what was from the beginning*. To what does this refer? According to the Greek grammar, *what* (as neuter gender) cannot refer to any of the specific nouns in this unit. Our clearest hint of what the author has in mind is found in the words *from the beginning*. Still, what exactly was *from the beginning*? Some scholars have argued that this is a reference to creation in Genesis 1:1. Others see *the* beginning as the unfolding of OT history. Still others associate this use of *the* beginning with the opening verse of John's Gospel: "In the beginning was the Word, and the Word was with God, and the Word was God." I agree with the third view.

While the initial clause does not refer to a specific noun, it is closely tied to the sentence's main verb *declare* (NRSV) or *proclaim* (NIV, RSV) in verse 3. This becomes apparent when reading the NRSV translation: *We declare to you what was from the beginning*. Additionally, in the second verse the author places *declare* next to the verb *testify* when referring to the incarnation (*this life was revealed*). These two verbs appear to be used interchangeably. Furthermore, it is clear from the NT that God's action in Jesus of Nazareth is the content of the early Christian witness and testimony. *What was from the beginning* may be a general reference to the entire ministry of Jesus that became the core of the Christian message (Brown 1982: 154). This suggestion is supported by the four verbs found in the following three clauses.

John selects four sensory verbs that are intended to counter anti-traditional docetic influence that may have taken root within his community. The crucial issue is denial of Jesus' humanity [*Docetism, p. 304*]. *We have heard, we have seen, we have looked at*, and [*we*] *touched* all speak of concretely experiencing one's world and events; therefore they are employed so as to reaffirm the church's inherited understanding of Jesus and his nature as a real material being. This stands in opposition to an understanding that views Jesus as only a spiritual being, which seems to be the teaching of the secessionists.

The first two verbs are in the perfect tense, which denotes the lasting effect of an action. They might be translated "We have heard and continue to hear" and "We have seen and continue to see." Although some scholars doubt a theological motivation for John's selection of this particular tense, their conclusion here is dubious. John may well be stressing the essential and continuing truth of the gospel message despite current attempts to significantly alter and revise the community's christology along docetic lines.

The phrase *what we have heard* likely refers to Jesus' earthly ministry, especially his teachings. This phrase about hearing is associated with *what was from the beginning*. Interestingly, these two phrases are used in combination in later passages (2:7, 24; 2 John 6; and similarly in 1 John 1:5 and 3:11). Even more interesting is the fact that three of the places where the author combines the concepts of *what we have heard* and *from the beginning* also mention *loving one another* (2:7 implied; 3:11; 2 John 6). It appears that in the author's mind Jesus' ministry is always connected to the ethics of the Christian life. It may be that the author also speaks of "seeing" as a reference to Jesus' healing ministry, but this is purely speculative. At the least we can say that sight reinforces hearing. Both are reasons the community continues in the faith that they have received.

The verbs of the third and fourth clauses, *we have looked at* and *touched with our hands*, are in the past (aorist) tense. This verb tense, unlike the perfect tense used in 1a and b, implies past one-time action. There is little difference between *we have seen* in the previous clause and *we have looked at* in the third clause. In fact, the difference is so slight that some scholars attribute the presence of both to an artistic or literary concern for variety. While this may be so, another option merits consideration. Perhaps the author uses these two verbs, one in the past tense (aorist) and one in the perfect tense, to stress the gospel's origin in events that were rooted in particular past events and in its ongoing manifestations in the lives of second- and third-generation believers. In this case, the first two clauses refer to the continuing power of the gospel of Christ to reach people and transform lives, while the third and fourth clauses remind the reader that the continuing message was and is based on specific past events: the life of Jesus.

This would help explain why the third and fourth verbs take on a decidedly material bent. How does one look at or touch a theological message? The verbs are clearly awkward if the author has only a spoken message in mind. However, this is not the case, for we are reminded that not only have the early witnesses *looked at* what was *from the beginning*, but they have also *touched with our hands*, which is literally translated as "our hands felt." In some biblical contexts this word implies "groping" as in the Septuagint (LXX) of Genesis 27:12. And while the verb can be translated "grope," we should not conclude that its use here implies uncertainty. As a matter of fact, it is used in Luke 24:39, at the resurrection scene, to reassure those present of the reality of Jesus' physical presence. All four verbs, then, are used to stress Jesus Christ's past and present ministry.

Likely the writer of 1 John was keenly aware that his opponents were denying Jesus' full humanity, refusing to declare that *Jesus Christ has come in the flesh* (4:2; 2 John 7). No doubt he knew of the inroads these secessionists were making into the Johannine circle of believers. Perhaps because such denial jeopardized the meaning of Jesus' atoning death for sin, he makes a strong accusation against those who consider themselves to be Christian (1 John 2:19). Clearly the full reality of Jesus' earthly ministry and that ministry's continuity with the Johannine community's contemporary beliefs and practices is being emphasized with these verbs. Moreover, the author selects these words so as to undercut the teaching of those who would lead Christian believers away from the core of gospel truth by a divergent understanding of Jesus' identity and role.

To whom do these *we* verbs refer? Does the writer actually mean "I" but uses the polite, editorial *we*? Might *we* refer to those who walked with Jesus during his earthly ministry, particularly, the beloved disciple? Early tradition, after all, assigned authorship of the epistle to John the beloved disciple. If this were the case, the term *we* would comprise a group distinct from the audience or readers—*we* and *you*. The four verbs seem to emphasize a firsthand experience of Jesus (Marshall: 106). If, however, this document is to be dated around the end of the first century, such an assertion may be possible but is not probable. After all, some sixty to seventy years have transpired since the earthly ministry of Jesus. Many, if not all, of his original and more intimate disciples would likely have died.

In addition to this time factor, there is another consideration that undercuts understanding the term *we* as referring to eyewitnesses of Jesus' earthly ministry. Many assume that the writer is the beloved disciple and further assume that John ben (the son of) Zebedee is this figure. This makes an apostolic connection; but the few uses of the word *apostle* in Johannine literature (John 13:14; Rev 2:2; 18:20; 21:14) do not connote the apostolic authority of one of the twelve. The appeal to "eye witnesses," however, is important (John 19:35; 21:24: 1 John 1:1-4; 3 John 12b). Apostleship as such appears to be a nonissue in these documents, whereas false teachers are of much concern (cf. Rev 2:2). So these considerations suggest that this document was written during the post-apostolic period or close to its beginning.

Additionally, *we* may refer to an author and his associates who were not eyewitnesses of Jesus themselves, but were nonetheless close followers of the beloved disciple or of others who were eye-witnesses. This hypothetical group has come to be known as "the Johannine Circle" (Cullmann) or "the Johannine School" (Culpepper 1975), and more recently as "the Johannine community." It is not altogether unusual for people of a later generation who stand in the same tradition as that of their ancestors to speak of their ancestors' events as if the younger generation has experienced those events themselves. In Amos 2:10 God says, "I brought you up out of, the land of Egypt, and led you forty years in the wilderness." Likewise in Joshua 24:7 we read, "Your eyes saw what I did to Egypt" (even though those addressed had not been present at the actual event). Similarly, Deuteronomy 5:1-3 makes the same use of this sense of solidarity (cf. Deut 26). As Brown notes, it is not uncommon in both secular and religious literature from the ancient world for "verbs of sensation [to be] used by people who participated in the sensation only vicariously" (1982: 160). This same feature, vicarious use of language, appears in 2 Peter 1:18 (also in Polycarp's letter *To the Philippians* 9.1; Irenaeus, *Against Heresies* 5.1.1; Tacitus, *Agricola* 45). At any rate, through the use of these sensory verbs, the author is clearly trying to identify with earlier generations of believers who have stood in the original Christian tradition.

Such observations, however, do not resolve another issue associated with these verbs: the *we/you* distinction. What exactly would be the relationship between this "school" and the congregation(s) that received this writing and the following two letters? Are we to believe that some "college" of elders or guardians of truth assumed responsibility for keeping local congregations on the correct theological track?

Yet another and more probable view points to both the author and readers. Judith Lieu observes that "for most of the letter 'we' denotes not the author and his fellow authorities, an exclusive circle, but the community together with the author" (1991: 26). Support for this view occurs at various points in 1 John. In 1:6-10 the author addresses the issue of sin, fellowship, and forgiveness. Here the author uses the first-person plural (*we/us/our*), clearly placing him-self on the same level as the readers. Additionally, between 2:1b and 2:18d the writer uses *we* when he means "I and you." This corporate association between the author and the readers is accentuated in 2:19, which draws a distinction between *us* and *them* (*They went out from us, but they did not belong to us*). Similar thinking may stand behind 3:2 and 5:18-19.

I am inclined to conclude that one Christian leader is addressing his fellow believers because he is the group's recognized teacher and guide. However, we need to be more specific about his role. While the author sees his function as "teacher and guide," he does not function in a hierarchical or authoritarian fashion. The verses cited above show the author's awareness of his own potential for sinfulness, and in this respect he is no better than his readers. The author seems to have a strong sense of the importance of the entire community's working together in order to successfully overcome the challenge they face. As Lieu concludes, "For 1 John authority lies within the life and experience of the believing community; finding the way forward is a shared enterprise, and examination of their present Christian life is done from within and not from outside" (1991: 27).

In essence, 1 John 1:1a-d refers to a commonly held Christian conviction about the significance of the Christ event, or the tradition about such. Both the author and the readers believe this theological truth and its historical foundation even though "others" do not. Brown suggests that through the use of this language, the writer and the audience affirm their covenant identification with earlier generations of believers. This language authenticates the writer's interpretation of the Johannine tradition (1982: 161). The author sees himself and his readers as standing within the original christological tradition.

The Content of Our Writing 1:1e-2

The end of verse 1 introduces a theme, *the word of life*, which is the jumping-off point for a brief and subtle digression in verse 2. The digression begins and ends with the theme of incarnation (*revealed*, NRSV; *made manifest*, RSV; *appeared*, NIV). Between these two references the author writes about human observation of and testimony to this incarnation of God in the midst of human affairs.

The use of *word* in this context immediately connects us as readers to the prologue of John's Gospel. In this Gospel, *only* in the prologue is the Greek word *logos*, "Word," used as a personalized reference to Jesus, and thus it is capitalized. A number of scholars see the same usage of the term here. However, the evidence does not support such an assertion. Nowhere does 1 John's use of *word* depict personalized action (cf. 1:10; 2:5, 7, 14; 3:18; 3 John 10 KJV), thus suggesting that the term as used here has a different meaning than in the Gospel of John. The more likely alternative is to view *word* in the sense of "message." In this case it would be equivalent to *we declare* in verse 3b, and it is probably a reference to the message about Jesus' entire ministry (Brown 1982: 164). The weight of numbers supports this understanding in that the term *word* is used twenty-five times in the Johannine literature to denote the concept of "message."

The genitive *of life* qualifies *word*. How that qualification is to be translated is less certain. Among the possibilities are phrases like *the word that is life, the life-giving word*, and *the word that gives life*. Regardless of the exact translation we give the phrase, the author's point is to make a connection between the Christian message (*word*) and its function as a source of authentic *life*. This same idea appears in the Gospel of John where Jesus says, "Truly, I tell you, anyone who hears my word and believes him who sent me has eternal life, and does not come under judgment, but has passed from death to life" (5:24).

In 1 John 1:2 it is not immediately apparent why the author digresses to write about *this life* that is probably a reference to Jesus' earthly ministry. This shift is confusing because one might reasonably expect an excursus on *the word*, the Christian message, but the author clearly focuses on incarnation. This is evidenced by the use of *was revealed* to bracket the beginning and end of verse 2. And yet, adding to the confusion, in the middle of this bracket is language more related to the theme of message: *testify* and *declare*.

Our understanding gains clarity when we turn our attention to the verb *revealed* (NRSV) (*made manifest*, RSV; *appeared*, NIV; *phaneroō*, Greek). The verb's meaning varies from "revealing that which was unknown" to "making visible the invisible." It is used eighteen times in the Gospel of John and 1 John; eleven of these are in a christological context. In 1 John 2:28 it refers to Jesus' return; in 3:5, 8 it refers to the Son's earthly ministry. It therefore seems likely that the author's dual use of *phaneroō* is intended to point to the earthly career of Jesus and the divine revelation that took place therein. This career/event then became the core message of the Christian movement, including the Johannine community, but is now disputed by the separatists, those who left the community.

The three verbs bracketed between the two uses of the term *revealed* (*we have seen it and testify to it, and declare to you*) show the movement from incarnation to sharing a message about the incarnation. *Have seen* is the same verb used in verse 1c. Having *seen* the Christ event, the early believers then *testify to it*. This verb and the noun *testimony* occur sixty-four times in the Gospel and letters of John. It is a distinctive Johannine concept because the synoptic Gospels employ the verb only twice. For our purposes the use of the verb in 1 John 4:14 clarifies the author's thought when using *testify*.

There he writes, *We have seen and testify that the Father has sent his Son as the Savior of the world. Declare* is a verb that is thematically connected to *testify*. That connection in the sense of "reporting" and the Greek phrase could be translated "and we report to you." Again, the primary task facing the author and his community is to pass on accurately (*testify to* and *declare*) *the word of life*, or the message about the incarnation, which has been entrusted to their care. As discussed later, this proclamation involves both word and deed.

The phrase *the eternal life that was with the Father* further clarifies *the life* that *was revealed*. This *life* then became the subject of the Johannine community's testimony and reporting. The use of *eternal* in our text speaks of both quantity and quality; however, the latter element is of primary importance for John (Brown 1982: 168; Smalley: 10). This verse subtly touches upon a theme that comes to the foreground in verse 3 and is central for the remainder of the letter: Jesus Christ revealed a type of life that enables positive connectedness to God. Moreover, this quality life is accessible to anyone who hears and accepts the Christian community's testimony and proclamation about Jesus Christ. Finally, in accepting the community's testimony, one is then accepted into the community of faith.

The Reason We Proclaim 1:3

With this verse the writer returns to the thought of the first verse by repeating two verbs, *we have seen* and *heard*, initially encountered in the opening clauses. Finally we locate the main verb that carries this long, involved sentence: *we declare* (NRSV; *we proclaim*, RSV, NIV). We saw this verb in the previous verse and will see it again, with slight modification, in verse 5. The reason for the proclamation is stated here: *that you also may have fellowship* with the author and like-minded believers. Furthermore, to have this fellowship is to also have fellowship with God and Jesus Christ. In short, John envisions fellowship as a phenomenon in which positive human-to-human relationships and positive human-to-divine relationships intersect.

The Greek word *koinōnia* stands behind the English translation "fellowship." *Koinōnia*, which occurs four times in 1:3-7, is fundamental to the identity of the early Christian community. The term can be translated many ways: "communion," "partnership," "fellowship," and "community" (for further discussion, see Explanatory Notes on 2 John 11). Briefly put, *koinōnia* refers to active involvement with the believing community or being in partnership with it.

But *koinōnia* in the early church is not limited to the human-to-human partnership. The author clearly claims that one can also have *koinōnia* with the divine: *and truly our fellowship is with the Father and his Son Jesus Christ.* An end result of the incarnation and gospel message is that fellowship can take place both on a horizontal level (human to human) and on a vertical plane (human to divine).

Moreover, it is implied that these two planes are inextricably intertwined and that one impacts the other. Whoever is apart from fellowship with the earthly community of faith has no fellowship with God. And true fellowship with God in Christ leads to fellowship with other like-minded humans. Given the probable schismatic context of this writing, we can understand why the author introduces this dual aspect of *fellowship.* The faith community has fragmented over the issue of Christology, which should be the source of their unity (see 3:23; 4:2-3; 5:1, 6-12; evidence of a split is seen in 2:19). Thus the author logically calls into question the authenticity of the secessionists' relationship with the divine because they have divided the community and threatened the fellowship (see the use of *antichrist* to describe the separatists in 2:18-25). Finally, he argues that without a proper understanding of Christ, one cannot find true *fellowship* with other humans (see Explanatory Notes on 3:11-17 and 4:7-21).

By now a congregation listening to the reading of these three opening verses would notice the repetition of several words. Smalley (4) observes that the passage points ever forward: "The suspense is built up and intensified in the movement . . . by a series of similar, short (and sometimes repeated) phrases." Then comes the momentous announcement that *the word of life* has been revealed, and the further declaration that this *word* is even now disclosed to the reader! The *word* is the good news of *life* in Jesus Christ and the possibility of *fellowship* with God and one another. This is the reason for Christian proclamation.

The Reason We Write 1:4

An additional statement concludes this introduction; in it John offers a reason for the writing: *so that our joy may be complete.* Although the NIV, NRSV, and RSV all opt for *our joy,* this could also be rendered "your joy." The same textual variant occurs elsewhere in the Johannine, NT, and other Greek writings. This is due to the fact that the two words are so similar and are essentially pronounced the same. The writing of the verb easily could have become confused when the text was reproduced via dictation to copyists, as was common in the ancient world. Still, the oldest manuscripts of 1 John read *our*, which thus is the reading found in the above-noted translations.

Joy (noun, *chara*) occurs twelve times in John's Gospel and epistles (John 3:29 [2x]; 15:11 [2x]; 16:20, 21, 22, 24; 17:13; 2 John 12; 3 John 4); the verb *rejoice* (*chiarō*) occurs thirteen times. This is an important term. Perhaps its use here harks back to the Lord's words in John 15:1-10 regarding abiding in the vine and John 15:11 ("I have said these things to you so that my joy may be in you, and that your joy may be complete"). Other evidence reveals *joy* as an important early Christian concept. In Galatians 5:22, Paul lists it as a fruit of the Spirit, and Luke views it as a result of the Spirit's work, despite resistance and difficulties confronting the disciples (Acts 13:52). In the short book of Philippians, it occurs sixteen times (noun and verb).

It is clear that this *joy* is somehow a result of the proclamation mentioned earlier in 1 John 1:1-3a. That proclamation leads to a present potential for *fellowship* with both God and humans (vv. 3b-c), and in turn that *fellowship* results in *joy*. The interesting twist is that the present *joy*, while no doubt including a futuristic element, is founded on the past: *we have heard, we have seen, we have looked at* and *touched*. In other words, the incarnation and good news associated with it results in a present *joy*, not a merely hoped-for future *joy*. Moreover, the author writes so that this *joy* may be *complete*. Literally, the verb is "filled" or "made full," thus suggesting that nothing is lacking from the joy available to believers. The author's reason for writing is to offer the readers a sense of complete joy that results from a clear understanding of who Jesus Christ is, what God has done through him, and how that action impacts one's relationship with both God and other believers.

THE TEXT IN BIBLICAL CONTEXT

Connection to the Gospel of John

The reading of these opening verses readily jogs one's memory to recall something like this said before. We first encounter these concepts in the prologue of John's Gospel (1:1-18). Virtually all scholars see some type of connection between John's prologue and 1 John 1:1-4. There are at least six verbal points of contact between the introduction of the letter and the Gospel of John's prologue:

we have seen	John 1:18, with both texts using the same verb form
we have looked at	John 1:14, with both texts using the same verb form
word of life/life	John 1:1, 14
we testify to it	John 1: 7-8
eternal life that was with the Father	John 1:1-2
our fellowship is with the Father and with his Son Jesus Christ	John 1:18

Stott (66-67) further observes that both writings open with emphasis on *the beginning*. Both identify Christ as the Father's Son, and both declare that the eternal has entered into history. Such evidence leads some scholars to firmly assert a connection between the two texts. Some even go so far as to propose that 1 John was modeled after the Gospel's prologue.

Others, including Stott, avoid such bold declarations, mainly due to the equally obvious differences between the two texts. Many scholars recognize that while there is overlap of words and concepts, these terms are not used the same way in both works. Stott (67), for example, notes the alternate use of *the word* in 1 John. In John's Gospel this expression is used absolutely; in 1 John the author qualifies it by adding the phrase *of life*. Stott further adds that the emphasis in the phrase *the word of life* seems to be on *life*. Stott sees this as a reference to the gospel of Christ as opposed to placing the emphasis on *Word*, which thus refers to Jesus in the Gospel of John. Given a tendency to employ common words differently, many scholars admit some connection but are unable to firmly argue that the author of 1 John wrote with a copy of the Gospel of John before him, nor do they conclude that the same author is responsible for both texts. Instead, a popular way of explaining the relationship is to suggest that both 1 John and the Gospel's prologue echo the theology of the Johannine community.

Incarnation

Quite apart from the issue of literary connections, one can conclude that 1 John's and the Gospel of John's openings share a concern for the complexity and importance of the incarnation. Both texts assume that the eternal has manifested itself in the presence of humans. God, in the person of Jesus of Nazareth, has lived in the midst of human affairs and has impacted human undertakings. In a large measure, John's Gospel is written to encourage believers to continue in their faith, believing that Jesus is the Christ (20:30-31) despite resistance and persecution from the Jewish leaders (7:13; 9:22; 12:42; 16:2).

John and his fellow believers must have been baffled by Jewish resistance to their message of God being revealed in Jesus. A fairly fertile OT tradition anticipates that one day the Lord would come to dwell in their midst (Isa 7:14; 8:8-15; 9:1-17). Moreover, the Davidic kings had come to be viewed as representatives "of the LORD" (2 Sam 7:14; Ps 2:7). Ben Witherington (90-96) further explains that the first century was a time of ripe messianic expectation. Drawing upon Gerd Theissen, Witherington points out that people involved in the messianic movements of this time period believed that "God was or would soon intervene and establish direct divine rule because God alone is king" (90). While some scholars point to a general "salvation hope" in the first century AD, Witherington argues for a focused element as well. There was

> a significant focus . . . on one or more messianic figures, who are properly understood in the larger context of messianic hope. In short, although messianic hope involved more than an interest in a coming anointed one, such a coming one was often the focal point of that hope both during and before Jesus' day. (91-92)

Because this idea of God's representatives being present in human history is not a totally novel concept, the early believers' affirmation of Jesus' divine sonship would have been a logical next theological step. The early believers clearly were convinced that Jesus fulfilled this OT Davidic Son of God and messianic role (Matt 1:1; 15:22; 20:30-31; Rom 1:3; 2 Tim 2:8; Rev 3:7; 5:5; 22:16). For example, James Dunn (1980) argues that Romans 1:3, probably drawing upon an early Christian formula, makes such an apologetic use of Psalm 2:7. Dunn further notes that Psalm 2:7 was an important proof text in the early decades of the Christian movement, and its use can be seen in Mark 1:11; Luke 3:22; Acts 13:33; Hebrews 1:5 and 5:5.

The reason for Jewish reservation on this issue may be found in the extent to which the first believers took the point. For example, Paul asserts that Jesus "was in the form of God" (Phil 2:5-8; cf. Col 1:19; Eph 1:19-20; Heb 1:3). Paul and other believers proclaimed that God's fullness was seen in Jesus of Nazareth, thus producing a high Christology. This differs significantly from the Jewish assumption that the Lord had human monarchical representatives, and it explains why so many Jews could not accept the Christian message, which focused on God's incarnation in Jesus of Nazareth.

But not only Jews who rejected Jesus as the Messiah were among those who questioned this high incarnational theology. The author of 1 John repeatedly addresses the topic to counter the teachings of a group that had left the Christian fellowship over this issue (1 John 2:18-25; 4:1-2, 9-10; 2 John 7). Generally speaking, the three Platonic ideas that God ("the One") was separated from humans ("the many") and was "unchanging" and "incorruptible" were popular ideas in the early church period. And so people who had been influenced by what one might call "popular Greek philosophy" would also have struggled with the Christian concept of incarnation. For them it was a given that a divine being was essentially and totally unlike human beings (Kearsley: 81-82). Not only was the salvific nature of Jesus' death on the cross a foolish notion to the Greeks (1 Cor 1:22-23; cf. Acts 17:16-34), but also the entire notion of God in human form was foolishness!

Fellowship

The author of 1 John assumes that the incarnation is not merely an abstract theological category upon which one might intellectually reflect and meditate. Like other early believers, he regards this act of incarnation as impacting human affairs and presenting us with a new model for human relationships. This model is summed up in the word *fellowship*.

The word *koinōnia* is used only eighteen times in the NT, in a variety of contexts. It can depict the relationship of the believer to the Spirit (2 Cor 13:13; Phil 2:1), to the gospel (Phil 1:5), or with God (1 John 1:6). Equally important is the concept that by individually sharing with the Spirit, the gospel, and God, we also share or have *fellowship* with one another. Fellowship characterized the early church's life (Acts 2:42). Paul understood that all believers were called into this *fellowship* by God's faithfulness (2 Cor 9:13). The author of 1 John would have agreed, for he wrote, *If we walk in the light as he himself is in the light, we have fellowship with one another* (1:7). This concept of fellowship was not limited to the spiritual realm, as can be seen in Paul's repeated use of the word when referring to the financial collection taken up on behalf of the poor in Jerusalem (Rom 15:26; 2 Cor 9:13; cf. Heb 13:16).

This basic concept of sharing can also be seen behind other familiar passages and images. Although the Gospel of John does not use the word *koinōnia*, the well-known image of the vine and branches in chapter 15 can be viewed as a vivid imagery of *fellowship* with both Jesus Christ and other humans who are also connected to him. This idea is probably also in the Gospel writer's mind as he penned the well-known prayer for unity in John 17. Moreover, one of Paul's favorite images for the church was that of the human body. In Romans 12:5 he wrote, "So we, who are many, are one body in Christ, and individually we are members one of another." He used the same imagery, but with more anatomical detail in 1 Corinthians 12:12-31 (cf. Eph 1:23 and Col 1:15-20).

Therefore, *fellowship* is a bi-dimensional concept involving our relationship with both the Divine and each other. As Stott (63) writes, "'Fellowship' is a specifically Christian word and denotes that common participation in the grace of God, the salvation of Christ and the indwelling Spirit that is the spiritual birthright of all Christian believers. It . . . makes them one."

And this *fellowship* is the end result of God's incarnation in Christ, the receiving of the message proclaimed about that event, and the continuing presence of the Holy Spirit (for wider treatment of NT use of *koinōnia*, see Swartley 1998: 24-29). The individual's acceptance of the gospel message simultaneously places that person in *fellowship* with God and other believers who respond similarly to the gospel message.

THE TEXT IN THE LIFE OF THE CHURCH

Incarnation as Foundation

First John is clearly an in-house religious document, as is evidenced by various verses. It is written to fellow believers (5:13), is offered to those who already know the truth (2:21), and it adds nothing new (2:7). Moreover, the recipients' sins have been *forgiven* (2:12). They are *children of God* (3:1; cf. John 1:12). This letter also calls the believers back to the essentials of the faith. Furthermore, it reminds believers of the light that *is already shining* in their midst (1 John 2:8), and so it is given, at least in part, as a word of encouragement. In its opening verses the letter begins with a long and complex reminder that they have inherited a message that is life-giving and a source of joy.

Nowhere do the Johannine Epistles recall a specific incident from Jesus' earthly life or directly quote one of his sayings and attribute it to him. It is, however, in the opening verses of this text that we most nearly approach the earthly life of Jesus when we read *we have heard, we have seen,* and *we have touched.* Without ever quoting Jesus' teaching or pointing specifically to his deeds or life model, these initial verses provide a clear call to the church to return to one essential element of the faith: God has lived among us in the person of Jesus of Nazareth. The incarnation is the author's assumption behind the remainder of this letter and the two that follow. His particular assumptions were not shared by everyone, however.

This topic continued to be debated into the second century and beyond. Various apostolic fathers defended the higher Christology of early believers. Polycarp (in his letter *To the Philippians* 7.1) alludes to 1 John 4:2-3 and 2 John 7. Ignatius of Antioch writes, "There is one Physician, who is both flesh and spirit, born and yet not born, who is God in man, true life in death, both of Mary and of God, first passible [subject to suffering] and then impassible, Jesus Christ our Lord" (*To the Ephesians* 7.2; cf. *To the Smyrnaeans* 5.2). Irenaeus, the second-century apologist, and Tertullian, a third-century Christian theologian, both saw a need to counter developing Gnostic thought that "took to a rigorous conclusion the Platonist assurance that the One stood apart from the Many, the Unchanged from the Changeable, the Incorruptible from the Corruptible" (Kearsley: 84). John, along with other NT writers and early church leaders, emphasizes Jesus' divinity but does not thereby discount his humanity.

Menno Simons would affirm 1 John's assumption that God was incarnate in the person of Jesus of Nazareth. In his *Brief Confession on the Incarnation*, written in 1544, he explains his unique view of how Jesus was both human and divine (in Wenger: 422-54). In the introduction to the essay, J. C. Wenger writes, "Menno rejected any tendency to divide Christ into two parts: a heavenly and divine Being who came down to earth, and a natural man begotten of a human mother" (420; cf. TLC for 1 John 2:18-27). Menno's creative explanation was not widely accepted by his fellow Anabaptists, but they strongly agreed with his belief that is printed at the beginning of his publications: "For other foundation can no man lay than that is laid, which is Jesus Christ" (1 Cor 3:11 KJV).

Incarnation and Worldliness

How does this vital manifestation of God in our world relate to today's disciples as we journey through the life span? Often it takes on an abstract "spiritual" overtone. Still, 1 John assumes that the incarnation is more than a source of abstract spiritual solace. It serves as an encouragement to live as Jesus' disciples in this world. Some traditions express justifiable concern for "worldliness." However, in those circles there is also some confusion on this matter. This is probably due, in part, to the frequent (ninety-seven times) and somewhat ambiguous use of the word "world" in the Johannine corpus. Often it refers to a mind-set of the forces that are anti-God or anti-Jesus (John 1:29; 7:7; 8:21-30; 12:31;

14:17; 15:18; 16:8; etc.). The "world" is viewed as a realm of evil and one dominated by an anti-God ruler (John 12:31; 14:30; 16:11; 1 John 5:19). And yet, ironically, the "world" was created by God and the Word (John 1:3, 10); this alone should cause some confusion and second-guessing for anyone wanting a simple and negative view of the "world" (see Swartley's extensive discussion in 2006: 289-95). Even more problematic for this negative view of the "world" is the fact that God loves the "world" (John 3:16), sent the Son to save it (John 3:17; 4:42), and willingly took on physical form to do so (John 1:1-18; 1 John 4:9, 14).

Like the early believers, we face a dilemma. What are we to think of the physical "world"? Is it essentially evil or good? In the early days of the movement, the church was persecuted by nonbelievers; believers faced the failings of their own human nature and were tempted by Gnostic thinking to conclude that the physical world and everything in it was evil. Similarly, early Anabaptists, who were often persecuted, tended to conclude that the "world" was evil and to be avoided. For example, in 1526 Michael Sattler published a document responding to reformers Capito and Bucer in which he writes, "Christ is despised in the world. So are also those who are His; He has no kingdom in the world, but that which is of this world is against His kingdom" (in Yoder 1973: 22). In about 1557, Dirk Philips echoes this negative view: "However, it is impossible for one to observe simultaneously the [commandment] of God and human commandments. . . . For God and the world are opposed to each other. . . . Therefore, if anyone wishes to serve God, he must forsake the world" (in Dyck, Keeney, and Beachy: 70-71).

Philipp Jacob Spener, speaking for many seventeenth-century Pietists, was also concerned about worldly influences on believers. In *On Hindrances to Theological Studies*, written in 1680, he expresses his reservations about people "who enter the service of the church for worldly reasons" never having "been purified of their youthful and worldly loves" (Erb: 65). Elsewhere he writes, "The joy of the world hinders spiritual joy to the greatest degree and make minds incapable of it. Worldly joy is gross, spiritual joy is subtle. Worldly joy draws man into the flesh, spiritual joy lifts him. Worldly joy puts him ill at ease, spiritual joy gives him peace" (96).

And yet both groups of spiritual ancestors were left in the world for a purpose. They were the continuing witness and sign markers of hope. They were, no doubt, encouraged in their walk by the fact that God, in Jesus Christ, lived in their world and midst. Jesus also faced persecution and temptation, and yet his message, and the message about him, is essentially one of hope and the source of life.

We, like our forebears in the faith, have been given the opportunity to continue the witness to the world, which God loves. While life is certainly more technologically complex today, the basic options are essentially unchanged: Is God primarily the creator and redeemer of this world, or the judge and destroyer of this world? We know all too well the temptations to choose the latter; and still the Scripture witnesses to the former as an essential Christian truth. Thus Louis Evely writes: "I often say to myself that, in our religion, God must feel much alone: for is there anyone besides God who believes in the salvation of the world? God seeks among us sons and daughters who resemble him enough, who love the world enough that he could send them into the world to save it" (Job and Shawchuck: 336).

First John's stress on God's presence in Jesus of Nazareth should stand as an intense reminder of the hope and salvation available to both the church and the world.

Fellowship Through Incarnation

Through Jesus' incarnation the opportunity for humans to hear, see, gaze upon, and touch the divine results in fellowship. As people throughout the ages come in faith to Christ, the focal point of their faith, they meet others on the same journey. In fellowship with Christ, they have fellowship with each other, and that fellowship is sanctified by the Father and the Son. The vertical and horizontal aspects of fellowship are so intertwined in the author's thinking that apart from the earthly fellowship of discipleship, love, and faith, there is no fellowship with God. In 1 John there is no middle ground. If one does not have fellowship with the community of faith, one is part of the unbelieving world. The Divine partakes of koinōnia, claims ownership in it, and shares it. This is a source of real joy!

Yet 1 John 1:3-4 speaks of a fellowship and a joy that is always in process of becoming. The fellowship is partial; the joy is incomplete. There are those who run ahead (2 John 9). There are those who pull away (1 John 2:19). There are those who cannot love (4:20). There are those who will not confess that Jesus Christ has come in the flesh (4:2-3), which results in a broken community. We also live in a pained and fragmented world, which has impacted our communities and influenced our understanding of fellowship. When disagreements over direction, purpose, worship styles, and so on occur, the great temptation is to withdraw, to go somewhere else for church fellowship, or to split from the church entirely. But doing so allows the values of the world to influence our decisions and warp our understanding of discipleship.

Instead of following a consumerist understanding of the church, we are better off by realizing that the fellowship we have currently, flawed as it may be, has greater potential for joy than repeatedly starting afresh—only to learn that the new congregational fellowship, like all fellowships, is also imperfect and in process of being formed. Rather than running to locate the elusive perfect fellowship, often it is best to stay where one is and to resort to dialogue and acts of love. The author of 1 John undertakes this first step of dialogue when he decides to write his letter. He takes up the second agenda when he encourages acts of love in his writing. Both themes are followed in the hope of producing a less flawed fellowship. Finally, we must be ever mindful that the fellowships in which we participate are not only human institutions. The risen Lord, who was *heard*, *seen*, and *touched* by other first-century believers, is present in each fellowship that takes seriously the divine call to discipleship.

Section 1: 1 John 1:5–2:17

Knowing *and* Doing

OVERVIEW

How does one address a church that has experienced division and knows the pain of failure, anger, and even hatred? Forthrightly, but with endearing language and pastoral concern, is what we learn from this epistle.

John addresses a division within the church that has degenerated into open hatred. In essence Jesus' commandments, especially the command to love one another, have been ignored (2:3-11); and so sin, as John sees it, is all too evident in the church. The author reminds his audience that the current situation runs counter to their understanding of both Christian theology and the Christian life (2:12-14). They claim to have had their sins forgiven and to know the one who is from the beginning and has overcome the evil one. And yet they continue to live in broken fellowship and flirt with flawed theology. In reality, their experience is more akin to that of "the world," which John warns against (2:15-17).

This first unit of the letter's body begins with a brief and abstract theological statement, but then quickly moves to issues of ethical behavior and sin (1:5-2:2). This pattern of interweaving theology with ethics is found throughout the unit. The author views Christian theology as having an impact on Christian behavior and vice versa. In reality, for John, what we *do* is a clear indicator of whether or not we *know* God. Moreover, he argues for an acceptance of the church's traditional teaching on sin and forgiveness.

What is not so clear is the thought process behind John's writing. The topics move rapidly from one thought to the next. Progression is often difficult to observe as he repeats central ideas. This has led some commentators to conclude that the epistle is nothing more than a compilation of sermonettes placed side by side. However, it can be viewed as a relatively well-constructed letter, addressing a delicate and difficult church situation.

OUTLINE

Our Claims and Reality, 1:5–2:2
To Know Is to Obey, 2:3-11
Why I Write to You, 2:12-14
Do Not Love the World, 2:15-17

1 John 1:5–2:2

Our Claims and Reality

PREVIEW

This unit deals with a topic that permeates the biblical message but seems to be a peripheral concern for large portions of contemporary Western societies: sin. The passage begins with the theological affirmation: *God is light and in him there is no darkness at all* (1:5). The words *light* and *darkness* are used metaphorically and repeatedly in this unit and the next (*light* in 1:5, 7; 2:8, 9, 10; *darkness* in 1:5, 6, 7; 2:8, 9, 11) as a way to highlight the two distinct options before humanity. This duality of *light* and *darkness* enunciates one of the writer's basic assumptions: there are two exclusive realms. The author assumes that believers, upon conversion, move from the realm of *darkness* to that of *light*. The problem is evidence of sin in the believers' lives, an element found in the *darkness* but not in the *light*. What is one to make of this phenomenon? Verse 5 also serves as a link between the introductory verses (1:1-4) that focused on the incarnational nature of the Christian message and 1:6–2:2, which address the implications of that message for everyday living.

The final seven verses contain conditional clauses that are probably designed to counter false assertions circulating in the community that 1 John addresses. The three main assertions are found in verses 6, 8, and 10, and each begin with *If we say*. These clauses are followed by statements identifying the consequences of the previously noted behavior and a positive contrasting statement. The point is clearly designed to show a contrast between erroneous thoughts regarding sin and correct ones. The structure of these three verses, especially verses 8 and 10, highlights the "inconceivable" nature of

any claims to be sinless, as Neufeld notes (90). Smalley (21) offers the
following structure:

Negative	*Positive*
6: *If we say* that we have fellowship with him, while we are walking in darkness, we lie and do not do what is true;	7: *but if* we walk in the light as he himself is in the light, we have fellowship with one another; and the blood of Jesus his Son cleanses us from all sin.
8: *If we say* that we have no sin, we deceive ourselves, and the truth is not in us.	9: *If* we confess our sins, he who is faithful and just will forgive us our sins and cleanse us from all unrighteousness.
10: *If we say* that we have not sinned, we make him a liar, and his word is not in us.	2:1b: *But if* anyone does sin, we have an advocate with the Father, Jesus Christ the righteous. . . .

Admittedly, the final "negative-positive" format breaks the pattern of the first two in that 2:1a is an explanatory introductory comment and 2:2 offers a more detailed explanation of Jesus' role in dealing with sin. In essence these clauses and verses all focus on the deeply rooted problem of sin, and there is a progressive intensity in the author's attempts to articulate a Christian approach to dealing with sin. As Robert Kysar writes, this section expresses "the conviction that God's revelation in Christ demonstrated the sinfulness of the human condition and God's willingness to correct that condition. Only by affirming the brokenness of their lives do humans avail themselves of that divine restructuring of existence" (1986a: 41-42). The entire unit comes together to accentuate the commonness, gravity, and complexity of sin. At the same time it resoundingly affirms the Christian hope found in Jesus Christ as a solution for this aspect of the human condition.

OUTLINE
Theological Introduction, 1:5
Claiming Fellowship, Walking in Darkness, 1:6-7
Claiming Sinlessness, Deceiving Ourselves, 1:8-9
Claiming Not to Have Sinned, Making Him a Liar, 1:10–2:2

EXPLANATORY NOTES

Theological Introduction 1:5

Verse five is connected to the introduction in that both focus on a message that has been *heard* (vv. 1, 3, and 5) and is now being *proclaim[ed]* (*apangellomen*, v. 3; *anangellomen*, v. 5). In the opening verses the message is about the incarnate Word, and in verse 5 the message accords with Jesus' teaching in John's Gospel, in which Jesus himself reveals God: *God is light and in him there is no darkness at all* (cf. John 8:12; 12:35-36, 45-46). The light/darkness contrast was a common image for good and evil in early Christian circles (as in John 1:4-9; Matt 5:14; 6:23; 10:27; Rom 2:19; 13:12; 2 Cor 6:14; James 1:17; 1 Pet 2:9). Such popularity of this imagery likely stems from Jesus' own use of it.

At the same time, the metaphorical use of light and darkness is quite widespread in the ancient world. In the OT, God is specifically associated with light (Pss 27:1; 36:9; 56:13; 104:2; Isa 9:2). The Qumran sectarians also employ the metaphors of light and dark. Their *Community Rule* (1QS 3.20) reads, "Those born of truth spring from a fountain of light, but those born of injustice spring from a source of darkness" (Vermès 1997: 101pb; 1995:73hb). The same imagery is found more broadly in Qumran passages, such as 1QS 1.9-10; 1QS 3.24-4.26; 1QH 18.29. The use of light and darkness is also common outside of Jewish circles, appearing in Gnostic, Hermetic, and Zoroastrian texts. Given the vast popularity of the image, this verse and following ones clarify what is meant by the Christian affirmation *God is light and in him there is no darkness at all*.

John is probably relying on the Jewish use of the image of *light* as a way of explaining God's flawless nature. This perfection motif is reinforced emphatically by the phrase *in him there is no darkness at all*. But we would miss John's opening point if we see this verse as a speculative exercise about divine essence and nature. John uses the categories of *light* and *darkness* with a much more practical concern: character. When he affirms that *God is light*, he is saying that God is truthful, authentic, and good (Kysar 1986a: 35) and thus the "source" of truth, authenticity, and goodness for humans who hear and respond to the *message*. Because there is no *darkness* in God's character, we cannot associate any trace of falsehood, inauthenticity, or evil with God.

The point is that by virtue of divine flawlessness God cannot associate with imperfection. The practical dilemma is that, as we see in the following verses, humans are flawed. Added to this is the earlier affirmation that both the Father and Jesus Christ seek fellowship with humans (v. 3). The end result is a perfect God seeking fellowship with imperfect humans. Our sin, however, stands between us and God. The question then is posed: How does one then deal with sin, that which fractures our fellowship with God?

Claiming Fellowship, Walking in Darkness 1:6-7

The first two "if" clauses, *If we say that we have fellowship with him while we are walking in darkness* and *but if we walk in the light as he himself is in the light*, are in contrasting parallelism. Verse 6 provides the negative, and verse 7 follows with the positive. Haas, de Jonge, and Swellengrebel (25) have observed that the use of *if* with the aorist subjunctive (the Greek *aorist* is similar to the simple English past tense, and the subjunctive is used when making a general reference to what *might* be) or present tense actually results in an "exception" clause rather than a "conditional" or "hypothetical" clause. In other words, a better translation here would be *when* (or *whenever*) *we say*. This translation suggests, as many commentators recognize, that a group is actually claiming to be in fellowship with God even while their lives point to a different reality. Clearly John writes these opening words because some influential person or group is claiming to be a model of how to relate to God, and yet the reality of their lifestyle leads the believing observer to draw the opposite conclusion.

The first portion of verse 6 highlights this inconsistency. The claim is that some see themselves in fellowship with God. In just the previous verse the point is made that God is *light*, meaning authentic and good, and there is no *darkness* in him. Therefore one may assume that those people claiming fellowship are authentic and good as well. But as the author reflects on their lives, he concludes differently. They *are walking in darkness*. The use of *walk* probably is rooted in the Hebrew world. In the OT the word is employed to describe one's behavior (Gen 17:1; 1 Kings 2:4; 2 Kings 20:3; Ps 1:1 KJV; Prov 8:20; Isa 2:5), and it is similarly used in the Qumran community (1QH 15.7; 1QS 3.17-19; 5.25; 7.18; 8.15). It is frequently found in both Johannine (1 John 1:7; 2:6, 11; 2 John 4; 3 John 3-4, as well as John 8:12 and 12:35) and Pauline material (Rom 6:4; 14:15; KJV: Eph 2:2; 5:2; Col 3:7; 4:5). Here *walk* is in the present subjunctive in the phrase *while we are walking*, suggesting that this possible condition is a continuous or habitual pattern of behavior, and that such people are repeatedly and consistently choosing *darkness* over the *light* of God's revelation in Jesus Christ (see 1:1-4).

As the second parallel clause notes, to live at this level of inconsistency means at least two things: such people *lie* and *do not do what is true. Darkness* and *lie* are closely related. Just as *light* and *truth* relate to one another, so also do *darkness* and *lying*. In typical Johannine duality, *truth* and *lie* are opposites just as *light* and *darkness* are opposites. In the OT those who tell lies are opponents of God (Jer 9:3). The enemies of the Qumran covenanters are liars (1QpHab 2.1-2 [Martínez: 198]; 5.11; 1QH 12.10, 16; CD 5.21–6.2). For John, this is a grave matter and not a mild case of ignorance or self-deception. To the author *no lie comes from the truth* (1 John 2:21), and the antichrists are lying prophets (4:1). The secessionists' habitual inconsistency—claiming fellowship with God while walking in darkness—is to *lie*, and to *lie* is to place oneself in *darkness* and opposition to God, not in *fellowship with him*, as they erroneously claim (1:6).

Moreover, such inconsistency means that one does not *do what is true. Do not do what is true* is, literally, *do not do the truth*. To use the verb *to do* is simply another way to stress the concrete or specific behavior of those making the false claims. In 1 John the concept of "doing" is associated with the will of God (2:17), what pleases God (3:22), justice (2:29; 3:7, 10), sin (3:4, 8-9), and lawlessness (3:4). What is crucial for this verse and subunit is the fact that the use of this "idiom of 'doing' applied to divine realities suggests that they can be concretized in human behavior" (Brown 1982: 199). John fully expects that believers will find ways to apply abstract theological categories to daily human affairs. The gospel is to be "lived" and not merely thought about.

John's main focus for "doing" is the *truth*, which first appears in this verse. The term *truth* appears 109 times in the NT, and 45 of these occurrences are in either the Gospel of John (25 times) or the Johannine letters (20 times). In the Johannine literature the tendency is to associate *truth* with the revelation in Jesus, and we should not be surprised that the word is introduced so close to 1 John 1:1-4, which reflect upon the incarnation, and verse 5, which refers to a message that John thinks Jesus taught. In other words, the author does expect that a believer's life and behavior will be regularly informed and molded by the teachings of Jesus. To be in fellowship with God is to endeavor to pattern one's own life after the truth revealed in Jesus' life.

To turn one's back on that message and live inconsistently with it is to reject the *truth*. Such rejection is a grave matter. As Brown notes, *truth* "conveys the notion of firmness or solidarity as a basis for trustworthy acceptance. When the truth of God's revelation is accepted by the believer, it becomes the basis from which that person lives; and if one acts in truth . . . , one is not simply following an outside model of what is right . . . but is acting from an interior principle" (1982: 199-200). According to John, some people's lives show how they have never internalized this principle that *God is light* or other aspects of *truth* associated with the incarnation.

Having challenged the erroneous view in verse 6, the author offers a positive scenario in verse 7. He connects this view to the previous one by reemploying the walking metaphor and listing two benefits of walking *in the light: fellowship* and purification *from all sin.* Despite a similar format to verse 6, this verse presents the reader with two oddities. First, whereas verse 5 tells us that *God is light,* verse 7 says *he himself is in the light.* Second, one would expect to have *fellowship* with God if one is walking *in the light.* However, the text says *we have fellowship with one another.*

Why does the author move from *God is light* (v. 5) to the phrase *as he himself is in the light* (v. 7)? How is this to be explained? Most commentators see little significance in the difference. Some see it as John's use of more poetic language; others take it as a shift in function. Earlier the author is writing about God's character as the foundation for the Christian experience, and in verse 7 he talks of God as a model for Christian behavior. God is pure and holy and so is found *in the light.* If we want to be pure and holy, then we must *walk in the light* as God does. At any rate, we should conclude that John's use of metaphors is rather flexible, and we need not belabor the subtle difference between the expressions in these verses.

The verse closes with two benefits of meeting the condition of walking *in the light.* The first, *we have fellowship with one another,* brings us to the second and more problematic oddity of verse 7. This is the fourth and final time *fellowship* is used in 1 John. The immediate context of verses 6-7 creates the problem, while the earlier usage of the word (v. 3) helps resolve the dilemma.

The phrase *if we walk in the light* is readily understood: it is the converse of *we are walking in darkness* (v. 6). Just as *walking in darkness* is habitual rejection of God's character and the truth of revelation in Jesus Christ, to *walk in the light* is a metaphor for continual openness and desire "to live out the implications of God's character and action" (Kysar 1986a: 37). This same metaphor is used in John 8:12 and 12:35-36, where it describes discipleship. For John, authentic discipleship is not merely making appropriate claims or affirming correct doctrine. True discipleship is exemplified in "doing" the good, which is defined by God's truth and revelation in Jesus Christ.

While verses 6 and 7 form a "contrasting parallelism," that form breaks down here. A purer form would be something like:

. . . if we walk in darkness, we cannot fellowship with God.
. . . if we walk in light, we can fellowship with God.

But the author says the benefit of walking in the light is *fellowship with one another*, not with God, as we might expect. Thus these verses present this modified parallelism:

. . . if we walk in darkness, we cannot fellowship with God.
. . . if we walk in light, we can fellowship with one another.

This observation must be tempered by looking at John's first use of *fellowship* in verse 3. There he states that the proclamation of the gospel results in a dual *fellowship*. On the one hand, to accept the message results in *fellowship* with God and Jesus Christ. On the other hand, the recipient has *fellowship* with others who also accept the message. His opening assumption is that human *fellowship* is a result of *fellowship* with the divine. Moreover, as we have seen in verse 6, the author fully expects that accepting the divine revelation of Jesus Christ will impact the ethical and moral life of those accepting the message he proclaims. If one takes God seriously and has fellowship with God, one will internalize God's character. The everyday result of this *fellowship* will naturally be *fellowship* with other like-minded people. John clearly assumes that "a saving relationship with God yields a sense of community among those who share that relationship" (Kysar 1986a: 37).

The reason for this shift from *fellowship with him* to *fellowship with one another* is probably due to the fact that the community of faith has been fractured along theological lines. Some have sided with John and his followers; others have banded together in opposition while making the erroneous claim in verse 6 (see 1 John 2:19; 2 John 7; 3 John 9-10, which specifically mention community tensions and splits). In the author's mind it is logical to conclude that the secessionists' theological error has resulted in their broken fellowship with both God and the faithful followers of God. At any rate, John clearly recognizes that human community is a result of finding community with God.

The final clause of verse 7 points to a second benefit of walking in the light: *the blood of Jesus his Son cleanses us from all sin*. The metaphor finds its setting in the OT in prescriptions of animal sacrifices for sin and in details for the observance of the Day of Atonement (Lev 4:1-12; 19:1-35; cf. Lev 16). The idea of Jesus' *blood* is important in the NT, which mentions *blood* ninety-seven times. The common point is that Jesus' obedience on the cross has resulted in the true, once-for-all, and thus perpetual sacrifice for sin (Rom 3:25; 1 Cor 5:7; Heb 9:12-14; 10:19-22; Rev 1:5). John views the shed blood and death of Jesus as fulfilling such a function without actually explaining how this occurs. However, further details will be offered in 1 John 2:2 and 4:10. The end result is that Jesus' death *cleanses* us. The verb is in the present tense, suggesting an ongoing or continuous process. When coupled with *from all sin*, the point is that our sins are continually washed or wiped away. It is not a select few sins that are removed. Rather, the singular collective *all sin*, which includes everyone's sin(s), is dealt with in Jesus' death.

Both Greek and Hebrew have various meanings for *sin*. However, the most common sense of the word revolves around lawlessness and unrighteousness. First John touches upon the former in 3:4 and the latter in 5:17. But 1 John also sees *sin* as opposition to revealed truth, as in the next verse, 1:8. As Smalley (24) notes, "In 1 John sin is regarded as a universal condition (1:10), resulting, apart from Christ, in alienation from God (2:15) and spiritual death (3:14). But in Christ, sin (and sins) can be removed (2:2; 3:5; cf. John 1:29)." While 1 John is probably not suggesting that the *blood of Jesus* removes deliberate and habitual sin that rejects God's truth (see v. 6), it is sufficient for specific sins and even defilement from our fallen nature (Stott: 76).

Claiming Sinlessness, Deceiving Ourselves 1:8-9

In 1:8 the author moves to a second claim made by his opponents. It is couched in the same fashion as verse 6, where *If we say* is followed by a statement. As in verses 6-7, the author also follows this opening clause by citing two negatives associated with such a claim, and the second verse (v. 9) provides the reader with a positive alternative action and two benefits resulting from that action.

The claim is that *we have no sin*. Scholars are divided as to the exact nature of this claim. Some argue that the opponents were articulating a "perfectionist" view: we have never lapsed into sin. Other see these words as referring to a more "libertarian" understanding of their religion: since we are religious people, no behavior we engage in can be described as sin. It is quite difficult to decide which is more probable, since we do not have sufficient information about these opponents. Our clearest help comes from the Johannine use of the phrase *we have no sin*.

The author frequently employs *to have* with an abstract noun, which names a quality or state such as "wisdom" or "fellowship," so as to convey the sense of being in a particular state or condition. In

1 John 1:3, 6, and 7 he writes about having fellowship; then 2:28; 3:21; and 4:17 talk of having boldness; 3:3 refers to having hope; and 3:15 and 5:12-13 speak about having life. The actual expression of having (or not having) sin is found also in the Gospel of John (9:41; 15:22, 24; 19:11 KJV). The emphasis here in 1 John 1:8 seems to have the same sense as the above uses of the expression. Therefore, we need not conclude that the claim is based on a libertarian lifestyle. Rather, the opponents may well be denying a general condition of sinfulness as opposed to engaging in specific sinful deeds. As Brown notes, their argument, which John challenges, may have been that, once they had faith or belief, sin was not a serious threat to their relationship with God (1982: 206).

The secessionists' line of thinking has two results: self-deception and an absence of truth. The note of deception is found in the reflexive expression *we deceive ourselves*, which stresses personal responsibility for this viewpoint. No one else has led these people astray because they have deliberately made this decision to hold to this perspective.

The second result is that *the truth is not in us*. The use of *truth* here parallels its use in verse 6. As we noted there, Johannine literature associates *truth* with God's revelation in Jesus Christ. This expression is yet another way of saying that to take sin lightly reveals one's tenuous grasp of the revelation that God has given in Jesus. According to John, people who doubt that humans have a general condition of sinfulness also fail to understand fully the implications of God's revelation in Jesus Christ. And building upon the previous verses' concepts, such as self-deception and absence of truth, this further proves that one is walking in darkness. Moreover, such a viewpoint is a serious challenge to the assertion in verse 7 that one needs redemption through Jesus Christ for the sins we commit and the sinful state in which we find ourselves.

Verse 9 then introduces the positive alternative to denying one's sin: *confess[ing] our sins*. Again the author introduces this option with the word *if*, thus beginning the verse with the conditional clause *if we confess our sins*. Although the statement is a conditional clause, Marshall (113) and others see it as having the "force of a command or obligation." So we ask, What is the meaning of the word *confess*? And to what practice is the author referring?

Forty percent of the occurrences of the term *confess* are found in the Johannine literature: four times in the Gospel of John, five times in 1 John, and once in 2 John. Essentially the word means to "acknowledge" or "avow" something, such as one's sins, in this case. This concept of confessing sin probably is inherited from Jewish religious culture, especially the process associated with the Day of Atonement (Lev 16:21; cf. 5:5; Josh 7:19; Ps 32:5; Prov 28:13; Dan 9:20). In this OT context, the confession is made to God, the covenant partner offended by sin.

Unfortunately, 1 John 1:9 does not inform the reader about the protocol for confessing sin. Some scholars see the acknowledgment of sin as a public act; otherwise the self-deception could continue. Others argue that the author envisions private individual confession to God. The verse offers no specific evidence for deciding one way or the other. What is clearer is the fact that the entire community is to engage in the confessing process. The author uses the first-person plural with the verb as opposed to the second- or third-person singular or plural. Everyone needs to confess their sin. That being the case, coupled with the above suggestion that the OT is the probable religious context for this verse, we might well conclude that John envisions this confession as taking place within the context of corporate worship.

The confession of sin results in the dual benefits of forgiveness and cleansing, not because of what we do, but because of God's character, especially God's faithfulness and justice, which is the theme taken up in the second clause: *he who is faithful and just*. Unlike the pagan gods of the ancient world, God is *faithful*, not fickle. *Faithful* means that God is "trustworthy" or "dependable." This divine attribute is affirmed in Scripture (Deut 7:9; Pss 36:5; 89:1-8; 1 Cor 1:9; 10:13; 1 Thess 5:24; 2 Thess 3:3), and occasionally God's faithfulness is associated with covenantal promises (Ps 89:1-4; Heb 10:23). Due to God's consistency in faithfulness to his promises, believers can confidently *confess our sins*, expecting forgiveness and cleansing and not judgment or retribution.

Just (*dikaios*) is the more challenging of the two words describing God's character. To speak of *just* conjures up images of judgment or punishment. However, that is not the thrust of this word. A better translation of *dikaios* is *righteous*, as in 1 John 2:29, *If you know that he is righteous*. Moreover, the opposite of God's *dikaios* is noted at the end of 1:9, where the author refers to our *unrighteousness* (*adikia*), from which God cleanses us. In fact, to characterize God as *faithful* and *righteous* emphasizes the element of divine nature that serves as the foundation for confessing sin. God forgives because he acts consistently according this nature: faithfully and rightly. And a key element of that nature is to be merciful to humans.

Equally challenging is the first word of the next clause: *and will forgive our sins* (RSV; NRSV omits the word). The English word *and* is far too weak to convey the thrust of the Greek word *hina*. Usually *hina* is translated *in order that*, producing a purpose clause with an intended result. However, *hina* clauses can also convey a "consecutive" sense: *which is why* or *which means that*. As Moule (142) points out, "The Semitic mind was notoriously unwilling to draw a sharp dividing line between purpose and consequence." It seems clear that the clause regarding forgiveness of sins is tied to God's attributes of faithfulness and righteousness, and the *hina* clause may be conveying both purpose and result. Therefore the two clauses together could be translated like this: *He is faithful and righteous, which is why he will forgive our sins.* The point is that God's nature and action are the core of forgiveness.

In this clause the author employs another verb to describe how God deals with our sin. In verse 7 we were told that God *cleanses us from all sin*; that verb will be used again in the next clause. But here in verse 9 John says that God *forgives our sins*. The verb *forgive* literally means "he releases" or "he lets go" and probably points to a legal background where one would be released from a debt, as in the OT sabbatical practice of releasing from debts. The presence of this verb, as opposed to *cleanses*, may well be connected to John's conviction that humans, apart from God, are found in a state of sin. Acceptance of the divine revelation in Jesus Christ and confession of our sinfulness results in being "released" from this bondage.

In the final clause we are told that [*he*] *cleanses us from all unrighteousness*. The expression *cleanses from* has been addressed above in verse 7, and all that remains to be noted is the word *unrighteousness* (*adikia*). The opposite of "righteous," one of God's attributes, *adikia* could be translated as "wrongdoing." It is used in 1 John 5:17, which says, *All wrongdoing is sin.* Additionally it is found in John 7:18 (KJV), where "unrighteousness" is set over against "truth." Given these two observations, we can conclude that our confession of sin results in God's releasing us from our anti-Godly ways, setting us free to live godly lives.

Both *forgive* and *cleanse* are in the aorist, the past point-action tense, which also may connote durative effect. This does not mean, however, that forgiveness or cleansing is continuous based upon one confession. For forgiveness and cleansing to take place regularly, one must confess one's sins regularly (cf. the Lord's Prayer). This repeating of the process points toward the author's understanding of the power and pervasiveness of sin. While it is dealt with decisively in the death of Jesus Christ (1 John 1:7), it is never totally overcome in humans. Therefore we must repeatedly admit and confess our sinful condition.

Claiming Not to Have Sinned, Making Him a Liar 1:10–2:2

In 1:10, John moves to a third and final claim made by the secessionists. Again it is set out in the same fashion as in verses 6 and 8,
where *If we say* is followed by a statement. As in verses 6-7 and 8-9,
the author also follows this opening line with two negatives associated with such an erroneous claim, and 2:1b-2 offers the readers a
positive alternative: *Jesus Christ*, the believers' *advocate* and *atoning
sacrifice* for the world's sin.

There is considerable debate as to the relationship between 1:10 and
1:8 due to the clauses *we have no sin* (v. 8) and *we have not sinned* (v. 10).
We are inclined to view verse 10 not as a mere parallel to verse 8 but as
a climactic point in the argument of 1:6-10. Though verse 8 probably
refers to guilt associated with sin, the use of the verb for sinning
(*hamartanō*) in verse 10 clearly refers to the fundamental actions upon
which shame or guilt rests. Further evidence for the climactic nature of
this verse is the lack of parallelism in the respective negatives: verse 8
focuses on self-deception, but verse 10 suggests that those who claim
not to sin are calling into question the nature of God.

What exactly is meant by *we have not sinned* is not certain. Are the
author's opponents asserting that they are not sinners by nature or
that since their conversions they have stopped sinning? What is clear
is the fact that this topic was hotly debated and complex. John returns
to it in 3:6-9, where he tries to clarify the inconsistency between abiding in God and practicing sin. A fuller discussion of this issue will be
offered at that point. For now we can say, the author accepts that
even believers have the capacity to sin (2:1). And when that occurs,
one had best confess the sin (1:9) and turn to Jesus Christ, our *advocate*
(2:1) and *atoning sacrifice* (2:2).

To assert *We have not sinned* places the speakers in the grave situation of making *him a liar*. *Him* most probably refers to God. God
becomes a *liar* if one were to correctly claim to be sinless. This is so
because God has repeatedly acted to redeem sinful humankind and
has most recently done so in the person of Jesus Christ. This pervasiveness of sin has been asserted both in the OT (Gen 8:21; 1 Kings
8:46; Pss 14:3; 53:2; Prov 20:9) and in the Gospel of John (8:21-30;
15:22-24; 16:8-9); God's purpose to redeem is also asserted (1:29;
3:17). The author of 1 John ascribes to these theological assertions.
However, his opponents do not, for they deny their sinning or being
sinful. If they are correct, then God must be the *liar*. This is the ultimate slander. To make God out to be *a liar* is to place the Creator,
Sustainer, and Redeemer of the universe in the same category as the
devil, who according to the Gospel of John is a liar (8:44).

In addition to impacting the nature of God, such a denial also says something about people who would advocate this opinion: *his word is not in us* (1 John 1:10). While the *word* can be a reference to the incarnation of God in Jesus Christ, it can also refer to the revelation of truth surrounding the incarnation. This is how John uses "word" in 1:1; 2:5, 7, 14; its use in this fashion occurs similarly in the Gospel of John (5:24; 8:51; 14:23-24; 15:3). Again, to assert one's sinlessness is evidence of one's failure to grasp and internalize the truth of the gospel message, which is the author's recurring accusation against the separatists.

With 2:1a, *My little children, I am writing these things to you so that you may not sin*, John moves along a tangent that briefly interrupts the parallelism of 1:6–2:2. These eight Greek words are interjected apparently out of a pastoral concern. As many observe, 2:1a qualifies his previous stern counter against the secessionists' claim to be sinless (1:10). The writer does not want to be misunderstood: sin must be taken seriously (Bultmann 1973: 22). And because sin is such a complex subject, it is not best understood in light of extreme viewpoints such as the secessionists' apparent stance that there comes a point when one stops sinning or ceases to have a sinful nature. The other extreme is that we have no hope in the face of sin's strength and pervasiveness. John does not want his readers to be either naive or without hope on this matter, and this is seen in his pastoral concern in this tangent.

Here in 2:1a the writer addresses the Johannine believers in the first-person singular, *I*, in contrast to *we* of chapter 1. In his concern that they not sin, he calls them *little children*. This word is used in 2:12, 28; 3:7, 18; 4:4; 5:21. *Little children*—as compared to the term *children* in 3:1, 2, 10; 5:2; 2 John 1, 4, 13 and 3 John 4—is probably employed to communicate the author's affection for those whom he considers his "spiritual children." Raymond Brown (1982: 214) suggests that this parent/child imagery was influenced by the wisdom tradition's category of fathers instructing their sons (Sirach 2:1; 3:1; Ps 34:11; Prov 4:1). John personally appeals to his readers *not to sin*, yet he realizes the all-pervasive character of sin.

Although sin is pervasive and powerful, one need not be resigned to be its slave, which would be the opposite extreme to the secessionists and a position of dire hopelessness. The author writes so as to encourage resistance: *so that you may not sin*. As Thomas Johnson (34) notes, "The Christian ideal remains *not to sin*." Specifically, the author probably has specific sinful actions or deeds in mind because the verb is found in the past (aorist) point-action form. He is encouraging his readers to avoid sinful actions, thus assuming a more moderate position on the issue of sin's strength and pervasiveness than either the secessionists' overly optimistic view or a hopeless view which 1:10 may be understood to advocate.

Mention has already been made that the blood of Jesus cleanses from sin (1 John 1:7), and the confession of sin results in cleansing due to God's justice and faithfulness (1:9). Lest the readers become discouraged in their efforts to avoid sin or doubt the possibility of forgiveness, the writer reminds them *we have an advocate*, which is introduced by the final occurrence of the conditional clause, *if anyone does sin*. The English word *advocate*, based on the Latin *advocatus*, corresponds to the Greek word *paraklētos*, from which *Paraclete* is derived. It literally means "one called alongside (to help)." The word undoubtedly points to a legal context where one is provided counsel for defense, and the NIV tries to convey this by offering *we have one who speaks to the Father in our defense* as the translation. The sense of 2:1 is that Jesus Christ stands before the Father, is pleading the case for sinners, and is interceding on their behalf. Paul communicates this same idea in Romans 8:34.

On what does Jesus' excellence as an *advocate* rest? He is *righteous*. This word was used in 1:9 to describe one of two primary attributes belonging to God, and so Jesus shares this attribute with God. In 3:5 and 7, Jesus is described as both *sinless* and *righteous*, and it is probably this sense of sinlessness upon which his role as advocate rests. The fact that he shares *righteousness* with the Father simply increases his effectiveness as an advocate for believers.

In 2:2 we read, *and he is the expiation for our sins* (RSV; *and he is the atoning sacrifice for our sins* in NRSV). Two items merit notice. First, 1 John literally reads *and he* (*autos*), *he is expiation for the sins of us*. The unnecessary presence of the pronoun *autos* emphasizes *Jesus' self* as the *expiation* or *atoning sacrifice* for sin. A possible translation reflecting this emphasis might be *and he himself is expiation*. Through the emphatic usage of the pronoun, the author is able to stress the centrality of Jesus Christ as the resource for dealing with sin. Denying one's sinfulness is not a Christian option. Rather, believers turn to Jesus Christ alone, who is both our *advocate* and *expiation* for sin.

The second item is considerably more complex and revolves around the Greek word *hilasmos*. The complexity of the issue becomes obvious as one compares how translation committees have tried to communicate the essence of the word for English-speaking readers. The RSV uses *expiation*, the KJV and NASB use *propitiation*, the NIV and NRSV use *atoning sacrifice*, and the REB uses *a sacrifice to atone*, which is a considerable improvement over the NEB's *remedy for the defilement*.

The diversity of translation is based on the fact that *hilasmos* is used at least three ways in the ancient texts. In the pagan and Greek world, it was used to describe the human act of sacrificing in order to appease the anger of the gods, and this usage stands behind the KJV and NASB's *propitiation*. Although that sense of *hilasmos* does appear in the OT and NT, a more-common sense of the word there places emphasis on cleansing or removing the taint of sin from the person offering a sacrifice. It is this thinking that stands behind the RSV's translation. In the LXX, the Greek translation of the OT, *hilasmos* and other words from the same root are used to translate the Hebrew *kpr* (*atone*, cf. Lev 25:9), where the Hebrew phrase for "Day of Atonement" is translated by the Greek words for "the Day [of] *hilasmou*." Here the point is not that God is appeased or placated; rather, that which is blocking reconciliation with God is removed. We see this line of thinking in 1:9, where the author writes, *If we confess our sins, he is faithful and just, and will forgive our sins and cleanse us from all unrighteousness* (RSV).

The final usage of *hilasmos* reflects a uniquely Jewish and Christian twist. In the pagan world only humans performed acts of *hilasmos*. But there is a line of thinking in both Christian and Jewish circles that God offers *hilasmos* instead of merely receiving these acts. In this way the word takes on a sense of "forgiveness," with God doing something to remove that which stands in the way of reconciliation. We have already seen this line of thinking in *the blood of Jesus his Son cleanses us from all sin* (1:7), assuming that the Johannine community receiving this letter believed that God was present (incarnate) in Jesus for this purpose (John 1:29, 35; 3:16).

The sinless Jesus was worthy to become the sacrifice that would wipe away sin before a holy God. His shed blood alone atones for the sinner. It was not that the Father had to be wrestled into an agreement, that he demanded a blood sacrifice wherewith to be placated, but God himself gave the sacrifice: God's only Son. In order to catch the meaning of both *expiation* and *propitiation*, the NIV and NRSV translated *hilasmos* as *atoning sacrifice*.

This section closes with the words *and not for ours only but also for the sins of the whole world*. In a sense these words almost seem like an afterthought to the previous phrase's affirming that Jesus intercedes and atones for the sins of the Christian community to which John is writing. However, to leave the reader with this narrow focus for the scope of Jesus' salvific action is quite misleading. In reality Jesus' pre- and post-resurrection activity is for *the whole world* (*holou tou kosmou*). But what is meant by *the whole world*?

World (*kosmos*) is found 185 times in the NT, and 55 percent of those occurrences are in the Johannine literature (78 times in the Gospel, 23 times in 1 John, and once in 2 John). Though some Christian traditions have tended to use *world* with primarily negative overtones, the NT usage is more complex and nuanced. This is especially clear when analyzing its usage in the Gospel of John and 1 John. The first twelve chapters of the Gospel use *world* as a positive descriptor for the realm of human activity by an approximately two-to-one margin. This may be due to the fact that in that section of the Gospel, Jesus' ministry is still generally received and the writer's agenda is to communicate God's incarnational love to the whole of humanity. Beginning with chapter 13, this positive usage gives way to a roughly four-to-one negative employment of the word. The mostly negative ratio continues into 1 John. Not surprisingly, both John 13–21 and 1 John have a heightened sense of conflict between Jesus and his followers and those who reject him and his disciples.

This one word is used to express two fundamental truths: God's inclusive love for all humanity (cf. John 3:16) and humanity's tendency to reject this love (cf. John 3:19). With these closing words the author reminds his readers of the universal significance of Jesus' death. It is not a possession of a single faith community. It is not undercut or destroyed by anyone's denial of needing the salvation it offers. All are sinners, and because of God's broad and deep love for all people, Jesus is the atoning sacrifice for *the whole world.*

Summary

First John 1:5–2:2 constitutes the first of three small sections in the larger ethical unit consisting of 1:5–2:17. In this section the writer's opponents claim to have fellowship with God even though they live immorally. Furthermore, they claim to be sinless because they allegedly have a relationship with God. And finally they claim to have no need for the benefits of Jesus' atoning death and intercession before God. The author counters these three claims with what he understands to be generally accepted Christian beliefs: fellowship with God results in living a life of authentic Christian behavior, not a naive denial of one's sinfulness; all people, including Christians, can and do sin; but God is faithful and just to forgive confessed sin. To deny our sinfulness is to make God a liar; instead, we should rely on Jesus Christ, who intercedes for us and serves as our atoning sacrifice.

THE TEXT IN BIBLICAL CONTEXT

Sin

Unlike the NT, the OT does not have one or two primary words for sin; yet sin is viewed as both universal and a deadly serious concept, as it is in the NT (Gen 6:5; 8:21; Isa 64:6-7). We see the universality of sin in humanity in the first couple, Adam and Eve, who are prototypes for all humans who follow. Sin is first noted in Genesis 3 when they both disobey a direct command from God. The end result is both personal pain and estrangement from God.

The eight chapters following Genesis 3 depict increasingly grave results from human rebellion against God. In Genesis 4 sin leads to jealously and fratricide, with Cain killing Abel and wanton interpersonal violence as reflected in Lamech's song regarding vengeance (4:23-24). By chapter 6 humanity's sin is so widespread that God resolves to destroy creation:

> The LORD saw that the wickedness of humankind was great in the earth, and that every inclination of the thoughts of their hearts was only evil continually. . . . So the LORD said, "I will blot out from the earth the human beings I have created—people together with animals and creeping things and birds of the air, for I am sorry that I have made them." (6:5-7)

The few people saved from this destruction are Noah and his family, because of Noah's righteousness (6:8-9). Once the flood has run its course, a new concept is introduced that will dominate the rest of the OT's understanding of sin: covenant. In Genesis 9 God blesses Noah and his family and establishes a covenant with them. God promises to provide for their needs and never destroy humanity again with a flood. In return, humans are to avoid eating blood. But as soon as this rudimentary covenant is established, sin reappears in an incident involving Noah's drunkenness and Ham's (or Canaan's) viewing of Noah's nakedness. Again the end result is broken human relations when Noah cursed Canaan. By chapter 11 human arrogance against God has grown to the point where humans try to build a tower to heaven, thus making a name for themselves.

A second covenant is attempted once Abram is called by God to leave Haran for Canaan (12:1-3). In that covenant "the LORD" promises divine protection for Abram and his heirs, as well as a land of their own once they are released from slavery in Egypt (Gen 15:7-21). For his part, Abram, now renamed "Abraham," was to "walk before me [God Almighty], and be blameless" (17:1). This included circumcising all male heirs as a sign of the covenant relationship.

More description of "walking blamelessly" before God is given upon the exodus from Egypt, when Moses receives the Ten Commandments (Exod 20:1-17) and the various detailed laws governing Hebrew life (20:22–23:19). Since all the commandments and many of the ensuing laws are directed at defining interpersonal and divine/ human interactions, it is clear that much of the Hebrew understanding of sin is offense against God and the community. Individual sin stains the relationship with God and has an impact upon the community and the whole nation (cf. Judg 2:6–3:6; Pss 26; 32; 43; 50; 51; 78; 94). For the individual or nation to ignore the commandments and laws is to reject the Lord who gave them and upon whose nature they are based. Such rejection thus violates covenant law and jeopardizes covenant relationship with God. The end result is not only estrangement from God but also punishment as a natural consequence of no longer being protected by God.

The good news of the OT is that, while humans may repeatedly sin and forsake their covenant relationship with the Lord, he is always faithful to the covenant. God's nature is always to forgive. When Solomon prays at the dedication of the temple, he prays to God that upon confession of their sins, the Lord will forgive them (1 Kings 8:22-53). Jeremiah (31:34) tells Israel that God's desire is a new covenant with the opportunity to forgive and to no longer remember their sins (Jer 36:3). Psalm 103 reminds us that God's attributes include a willingness to "forgive all your iniquity" (v. 3), and God "does not deal with us according to our sins, nor repay us according to our iniquities" (v. 10). Rather, "as far as the east is from the west, so far he removes our transgression from us" (v. 12).

Moreover, a task for the prophets, sent personally by "the Lord," was to remind Israel of the covenant, call for repentance, and hold before them the promise of forgiveness. Isaiah begins his prophecies with "Come now, let us reason together, says the Lord: though your sins are as scarlet, they shall be as white as snow; though they are red like crimson, they shall become like wool" (1:18 RSV). With poignant tenderness Jeremiah recalls the Lord's remembrances, "I remember the devotion of your youth, your love as a bride, how you followed me in the wilderness, in a land not sown. Israel was holy to the Lord" (2:2-3). Ezekiel's words of assurance are these: "I will save them from all the backslidings in which they have sinned, and will cleanse them; and they shall be my people, and I will be their God" (37:23 RSV). Micah asks, "Who is a God like you, pardoning iniquity?" (7:18); and Micah further speaks of God's compassion, delighting in steadfast love and casting all sins into the depths of the sea

(7:18-19). Nehemiah, the rebuilder of Jerusalem's walls, confesses, "But you are a God ready to forgive, gracious and merciful, slow to anger and abounding in steadfast love" (Neh 9:17).

While recognizing that God alone could forgive and deliver people from their sins (Ps 3:8), the ancient Hebrews came to view temple sacrifices as the means through which forgiveness was facilitated. This complex system was seen as a gift to Israel from the Lord as a way of removing sin's taint and renewing covenant relationships with God. The early chapters of Leviticus describe the details surrounding sacrifices to the Lord, including "sin offerings" in chapters 4–7. While some may be inclined to look upon these details as rigid legalism that undercuts grace, another way of viewing these sacrifices is that God graciously provided a powerful ritual to deal with the emotional and psychological traumas surrounding the guilt of sin. If one followed the divinely prescribed rituals, one was assured forgiveness—not because the Lord was appeased by blood sacrifice, but, as noted above, God's nature is to forgive.

In Jesus' ministry we encounter a transformation of thought regarding sin that is seen in his definition of sin, his attitudes toward sinners, and his solution for sin. Initially Jesus, like some Jewish teachers before him, rejects the simple behavioral definition of sin as acts of disobedience to God and a breaking of the covenant or of some Pharisees' popular oral interpretation of these laws. A sinner is not simply someone who commits adultery: a sinner is anyone who even lusts for another person (Matt 5:27-30). Not only is the act of murder a sin; even being angry with another is sin (5:21-26). Behavior alone is not how Jesus defined sin. Sin also includes the private thoughts and attitudes upon which the behavior rests.

In this respect *all* people are sinners, not only those whose behavior violates the covenant with God and God's laws. Because of this universality of human sin, all people—pious Jews and morally good Gentiles, faithless Jews and immoral Gentiles—all stand before God in need of the salvation that Jesus offers. This is clear from many of Jesus' parables and is especially obvious in his parable of the Pharisee and the tax collector (Luke 18:9-14). Nowhere in the Gospels do we gather the impression that Jesus thought non-Jews were necessarily worse sinners than Jews. In fact, he occasionally affirms them as having a clearer understanding of themselves and their need for God than their Jewish contemporaries (Matt 8:5-13; 15:21-28).

Equally radical was Jesus' attitude toward sin and sinners. Jesus taught that God's primary attitude toward sinful humanity was a deep love and desire for reconciliation (Luke 15:1-32; John 16:27).

Whereas John the Baptist associated the judgment of sinners with the Messiah's arrival (Luke 3:7-9), Jesus announced that his ministry was one of healing and release (4:16-21). Therefore he freely interacted with socially recognized sinners, such as tax collectors and prostitutes, while proclaiming his message: "The time is fulfilled, and the kingdom of God has come near; repent and believe in the good news" (Mark 1:15). While many of his Jewish contemporaries viewed sin and sinners as a grave personal threat, Jesus saw sinners as the primary object of his ministry (Matt 9:9-13).

But most radical of all is the solution to sin. God is still the source of forgiveness offered to humans; however, Jesus saw himself as the focus of God's redeeming work. Throughout his ministry he submitted to God's will, and this is especially true in his death on the cross. In Mark we are told three times that Jesus spoke of his death (8:31–9:1; 9:30-32; 10:32-34), and the third time he describes that death as "a ransom for many" (10:45). In John's Gospel Jesus tells Nicodemus,

> No one has ascended into heaven except the one who descended from heaven, the Son of Man. And just as Moses lifted up the serpent in the wilderness, so must the Son of Man be lifted up, that whoever believes in him may have eternal life. For God so loved the world that he gave his only Son, so that everyone who believes in him may not perish but may have eternal life. (3:13-16)

Jesus' death renews humanity's relationship with God, evident in his actions at the Last Supper. There he blesses both the meal's bread and cup: "This is my body, which is given for you. . . . This cup that is poured out for you is the new covenant in my blood" (Luke 22:19-20; cf. Matt 26:26-28; Mark 14:22-24).

While there can be little doubt that John the Evangelist shared many of the biblical ideas relating to sin, for him the gravest sin of all was to reject Jesus Christ, because he is, in John's mind, "the Lamb of God who takes away the sin of the world" (1:29). Repeatedly in conversations with the Jews, Jesus is depicted as stressing the importance of believing in him, as in 8:21-30: "I told you that you would die in your sins, for you will die in your sins unless you believe that I am he" (v. 24). Similar thoughts are found in 8:31-38; 9:35-41; and 15:18-27. A primary function of the Paraclete is to "convince the world concerning sin and righteousness and judgment: concerning sin because they do not believe in me [Jesus]" (16:8-9 RSV). Finally, in Jesus' trial before Pilate—whom John depicts as feckless and torn between accepting Jesus' innocence and the crowd's demand for his death—Judas is described as having "greater sin" than Pilate because he collaborated with the religious leaders seeking to kill Jesus (19:11). As one of the Twelve, he "betrayed" Jesus (18:2, 5).

The letter to the Hebrews also accords Jesus a central role in the discussion of human sin and redemption. In addition to reflecting God's glory and upholding the created order, Jesus Christ "made purification for sins" (1:3): "He had to be made like his brothers and sisters in every respect, so that he might become a merciful and faithful high priest in the service of God, to make a sacrifice of atonement for the sins of the people" (2:17). The writer of Hebrews focuses on this highpriestly imagery and repeatedly applies it to explain Jesus' intercessory work. For example, he writes, "Let us therefore approach the throne of grace with boldness. . . . Every high priest chosen from among mortals is put in charge of things pertaining to God on their behalf" (4:15–5:2; cf. 2:17 for emphasis on mercy). In 9:23–10:18 the writer explains, similar to 1 John 2:1, that Jesus as advocate sits in the presence of God and is interceding on our behalf (Heb 7:25). And the reason he can sit there is due to the fact that he had "been offered once to bear the sins of many" (9:28), thus ending the need for animal sacrifices required in the OT.

The most detailed NT attention to sin and forgiveness is found in Romans. In the opening three chapters, Paul makes a case for universal sinfulness; neither Jew nor Gentile is sinless before God. He concludes his opening argument with sentences and phrases like this: "All, both Jews and Greeks, are under the power of sin (3:9)," and "all have sinned and fall short of the glory of God" (3:23). The power of sin over humanity is so pervasive that it touches all aspects of human existence: our minds (1:21), our physical bodies (6:19), and our wills (7:15). For Paul the only solution is God's activity in Jesus Christ: "They [all sinners] are now justified by his grace as a gift, through the redemption that is in Christ Jesus, whom God put forward as a sacrifice of atonement by his blood, effective through faith" (3:24–25; cf. 4:25; 5:21; 7:25; 2 Cor 5:21). Additionally, Paul firmly believes that transformation accompanies justification, for he writes,

> But you are not in the flesh, you are in the Spirit, since the Spirit of God dwells in you. Anyone who does not have the Spirit of Christ does not belong to him. But if Christ is in you, though the body is dead because of sin, the Spirit is life because of righteousness. (Rom 8:9–10; cf. Gal 2:20; 2 Cor 5:17)

Believers are to continue onward in this transformation process, becoming more Christlike and less worldly (Rom 12:2).

Confession

Related to the biblical theme of sin is confession. Repeatedly in the OT, confession is a human activity essential to restoring relations with the Lord. Both individual and corporate sin are to be confessed. In Joshua 7:16-26 Achan must confess his sin, and in Psalm 32:5 David confesses his sin to the Lord. At the dedication of the first temple, Solomon prays that when Israel sins against the Lord, the people are to come to the temple, "confess your [God's] name, pray and plead with you in this house" (1 Kings 8:33; cf. 1 Kings 8:35; 2 Chron 6:24, 26). Ezra 10:1-44 depicts the people gathering publicly to confess their sins against Yahweh, "the LORD," which includes their forsaking the covenant and transgressing God's law (cf. Dan 9:1-27). All of this is based upon the assumption that the Lord is forgiving and just, but the creature must admit wrongdoing before a transcendent and holy Creator (Prov 28:13).

This line of thinking continues into the NT. A major element of John the Baptist's ministry was to bring people to a confession of their sins and baptize them upon that confession (Matt 3:6; Mark 1:5). Similarly, in response to Paul's ministry in Ephesus, people "confessed and disclosed their practices" (Acts 19:18). In James 5:16, we read, "Confess your sins to one another, and pray for one another, so that you may be healed." Repeatedly this act of "confessing" is related to one's understanding of Jesus as Lord and Savior (see Matt 10:32; Luke 12:8; John 9:22). Paul's well-known line best sums this up: "if you confess with your lips that Jesus is Lord and believe in your heart that God raised him from the dead, you will be saved" (Rom 10:9-10).

Clearly in early Christian circles, confession was an act of recognizing one's sinfulness and God's redeeming work in Jesus Christ, and to do this signaled renewed relations with God.

THE TEXT IN THE LIFE OF THE CHURCH

A Balanced View of Sin

Though 1 John was written to a specific congregation in the ancient world, these words have continuing validity throughout the ages. This is true, in part, because people continually struggle to arrive at a balanced view of sin. Some of our contemporaries seemingly line up with the secessionists who have left the congregation to which John writes. They believe that sin is either insignificant or nonexistent in their lives. They are essentially good people who must surely be acceptable to God. I have a friend who typifies this attitude toward sin and her own supposed lack of sinfulness. In a conversation about faith and salvation, she stated that she did not believe Jesus' death or resurrection is important for a relationship with God. Her sole reason: "I'm too good for God to send me to hell." By her own admission, however, she loves money and hates people of color. Too good? Without sin? No need of Jesus Christ?

At the other extreme are people who are overwhelmed and debilitated by their sins. They sense that they are unworthy of forgiveness because of the lives they live or have lived. Occasionally they are victims of another's sinful behavior and carry that burden as their own. They are certain that no God with an ounce of holiness would allow them into the divine presence, let alone offer reconciliation and forgiveness. And so they stay far from God's love. In reality the good news (gospel) is too good to be true for people who think like this.

As Christians we need to remember and find ways of communicating a balanced view of sin. Sin is not a stray cat that, if ignored, will simply go away. Nor is sin a vicious pit bull terrier that will continually savage its victims until they are lifeless. John says that sin is a serious problem for humans, and he also reminds us that God has provided a serious solution: Jesus Christ, who *cleanses us from all sin* and is our *advocate with the Father.* Such a balanced view is exemplified by a young man who, upon his baptism, made his confession of faith this way. For him the Christian life could be summed in three words: "responsibility," "risk," and "redemption." He shared that he had held back from making a Christian commitment because of the "responsibility" it involved. Baptism, to him, meant keeping a covenant with God, even in the face of death. Additionally, it involved "risk." No one could perfectly keep that covenant, and so there was a fear of failure and sin. But what moved him to baptism was his realization that God provides "redemption" and cleansing in Christ Jesus. Redemption and freedom from the power of sin comes from God, not from us.

This balanced witness is not new. Anabaptist leader Pilgram Marpeck (d. 1556), in a letter to Magdalene von Poppenheim and several others, quotes from the first chapter of 1 John, as he deals with the paradox that Christians are at the same time justified and sinners. Marpeck was a much appreciated and highly respected Strasbourg city engineer, living life intensely where the secular and the life of faith intersected. He writes,

> In the judgment of acquittal, there are first of all sinners. "If we say we have no sin," says John, "we deceive ourselves and the truth is not in us. If we confess our sins, He is faithful and just, and He will forgive our sins and cleanse us from all unrighteousness. If we say we have not

sinned, we make Him a liar and His word is not in us." This text clearly shows that there are sinners and penitents in the judgment of grace. If someone has sinned and does not confess it, he makes God a liar, and His Word is not in that man. Nor does he desire any intercession to give him life again. He thinks he lives. Really he is dead. But those who confess their sins, in the hope that Christ will cleanse them from all stain, are penitents and forsake sin. If Christ the Savior cleanses such a person, he is acquitted and no longer a sinner; he is born anew of God. (Klassen and Klaassen: 471)

Alan Culpepper summarizes the message of this section:

This section offers us a penetrating exhibition of the dangers of denying the presence of sin in our lives. That denial, of course, can take on a variety of forms, all dangerous. How do we deny sin today? By refusing to take God seriously? By assuming that how we live does not matter? By refusing to see how we are compromised and corrupted by impure motives and desires while exposing the dirty laundry of others? The splinter and the beam syndrome can be practiced by individuals, nations, ethnic groups, religious denominations or a church within a denomination. Perhaps one factor in the contemporary neglect of sin is that we do not seriously believe that any other style of life is possible. We do not actually believe that the Word of life can enable us to enjoy an entirely different quality of life as children who share the fellowship of a faithful and just God. (1985: 22)

1 John 2:3-11

To Know Is to Obey

PREVIEW

In the previous section, 1:5–2:2, the author focused on the topic of sin. He clarified for his readers the Christian understanding of sin's pervasiveness and power, as well as the solution to these two daunting characteristics. The author achieved this agenda by citing three erroneous claims made by the secessionists: claims to have fellowship (1:6), to be without sin (1:8), and not to have sinned (1:10). In fact, John counterclaimed,

> To claim fellowship with God while walking in darkness is a lie (1:6).
> To claim to be without sin is self-deception (1:9).
> To claim not to have sinned makes God a liar (1:10).

Rather, the Christian way to deal with sin is to walk in the light (1:7), confess our sins (1:9), and rely on Jesus Christ, our advocate before God (2:1b).

It is one thing to counter self-understanding that allows a person to think he is sinless, as in 1:5–2:2. But that is a different issue than what it means to actually know God, the issue the author now addresses. What is the evidence that a person has a reasonable understanding of who God is? In 1 John 2:3-11 the writer argues that to know God is to obey God's commandments. Urban von Wahlde (60) observes, "They [the commandments] function as an integral part of the author's defense in the conflict raging within the community."

In this section John continues to counter the flawed thinking of the separatists, but he moves his argument forward. Here he tackles the issue of how to prove that a person knows God. The author's general answer is clear: one who keeps God's commandments knows God

(v. 3). This keeping of the commandments is based on Jesus' model of the same behavior. As von Wahlde (60) concludes, "The believer is to walk 'as he walked' (v 6); . . . the commandment which the believer is to obey has been realized in Jesus and so it should be realized also in the life of the Christian (v 8)." Also, similar to the previous unit is the recurring use of the polar images *light* and *darkness* (1:5, 6, 7; 2:8, 9, 10). After 2:3-11 John does not employ this imagery again.

With this continuity of images, there is also a degree of discontinuity between this unit and the previous one in style. Instead of using a conditional clause (*If we say*) three times to highlight the secessionists' views, now the author employs a participial phrase (*ho legōn*, literally translated as *the saying* [*one*] or *the* [*one*] *saying*) three times to expose the separatists' tendencies. Additionally, John now addresses an even more basic question than the nature of sin: How can we be sure we know God? Are there any tests that can be applied to ascertain the validity of someone's claim to know God?

These nine verses are crucial to the entire letter's development in that they introduce four themes that will frequently recur:

- knowing God (vv. 3-4)
- obedience: keeping the commandments (vv. 3-8)
- eschatology: this era is giving way to the next age (v. 8)
- loving one another (vv. 9-11)

All four are interwoven and will continue to intersect with one another in the following chapters. (See Table 1)

OUTLINE

Introduction of a General Principle, 2:3
A General Test of the Principle, 2:4-6
A Parenthetical Clarification on the Principle's Origin, 2:7-8
A Specific Test of the Principle, 2:9-11

EXPLANATORY NOTES

Introduction of a General Principle 2:3

Many scholars note that the opening phrase of verse 3, *by this* (*en toutō*), can refer to ideas or concepts that precede or follow the phrase. Though that is generally true, here the phrase clearly refers to something that follows. For one reason, the presence of *now* (*kai*) signals a shift in argumentation, as it did at the start of 1:5 (GNB). Moreover, it is difficult to understand how the previous content in

Table 1

The Principle Generally Introduced 2:3
Now by this we may be sure that we know him,
  if we obey his commandments.

A General Test for the Principle: 2:4-6	A Specific Test for the Principle: Hating or Loving 2:9-11
Whoever says, "I have come to know him," but does not obey his commandments, is a liar, and in such a person the truth does not exist; but whoever obeys his word, truly in this person the love of God has reached perfection. By this we may be sure that we are in him: whoever says, "I abide in him," ought to walk just as he walked.	*Whoever says, "I am in the light," while hating a brother or sister, is still in the darkness. Whoever loves a brother or sister lives in the light, and in such a person there is no cause for stumbling. But whoever hates another believer is in the darkness, walks in the darkness, and does not know the way to go, because the darkness has brought on blindness.*

A Parenthetical Clarification: Old and New Commandment 2:7-8

Beloved, I am writing you no new commandment, but an old commandment that you have had from the beginning; the old commandment is the word that you have heard. Yet I am writing you a new commandment that is true in him and in you, because the darkness is passing away and the true light is already shining.

1:5–2:2, especially the immediate subject of Jesus as *atoning sacrifice for our sins* in 2:2, is an assurance for John's present concern: how do we know that someone knows God? Can we provide evidence of *our* knowing God by an action undertaken by God? Finally, as Brown states, if *by this* refers to a previous thought, the following conditional clause, *if we keep his commandments,* is left hanging alone (1982: 248-49).

In fact, what we have in the opening phrase of verse 3, *Now by this,* is one-half of what David Rensberger (60) refers to as a "discernment formula." In the midst of the chaos and controversy in which this community is embroiled, John uses a number of these formulas in order to help clarify their thinking and situation. These formulas show up in varied forms: in 2:18; 3:10, 16, 19, 24; 4:2, 6, 9, 10, 13, 17; and 5:2. In this particular instance, the vague phrase *by this* is connected to and clarified by the conditional clause *if we obey his commandments*. Haas, de Jonge, and Swellengrebel (38) argue that the decision to separate *by this* from the conditional clause by using the words *we may be sure that we know him* intensifies or emphasizes the importance of keeping the commandments.

An ambiguous point relating to the second half of the discernment formula is the identity of the person designated by *his* in the clause *if we obey his commandments*. This ambiguity recurs numerous times in 2:3-6 because the third-person masculine pronoun is used in varied forms: *his, him,* and *he*. These occur as follows: we know *him* (v. 3); *his* commandments (vv. 3-4); I know *him* (v. 4); the truth is not *in such a person* (v. 4; literally, *in him*); *his* word (v. 5), *in him* twice (v. 5: once the NRSV renders it as *in this person*); abides *in him* (v. 6); and *he* walked (end of v. 6). So to whom is John referring when he writes *his, him,* and *he*?

The easiest occurrence to resolve is the *in him* in 2:4, *in such a person the truth does not exist*, and the first use in verse 5, *in this person the love of God has reached perfection*. Here the sentences are clear: the text refers to the believer. What of the other usages? The obvious choices are either God or Jesus. Some scholars see great complexity behind the use of the word in vv. 3-6. Sometimes it refers to God, as in *we know him, if we obey his commandments* (v. 3), and at other times it is a reference to Jesus, when John writes, *as he walked* (v. 6). The logic is simple enough. God gave commandments and Jesus walked on earth. I propose, however, that all of these uses of the pronoun refer to Jesus, except those referring to the believer, as mentioned above. The strength of this proposal is its consistency with the christological tenor of the Epistle's focus. How one views Jesus is at the heart of the controversy between the Johannine tradition and the views of the secessionists.

First, we must recall that John's thinking here is a continuation of his thoughts in the previous section. The last figure mentioned in 1:5–2:2 is Jesus Christ, who is our expiation. Moreover, in the Johannine tradition, it is not only God the Father who gives commandments. Jesus himself is depicted as giving at least one commandment (cf. John 15:12), and the Gospel of John reports that Jesus gave more than one commandment (cf. John 15:10; see chart on "Commandment(s)" in Swartley on John 15, forthcoming). The author of 1 John is aware of that tradition, which depicts Jesus as a giver of *commandments*, as he notes in verse 3. Thus *his commandments* in verse 4 and *his word* in verse 5 parallel the use of *his commandments* in verse 3. That leaves us with *We are in him: whoever says, "I abide in him," ought to walk just as he walked* (vv. 5b-6). Clearly *he walked* in 2:6 is a reference to the incarnate Christ. Thus I suggest that abiding *in him* is an appeal to and use of the Johannine tradition of remaining/abiding (*menō*) in Jesus Christ (John 6:56; 15:1-11). The content of these verses may well be in the author's mind as he pens this section of the letter. At any rate, we are best advised to avoid attempts to neatly separate God the Father and Jesus Christ the Son, because the ample evidence within the Johannine tradition emphasizes their intimacy and oneness. This relationship is evident from the Gospel's very first verse, and it is developed in a number of ways. For example, John 10:22-39 depicts a tense dialogue between Jesus and the Jews regarding his messianic role. There Jesus claims to work in the Father's name (10:25; cf. 5:17-18), and he even claims "The Father and I are one" (10:30; cf. 10:38). Ultimately, within the Johannine tradition, knowing Jesus means knowing God (cf. John 1:18; 14:9-11a; 15:15).

This discernment formula's core is the conditional clause *if we obey his commandments*. The theme of keeping commandments is one of John's central concerns. Whereas Paul tends to prefer the verb *guard* (*phylassō*) when referring to keeping the commandments (Rom 2:26; Gal 6:13; 2 Thess 3:3; 2 Tim 4:15; cf. Phil 4:7) where Paul uses the word in different contexts), the author of 1 John uses the verb *tēreō*, which can be translated as *obey* or *keep* (see 1 John 2:3, 4, 5; 3:22, 24; 5:3; cf. John 8:51, 52, 55; 14:15, 21, 23, 24; 15:10 [2x], 20 [2x]; 17:6). The verb appears in other NT passages in the context of keeping commandments or words (Matt 19:17; 1 Tim 6:14; Jas 2:19; Rev 12:17). It would seem as though John views this word as synonymous with *doing*, for in 1 John 5:2 the author literally writes, *We do his commandments*. For John and his community, the concern is how one lives in relation to the commandments. One does not simply acknowledge the existence of the commandments. Rather, one internalizes them and tries to embody them in the course of everyday living. As OT prophets anticipated, the law will be written "on their hearts" (Jer 31:33; cf. Ezek 36:26-27).

What are to be embodied are the *commandments* (*entolai*). This word has its roots in the OT's concept of the law as based on the Lord's nature and given by the Lord to the people of Israel. This law or Torah is summarized in the Ten Commandments (Exod 20:2-17), the core teachings that are to govern the Israelites' social interaction. The word *commandment* is found 14 times in 1 John (in the plural form in 2:3, 4; 3:22, 24; 5:2, 3 [2x] and in the singular form in 2:7 [3x], 8; 3:23 [2x]; 4:21. See also 2 John 4, 5, 6 [2x]). As is soon evident, John, similar to the tradition in the OT, comfortably summarizes a broad body of commandments with a specific commandment: love one another. For now, he generally and broadly introduces his guiding principle that reveals one's knowledge of the Divine: one obeys the commandments.

The final element of the general discernment formula is this: *We may be sure that we know him* or, literally, *We know that we have known him.* The author of these epistles uses two different verbs to communicate the idea of knowing. In reality there is little or no meaningful difference between them, and in this case John uses *ginōskō*. However, there are shades of meaning when he employs *ginōskō*. Some scholars see as many as seven different nuances associated with the words (Kruse: 77), but for our purposes we will mention just two. The first use of *know* has to do with knowing that something is accurate or certain. The second usage of the word connotes involvement or intimacy.

In short, John is saying that his fellow believers can be confident that they know God, based on their involvement with Jesus Christ and obedience to his commandments. This involvement with Jesus Christ is hinted at in that the verb is in the perfect tense, indicating a past experience. Thus far in the letter the author has stressed the experience of the incarnation (1:1-2), fellowship with God and Christ (1:3), and fellowship with other believers (1:3, 7). So it is probably these events to which he points as the basis of one's knowledge. This assertion is placed over against the secessionists' more speculative and abstract ways of knowing God [*Gnosticism, p. 308*]. For John, both the basis for knowing God and the continuing evidence of knowing God grow out of and find concrete expression in the midst of human events. Solid evidence of one's knowledge of the divine is not found in one's grasp of abstract theology or philosophy, but rather in daily obedience to Christ's commandments. As Schnackenburg declares, "Despite all the speculation and mystical profundity that impresses us so much in the Johannine writings, they are eminently practical and down to earth in their moral concern" (1992: 96).

Here the author also differs from those OT prophets who lamented their contemporaries did not have a full knowledge of God in view of their consistent disobedience (1 Sam 2:12; Job 36:12; Isa 1:3; 5:13; Jer 9:6) and who projected the hope that one day the people would have this knowledge (Jer 9:23-24; 31:34; Hos 4:1; 6:1-3; Hab 2:14). I suggest that John does not invoke this prophetic tradition because he believes that the Christ event is the divine act that now makes the prophetic hope a reality for humanity. John's outlook is not that of the more pessimistic OT prophets but is shaped by the knowledge of Jesus Christ.

John's view also stands against the overly optimistic, abstract, and contemporary secessionists. Although they claimed a superior knowledge of God, their sinful lives—already challenged in the previous section—undercut their claim. By introducing this general principle in verse 3, the author makes it quite clear that true knowledge of the divine realm works itself out in a life of obedience to the revealed commandments of Jesus Christ. As he firmly states, keeping divinely given commands is strong evidence that a person knows the source of the commandment.

A General Test of the Principle 2:4-6

In beginning this subunit, the author takes the general principle in verse 3 and clarifies it by rephrasing it in a negative form and alluding to claims made by the secessionists. In verses 4 and 6, as noted above, we see the same expression *whoever says* (*ho legōn*), and we will see it again at the beginning of verse 9. Many commentators see a parallel between these sections (vv. 4-6 and 9-11) and what the author did in 1:5–2:2. There John is seen as highlighting three false claims of his opponents by the use of the same conditional clause in 1:6, 8, and 10. Some think John is perhaps citing direct quotes in this section instead of using his own paraphrasing of his opponents' views, as in 1:5–2:2 (Brown 1982: 253). To make such a claim goes too far. What we can certainly say is that John continues his polemic against the separatists, and this time he takes his argument forward by moving from the abstract theological plane to the mundane field of daily living. Instead of challenging his opponents' theories about the nature of sin, John in 2:3 has asserted his principle that knowing the divine plays itself out in obedience to divine commandments. In verses 4-6 (and 9-11), he cites the discontinuity between his opponents' lives and their theological claims so as to accentuate the flaws of their worldview.

At one level 2:4 does not introduce any new ideas. We have seen John's tendency to refer to his opponents' views. We have heard the charge of lying and not following the truth in 1:6. Further, *does not obey his commandments* in 2:4 is simply a negative form of *we obey his commandments* found in verse 3. While the content has not changed, the intensity of John's charges certainly has been altered. Now he moves away from the inclusive words *We lie and do not do what is true* in 1:6 to much more personalized and accusatory language: *The one who says . . . but does not obey . . . is a liar, and the truth is not in him* (2:4 AT). It is no longer a matter of we may be lying and not doing the truth. Now it is So-and-so is a liar, and not only does he not do the truth, he doesn't even understand the truth. At this point the author is thinking in terms of "us" and "them."

As secondhand readers we will never fully grasp the meaning of this verse in the same fashion and with the same intensity as John's original audience. They knew the people about whom John was writing. They could offer illustrations of inconsistent behavior. They knew not only the inconsistency but also the tensions, shame, and pain that resulted from the divisions within the community. After all, some of the separatists were probably relatives and old friends. Angry words may have been exchanged. The situation was in danger of total collapse. What was one to do?

It may look as though the author is convinced that finding scapegoats is the best way to deal with this situation, but that is not the case. Though he does not let his opponents off lightly, he does remind the faithful that they carry the burden of proof. The principle that is negatively stated in 2:4 reinforces the importance of keeping the commandments. In essence John says, Do not behave like those who have left. Be faithful to what you have been taught. Verses 5 and 6, as well as 9-11, will clarify the content of that teaching. And 3:23 will specifically state the core of the "commandments": *And this is his commandment, that we should believe in the name of his Son Jesus Christ and love one another, just as he has commanded us.* These are the two topics with which 1:1–2:11 is dealing.

In 2:5a the core charge against the secessionists is reformulated into a positive statement: *but whoever obeys his word, truly in this person the love of God has reached perfection.* The presence of the word *but* (*de*) indicates the author's attempt to subtly draw a contrast between the claims and behavior of the separatists and the ideal Christian lifestyle. Simply put, the difference is this: one way claims knowledge of God while disobeying divine directives; the other way allows God's primary character, love, to be embodied in lives of obedience.

Additional evidence that John is continuing his argument about the importance of obedience is found in the close parallelism between *but does not obey his commandments* in verse 4 and *obeys his word* in verse 5a. In both instances the same Greek verb is used for *obey*. Moreover, both verses use the present active form of the verb, suggesting that John views this obedience as an ongoing process. This note of consistency will be reinforced by the theme of "perfected" love in verse 5 and the themes of "abiding" and "walking" in verse 6.

The obvious difference between these two phrases, apart from the negative form of 2:4, is the use of *commandments* and *word*. Some scholars see this change of wording as an indication of John's broadening his argument. They suggest that the reference in verse 4 is to the law given by God and that verse 5 further includes Jesus' teaching. Such a suggestion is based upon speculation: we simply cannot know if that is the case. Conversely, we have already seen that the author tends to "collapse" God the Father and Jesus the Son into one, thus making it somewhat unlikely that the author makes a clear distinction between *commandments* and *word*. Instead, he is highlighting the importance of believers conforming their life to the patterns established in the teachings they have received.

Much more challenging and crucial for understanding John's argument is the statement: *Truly in this person the love of God has reached perfection.* Two issues arise here. First, what does John mean when he writes, *the love of God* (*hē agapē tou theou*)? And second, what concept stands behind the verb *reached perfection* (*teteleiōtai*)?

The Greek words for *the love of God* are more than a little ambiguous. In fact, the phrase *the love of God* (*hē agapē tou theou*) can be translated three different ways. First, it could be viewed as an objective genitive: "love *for* God." If translated this way, the verse would be communicating the idea that through our obedience our love for God is perfected. Second, the phrase could be a subjective genitive, meaning "God's love" and suggesting that the believers' obedience is a conduit for the perfecting of God's love for believers, not the believers' love for God. Finally, it could be translated as a qualitative genitive: "God's *kind* of love." Here the author would be suggesting that the life of obedience facilitates the believer's embodiment of a love like God's love.

The trend among recent translations is to view the phrase as a subjective genitive. Therefore, the NIV translates these words as *God's love*, and the NRSV reads *the love of God*. The older RSV opted for the objective genitive when its translation committee accepted *love for God*. Though the modern mind may debate which option is preferable, we cannot be sure that the author was so exacting. Perhaps he intentionally selected an ambiguous phrase because he preferred the full range of meaning. As Garrett Kenney (23) states, John has a strong sense of the Christian life involving an intimate and personal relationship with the divine and a love that can only be viewed as reciprocal. In this case, one's obedience could be the result of one's love for God, the conduit for God's love, and the embodiment of a love like God's own love—all three meanings.

The other challenge for the modern translator and reader is the author's choice to use the verb *teleioō*. The verb can be translated as having the sense of "perfected": so the RSV reads *love for God is per-*

fected; the NRSV has *love of God has reached perfection*. For a variety of reasons, both are misleading. First is the assumption of flawlessness that goes with the English word *perfect*. Second, both translations further this misunderstanding by inadvertently suggesting that this state of flawlessness can actually be achieved at some point. The previous unit on sin has certainly ruled out that conclusion as one of John's beliefs. There he never assumes that the power of sin is fully overcome by the believer. We instead rely on our advocate, Jesus Christ, not our own state of *perfection* or flawlessness. A better way to translate *teleioō* is to use a word that tries to communicate its underlying sense of "fullness." The NIV did this when the committee agreed on *God's love is truly made complete*. Better still is Eugene Peterson's phrase in *The Message*: *God's mature love*.

This idea of "perfected" or "complete" love is a crucial concept for the author of 1 John and is first introduced here. This verb *teleioō* is found again in 4:12 and 17-18, where it is further developed. Again it is associated with obedience to divine commandments, but an additional theme is confidence before God on the *day of judgment* (4:17). As we will see, this theme of eschatology, about the final events, is always or nearly always lurking in the back of the author's mind. We see evidence of it in his choice of words here in 2:5, the theme of *passing away* in 2:8 and 17, the arrival of the *antichrist(s)* and the *last hour* in 2:18-27 and 4:3, and the second coming in 3:2. One cannot help but wonder if the crisis facing the Johannine community was so intense that it rekindled older and more traditional eschatological theology. At any rate, we can say that John's immediate solution to the crisis is for his followers to obey the commandments, thus placing themselves in a position whereby God can "perfect" or "mature" the love they know.

The closing words of verse 5, *By this we may be sure that we are in him*, could refer either to what went before or to the words of verse 6. Some scholars point to *By this we may be sure* in verse 3 and suggest that the use of exactly the same phrase in verse 5 forms an *inclusio* (a literary unit beginning and ending with the same theme), running from verse 3 through the end of verse 5. If that is the case, verse 6 is merely a recapitulation of the theme in verses 4-5. However, as noted above, verse 3 is a general introduction to the whole of 2:3-11. Additionally, *we are in him* in verse 5b clearly introduces and connects with *I abide in him* in verse 6, which is another crucial theme for this letter *["Abiding" in the Johannine Letters, p. 300]*. Finally, verse 6 does not appear so much as a recapping of the previous line of thought as it functions as a climax for verses 4-6. In verse 6 the author seeks to concretize his earlier general admonition to obey *his word* (v. 5).

Verse 6 begins with the same words that begin verse 4: *Whoever says* (*ho legōn*). If there is an *inclusio* in this unit, it consists of this phrase and not *we may be sure* in verses 3 and 5. At any rate, the repeated use of *whoever says* is used to contrast two options that lie before the Johannine community. The first, the rejected alternative, is to claim knowledge while disobeying divine commandments. The second option, advocated or even demanded in verse 6, is to *abide in him* and to *walk just as he walked*. Despite the awkwardness of the Greek (literally translated by Haas, de Jonge, and Swellengrebel [43] as "he . . . has-the-obligation (that) just-as that-one walked he-himself also be-walking"), it is clear that John is arguing for an imitation of Christ as a sign of faithfulness and the foundation for Christian confidence. Simply saying one *abides in him* is insufficient. The genuine evidence of one's abiding is *to walk just as he walked.*

The first question raised by this verse is this: to whom do the pronouns *him* and *he* refer? The *he* of *he walked* is *ekeinos*, "that one." In 1 John *that one* is used repeatedly as a reverential expression for Jesus (as in 3:3, 5, 7, 16; 4:17). This is especially clear in 3:16, where the author writes, *He* [*ekeinos*] *laid down his life for us.* The use of the verb *walked* simply reinforces the conclusion that *he* is a reference to Jesus, because it again points to his incarnation and earthly ministry—a theme that is found at the beginning of the letter and is an issue that gives rise to the letter's writing. Having established this fact helps establish that *abiding in him* also refers to Jesus. There is a connection between the two. If one is *in him*, then one will walk *as he walked.* In essence, John is saying that if one has a genuine relationship with Jesus, then one will live as Jesus lived.

The question then becomes clear: What is the nature of this relationship? To communicate this idea, the author repeatedly uses the verb *abide* (*menō*), which first appears here in this letter. As many scholars note, it is one of the author's favorite verbs and probably a core concept of his theology. Fifty-five percent of all the NT occurrences of the word are in the Johannine writings. It is used forty times in the Gospel of John, twenty-four times in 1 John, and three times in 2 John. As Brown notes, it has a wide range of meaning and can be translated by many different English words, including "remain," "dwell," and "rest" (1982: 259).

Unfortunately, none of these words communicates the "vitality" or "dynamic" nature of what the author has in mind when he uses it. However, a brief survey of its usage in the letter yields understanding. In particular, we are interested in those verses where the verb is used to express "the abiding presence of the Christian in God and Jesus, and vice versa" (Brown 1982: 259). John employs the phrase *abide in* (*menō en*) to communicate the idea of the believer in relationship with Jesus in this verse and in 1 John 2:27, 28 and 3:6 (cf. John 6:56; 15:4, 5, 6, 7). A similar relationship between the believer and God is expressed through these words in 1 John 3:24; 4:13, 15, and 16. And once, in 1 John 2:24, *abide in* is used when communicating the believer's relationship to both God and Jesus. This act of "abiding," however, is not a one-way avenue in the author's mind. Not only does the believer *abide in* God or Jesus, but God and Jesus also *abide in* the believer, as is evidenced by 1 John 3:24; 4:12, 13, 15, 16 (God/believer) and John 6:56; 15:4, 5 (Jesus/believer). When the author uses this verb, he is trying to communicate his belief that genuine religious experience is essentially an intimate and reciprocal relationship between the human and the divine.

Such a relationship carries with it at least one obligation: [*one*] *ought to walk just as he walked*. What the author is suggesting here is not mere conformity to a law code or, even worse, legalism. He is arguing that if one wants to claim unity with Jesus Christ and the Father, then that person's life must reflect the nature of the divine figure in which one is supposedly abiding. The author has made this point in a more general fashion in verses 3, 4, and 5, when he writes about keeping or not keeping commandments and teachings. As we will see in the TBC section below, John's argument is based on the biblical ideal of a covenant relationship and the people of God living lives that reflect the divine nature. In particular, as we would expect from someone in the Johannine circle, the life of Jesus (*as he walked*) is *the* model for the believer. The author of the letter believes that the Johannine tradition regarding Jesus reveals all the crucial truth one needs to live a moral life that is pleasing to God. And that is why John gives this as his one concrete illustration for the more general point of keeping *his commandments* (v. 4) and *word* (v. 5). When we return to this theme in verses 9-11, after the parenthetical clarification in verses 7-8, the author will offer an even more specific pattern of behavior for those who *abide: they love*.

Having said this, an important qualification must be made. This verse, just like the word *perfection* in verse 5a, could easily be misunderstood by the modern reader. Even a notable scholar like Rudolf Schnackenburg flirts with this confusion when he writes, "If fellowship with God is to be real and lasting, it requires constant fidelity to the great paradigm, . . . that is, Christ himself" (1992: 99). Many people think that a relationship with God is solely dependent upon *our* faithfulness to Christ. By living like Christ we can somehow prove ourselves. Yet as Georg Strecker (43) notes, "There is, however, no notion of earned merit associated with this idea." What 1 John is trying to communicate in verses 5b-6 is this: a genuine and lasting relationship with the divine or authentic religious experience, unlike the religion of the secessionists, naturally results in a life like Jesus' own life. The cause and effect flows from the relationship to the life lived, not the reverse. The separatists have religious experience, but it is not Christian religious experience. If it were Christian religious experience, if the risen Christ were present in their lives, they would live like Christ; but they do not *walk just as he walked.*

A Parenthetical Clarification on the Principle's Origin 2:7-8

As we come to verses 7-8, we encounter a short parenthetical clarification that has probably been triggered by the reference to *commandments* in verse 4 and the general theme of obedience that reflects Jesus' own life in verses 4-6. Perhaps John suddenly realizes that a word is in order regarding the nature of the *commandments* and obedience to which he has just referred. Some scholars have justifiably suggested that the author is defending his views against those of the "progressive" and innovative separatists, and this defense is the foundation for these verses. Here the author certainly appeals to the Johannine tradition if not to the Gospel of John itself. Two items are of primary importance in these verses. First, what does John mean when he says the commandment is both *old* (v. 7) and *new* (v. 8)? Second, there is some confusion as to the referent for the relative pronoun *which* (RSV; *that* in NRSV) in the phrase *which is true in him and in you* (v. 8). The closing expression, *The darkness is passing away and the true light is already shining* (v. 8), helps to resolve both issues.

John begins these verses with *beloved,* a term of endearment, which he uses six times in this letter (here and 3:2, 21; 4:1, 7, 11). Its presence indicates both the author's affection for his audience and a shift from exposition to direct personal address (Haas, de Jonge, and Swellengrebel: 43). John wants to remind his readers that he is not introducing a new teaching as his opponents have done. In fact, he is appealing to *an old commandment which* [*that,* NRSV] *you have had from the beginning. . . .* Furthermore, this *old commandment* is described as *the word which* [*that,* NRSV] *you have heard* (RSV).

While the commandment could be described as *old* because the author has a passage like Leviticus 19:18 in mind, this is rather unlikely. It is, after all, something they have had *from the beginning* and *the word* they have heard (see comments on 1:1-4 and on 2:5). It is more probable that the author has in mind either the Johannine tradition behind John

13:34 or that specific verse from the Gospel of John ("I give you a new commandment, that you love one another. Just as I have loved you, you also should love one another"). Therefore the commandment can justifiably be described as *old* because it goes back to the beginning of the Christian movement. It is a basic teaching of the Johannine community, and every new member is given this commandment as part of the initiation process. The fact that it is a core teaching will be seen when we turn to 2:9-11, where this one command is used to sum up all the commandments generally referred to in 2:4. Here the author describes it specifically as *the word* (*ho logos*) as opposed to "a word" because it is a specific and well-known word in John's community (Brown 1982: 265).

That explanation of *old* is plausible. The difficulty with it comes in the next verse, when John writes, *Yet I am writing you a new commandment that is true in him and in you.* The presence of *yet* (*palin*) reveals that the author may well be thinking on the fly here, because the word carries with it a sense of firm contrast. *Palin* could be translated *on the other hand* (as in *The Message*), which would help English readers better understand John's awareness of the complexity associated with this *old/new* teaching.

We come to grips with the newness element only when we consider the second challenge in these verses. The phrase *that* [*which*] *is true in him and in you* begins with a relative pronoun and therefore must refer to some earlier concept. The obvious choice would be the noun *commandment* (*entolē*), thus resulting in the sense that it is the *commandment* itself that is *true in him and in you*. The problem is that *entolē* is a feminine word and *ho* is neuter; therefore, *ho* (*which/that*) cannot be referring to *entolē*, or *commandment*.

The option is that John has the concept of *new* in mind when he writes that "something" (neuter) is *true in him and in you*. If he is suggesting a connection between *new* and *true*, he is thinking along the following lines. The original *old* command to love one another took on a radically *new* twist in the life of Jesus Christ, especially in his willingness to lay down his life for those he loved (cf. John 15:13). And even more phenomenal is the fact that this type of love continues to be manifest in the ongoing life of the Johannine community (*in you*; note that *you* here is in the plural form). In this sense it is ever *new* and fresh when the community of faith loves one another. The fact that the author decides to describe this as *true* supports this, for *true* (*alēthes*) carries with it a sense of "manifest" (Haas, de Jonge, and Swellengrebel: 46), "genuine," or "real" as in John 6:55; Acts 12:9; 1 Peter 5:12.

The final words of verse 8 further support the previous line of thinking. The reason this radical love commandment can be *true* in the Johannine community of faith is *because the darkness is passing away and the true light is already shining.* This verse is founded upon a crucial NT and early Christian presupposition. C. H. Dodd (34) refers to this: "It is the universal assumption of all NT writers that with the coming of Christ a new age has dawned." We see evidence of this in 1 Thessalonians 5:4-8 and Ephesians 5:8-14. In the Gospel of John, Jesus is described as "the true light, which enlightens everyone, was coming into the world" (1:9; cf. 3:19; 8:12; 9:5). And in the Johannine tradition, Jesus is depicted as offering this light to those who follow him (John 8:12; cf. 12:35-36, 46).

This theme of light and darkness was introduced in 1:5-7 and now is qualified eschatologically in 2:7-8 *[Eschatology, p. 306]*. It will be further addressed in the next three verses. The writers of 1 John and the Gospel of John are clearly aware that the Christ event was a watershed type of occurrence. Unlike the synoptic Gospel writers, who have a more future-oriented eschatology, the Johannine eschatology is balanced between past, present, and future. All three time periods are important. What Jesus Christ has done in the past has a positive impact on the present in that it has begun the process of transition from one age to another, and this process will come to full completion in the future. Especially important to John is the present. He is convinced that "the Christian can 'walk in the light' *now,* and share this light with others" (Smalley: 58). And the primary way the community of faith shows that it walks in the light is by the manifestation of the *old/new,* and as yet unspecified, commandment in its midst.

A Specific Test of the Principle 2:9-11

In this last subunit of 1 John 2:3-11, the author's argument finally reveals a specific test and commandment that he probably has had in mind since writing *Now by this we may be sure that we know him, if we obey his commandments* (v. 3). The shift from the plural to singular in the repeated use of *commandment* in verses 7-8 further reveals that John has a specific commandment in mind. And that particular commandment is the one that he writes about in verses 7-8: love one another.

He begins verses 9-11 by using a third time the participle *whoever says (ho legōn).* This continues the pattern set in 2:4 and 2:6 and also harks back to the previous unit, where John probably cites his opponents' views in 1:6, 8, and 10 with the phrase *If we say.* Clearly part of this community's dilemma has to do with people making claims (*saying*) but not showing evidence of their claims by what they do. The author highlights the importance of tangible support for one's claims when he further uses two more participles—*whoever loves* (*ho agapōn*) in verse 10 and *but whoever hates* (*ho de misōn*) in verse 11—which are intended to relate to and contrast with *he who says* in verse 9. In other words, the true test of one's awareness of God is not based on what one says about one's relationship to God but how one actually relates to others in the community of faith.

The specific test is first articulated in a negative form. John returns to a metaphor that he first uses in 1:5 (*God is light*) and that recurs in 1:7 (*We walk in the light as he himself is in the light*). The author there suggests that being *in the light* results in *fellowship with one another*. The light theme recurs in the parenthetical clarification in 2:8, when John writes that *the true light is already shining*. In essence this metaphor is used to describe one's awareness of God and intimate involvement with God, which is a divisive issue for the Johannine community. The secessionists claim intimacy with God based upon their definitions and categories; John and his supporters adhere to a different set of standards. The end result is a conflictive relationship between the two groups.

Because John firmly believes that fellowship with God naturally results in fellowship with others who have a similar relationship with God (see 1:7), he asserts that anyone who hates *a brother or sister is still in the darkness*. In an attempt to stress the gravity of their situation, he uses an emphatic phrase for *still* (*heōs arti*). Despite the fact that the *darkness is passing away and the true light is already shining* (v. 8), these people, who hate the members of John's community, show that they are *still* in darkness and not in relationship with God, who is light. Hatred is a sign of the old age or darkness that is fading. Love is indicative of the light and the coming new era.

Finally, a word regarding *brother or sister* is in order. The original Greek text reads *adelphon autou* or, literally, *his brother*, as the RSV presents it. Although the author uses a masculine noun here, it is clear that he generally means a person who is a member of the Christian community and not just males in that community. As Brown notes, the word *adelphos* is used sixteen times in the letter for "spiritual relatives" (1982: 269). Those spiritual relatives could be either male or female. In fact, the word *brother* is a common NT expression for a believer's "spiritual relative." Only Titus, Jude, and some of Paul's references to a particular brother (e.g., 2 Cor 1:1; 2:13; 8:18, 22, 23) do not use it in this fashion, but the remaining books of the NT employ it over two hundred times. Only rarely does a NT writer take time to specifically refer to "brother and sister" (cf. 1 Cor 7:15; James 2:15).

This use of *brother* for both male and female spiritual relatives was probably due to the strong patriarchal influence of the ancient world and Middle Eastern cultures in particular. Brown convincingly argues that the author of the fourth Gospel and this community based on his teachings move significantly away from these patriarchal norms. Brown concludes, "In researching the evidence of the Fourth Gospel, one is still surprised to see to what extent in the Johannine community women and men were already on an equal level in the fold of the Good Shepherd. This seems to have been a community where in the things that really mattered in the following of Christ there was no difference between male and female" (Brown 1979: 198). If this is so, then modern translators, such as those who worked on the NRSV, quite appropriately translate the Greek word *adelphos* as *brother or sister*. A more challenging issue is this: What does the author have in mind when he refers to a brother and sister? How broadly or narrowly does he define the Christian community? Is John "sectarian" (cf. comments on 3:11 on this matter)?

Verse 10 places a positive emphasis on the point the author makes by highlighting "doing." "Saying" is simply not enough to reveal one's relationship with God. One's actions are the solid evidence that indicates a person's orientation to either *light* or *darkness*. Here John makes the point that if one loves a brother or sister, one can conclude that such a person *is in the light*. This is the first of numerous times when John will raise this issue of loving one's brothers and sisters (cf. 3:10-23; 4:7, 11-12, 20-21). Schnackenburg correctly sees the repetition of this theme as an indication of just how serious are the interpersonal tensions facing John's community (1992: 107).

In addition to taking up a positive statement of his specific test for whether or not one is in the light, the author uses a phrase, *in such a person there is no cause for stumbling (kai skandalon en autō ouk estin)*, that moves his argument forward but presents a challenge for translators. The challenge is that the words *en autō* can be translated as either *in it* or *in him*. Thus the entire phrase can be translated as either "and in it [the light] there is no cause for stumbling," or "and in him [the one who loves] there is no cause for stumbling." Most translators opt for the second alternative, as is clear from the NRSV text above or the REB's *there is no cause of stumbling in him*. Some commentators, such as Schnackenburg (1992: 108) or Smalley (62), argue that the phrase is a reference to the light and so opt for *in it*, as does the RSV. However, such an affirmation is unnecessary. John and his readers already know and accept that being in the light is being in relationship with God. How can the light then be a cause for stumbling?

It is better to conclude with Brown (1982: 274), Marshall (132), and others that John had "in him" in mind as he wrote this phrase. In 1 John we see that the author repeatedly uses similar phrases (*in . . .*) in this manner (1:8, 10; 2:4, 8). Since schism is the historical context that gave rise to the letter's writing, reference to humans as the cause of *stumbling* is the more plausible way to understand this phrase. Some modern writers further refine the question by asking if John meant to suggest that the stumbling has an impact on the individual, such as a hateful person causing oneself to stumble, or if the author meant that a hateful person was a source of stumbling to others. Such refined musings probably go too far. It is not inconceivable that he saw both involved. *To hate* destroys fellowship. This, in turn, harms both the individual and the community of faith. Conversely, *to love* builds up the faith community, which in turn encourages persons individually and the community corporately.

With verse 11 the author returns to the earlier theme of hating one's spiritual siblings. Returning to that theme is evidence that the author considers this particular behavior to be dangerous and un-Christian. Further evidence of this assumption is the way this verse asserts three times that such behavior indicates how the person who *hates another believer is in the darkness*—a darkness mentioned in 2:9 and introduced in 1:5. For one to hate members of the Johannine community reveals beyond the shadow of a doubt that that person is not functioning under the influence of God's revelation in Jesus Christ (2:8).

To depict the pervasive nature of the spiritual barrenness afflicting anyone who hates a member of John's community, the author progressively traces the result of the darkness that influences that person's life. Initially he says that such a person simply exists or has his being in *the darkness*. This is the general realm to which the hateful person is oriented. However, that person is not only generally oriented toward darkness; he also *walks in the darkness*. Significant damage can be done by a person who insists on moving about in a dark room. Injuries can be inflicted to that person and others. Material items may be knocked over and broken. To move about in a darkened room has much more potential for damage than simply standing still in the darkness. Finally, we learn that the author sees little hope for people who hate: *the darkness has brought on blindness*. The darkness has resulted in a serious defect for the person under its influence. He now is blind (cf. John 9:39-41). The matter cannot be easily resolved by lighting a lamp. To fall into hatred is to fall utterly and totally. And serious damage is done to the self.

Summary

Ultimately the author's specific test is extremely focused. In his mind people fall into one of two categories: they are either in the light or in darkness, either they know God or they don't (see "Duality" under "Main Themes" in the Introduction, and [Duality in the Epistles, p. 304]. A general way to access a person's knowledge of God is not by what they say or claim, such as with the secessionists' speech, but by looking at what they do. More specifically, do they obey the commandments? Keeping the commandments shows that a person's love is mature. And love is the crucial point for John in this unit. He will repeatedly address the issues of Christology; and, indeed, he is concerned about orthodoxy in this regard. This entire section and the next one also, however, make it equally clear that John is also concerned about orthopraxy. Specifically, he holds out one simple and central test: does a person love or hate others in the community of faith? Answer that question, and you know if a person is in the light or darkness.

THE TEXT IN BIBLICAL CONTEXT

Knowing God

Numerous writers report that "knowledge of God" is a widespread religious motif in the ancient world. Brown, drawing on Dodd, states that in the classical Greek period human reason was hailed as the avenue for achieving this goal. However, this confidence failed in the Hellenistic period. The various mystery religions that then began to flourish emphasized special revelation, which in turn became the popular way to achieve knowledge of the divine (1982: 277-78). On this point Judaism and early Christianity shared more with the mystery religions and their stress on revelation than with the rationalistic approach of classical Greek philosophy.

Where they differ from the mystery religions is the biblical emphasis on this knowledge as practical and experiential as opposed to the more abstract, theoretical, and secretive knowledge of the pagan religions. To know God was "to live in a relationship of love and obedience," as is reflected in the use of the Hebrew word da'at (knowledge) in Hosea 4:6 (Kysar 1986a: 44). However, as this verse notes, lack of knowledge of God is a prophetic critique of Israel, when they disobeyed God's covenantal revelation, as is evident in texts such as Job 36:12; Jeremiah 9:6; Isaiah 1:3; 5:13; and Hosea 4:1. Thus within the prophetic tradition the hope develops that one day full knowledge of God will be available to humans (as in Hos 6:1-3; Hab 2:14; Ezek 36:26-27; Jer 9:23-24). A classic and well-known text,

Jeremiah 31:31-34, reads (which Heb 8:8-12 quotes in full, and 10:16-17 quotes again in part),

> The days are surely coming, says the LORD, when I will make a new covenant with the house of Israel and the house of Judah. It will not be like the covenant that I made with their ancestors when I took them by the hand to bring them out of the land of Egypt—a covenant that they broke, though I was their husband, says the LORD. But this is the covenant that I will make with the house of Israel after those days, says the LORD; I will put my law within them, and I will write it on their hearts; and I will be their God, and they shall be my people. No longer shall they teach one another, or say to each other, "Know the LORD," for they shall all know me, from the least of them to the greatest, says the LORD; for I will forgive their iniquity, and remember their sin no more.

In the NT, Paul walks a fine line with regard to knowledge in his first letter to the Corinthians. At one point he can write, "I give thanks to my God always for you because of the grace of God that has been given you in Christ Jesus, for in every way you have been enriched in him, in speech and knowledge of every kind" (1 Cor 1:4-5). Later in the same letter he follows a more cautious line when he writes, "Now concerning food sacrificed to idols: we know that 'all of us possess knowledge.' Knowledge puffs up, but love builds up" (8:1; cf. 8:10; 13:12). The tension here between claiming to possess knowledge and needing to display love is similar to the concern in 1 John 2:3-11.

Matthew 7:15-23 connects thematically with 1 John 2:3 but approaches the issue from a slightly different angle. Like the author of 1 John, Matthew stresses the importance of connecting one's knowledge of God to appropriate behavior. The evangelist argues that a person's "fruits" reveal his orientation toward or away from God. The twist is this: it is Jesus who will refuse to acknowledge anyone who does not do the will of God. As 7:23 reads, "Then I [Jesus] will declare to them, 'I never knew you; go away from me, you evildoers.'" The final authority for confirming one's knowledge of God rests not with the person claiming to know God. The final decision is based on behavior that either conforms to or deviates from the will of God.

First John, not surprisingly, comes close to the Gospel of John with regard to this topic. In the Gospel one's knowledge of God is tested by fidelity to Jesus, who has revealed God (Rensberger: 61). This is evidenced in such places as John 8:19, 54-55; 14:7; 17:3, 25-26. First John makes a similar point in 1:1-3; 4:8-10, 14-16; 5:20. Both pieces of Johannine literature are concerned that people do not simply settle for knowing facts about God. Rather, the main agenda is personal involvement (Kruse: 78) or "an intimate relationship with God" (Rensberger: 61).

Obedience

A second important theme in this unit is "obedience." The opening
three verses refer to this topic three times: twice in a positive form—
obey his commandments or *word* (vv. 3, 5), and once in a negative form—
disobeys his commandments (v. 4 RSV). Rensberger (62) correctly
observes that this idea of knowing and obeying has "deep roots in
[the] Johannine tradition . . . and beyond that in Hebrew Scripture"
(cf. M. M. Thompson: 55). This belief, that knowing God results in
obedience, is not limited to Johannine literature and the OT. As
Schnackenburg points out, the theme also connects 1 John to Jesus'
teaching in the synoptic Gospels and the moral teachings of earliest
Christianity (1992: 96). This is not a narrow sectarian assumption, but
a core conviction of both Judaism and Christianity.

Intimate relationship is foundational to both "knowing God" and
"obeying God." Obedience in both the OT and the Johannine tradition
grows out of humanity's covenant relationship with God; it is not
simply a blind following of the rules. In the Hebrew Scriptures, "the
Lord" repeatedly establishes covenants with various figures, and the
covenant is periodically "recalled" (Gen 6:18; 15:1-21; 17:1-27; Lev
26:9; Num 25:12; Deut 4:31; 7:9). As Deuteronomy 7:9 reveals, an
important element of this covenant relationship is the human role of
loving God and "keep[ing] his commandments." The fact that love
and obedience are paired shows that from the beginning there is
more to the biblical understanding of obedience than mere legalism.

This basing of obedience on more than legalism is clearly revealed
in the Ten Commandments (Exod 20:1-21). Within Christian circles
there is a tendency to begin counting these commandments with
Exodus 20:3 ("You shall have no other gods before me"), in part
because that is the verse where the first commandment appears. In
reality, however, verse 3 picks up in the middle of a sentence that
begins in Exodus 20:2: "I am the Lord your God, who brought you out
of the land of Egypt, out of the house of slavery." In recalling the
entire first sentence of the Decalogue, as the Jewish tradition certainly does, we are constantly reminded that these ten laws are based
on the Lord's merciful and redemptive nature; they are not simply
rules to which we must conform. To obey the Ten Commandments is
to respond to a God whose nature is to be merciful, who desires to
save, and who is revealed in Israel's exodus from slavery.

The idea of obedience as more than rigid conformity to rules is
evidenced in Deuteronomy. At least twice the reader is told that the
act of obedience is for one's "own well-being" (4:40; cf. 29:9:
"Diligently observe the words of this covenant, in order that you

may succeed in everything that you do"). And twice we read that obedience is a personal response to God: "Keep the commandments of the LORD your God, by walking in his ways and fearing him" (8:6). "The LORD your God you shall follow, him alone you shall fear, his commandments you shall keep, his voice you shall obey, him you shall serve, and to him you shall hold fast" (13:4).

The prophetic tradition shares this basic assumption that obedience grows out of knowledge of God, but in their role as prophets they often remind Israel of its immorality and disobedience and failure to obey. When Israel forsook the Lord, Micah reminds the nation that their God redeemed them from bondage in Egypt (6:4) and asks: What will please "the LORD"? He answers: It is not sacrifices and ritually proper worship forms. "The LORD" desires that they "do justice, and . . . love kindness, and . . . walk humbly with your God" (6:8). Similarly, Hosea's shocking prophetic action of marrying Gomer, a prostitute, symbolizes the agony that Israel was creating for the Lord because of the nation's disobedience (1:2-9). We also hear the prophets reminding Israel of God's merciful and just nature to encourage obedience (as in Isa 1:18-19; 55:7; Jer 3:12-13; 26:13).

In the NT, Matthew shows continuity with the Hebrew Scripture when he writes, "Not everyone who says to me, 'Lord, Lord,' will enter the kingdom of heaven, but only the one who does the will of my Father in heaven" (7:21; cf. 5:19; 19:17; 23:23). Paul tells the Romans, "For he will repay according to each one's deeds: to those who by patiently doing good seek for glory and honor and immortality, he will give eternal life; while for those who are self-seeking and who obey not the truth but wickedness, there will be wrath and fury" (2:6-8; cf. 1 Cor 7:19; Gal 5:15-21). Paul also seems to tap into a similar early Christian tradition as the author of 1 John does when he writes, "For the whole law is summed up in a single commandment, 'You shall love your neighbor as yourself'" (Gal 5:14; cf. Rom 13:8-10; 1 Tim 6:14). James strongly encourages his readers to obedience when he writes, "Be doers of the word, and not merely hearers who deceive themselves" (1:22; cf. 2:14-18).

While the author of 1 John shares much with these OT and NT writers, he is closest to the author of John's Gospel. He, like the Gospel writer, is aware that the best obedience is that which develops from love for Christ and attempts to reflect Christ's own obedience. In the fourth Gospel we read, "If you love me, you will keep my commandments" (14:15). "They who have my commandments and keep them are those who love me; and those who love me will be loved by my Father, and I will love them and reveal myself to them" (14:21). "I give

you a new commandment, that you love one another. Just as I have
loved you, you also should love one another. By this everyone will
know that you are my disciples, if you have love for one another"
(13:34-35). John, in both the Gospel and the letters, seems to narrow
the focus of one's love to those within the community, whereas Paul
and Jesus extend love to the enemy. In the Gospel, however, Jesus
speaks of drawing "all people to myself" (12:32; cf. 3:14-16; 7:17a, 37c;
20:30-31). Swartley (utilizing the works of Rensberger; Karris; and
Volf) contends that John's love ethic embraces the enemy as well,
notably in the *necessity* for Jesus to go through Samaria. Mission and
peacemaking in John extend the love of God and neighbor beyond the
borders of the faith community (2006: 296-300, 304-20; forthcoming
BCBC commentary on John 4 and essay "Love Ethic in John").

THE TEXT IN THE LIFE OF THE CHURCH

Christian Behavior

Their acceptance of the biblical notion that obedience is an integral
element of the Christian life marked the early Anabaptists as unique
and even dangerous. While most Reformers stressed God's actions that
resulted in salvation, the Anabaptists stressed that human effort to live
obedient lives was equally important. As Judith Lieu declares, this is a
long-standing point of tension in Christian thought (1991: 57). The
radical reformers generally agreed with the author of 1 John and would
have concurred with Lieu: "Behaviour can in no way, even miscon-
ceived, be seen as creating or maintaining a relationship with God; it is
rather the fruit and the test of such a relationship" (1991: 58).

   The early Anabaptists were repeatedly accused of "works righteousness." In his 1552 pamphlet *Reply to False Accusations*, Menno Simons
responds to the slanderous charge that he and his fellow Anabaptists
are "heaven-stormers" and "merit men" (Wenger: 543-77). His reply
echoes 1 John. First, Anabaptists are accused of this simply because they
take Jesus seriously when he said his followers "must keep the commandments" (569). Moreover, the opponents who make these charges
reveal their true orientation. Menno writes that they are "bold despis-
ers and transgressors of the commandments of God who prove plainly
by their deeds that they do not confess the saving grace of God, do not
believe in Christ Jesus, and according to Scripture abide in damnation,
wrath, and death. For whoso doeth unrighteously showeth by his works
whose disciple he is" (569).

   Menno argues that a desire to follow the commandments and
live a life of obedience grows out of an awareness of God's gracious-

ness, as he writes in *True Christian Faith*: "All who comprehend with
a sincere, unwavering, believing heart, the great solicitude and diligence of God for us . . . and His unbounded kindness, mercy, and
love, as paternally manifested toward us through Christ Jesus, . . .
can never be prevented . . . from loving this gracious Father . . . [and]
praise, honor, thank, serve, and obey Him all the days of their life."
The greatest "delight and joy" of true Christians is "the keeping of
His commandments" (Wenger: 337-38).

For Menno, all of this is based on his position that one must
repent and be born again. In 1537 he writes, "The birth from above
and true repentance must take place. We must believe Christ and
His word and abide constantly in His Spirit, ordinance, and example, or eternal misery will be our position. This is incontrovertible"
(Wenger: 95). In the same way, Menno continues his argument by
pointing to a common claim that he heard from his opponents: We
do believe Jesus is God's Son and that he purchased us with his
blood. Menno pointedly asks those who make such a claim: "If your
faith is as you say, why do you not do the things that he has commanded you in His word? His commandment is: Repent and keep
the commandments" (96).

Though Menno's writings seem to indicate that his non-Anabap-
tists contemporaries casually disregarded the issue of obedience or
severed it from faith, we must be careful here. Calvin, for example,
is clearly aware that obedience is a crucial element of the Christian
life. In his commentary on 1 John 2:3-6, he writes, "After dealing
with the doctrine of the free forgiveness of sins, John comes to the
exhortations that belong to it and that depend on it. And first
indeed he reminds us that the knowledge of God, derived from the
Gospel, is not ineffectual, but obedience proceeds from it" (Calvin
and Henry 1998: 30).

Throughout the ages Christians have recognized that obedience is a
complex concept. In his *Adumbrations*, Clement of Alexandria (d. 215)
comments on 1 John 2:3 and names at least three contexts for obedient
behavior:

> The one who understands will also do the works that pertain to the
> duty of virtue, but someone who does the works is not necessarily
> among those who understand. For he may just be someone who under-
> stands the difference between right and wrong but who has no knowl-
> edge of the heavenly mysteries. Furthermore, knowing that some
> people do the right thing out of fear of punishment or for some kind of
> reward, John teaches that a man of perfect understanding does these
> things out of love. (Bray: 178)

Similarly, Anabaptist leader and martyr Michael Sattler (d. 1527) was well aware of more than one kind of obedient behavior. In his essay "On Two Kinds of Obedience," he identifies servile obedience and filial obedience (Yoder 1973: 121-25). Servile obedience is motivated by reward or self and "does nothing unless it be commanded." Filial obedience, on the other hand, springs forth from love for God and "does as much as it can (121). Sattler, interestingly, does not see these two types of obedience as contradictory. Servile obedience is better than no obedience at all, but filial obedience is "better and higher," and the person who is obedient in a servile fashion should "seek after a better [obedience] which is the filial, which needs the servile not at all" (121).

Any religious community or individual that takes ethics seriously would do well to read and reread Sattler's short essay. Granted, obedience to the commands of Christ is not an optional element of the Christian life. There is, however, a significant difference between servile and filial obedience. And we all know that the former has repeatedly manifested itself in believers-church circles. Most of us either know another person whose Christian life functions in this mode or we find ourselves trapped in this pattern of behavior. We know the weighty sense of duty and the small sense of reward associated with having done it. There is, however, much more to the Christian life than plodding obedience to Christ's commands. Paul knew that the Christian life could not be reduced to following or not following rules and regulations, as he says in Romans 14:17: "The kingdom of God is . . . righteousness and peace and joy in the Holy Spirit."

If we want our lives to come close to what John is writing about in this unit, the early Anabaptists, such as Sattler and Menno, will encourage us on our way. As noted above, Menno was clearly aware that the obedience that John envisions can only develop out of an awareness of God's basic attributes. We might even argue that joyful obedience grows out of an intimate and dynamic personal relationship with God through Jesus Christ. It is not good enough to be born to parents and grandparents who knew God and obeyed, and then think that all we need to do is obey community rules. In reality, both Jesus and Menno remind us that knowing God through "repentance" precedes "obedience." We must turn to God before we can respond by keeping God's commandments. We need to consider evangelism a task equal to ethics.

I suspect that many of us have been put off by evangelism because of what we see around us. Aren't there sufficient numbers of people who use the gospel for personal financial gain? Aren't we wearied by grotesque characters who shout "Repent" when they have been caught as people who need to repent themselves? And aren't we worried by the messages and messengers who confuse the beginning of the Christian journey with the end? Indeed, accepting God's gracious offer of salvation is only the start of our Christian lives. There is still much to learn and do, and much of the learning and doing has to do with obedience or discipleship. Commenting on 1 John 2:3-6, Marianne Meye Thompson writes,

> In *The Cost of Discipleship*, Dietrich Bonhoeffer penned the words, "Cheap grace is grace without discipleship, grace without the cross, grace without Jesus Christ, living and incarnate" (1959: 47). Cheap grace means living as though God ignores or condones our sins. But forgiveness means that sin is real, and must be dealt with. We cannot ignore it, because God does not ignore it. The denial of sin is not grace: it is a lie. Cheap grace means living without the demand of obedience upon us. (51)

The solution to one-sided evangelism that focuses on cheap grace is not to ignore evangelism in favor of an equally one-sided emphasis on ethical behavior. Rather, we are called to communicate the importance of *both* knowing God *and* obeying God.

1 John 2:12-14

Why I Write to You

PREVIEW

How do we respond to life situations in which there is seemingly no clear-cut right or wrong? Many of us seek out the counsel of a trusted friend. We want and need to know if the friend understands the situation the way we do. Not many of us would settle for only half a response, one affirming that the other party is wrong. We also desire assurance that *we* are right. These three verses are John's attempt to assure his readers.

This short but well-organized unit stands immediately after John's polemic against the separatists and just before the next unit, which is exhortatory in nature. In a real sense, it is a bridge between the previous and following material, but it also fulfills an important function of its own. That crucial role is to serve as words of assurance to the readers. As Robert Kysar observes, in this respect John wants to reassure his loyal followers of an impressive array of theological truth that applies to them (1986a: 55). They are not like the secessionists, who have been making false claims and so are relying on faulty theology. Instead, John reminds his readers that their sins are forgiven (2:12), they have a relationship with God (vv. 13a, c; 14a), evil is defeated (13b; 14f), they have spiritual strength (14b), and God/word of God abides in them (14b, e). In other words, they have victory in Christ and have no need for the separatists' lies. These same words of assurance also serve as the foundation for the exhortation that comes next. The fact that they do have victory and life in Jesus Christ does not mean they can simply rest on either his or their laurels. Next John reminds them they are to continue by resisting *the world.*

108

In 2:3-11 the author has introduced four crucial topics that are repeatedly stressed in this letter: knowing God, obedience, eschatology, and loving one another. His primary argument in the previous section is that real knowledge of God results in obedience to God. The author made this point before challenging a number of erroneous claims that the secessionists made regarding sin. This is why most of the letter up to this point has been polemical in nature. As Rodney Whitacre argues, the author of the letter challenges these secessionists and formulates his polemic on theological grounds and a particular view of God while appealing to the tradition of the Johannine community, but his polemic also includes reassurance for his readers (1-4, 141-45).

That is why there is a sudden change in verse 12. Up to this point he has been addressing weighty theological and ecclesiastical issues, and he has made a strong case for his views. Moreover, his argument is rather strident: John is not inclined to provide his opponents with room for maneuvering. But now it is almost as if he pauses to think, What if my supporters misunderstand me? What we have in 2:12-14 are words of reassurance and encouragement. The author does not want his readers to think that he places them in the same category as the separatists. Additionally, these verses serve as the foundation for what is written in the next unit, 2:15-17. There his readers are encouraged to eschew the world. They can do that only if they fully realize who they are and what their status is with the Father, which is addressed in this section.

Recognizing that these three verses are important to the author's overall argument, we should mention that they pose several challenges. Kysar writes, "These three verses constitute what is one of the most debated passages of 1 John" (1986a: 52). Alan Culpepper depicts the situation even more starkly: "For all the apparent simplicity of these verses, they present difficulties that have troubled scribes and commentators from the earliest centuries" (1985: 33).

Three main issues need to be addressed. The first hinges on a change in verb tense in verse 14. Up to that point John says *I am writing* (present tense) three times in verses 12 and 13. But in the final verse he shifts to the aorist/past tense, yet translated *I write*, and uses this verb tense for the final three references to his writing. The second issue focuses on his use of the terms *little children* (*teknia*), *children* (*paidia*), *fathers*, and *young people*. Specifically, commentators ask if John has one, two, three, or even four audiences in mind with his use of these four terms. Finally, there is debate as to how the six uses of *because* (*hoti*) in the NRSV should be translated. Does he intend to make declarative statements introduced by *that*? Or is he using the word causally, in which case *because* is the better translation?

What commentators do agree on is the fact that this section is well organized. Numerous Bible translation committees—including NIV, NRSV, and REB—have typeset these verses in a poetic fashion. This is due to the fact that this material is organized into two triplets following an "A, B, C, a, b, c" pattern (Kysar 1986a: 52). Each triplet's opening line is addressed to either *little children* or *children*. These opening lines are then followed by an address to the *fathers* and an address to the *young people*. Assurance is a driving agenda behind these words, and many modern writers have noticed this. As Kysar points out, these three short verses remind the readers of one key Christian idea: as believers they have victory in Christ Jesus (1986a: 55). The two triplets follow this pattern:

Triplet One 2:12-13
> *I am writing to you, little children,*
> > *because* [or *that*] *your sins are forgiven on account of his name.*
> *I am writing to you, fathers,*
> > *because* [or *that*] *you know him who is from the beginning.*
> *I am writing to you, young people,*
> > *because* [or *that*] *you have conquered the evil one.*

Triplet Two 2:14
> *I write to you, children,*
> > *because* [or *that*] *you know the Father.*
> *I write to you, fathers,*
> > *because* [or *that*] *you know him who is from the beginning.*
> *I write to you, young people,*
> > *because* [or *that*] *you are strong,*
> > > *and the word of God abides in you,*
> > > *and you have overcome the evil one.*

OUTLINE
Triplet One, 2:12-13
Triplet Two, 2:14

EXPLANATORY NOTES

Triplet One 2:12-13
The first triplet begins with a number of words that we have already seen in the letter. Two of the first three Greek words, *I am writing to you, little children*, remind us of 2:1, which reads, *My little children, I*

am writing. . . ." This short phrase introduces us to two of the three debated points found in this unit. The first is the author's use of the verb *write* in two different tenses. In 2:1 it is found in the present tense, but in 2:14 John shifts to the past tense (see my comments on 2:14 regarding this puzzling shift).

For now we note that this use of *write* helps connect this unit to the previous material. The verb is used six times in this short unit, and the author is quite aware that he is here continuing his written argument that begins in the first unit. In 1:4 he shows that he is aware that he is writing purposefully: *We are writing these things so that our joy may be complete.* He uses almost the exact same phrase in 2:1 and in 2:7: *Beloved, I am writing you no new commandment.* In 2:8 he uses a similar phrase, *Yet I am writing you. . . .* Not surprisingly, all these uses of *write* have one element in common: they show that John is trying to clarify or communicate doctrinal issues for his readers. As Smalley suggests, the author uses these words (*I am writing* [RSV] or *I have written* [NASB]) to "recapitulate and elucidate the grounds of true Christian experience and character already discussed in 1:1–2:11" (68). In this sense these words reveal a connection between this unit and the previous units.

The second debated point introduced by the opening phrase in 2:12 is the question of audience or audiences. As noted in the Preview, the author singles out four groups. By placing these four groups into their positions of occurrence in the two triplets, the following pattern emerges:

Triplet One	Triplet Two
little children (*teknia*, 2:12a)	children (*paidia*, v. 14a)
fathers (v. 13a)	fathers (v. 14c)
young people (v. 13c)	young people (v. 14e)

Fathers and *young people* are named twice in exactly the same order, and both occurrences come after the use of either *little children* or *children*. The author apparently expects the reader to view *little children* (*teknia*, v. 12) and *children* (*paidia*, v. 14) as synonyms for the same group and not as a reference to two different groups within the community.

Not only is there this obvious parallelism; the author also tends to use these two words interchangeably throughout the letter (cf. 2:1, 18, 28; 3:7, 18; 4:4; 5:21), although he does prefer *teknia* (employed seven times) over *paidia* (used twice, 2:14, 18). What is even more important in his use of *teknia* is the fact that this term tends to be used when referring to the entire community, as in 2:1 (*My little children, I am writing these things to you*) or 2:28 (*And now, little children, abide in him, so that when he is revealed we may have confidence*). Interestingly, in John 13:33 we read of Jesus addressing his followers with these words, "Little children [*teknia*], I am with you only a little longer." It may well be that this word was used within the Johannine community for the general membership of the community because the tradition viewed it as Jesus' own preferred term of endearment for his followers.

Drawing upon an analysis of Greco-Roman rhetorical patterns, Duane Watson offers an additional reason for considering this use of *teknia* and *paidia* as a general reference to the entire community. He convincingly argues that these verses in 1 John 2:12-14 are a classic example of *distributio* where the writer or speaker initially addresses the entire group and then mentions specific subgroups within the larger group (1989: 99). Watson (101) points out that these verses in 1 John are not the only examples of *distributio* in the OT and NT. Examples from the LXX include Exodus 10:9; Joshua 6:21; Isaiah 20:4; Ezekiel 9:6. Among NT examples are Acts 2:17-21; 1 Timothy 5:1-2; Titus 2:1-8; 1 Peter 5:1-5.

Added support for this suggestion that *little children* refers to the general populace of John's faith community is that what he ascribes as true of the *teknia* is doctrinally true of all Christians. All believers—whether fathers, young people, or little children—should know that their *sins are forgiven on account of his name*. In light of Watson's argument and the previous paragraph's observations on the structural pattern, one can certainly say that John uses *teknia* and *paidia* as general terms of affection for the members of his community. In verses 12a and 14a, John is probably addressing the entire community by using *little children* and *children*. He then directs further comments to two subgroups within the larger community, whom he identifies as *fathers* and *young people*.

These verses assert a number of facts, and the first one, *Your sins are forgiven on account of his name*, is basic and foundational. Certain elements of this phrase have already been addressed when commenting on 1:7 and 1:9. The concept of forgiveness (*are forgiven*), carries with it a sense of releasing or letting go. While sin is generally viewed as lawlessness or unrighteousness (3:4), the author has an additional sense that opposing divinely revealed truth is sin also. Thus what the author is saying in the first portion of his statement is clear. His readers are not bound by sin and unrighteousness, nor do they reject divine truth.

What is not nearly as clear is how this release from bondage to sin and acceptance of truth takes place. Specifically, the author views it as occurring *through his name*. It is widely, if not universally, accepted that *his* is a reference to Jesus, and so it is Jesus' *name* that facilitates the readers' release from sin. This general acceptance is due, in large measure, to the fact that a phrase like "because of my name" is frequently associated with Jesus in the NT (Brown 1982: 302; John 15:21; Matt 10:22; 24:9; Mark 13:13; Luke 21:17; Rev 2:3). Acts 4:30 and 1 Corinthians 1:10 use phrases similar to those in 1 John 2:12, and both verses make it quite clear that the reference is to Jesus' name.

Also in Semitic thought the "name" of an individual "stands for the whole person" (M. M. Thompson: 62). The author of 1 John seems to be thinking along these lines. Later in the letter he refers to *the name of . . . Jesus Christ* or *the name of the Son of God*. Thus he writes, *And this is his commandment, that we should believe in the name of his Son Jesus Christ* (3:23); and *I write these things to you who believe in the name of the Son of God* (5:13). These three uses of the phrase (2:12; 3:23; 5:13) make it clear that John is using *the name* as a shorthand reference to Jesus himself. In other words, he is pointing out to his readers that their sins are forgiven because of Jesus' actions (so also in 1:7; 2:1-2), and they acknowledge the truthfulness of this element of the Johannine tradition.

Verse 12 presents us with one final question, one of the three issues associated with all three verses of this unit: how are we to understand the small word *hoti*? There are two options. First, the word can be viewed in a causal sense. In other words, the author is using it to explain why he is writing this letter; and in that case it should be translated *because*. The alternative is a declarative sense, with John making a statement, and thus *hoti* would be translated *that*.

The use of *hoti* in these verses has produced an interesting cycle in the history of discussion: near consensus, challenge, discussion, near consensus, and so forth. Before 1900 most scholars viewed *hoti* as a declarative. The causal alternative then held sway until 1960, when Bent Noack (236-41) argued that the word should be viewed as a declarative. An emerging trend these days is to lay out the evidence for both options, suggest which one is to be marginally preferred, and then say that the original readers may not have distinguished between the two (Marshall: 136; Smalley: 71; Strecker: 57). Although these scholars are probably correct to note the possibility of both meanings, the context would certainly lead us to place more weight on the declarative option: *that*.

Noack is quite right when he argues that many have misapprehended the polemical nature of the letter up to this point (238). John knows that his readers are believers. Why would he need to tell

them he is writing *because* they do believe? But considering the crisis they face—a split in the community, new doctrines introduced,
and some people probably still wavering over the question of who is
correct (see comments on v. 14 below)—John is making declarative
statements about them and their status so as to reassure them of
their correctness in remaining true to the Johannine community.
Not only this, but John may also have envisioned some of his readers
as questioning whether or not they fit the negative categories that
he argues against in 1:6, 8, 10. In 2:12-14 he gives an assurance that
they are not to see themselves as members of the separatists' camp.
Moreover, 2:15-17 will make more sense if we understand 2:12-14 as
presenting declarative statements. Because his readers have a particular status before God, such as forgiveness of sins and knowing
the Father, they must then continue on and live out the "natural"
consequences of this status: *Do not love the world* (v. 15). At any rate,
the author's first words of reassurance are to remind his readers
that their sins are forgiven, implying that they need not look elsewhere for salvation.

In verse 13, the second portion of the first triplet, we notice that
John follows the same basic pattern established in the previous verse:
I am writing to you, then he specifies a group, and then he offers the
declarative and affirming statement introduced by *hoti*. The two
groups specified are *fathers* and *young people*, and their introduction
raises at least two questions. The first is one that was introduced
above and will now be resolved: how many audiences does the author
have in mind? The second question focuses on the assumed age difference between the two groups. Is John thinking of actual age
groups, such as senior citizens and young adults? Has he classified
these groups according to "spiritual maturity"? Or is he thinking
along other lines altogether?

Numerous solutions have been proposed to resolve the first question. We cannot review and weigh the merits of all these arguments
(see Marshall: 137-38 for a concise overview). These three verses, it
seems to me, best support the conclusion that in verses 12a and 14a
the author is addressing the entire congregation. He then singles out
two subgroups, which he designates as *fathers* and *young people* (cf.
M. M. Thompson: 63; Schnackenburg 1992: 116; Houlden: 70). As
Watson has shown, this explanation would conform to an accepted
rhetorical pattern in the ancient world (1989: 99-101). The cumulative
impact is that the entire group is affirmed and then specific subgroups are twice affirmed. By using this simple rhetorical device, the
author maximizes the assurance he is attempting to communicate.

Even more difficult to answer with any degree of certainty is the second question. Dividing a group into subgroups based on spiritual maturity or age is certainly not unknown in the OT, intertestamental literature, and the NT. The majority of OT passages that divide groups into subgroups of old and young do so on the basis of age (cf. Gen 19:4; Exod 10:9; Josh 6:21; Isa 20:4; Job 32:6; Ps 37:25). But Joel 2:28-29 is one classic OT passage that associates specific spiritual activities with particular groups. Specifically for our interest, the prophet first mentions the entire group and then identifies particular subgroups, including old and young:

> Then afterward
> I will pour out my spirit on all flesh;
> your sons and your daughters shall prophesy,
> your old men shall dream dreams,
> and your young men shall see visions.
> Even on the male and female slaves,
> in those days, I will pour out my spirit.

In the writings of the Qumran community similar distinctions are drawn among community members depending upon their level of acceptance and initiation into the religious life of the community (see 1QpHab 12.4-5; 1QS 6.13-24; CD 13.11-13). But the covenanters also are aware of simple groupings based on age as in 1QSa 1.6-19. In the NT, Acts 2:17-21 quotes Joel 2:28-29 with the age differences that the prophet specified: young men and old men. Titus 2:1-8 assumes that different spiritual attributes and ethical qualities are to be associated with various age groups. First Peter 5:1-5 charges elders with the task of pastoral care for a congregation, while the young are to accept the elders' authority; both groups are to be humble.

I am inclined to see 1 John 2:13-14 as using the terms *fathers* and *young people* primarily as categories denoting levels of spiritual maturity, but age as a secondary consideration cannot be ruled out entirely. The content of these two verses leads us to this conclusion. Though the author's agenda is to affirm his readers, he is aware that not all of them have reached the same level of spiritual maturity. Some are stable in their faith. Therefore he needs only to remind these *fathers* that they *know him who is from the beginning,* and he does this twice while using exactly the same words both times. The content of this unchanging affirmation hints at stability and perhaps spiritual maturity: they *know* (in the sense of "relate to") some long-standing figure. They are not reminded of any other important truth. *Know[ing] him* is sufficient, and so it is merely repeated twice.

Development and elucidation, however, is evident in the affirmation of the *young people*. Initially they are affirmed in that they *have conquered the evil one* (v. 13). Verse 14 affirms them for this as well, but the author also sees a need to add additional affirming truth. Thus he writes that they are *strong* and that *the word of God abides in you*. They have not conquered the evil one alone, nor is their strength their own. Their strength and their victory is a result of the *word of God* abiding in them (Malatesta: 168-73). The fact that John decides to develop this group's affirmation raises the question of whether it is possible, or even probable, that this group, the less spiritually mature members of John's community, have been and still are the targets of the secessionists. It is this group that is tempted to turn their backs on the Johannine teachings and traditions and leave the community to join the separatists. Therefore the author reminds them that they already have what they need to conquer the evil one and his followers (see the reference to the *antichrists* in 2:18-27). They have the strength that comes from being in relationship with the *word of God*, and so they are in a position to resist the temptation to leave the Johannine faith community.

In verse 13a the *fathers* are reminded and affirmed that they have known *him who is from the beginning*. The identity of *him* and the context of the affirmation are made clear when we look at how the author in the Johannine tradition has used the phrase *from the beginning*. The expression is frequently used in the letters and the Gospel of John, and it is used in a variety of contexts. One referent ruled out is the devil (as in 1 John 3:8; John 8:44). Rather, the phrase is used in a discussion relating to discipleship: as in *an old commandment that you had from the beginning* (1 John 2:7) or *Let what you heard from the beginning abide in you* (2:24; cf. 3:11; 2 John 5-6). Additionally, it is used with reference to either *the Word* (John 1:1) or *the Word of life* (1 John 1:1). We have already identified *Word of life* as Jesus when commenting on 1 John 1:1-4 (see above). Colin Kruse (89-90) points out that "the only person referred to as *being* from the beginning is the Word (identified as Jesus Christ)." Therefore Kruse is correct to conclude that this phrase, both here and in exactly the same form in 2:14, is a reference to Jesus Christ.

Although that is quite likely the author's primary referent and way the phrase should be understood here, it certainly could carry with it undertones of personal discipleship because the author also uses *from the beginning* as a shorthand code for the Christian life, as in 2:7, 24; 3:11; 2 John 5-6. John is probably reminding both the *fathers* and other readers, who may be wavering, of the crucial importance of a relationship with Jesus Christ that is sustained over a long period of time. Hence it is connected to a group whose maturity has developed over time.

Verse 13b shifts focus from the *fathers* to a group identified as *young people* in the NRSV. The word in the original Greek text is *neaniskoi*: if translated literally, it would be *young men*, as in the RSV and NIV translations. Again, the reason for the NRSV's gender-neutral translation is the same as that for the use of *brother or sister* in 2:9 (see comments above). This group is affirmed in that they *have conquered the evil one*.

The fact that the author affirms the *young people* because of their conquest may inform us about both John and his audience. The Greek verb for "conquer" (*nikaō*) is a favorite in the Johannine tradition. It is found 28 times in the whole of the NT, and 24 of those occurrences are in Johannine writings (Malatesta: 168-69). Six of the twenty-four uses are in 1 John (here, 2:14; 4:4; 5:4 (2x); 5:5; most are in Rev). All six usages refer to overcoming the forces that oppose God in some form or another. Here and in 2:14 the talk is of overcoming *the evil one*; people who refuse to confess Jesus as having come in the flesh are noted in 4:4; and 5:4-5 speaks of overcoming the world. A number of commentators remark that the author's choice of verb tense in this instance, along with all six affirmations, is significant. *Nikaō* (vv. 13-14), as well as *forgiven* (v. 12) and *know* (v. 13, twice in v. 14), are all in the perfect tense. By selecting this tense, the author is communicating the idea that although the action took place in the past, the event still has a present and ongoing impact. Smalley (75) explains this well: "The 'young' in Christ have known what it is to be victorious over evil, and they can still share this experience in their daily lives."

The *young people*'s conquest is over *the evil one* (*ton ponēron*). Later the author will also introduce the term *the devil* (*ho diabolos*) in 3:8, and these two terms seem to be synonyms. Given the author's dualist worldview, we should not be surprised that the personification of evil is noted here and will be referred to in future verses (2:14; 3:12; 5:18-19). God was incarnate in Jesus Christ, and evil is incarnate in some figure known to John and his community. As we will see in the next two units, John does not glibly or casually assume that this victory over *the evil one* is easy. The author implies that *the evil one* influences *the world* and is aligned with the *antichrist(s)*. Interestingly, in 2:13 John leaves his young readers with the impression that they have won the battle. This, however, will be clarified in the second triplet (v. 14).

Triplet Two 2:14

The form in the second triplet is essentially the same as that of the first triplet. As Marshall (140) notes, "These thoughts [vv. 12-13] are now repeated, and the effect is to emphasize the points already made." In fact, the address to the *fathers* is exactly the same as what is said in verse 13 apart from the change in verb tense from *I am writing* to *I write*. The affirmation for the *children*, meaning the entire church, has changed, and John expands the affirmation directed toward the *young people*. These three changes merit further comment.

The change in verb tense from *I am writing* to *I write* may simply be explained as a result of John's concern for style and word variation. That seems to be the conclusion of the NIV translation committee that has translated both verbs with the English words *I write*. Kysar (1986a: 53) is inclined to agree with this: he suggests that the author freely shifts between the present tense (1:4; 2:1, 7, 8) and the aorist tense (2:21, 26; 5:13). While that may be the case, an ancient literary device may also be at play in this intentional shift of tense. C. F. D. Moule (12) identifies 1 John 2:14 as an example of the "epistolary aorist," where the author "courteously projects himself in imagination into the position of the reader, for whom actions contemporaneous with the time of writing will be past." Other NT examples of this are found in 1 Corinthians 5:11; Ephesians 6:22; Philippians 2:28; Colossians 4:8; and Philemon 12. More recently Stanley Porter (36-37), writing partly in response to the unlikely suggestion that this change of verb tense indicates previous letters written by the author to the community, suggests that it is "especially common . . . to find the aorist used to refer to the entire writing process."

A more interesting change is the content of the general affirmation directed at the *children*. Initially they are affirmed in that their *sins are forgiven on account of his name* (v. 12), and now their affirmation is that they *know the Father*. This affirmation is likely to be an elucidation or development of the first affirmation of the *little children* in verse 12. Their affirmation there, *Your sins are forgiven on account of his name*, could be understood as a precursor to this one of *know[ing] the Father*. So far John has argued that one can have fellowship with both Jesus and the Father (1:3), that the Son cleanses us from sin (1:7), that the Son further acts as our advocate before the Father (2:1). By addressing these two related affirmations to the entire community, the author is stressing the fact that they already possess a basic Christian attribute. Through Christ, their sins—which separate people from God—have been dealt with, and they now enjoy an intimate relationship with God the Father. Having mentioned this, the author restates his affirmation of the *fathers* and then develops his affirmation of the *young people*.

In verse 13 the *young people* were left with the impression that they had *conquered the evil one*. In verse 14 this affirmation is repeated and clarified. The clarification is one point consisting of two elements: they *are strong* and *the word of God abides in* [*them*]. This is the only time John uses *strong* in the Johannine letters. But it is used nine times in Revelation, where as an adjective it modifies angels, humans, thunder, a city, and God. Therefore we cannot say that the word primarily relates to spiritual strength. Nonetheless, context leads to the conclusion that John uses it here to denote spiritual strength. Ephesians employs the noun form of this root (as "power") in a similar fashion: "Be strong in the Lord and in the strength of his power" (Eph 6:10). There the noun is clearly intended to be understood as spiritual strength.

The strength of these *young people* is a result of the fact that *the word of God abides* in them. Brown (1982: 305) and others rightly suggest that this phrase is designed as an explanation for the source of their strength. The addressees are not *strong* because they are *young*. Rather, they are *strong* because of the presence of God's word. Ultimately it is God who has *conquered the evil one* and not the *young people* themselves. The author is writing to remind them of this truth at work in their lives. In the Johannine tradition, the "word of God" is something that believers have and nonbelievers do not possess (cf. 1 John 1:10; John 5:38). The author likely refers to *the word of life* or message lived and taught by Jesus (Brown 1982: 306; cf. 1 John 1:1). An even more specific understanding may be the commandments that one *should believe in the name of his Son Jesus Christ and love one another* (3:23). In other words, the *young people* are strong because they have allowed the core of the Christian message to take root in their lives and be manifest in their social interactions.

THE TEXT IN BIBLICAL CONTEXT

Assurance

These three verses touch upon a crucial but often overlooked theme: assurance. We might even go so far as to agree with A. E. Brooke (40-41) that "the writer reminds his readers of what their position is and what is involved in it. He knows that they are harassed by doubts as to the validity of their Christian position, so he hastens to assure them of it, and to use his assurance as the ground of the appeal that he is making" (cf. Bass: 48-50; Carson: 73). Brooke's contemporary Robert

Law dedicates an entire chapter to the theme of assurance in 1 John in *The Tests of Life* (279-305). Most recent commentators, however, make only passing reference to this topic, if it is mentioned at all. One of the few notable exceptions is Colin Kruse (198-200), who identifies seven bases upon which John builds his case for assurance in 1 John. Bass and Carson make the point as well. Therefore an exploration of this subject is appropriate at this point.

From the outset it is absolutely crucial for us to realize that our assurance is not based on human effort, but is firmly founded on divine actions and characteristics. That point is subtly but surely made in 1 John 2:12-14. The readers' sins are forgiven not because of something they did or who they are, but because of *his name* (cf. 1:7; 2:1-2). Three times the readers are reminded that they *know him* or they *know the Father*, suggesting that they are privy to details and characteristics already revealed in Jesus Christ (cf. 1:2-3). They are reminded that they are strong because God's word abides in them, thus enabling them to *overcome the evil one*.

In the chapters that follow, John touches upon the theme of assurance at least four more times. In 2:28 the readers are encouraged to remain *in him, so that when he is revealed we may have confidence.* In a particularly touching pastoral section, 3:19-22, we hear the author reminding his readers that their willingness to love shows that they *are from the truth* and this *will reassure our hearts before him.* But even if our hearts condemn us, John compassionately points out, *God is greater than our hearts, and he knows everything.* Indeed, we have *an advocate with the Father, Jesus Christ the righteous* (2:1). Recall that 2:1 is in a section dealing with the complexity and pervasiveness of sin in the human experience, but that unit closes with reassuring words regarding Christ's intercessions and his *atoning sacrifice for our sins.* This is the basis of our assurance (2:2; Bass: 55-97). A third reference to assurance is found in the well-known verses in 4:17-19. Again the author is reminding his audience that the presence of love in their lives results in *boldness on the day of judgment,* and *there is no fear in love, but perfect love casts out fear.* Finally, 5:13-14 reassures the readers that God hears their prayers, but again the *boldness* and assurance is not found in them, but rather *in him,* which is probably a reference to Jesus Christ.

The assurance claimed in 1 John no doubt finds its roots in the Johannine tradition, of which the Gospel of John is a part. Early in the Gospel (John 1:12-13) the readers are reminded that through the incarnation and belief in Jesus Christ, they have been given the "power to become children of God." Their status as "children of God" is a result of

God's action, which makes it possible for people to be "born of the Spirit" and so enter the kingdom of God (3:1-21; cf. the discussion on "children of Abraham" versus "children of God" in 8:39-47). Later in the Gospel, when facing separation from Jesus, the disciples are promised the "Spirit of truth" or the "Advocate" (14:15-17) so that Jesus' followers are not left "orphaned" (14:18). Furthermore, those who are in Jesus are also in the Father; those who keep Jesus' commandments love him, and whoever does that will, in return, be loved by the Father (17:21). The Gospel has a strong sense of intimacy between the followers of Christ and the God who sent him, and this intimacy results in assurance for the believers. John Bogart notes this in his list of eleven themes relating to assurance in the fourth Gospel (66-76).

This reassuring imagery of being born of the Spirit and living as God's children is not limited to the Johannine tradition. Paul tells his readers that there is "no condemnation for those who are in Christ Jesus" (Rom 8:1). This is because the Romans live according to the Spirit of God that *dwells in* them (8:9). Furthermore, those who are "led by the Spirit of God are children of God" (8:14). They are God's adopted children and can call out to God as their heavenly *Abba*, God's name of intimacy (8:15).

Even when writing to the troublesome Corinthian congregation, Paul begins both letters with words of assurance regarding God's power to give confidence to the believers. In 1 Corinthians we read, "He will also strengthen you to the end, so that you may be blameless on the day of our Lord Jesus Christ. God is faithful; by him you were called into the fellowship of his Son, Jesus Christ our Lord" (1:8-9). In the second letter, Paul writes, "For in him [Jesus Christ] every one of God's promises is a 'Yes.' For this reason it is through him that we say the 'Amen,' to the glory of God. But it is God who establishes us with you in Christ and has anointed us, by putting his seal on us and giving us his Spirit in our hearts as a first installment" (1:20-22).

In a passage that seems to reflect similar contextual tensions to those of 1 John, Paul reassures the Colossians of their salvation. The apostle begins his letter with a thanksgiving section and a unit regarding Christ's supremacy, reminding the readers that God's fullness dwelled in Christ and that reconciliation between God and all things took place through the cross. Then Paul assures his readers of his desire that they "be encouraged and united in love, so that they may have all the riches of assured understanding and have knowledge of God's mystery, that is, Christ himself" (2:2). Paul further encourages the Colossians, "As you therefore have received

Christ Jesus the Lord, continue to live your lives in him, rooted and built up in him and established in the faith" (2:6-7).

Early in his letter to the Hebrews, the writer encourages his readers not to have evil and unbelieving hearts that would then turn them away from the living God; only those who "hold our first confidence firm to the end" can be considered partners of Christ (Heb 3:12-14). In Hebrews 6:9-12 the readers are reminded that God is not unjust nor will God overlook their work and love, shown "for his name" (v. 10 mg.). The writer then encourages them to "show the same diligence so as to realize the full assurance of hope to the end" (6:11). Both of these snippets of reassurance reflect the writer's assumption that Christians' confidence is based on the atoning work of Jesus (cf. 10:22). As Delling (311) states, "Purified thereby, the Christian can stand with 'full confidence' before God."

A final NT passage that relates to assurance and confidence is 1 Peter 5:6-11. Many of the same themes are present there that are in 1 John 2:12-14. The readers are told the devil is like a lion, looking for victims. The believers are encouraged to resist him and remain steadfast. They are reminded that God "cares for you" and "has called you to his eternal glory in Christ." Additionally, God will "restore, support, strengthen, and establish" believers (5:10). Again, just as in 1 John 2:12-14, we see words of assurance for believers facing difficult times.

In the OT we might expect to find minimal expression of conviction regarding assurance. The reasoning would be that the OT is dominated by the concept of law; and therefore the followers of the Lord are primarily under legal obligation to do the will of God. This, however, is not the case. If anything, we might argue that assurance and confidence before God are more widespread.

Much of the OT's sense of assurance is found in one word that generally sums up "the Lord's" nature: ḥesed. It is a rich word that has no single English equivalent. If we mixed "steadfast love" and "mercy," we would come close to understanding ḥesed. In essence the word communicates the Lord's radical commitment to maintaining a relationship with Israel, despite the nation's flaws and foibles. Or as my colleague Eric Seibert describes it, ḥesed sums up the Lord's "stick-to-us-ness."

Exodus 34:6-7, presenting a foundational OT "creed," uses ḥesed. There "The Lord, the Lord," is described as

> a God merciful and gracious,
> slow to anger,
> and abounding in steadfast love [ḥesed] and faithfulness,
> keeping steadfast love [ḥesed] for the thousandth generation,

forgiving iniquity and transgression and sin,
yet by no means clearing the guilty,
but visiting the iniquity of the parents upon the children
and the children's children,
to the third and fourth generation.

This basic aspect of the Lord's faithful nature is found repeatedly in the OT (such as Num 14:18-19; Deut 7:9; Pss 36:5; 108:4). Even the prophets who warn Israel of the Lord's wrath also stress God's steadfastness (Joel 2:12-14; Mic 7:18-20). This basic belief that the Lord is a faithful and loving God gave Israel assurance and confidence even in the most difficult situations. From the depths of the exile, the author of Lamentations writes, "The steadfast love of the LORD never ceases, his mercies never come to an end; they are new every morning; great is your faithfulness" (3:22-23).

Not surprisingly, this theme of the Lord's character and assurance for the believer is manifested in the context of worship as seen in the Psalms. Gordon Fee and Douglas Stuart (196-97) have identified a category of Psalms that they describe as "Songs of Trust." The thrust of these Psalms is "the fact that God may be trusted, and that even in times of despair, his goodness and care for his people ought to be expressed" (196). Included in this group would be Psalms 11; 16; 23; 27; 62; 63; 91; 121; 125; and 131. Other Psalms touch upon this theme as well. For example, Psalm 46:1-3 reads,

God is our refuge and strength,
    a present help in trouble.
Therefore we will not fear, though the earth should change,
    though the mountains shake in the heart of the sea;
though its waters roar and foam,
    though the mountains tremble with its tumult.

Psalm 105:6-8 sums up this entire section:

He is the LORD our God;
    his judgments are in all the earth.
He is mindful of his covenant forever,
    of the word that he commanded, for a thousand generations.

THE TEXT IN THE LIFE OF THE CHURCH

Confidence Before God

One of the best-known images from the *Martyrs Mirror* depicts Dirk Willems saving the life of another man. Willems was a Dutch

Anabaptist who had been arrested as a "rebaptizer," but he escaped from prison late in the winter of 1569. He was pursued across an ice-covered body of water by an official intent on arresting him again. His pursuer fell through the ice and struggled to save his own life. Willems stopped and returned to rescue the official. For his act of unselfish heroism, Willems was rearrested, imprisoned, tortured, and burned at the stake for his crime of being an Anabaptist.

In an engaging article "Why Did Dirk Willems Turn Back?" Joseph Liechty reflects upon this well-known story. It means different things to different people. Some are incensed at the injustice. Others are inspired by Willems's example of obedience to Christ's teaching to love our enemies. Liechty believes that Willems helps us overcome a weakness in the Anabaptist two-kingdom theology. The official was not simply a representative of the kingdom of the world and therefore an agent of evil: he was also a helpless victim. Although some Anabaptists, Liechty argues, may be tempted to settle for a simple dualistic worldview, Willems knew that life is much more complex, and his intuition moved him to action: he was not passive. Liechty speculates that if we were to ask Willems why he turned back, he would have responded, "Not I, but Christ in me."

I like Liechty's perspective on Willems's actions, but I want to push his thought one step further. Liechty believes that "as Dirk walked across the ice, he was sustained but not compelled by the hand of God" (12). I suspect that he was sustained by assurance. He had an assurance like that claimed in 1 John 2:12-14. He was sure his sins were forgiven. He was sure he knew him who was from the beginning. He was sure he had conquered evil. He was sure he knew the Father. He was sure he knew he was strong because the word of God abided in him. With that kind of solid foundation, Willems's act, while still amazing, is more understandable. Dirk Willems's knowledge naturally resulted in action.

One benefit of sound assurance is the ability to live the Bible's high ethical standards. Modern cognitive psychological therapies help us understand this phenomenon. Crudely and simplistically put, these cognitive therapies suggest that we tend to behave the way we think. If we think depressing thoughts, we will act like depressed people. Similarly, if we can begin to incorporate the biblical theme of assurance into our theology, we will find our Christian lives functioning at a higher level. For example, in the case of 1 John 2:12-14, the fact that our sins are forgiven will free us from primarily worrying about avoiding sin to being or becoming able to focus on doing the good. The assurance of God's protection enables us to be spiritually strong and capable of overcoming the evil. This will intensify our desire and confidence to resist evil.

A second benefit is identified by Gary Burge. He believes that the first threat to faith comes when a person doubts the validity of one's own salvation. This doubt then makes that person vulnerable to the influence of a person or group claiming to possess a more complete awareness of the divine. Ultimately the person who wrestles with doubt is potentially "swept up into a new religious movement" (119). Like John in these verses, the church has a responsibility to reassure members of the validity of their Christian experience. As Burge notes, this is not done simply to help people "feel better"; rather, the goal is "to help them know more completely that their Christian experience is true, authoritative, and complete" (119). If this is done well, believers are then released from self-doubt and directed away from the temptation to look elsewhere for fulfillment. One's focus can then be redirected to live a Christian life that is a natural response to the God who acts faithfully to redeem creation.

The greatest danger associated with "assurance" is the potential for complacency or a cavalier attitude toward sin. It is an old phenomenon, and Paul the apostle addresses the issue in Romans 6. If our sins are forgiven, why worry about avoiding sin? If God loves us regardless of what we do or don't do, we will never be convicted of our sins. We do not regard sin as a significant issue if we use assurance as an excuse for doing what we want while disregarding divine directives. But to employ assurance in this fashion is not Christian, nor is it acceptable in Johannine Christianity. In reality, the author sees the assurances he offers in 2:12-14 as a double-edged tool. On one hand, he uses it to reassure and build up the confidence of his readers: they are *not* like the separatists; the readers *know the Father.* On the other hand, these assurances are the foundation for the exhortation found in the following verses (2:15-17): *Do not love the world or the things of the world.* In John's theology, assurance and ethics go hand in hand.

1 John 2:15-17

Do Not Love the World

PREVIEW

Imagine what our lives would be like if our beliefs never translated into appropriate behaviors. Auto body repair shops would be busy if people believed they were to stop at red traffic lights, but never actually "acted" upon that belief. How long would one remain a college student if he said he believed he should study, but he never actually studied? How many relationships would last if the people involved only ever "said" that they loved the other person, but never found tangible ways to express their love?

In these verses we see more clearly the relationship of Christian belief and Christian behavior. In the preceding unit, the author focused on reminding his readers of three fundamental Christian doctrines: forgiveness of sins, knowledge of God, and empowerment to overcome the evil one. Ultimately all three doctrinal points are connected to a central issue of this letter: Christology (1:1-4). But Christology is not an abstract discipline that only engages scholarly minds.

In reality, Christology is a crucial subject for every believer who desires to be faithful—crucial for the mature, immature, or in-between. In John's view, who Jesus Christ was and what he did has numerous implications for how believers live. To take Jesus seriously is to live seriously, as Jesus himself lived. Christology and ethical behavior are not only connected; they are also inextricably intertwined like two strands of one rope. To accurately grasp who Jesus is results in the blessed movement from the realm of darkness to light (1:5-7); it results in the blessing of fellowship with like-minded people (1:7); and there is the obvious blessing that our sins are forgiven (1:7-10; 2:2). Moreover, there is the clear positive ethical consideration: those who understand Christology keep his commandments, especially his command to love one another (2:3-5). Finally, as we see in these closing verses of the unit, there is a "negative" implication associated with a firm grasp of who Jesus is: one does not love the world or earthbound desires associated with worldliness. To ignore the Christian life's ethical dimension is to risk losing the Christian life's blessings. As Garrett Kenney (25) writes, "The blessings declared flow from the proper christological base, stress the need for ongoing forgiveness, and affirm victorious Christian living. Believers are warned here . . . of being seduced from these blessings."

True to John's worldview, this current unit is primarily organized around the duality involving the Father and the world. Human beings are caught between the two: their love and basic orientation can drift to one side or the other. They cannot, however, love both the Father and the world. There are two reasons for this. First, each party is exclusive: there is nothing in common between the world and the Father. Second, the world is transitory and passing away; only the Father and his followers are permanent. But the question is, How does one know if one is "in love with" the world? John has already made it clear that those who have an intimate relationship with the Father show this by keeping his commandments, especially through loving fellow believers (2:3-11). John now gives the readers three illustrative traits that reveal a person's love for and orientation to the world. Clearly, in John's thinking, the Christian life links correct doctrine to correct living. The daily life of those who truly "know" God will reflect this—not only by what they do, but also by what they do not do.

While the structure of this unit is not as neat as some earlier units, duality continues. The author includes a small parenthetical statement (v. 16) between the two reasons given as support for his exhortation not to love the world. All this is offered to help the readers understand the importance of John's instructions about their relationship to the world.

Exhortation and First Reason 2:15
Do not love the world
> *or the things in the world.*

>> *The love of the Father is*
>>> *not in those who love the world;*

Parenthetical Statement 2:16
for all that is in the world—
> *the desire of the flesh,*
> *the desire of the eyes,*
> *the pride in riches—*

>> *comes not from the Father*
>>> *but from the world.*

Second Reason 2:17
*And the world and its desire
  are passing away,*

                              *but those who do the will of God
                              live forever.*

OUTLINE

An Exhortation and First Reason, 2:15
Behavior Revealing One's Orientation to the World, 2:16
A Second Reason for the Exhortation, 2:17

EXPLANATORY NOTES

An Exhortation and First Reason 2:15

The author's exhortation revolves around two key words that have
already been used in the letter: *love* and *world*. However, here the two
are placed together and qualified with a negative: *do not love [agapate]
the world or the things in the world.* The concept of "love" is terribly complex and nuanced for modern people. Simply think about these two
sentences: "I love my wife" and "I love the highlands of Scotland." The
same verb, "love," is used in two different ways. Unfortunately, English
speakers are often forced to use "love" in widely divergent ways.

Ancient Greek speakers, on the other hand, had three main words
from which to choose when addressing the idea of *love* (a less frequent
fourth use, *storgē*, as well as *eros* for passionate or sexual love, do not
occur in the NT). *Philia* described general "affection" or friendship.
Agapē was employed to express a more "spontaneous, unmerited, creative love flowing from God" (Brown 1982: 255). None of this is new;
most people are aware of these Greek words for *love*. But what is not
nearly as well known is the fact that *agapaō* (to love) has another
nuance in addition to being spontaneous and unmerited. In classical
Greek the verb *agapaō* carried with it a sense of "prefer" or "be content
with" (Haas, de Jonge, and Swellengrebel: 41; Brown 1982: 255).
Additionally, the LXX uses this Greek verb to translate a Hebrew verb
describing an act of the will rather than an emotional action (Haas, de
Jonge, and Swellengrebel: 41).

When John tells his readers, *Do not love the world,* he may be saying "do
not emotionally prefer the world." This nuanced meaning for *love* makes
perfect sense in this context. These verses are thoroughly dualist. On one
hand, we have the world; on the other, there is the Father. The believer
cannot "prefer" both, cannot "love" both. A decision must be made.
Which is preferred? Where is the believer's fundamental orientation?

Additionally, the preferential decision is not based on feelings. It is will-oriented: it is rational. John has just made the case that God came into the world to set us free from sin. God's light shines in the darkness because the eternal Word has become incarnate. Believers know God, are empowered by God, and have overcome the evil one, who is also in the world as ruler-claimant (4:4). Given all of this, it is unreasonable that they should prefer the world over the Father.

But what does John mean by *world*? Is it wrong to "love" the mountains and lakes of Scotland? After all, John 3:16, probably the best-known Bible verse, reminds us that even God loves "the world." Again the author's use of the word *world* (*kosmos*) is complex and nuanced. It can and does mean different things, depending upon context. For a fuller exploration of this diversity, see Brown (1979: 63-66); Schnackenburg's "Excursus 6" (1992: 125-28; Swartley 2006: 279-80). A few initial observations on the usage have already been made.

Additionally, the Johannine literature tends to use *world* in one of two primary ways: one positive and one negative. On the positive side, we are told that the world was created by God's word (John 1:10) and is loved by God (3:16). God desires to redeem the *world* and thus sends Jesus as Savior into the *world* (John 4:42; 1 John 4:14). This Savior, Jesus Christ, is the *expiation* for the *world* (1 John 2:2 RSV), the Lamb of God who removes the sins of the *world* (John 1:29), and the light of the *world* (John 1:9; 8:12; 9:5). On the other hand, the *world* also has a negative connotation. It is gripped by the evil one (1 John 5:19) and is under the influence of the spirit of the antichrist (4:3-4): it is against God. The *world* failed to recognize the light that was sent to it (John 1:10; 1 John 3:1), and it refuses to accept the followers of the light (1 John 3:1). The *world* hates the disciples (John 15:18–16:4a; 17:14; 1 John 3:13) even as it hated Jesus (John 7:7; 15:18, 23-25; Bruce: 60). Given this brief survey, it is obvious that John 3:16 uses *world* in the positive sense, while 1 John 2:15 employs *world* negatively to describe the forces that are in rebellion against God.

Verse 15 closes as the author sets forth the first of two reasons why a believer should not love the world: *The love of the Father is not in those who love the world.* As it stands in this verse, these words seem more like an assumption about the dual nature of reality and the way in which humans respond to the world and to God. Because John is probably thinking along the lines of "preference" when he writes, *The love of the Father is not in those who love [prefer] the world*, his assumption makes perfect sense. The *things* of the world (vv. 16-17) are diametrically opposed to the Father and the divine reality that is breaking into the humanity's mundane affairs through Jesus.

Therefore one must opt exclusively for either the world (negative use) or the Father, and reject the other. This reason is elucidated in verse 16 as the author expands his understanding of *the things . . . that* [are] *in the world.* They do not come from the Father.

Behavior Revealing One's Orientation to the World 2:16

Verse 16 specifies three illustrative traits. Despite the opening phrase, John is not offering an exhaustive list of characteristics that distinguish the world from the Father. These three traits are selected in order to make a strong case against the world's main flaw: it is enamored with material things and fails to recognize the new era in which the divine reality is now manifest. This is not a new topic for the author; he has already mentioned it in 2:8-12 (cf. 1:5-2:2). Recall that there he made the case for following and practicing godlike love if one truly knows God and belongs to the new era that God and Christ have initiated.

This section is frequently viewed as both an "admonition against pagan vices" and similar to other NT passages (e.g., Rom 13:12; Matt 6:24; Kenney: 25). Some scholars see a parallel between these three desires and the temptations of Eve and/or Jesus. However, it is more likely that verse 16 is a parallel to the threefold notation of sin in 1 John 1:5-2:2. Here the author is simply providing a threefold illustration of the root of sin, while there he explored the secessionists' attitude toward sin.

The first two characteristics are expressed in similar forms by using the word *epithymia: desire* or *longing.* Again, it is not necessarily a negative word. For example, in Philippians 1:23 Paul writes, "My desire is to depart and be with Christ." Or Jesus is depicted as saying, "I have eagerly desired to eat this Passover with you before I suffer" (Luke 22:15). It is, then, the context that supplies the negative overtone; we are specifically told that *the desire of the flesh* and *the desire of the eyes* are *not from the Father.* In addition to 1 John 2:16-17, the word *epithymia* is used only one other time in John's Gospel. In John 8:44 we read, "You are from your father the devil, and you choose to do your father's desires" (cf. Rev 18:14).

In addition to these *desires* not coming *from the Father,* their negativity is intensified by connecting them to *the flesh* and *the eyes.* In Greek thought the phrase *the desire of the flesh* is frequently associated with gluttony, drunkenness, and wanton sexuality. But as both Rensberger (74) and Kenney (25) urge, this phrase should not be taken narrowly to focus only on these three or on sexuality alone, as often occurs. Rensberger is correct to suggest that the real concern here is the human tendency toward "self-centeredness." This egoism can be seen as the foundation for many of "the desires of the flesh" that Paul identifies in Galatians 5:16-21, including idolatry, strife, jealously, and quarrels.

The expression *the desire of the eyes* is vaguer, yet the eyes are frequently viewed as the source or entry point for evil into a person's life (see Matt 5:27-29; 6:22-23). Haas, de Jonge, and Swellengrebel (57) and others think the author is pointing to the biblical theme that humanity's base desires are "aroused chiefly by what he sees." Especially interesting is an OT connection between the eyes and pride, as in Isaiah 5:15: "People are bowed down, everyone is brought low, the eyes of the haughty are humbled." Moreover, from the earliest times the eyes have been associated with covetousness in biblical literature (Schnackenburg 1992: 122). Finally, the eyes are frequently associated with resisting God's will (Gen 3:6; Num 15:39; cf. Mark 9:47; 1QS 5.4-5). At least we can conclude that John's concern in citing *the desire of the eyes* is to point toward a human tendency to reject God's influence and elevate another entity, usually the self, in God's place.

At least two issues emerge with the third trait. The first is how the Greek words should be translated. Little agreement exists among the various translation committees (see below). The less enigmatic issue is how we should understand the Greek genitive form in which the phrase is found. Most scholars view the first two traits as being "subjective genitives," meaning desires "coming from" the flesh or eyes, not desires "for" flesh and eyes. But oddly some scholars view the third characteristic as an objective genitive, meaning "the pride for life," instead of a subjective genitive, meaning "the pride of life" or "the pride arising from life." However, the three are best understood as trying to communicate desires that grow out of the flesh, eyes, or life. To view them in this way has the double benefit of consistency and awareness that the material world is not evil in itself. Food, drink, sexuality, and so forth can be misused, but they are not evil in and of themselves.

Assuming then that all three phrases are subjective genitives, what does the author mean by what the NRSV translates *pride [alazoneia] in riches [tou biou]*; RSV: *pride of life*; NIV and TNIV: *the boasting of what they have and do*; and REB: *the arrogance based on wealth*. We need to understand *alazoneia* and *biou* before we can suggest a meaning.

As the various translations suggest, *alazoneia* covers a wide range of meanings, including "pride," "arrogance," and "boasting." In classical Greek usage a good English equivalent would be "pretentiousness," and in later Hellenistic Greek, the meaning shifted toward "ostentation" (Brown 1982: 311). In the first century AD, James 4:16 employs the word in the sense of "overconfidence": "As it is, you boast in your arrogance; all such boasting is evil." So at least the first part of the formula has something to do with showiness and overconfidence. But what gives rise to this arrogance? The quick answer is *bios*; but what does John have in mind when using this word?

The term *bios* is used ten times in the NT and twice in 1 John. Its use in 1 John 3:17 carries with it the sense of material possessions: *How does God's love abide in anyone who has the world's goods [ton bion] and sees a brother or sister in need and yet refuses help?* Mark 12:44 uses the word when Jesus comments on the widow who contributed to the temple. Her two small coins were "all she had to live on." In these instances *bios* is certainly to be understood as "material" possessions or wealth. Thus the NRSV's *pride in riches* or the TNIV's *the boasting of what they have and do* are useful translations.

Still one question remains: If these three phrases are illustrative of one characteristic of the world, what is it that believers are to avoid? Marshall (146) believes this verse is a "timeless warning against materialism." According to Dodd (42), John is reminding his readers that they have been brought out of pagan society "with its sensuality, superficiality and pretentiousness, its materialism and its egoism." Bruce (61) notes that these "worldly" tendencies are quite complex: "It [worldliness] may manifest itself in petty but soul-stunting ambitions like 'keeping up with the Joneses'; it may manifest itself in unthinking acquiescence in current policies of monstrous malignity, as when too many Christians in Nazi Germany found it possible to go along with (or close their eyes to) their government's genocidal treatment of the Jews." At any rate, John is encouraging his readers to turn away from the shallow, material-bound selfishness and ultimately destructive orientation of the world. In the next verse he reminds them to keep in mind that God has begun a new order in Jesus Christ.

A Second Reason for the Exhortation 2:17

Verse 17 contains the climax for this unit and the entire section that began back in 1:5. These words, *And the world and its desire are passing away, but those who do the will of God live forever*, provide the unit's second reason for not loving the world and draw to a conclusion the unit's dually oriented argument that began with the fundamental proclamation *God is light and in him there is no darkness*. Throughout the larger unit, John has crafted the argument to convince his readers that two options lie before them. On the one hand, *darkness* essentially consists of rejecting Jesus Christ and his salvific works

and opting for a life of sin, including hatred and a primary orientation to the world and its desire. On the other hand, it denotes a life
that correctly understands Jesus and his provisions for dealing with
sin, a willingness to obey his commandments, especially the love
command. It means awareness of the believer's relationship to the
Father and awareness of victory over the evil one.

Along the way from 1:5, John may well be thinking ahead to the
content of 2:17. Having drawn firm boundaries between the darkness and God, the expressed duality of the world (those who reject
God and God's ways) and believers (those who accept Jesus and do
God's will), John leaves us with an obvious question: What is the end
result for those in either camp? Despite the contrary view of some
NT scholars (Bultmann 1973: 34; Schnackenburg 1992: 123), John's
answer is as eschatological as this entire unit is dualist: *The world . . .
is passing away . . . , but whoever does the will of God abides forever* (RSV).
If 2:17 is not sufficiently clear on this matter, the opening verse of
the next unit is. In 2:18 John writes, *It is the last hour! . . . Many antichrists have come. From this we know that it is the last hour.*

Jacob Elias's commentary on 1–2 Thessalonians provides an excellent essay on "eschatology," which he says is a theological term for
"the doctrine concerning final events"; the uniquely biblical view of
eschatology focuses primarily on "the end of history or another
worldly realm beyond this life" (1995: 355-57). Biblical eschatology
contains a paradoxical key belief that the world, while still existing, is
passing away, and that the kingdom of God, having initially arrived, is
still in the process of coming to completion. Biblical eschatology can
be summed up in the phrase "already but not yet." That is to say,
God's rule has already begun but it is not yet complete.

First John 2:17 must be seen against this already-but-not-yet
perspective. Here John reiterates a motif in 2:8: the world/*darkness
is passing away.* The Greek verb behind this English verb is used only
twice in the Johannine epistles, twice in the Gospel of John and
seven times in the rest of the NT. In 1 Corinthians 7:31, Paul uses it
in an almost identical way as John does when he tells the Corinthians,
"For the present form of this world is passing away." Our author
probably inherited this viewpoint from the larger Johannine tradition. In the fourth Gospel are at least three verses where the author
hints at his belief that the present age is in the process of giving way
to the new order inaugurated by Christ (see 8:12; 9:5; 12:46).

In addition to this broad understanding of eschatology, 1 John 2:17
also depicts a mild apocalyptic tendency. Elias's commentary also
offers an essay on the term *apocalyptic* (354-55), which comes from a

Greek word meaning "revelation" or "unveiling" and is applied to both a literary genre, such as Daniel and Revelation, as well as a theological orientation. Clearly 2:17 is nothing like apocalyptic literary genres, but the writer's theological worldview certainly appears "apocalyptic." As Elias explains,

> One of the characteristic features of apocalyptic thought is the dualistic doctrine of two ages: this present age is passing away, and the age to come is about to begin. Such duality also manifests itself both in the way apocalyptic writings depict the inner personal struggles between good and evil and in their portrayal of the cosmic tug-of-war between God and Satan. However, writers of apocalyptic envision that in the end God and good will triumph over Satan and evil. In fact, history moves relentlessly toward the time when God will win the victory. The faithful, therefore, just need to be steadfast until the end. (354; see also Elias's 2006 work on Pauline eschatological thought, *Remember the Future*)

Although 1 John's author seems to accept a number of characteristic apocalyptic traits, what is less certain, at least up to this point in the letter, is his attitude toward the common apocalyptic view that in the end God will dramatically intervene in human affairs to heap judgment upon the wicked while vindicating the faithful. John appears to have a much more gentle vision of the future, where the darkness and the world simply pass into oblivion, while the one who does God's will remains forever. Again, as in 2:12-14, John leaves his readers with a word of assurance after warning them about the dangers of worldliness.

THE TEXT IN BIBLICAL CONTEXT

The World

The Bible's use of *the world* is complex. Numerous passages indicate that this word is used positively. The most obvious is the first creation account. Throughout the process, God pronounces elements of the created order as "good" no less than six times and twice blesses elements of creation (Gen 1:4, 10, 12, 18, 21, 25; cf. 1:22, 28). The entire creation process is summarized with these words: "God saw everything he had made, and indeed, it was good" (1:31).

John's Gospel is another obvious text that picks up on this positive view of the world. This Gospel comes to mind primarily because of the well-known 3:16 verse, "For God so loved the world that he gave his only Son. . . . " However, as Raymond Brown observes, "The term 'world' becomes more common in John for those who reject the light" (1979: 63). Schnackenburg goes so far as to write, "The 'world' here [in Johannine literature] is a dangerous reality, and people have to be warned against it" (1992: 125). Additionally, it is not only John's writings that reflect this concern. It appears to be widespread in the NT; and even early OT writings speak of the dangers present in "the world."

The first commandment warns the Israelites to avoid making idols of "anything" found on earth (Exod 20:4-6). They are not to confuse the world's created things with the Creator, who made them; and they are specifically told to avoid worshipping these transient material objects (20:5). But a mere twelve chapters later they worship the idolatrous golden calf (32:1-24). It is thus no surprise that Israel repeatedly forgets God and worships a material object. The creation story reminds us of the fall and evil's influence in the world (Gen 3:1-24). This theme of humanity's bent toward rejecting God for the material things of the world continues throughout the OT and into the NT, where the fundamental themes found in the OT are accepted and expanded.

The NT writers accept that the world is under the control of the evil one and his minions, and even Jesus was tempted to forsake God for the world's material blessings. In Matthew (4:1-11) and Luke (4:1-13) the devil tempts Jesus three times. The most pertinent temptation is where the devil offers Jesus the kingdoms of the world:

> The devil took him to a high mountain and showed him all the kingdoms of the world and their splendor; and he said to him, "All these I will give you, if you will fall down and worship me." Jesus said to him, "Away with you, Satan! for it is written, 'Worship the Lord your God, and serve him only.' " (Matt 4:8-10)

Paul shares this worldview when he tells his readers that although they were once controlled by the "elemental spirits of the world," they are no longer in bondage to these forces (Gal 4:3; cf. Col 2:8, 20).

Because people are often under the influence of the evil one who seems to control the world, various biblical writers simply use *the world* as shorthand for forces that have rejected God. This is certainly true in the Johannine literature. We see this same conflictive relationship between God and the world in other NT writings as well. In his first letter to the Corinthians, Paul divides people into one of two categories: those who have the "spirit of the world" and those who have the "Spirit that is from God" (2:12). Earlier in this same letter, Paul identifies the source of the conflict to be the cross: "For the message about the cross is foolishness to those who are perishing, but to us who are being saved it is the power of God. . . . Where is the one who is wise?. . . . Has not God made foolish the wisdom of the world?" (1:18-20). Because *the world* has rejected God's work in Christ, *the world* is condemned (11:32; cf. John 9:39; 12:31); and as 1 John 2:8 and 17 say, "the present form of this world is passing away" (1 Cor 7:31). Ultimately Paul reminds all his followers that they should "not be conformed to this world, but be transformed by the renewing of your minds, so that you may discern what is the will of God" (Rom 12:2).

Ironically, the writer James, whom we often view as antithetical to Paul's thinking, agrees with him on this subject. James's letter has little commendation for the world. James believes that the world is a source of blemish for believers who wish to remain "undefiled before God" (1:27). Additionally, he comes close to 1 John when he writes, "Do you not know that friendship with the world is enmity with God? Therefore whoever wishes to be a friend of the world becomes an enemy of God" (4:4).

This basic view of *the world* continues into the late NT era and the period of the Apostolic Fathers. Like James, 2 Peter views the world as a corrupting influence (1:4). Moreover, he warns his readers to avoid again becoming entangled with the world once they are set free through Jesus Christ, for to do so is to end up in an even worse condition than before one's conversion (2:20). Similar to the dualist worldview found in 1 John 2:15, Ignatius, an early Christian leader who died around AD 108, writes *To the Romans*, "Do not speak of Jesus Christ, and yet desire the world" (7:2). Interestingly Ignatius even uses language that is found in 1 John. He makes the same point when writing *To the Magnesians* (5.2) by drawing on the two-coin imagery in Matthew 22:19: "Just as there are two coinages, the one of God, the other of the world, and each has its own stamp impressed on it, so the unbelievers bear the stamp of this world, and the believers the stamp of God the Father" (Lake 1912: 201).

Finally, the writer of the *Didache* (10.6) recognizes the world's transient nature: "Let grace come and let this world pass away" (Lake 1912: 325).

Desire or Lust

Related to *the world* is the topic of *desire(s)* (NRSV, NIV), *lust(s)* (KJV, RSV, NASB), or *cravings* (Weymouth), because *all that is in the world— the desire of the flesh, the desire of the eyes, the pride in riches*—creates such an attraction to one who is seeking to be faithful to God. The author uses one Greek word *epithymia* to sum up the desires of the flesh and eyes, as well as *pride in riches*. The word has a long and mixed usage.

In the classical Greek period the earliest usages were neutral, but later it takes on decidedly negative overtones from being associated with three other negative passions in Greek culture: fear, pleasure, and sorrow (Schönweiss: 456). The word is found about fifty times in the LXX, and it is used primarily three ways. It can be a neutral word, as in Deuteronomy 12:20-27: "When the LORD your God enlarges your territory, . . . and you say, 'I am going to eat meat,' . . . you may eat meat whenever you have the desire." It is also used positively, as in Genesis 31:30 and Isaiah 58:2. But the LXX uses the word negatively in Numbers 11:4 and 34 and in the final commandment (Exod 20:17) on coveting.

In the NT, *desire* is employed in both a neutral sense (Luke 15:16; Heb 6:11) and positively (Matt 13:17; 1 Thess 2:17), but its negative use predominates. In Matthew 5:28 it takes on the sense of sexual desire or lust; Mark 4:19 refers to desiring material goods and indicates that such desires are a serious threat to *the word* and will effectively separate the person with such desires from God. Additionally, Paul uses *desire* as an expression for things that rule a person (Schönweiss: 457). Such desires can be sexual in nature or directed at material goods and possessions belonging to other people, as is clear from passages like Romans 1:24; Galatians 5:16-21; and 1 Timothy 6:9-10. Ultimately, although these desires give pleasure, they also enslave the individual who yields to them (Eph 4:22); the Christian should only be a slave to Christ and righteousness (Rom 6:17, 20; cf. Paul's numerous self-identifications as a slave of Christ, as in Phil 1:1 mg.; Rom 1:1 mg.).

Like Paul, the writer of 1 Peter recognizes that these desires are antithetical to the Christian life. In 1:14 we read of Peter's warning against conforming to one's pre-Christian desires, and in the next chapter he writes, "Abstain from the desires of the flesh that wage war against the soul" (2:11). That these *desires* conflict with the divine will is evidenced in 1 Peter 4:2. Moreover, 2 Peter continues this "anti-*desire*" line of thinking in 1:4; 2:10, 18.

As Schönweiss (457) concludes, "When all is said and done it [*epithymia,* or *desire*] expresses the deeply rooted tendency in man to find the focus of his life in himself, to trust himself, and to love himself more than others." Because of this self-centeredness, "natural humans" act upon their desires and seek *the desire of the flesh, the desire of the eyes,* and *the pride in riches.* However, Revelation 18:11-14 reveals the ultimate destination of such *desires* and the objects upon which they focus. The objects are lost, and those who desire things such as gold, silk, fine food, military power, and so on are left empty and in mourning.

THE TEXT IN THE LIFE OF THE CHURCH

The World and Desires: Materialism

These few verses touch a raw nerve. They probably always have and always will. The harsh reality, amid the complexity of the issue, is this: humans tend to desire the creation over the Creator. We are easily tempted to seek things that are transitory. We look to the material world for meaning, stature, and pleasure. Still, the biblical tradition repeatedly asserts that such orientation is self-destructive at best and idolatrous at worst. Most early Christians who took Jesus and his teachings seriously saw danger in desiring the world. One classic example is Augustine of Hippo (354-430), who wrote,

> Let my soul praise you for these things [various elements of the material world], O God, Creator of them all; but the love of them, which we feel, through the senses of the body, must not be like glue to bind my soul to them. For they continue on the course that is set for them and leads them to their end, and if the soul loves them and wishes to be with them and find its rest in them, it is torn by desires that can destroy it. In these things there is no place to rest, because they do not last. (*Confessions* 4.10; Pine-Coffin: 80)

Furthermore, throughout the history of the church, those movements that took Scripture and earliest Christianity as their model are aware of the danger associated with the world and our desires to possess the things of the world.

This is true of the various leaders and documents associated with Anabaptism. In *Martyrs Mirror*, 1 John 2:15-17 is among the most-quoted verses of the letter. Additionally, around 1527, Michael Sattler wrote a letter to Martin Bucer and Wolfgang Capito, the Strasbourg Reformers, to explain why he could not support their agenda. The letter's core is a list of twenty points that serve as Sattler's "hermeneutic foundation, underlying all his particular convictions" (Yoder: 20). Sattler's eighth point is an allusion to 1 John 2:15-17 or James 4:4: "Christ is despised in the world. So are also those who are His; He has no kingdom in the world, but that which is of this world is against His kingdom" (22). As Yoder notes, two ideas permeate this letter: solidarity with Christ and history as the battlefield between Christ and the forces of evil (21).

Menno Simons also addressed this issue of the world's influence. In his essay *The New Birth*, dated 1536, Menno argues that believers bury their sins in baptism and rise with Christ "to a new life" (Wenger: 93). Among the sins left behind in baptism are avarice, pride, pomp and "all impure, carnal works," and believers "resist the world with all its lusts" (93). In the paragraphs that follow, it is clear that Menno expects believers to have a "detached" attitude toward material things, for he writes, "Their citizenship is in heaven, and they use the lower creations such as eating, drinking, clothing, and shelter, with thanksgiving and to the necessary support of their own lives, and to the free service of their neighbor, according to the Word of the Lord" (94; cf. *True Christian Faith*, in Wenger: 368-69, where his writing against wealth and profit takes on a more strident tone).

Menno would have found a kindred spirit in John Wesley (d. 1791), who recognized the powerful temptation associated with the world. In his *Plain Account of the Christian Perfection*, Wesley (79) declares that even mature believers need to be reminded not to love the world. Moreover, one of Wesley's best-known adages relates to material things: "Gain all you can, save all you can, give all you can" (sermon, "The Use of Money"). Lest we misunderstand what he meant, we remember that Wesley led a frugal lifestyle and died with little money and few possessions to his name.

Almost 150 years after Wesley's death, Dietrich Bonhoeffer wrote *The Cost of Discipleship*. Commenting on Matthew 6:19-24, Bonhoeffer writes,

> The life of discipleship can only be maintained so long as nothing is allowed to come between Christ and ourselves—neither the law, nor personal piety, nor even the world. The disciple always looks only to his master, never to Christ *and* the law, Christ *and* religion, Christ *and* the world. He avoids all such notions like the plague. . . . Worldly possessions tend to turn the hearts of the disciples away from Jesus. What are we really devoted to? That is the question. Are our hearts set on earthly goods? Do we try to combine devotion to them with loyalty to Christ? Or are we devoted exclusively to him? (154-55)

Those are still key questions decades later, especially important for people in churches that once stressed the centrality of not conforming to the world. Was our parents' and grandparents' commitment to nonconformity a quaint element of their rural context (cf. Amish today)? Or were these commitments honorable attempts to be faithful to Christ?

These are crucial questions to ask and faithfully answer considering that we live in a time when we are bombarded by media images regarding "the good life." One cannot go through a day without seeing a television commercial, hearing a radio advertisement, or reading a magazine that promises happiness if we simply purchase the right car, clothing, microwave oven, or house. Often the message is that the more we possess, the happier we will be. We rarely hear an "honest" commercial like the automobile ad that ran a few years ago. The thirty-second spot was filmed in an exclusive neighborhood where a luxury vehicle sat in every driveway. A voice-over extolled a particular nonluxury automobile's attributes: good gas mileage, dependability, and safety features. The voice-over's final words were "If you buy a car to impress the neighbors, you live in the wrong neighborhood." The advertisement ran for a short time. It challenged the system. It sounded too much like 1 John and the thinking of the early church.

That commercial was an oddity. The world rarely encourages us to be faithful to Christ. We have to do that ourselves, aided by the church community. Every believer and every congregation, every preacher and every Sunday school teacher—all of us need to continually ask, What does it mean to reject the world and live for Christ today? Yesterday's simple solution of rejecting and avoiding dubious cultural trends will not work for today or tomorrow. What does not loving the world or the things of the world look like today? More important, how do we foster "the love of the Father" and "do the will of God" each day?

Section 2: 1 John 2:18–3:24

The Present Situation: Confidence Amid Conflict and Confusion

OVERVIEW

In 1 John 1:5–2:17 John interwove doctrinal and ethical concerns. There he argues for accepting the church's teaching on sin and forgiveness. At the same time he urges his readers to love one another. That section strongly suggests that the community was facing both doctrinal and ethical challenges, but what is not clear is the exact nature of those challenges.

This second major section specifically reveals the central doctrinal issue before the community: *many antichrists have come* (2:18). Specifically, these *antichrists* deny that *Jesus is the Christ* (2:22). Not only are they challenging the church's doctrine regarding Jesus Christ; they have also created a schism for, as John reports, *they went out from us* (2:19). This division has resulted in a crisis of confidence, which the author addresses in this unit.

In addition to reminding his readers that they *know the truth* (2:21) and *have knowledge* (2:20), he reminds them they are *anointed* (2:20). Given these facts, their task is to *let what . . . [they] heard from the beginning abide in [them]* (2:24). That advice echoes his earlier advice; John again identifies the key test as to one's true orientation: those who abide in Christ are like him (2:28). They have turned from sin (3:1-10) and love one another (3:11-18).

We have heard all this before. Now, however, John employs this information toward a different end. Their turning from sin and loving one another is evidence *that we are from the truth and will reassure our hearts before him whenever our hearts condemn us* (3:19-20). Right belief and obedience to Jesus' teaching are again held up as hallmarks of the authentic Christian life, and these markers are offered as test patterns for the community's confidence.

OUTLINE

The Last Hour and Confusion, 2:18-27
Abiding and Doing Right, 2:28–3:10
Illustration, Encouragement, and Transition, 3:11-24

1 John 2:18-27

The Last Hour and Confusion

PREVIEW

When one is buffeted by conflicting information, confusion is a natural response. When the conflicting information takes on a personal edge, one might naturally experience a loss of self-confidence. What will restore clarity and confidence? For the readers of this letter, John points to their relationship with the Divine and with the Johannine tradition.

The author's opening reference to *the last hour* and the arrival of the *antichrists* may lead many modern readers to sigh with relief. At last our author addresses a theological subject that is popular in our time. Such a modern reader will be disappointed because John's theological agenda here only slightly touches upon eschatology. In fact, his concern about the *antichrist* brings him squarely back to previous issues of sin and Christology. He does not have the slightest interest in the number 666 or the relative merits of premillennialism, postmillennialism, or amillennialism. Rather, he begins by telling his readers why they should be confident despite finding themselves in conflicted and confusing times. They are *anointed by the Holy One* (2:20). Verses 18-20 function as an introduction to the entire unit (2:18-27), yet also introduce two ideas that will be clarified in 2:21-25 and 2:26-27. The theme of "antichrist" is initially addressed in 2:21-25, and the topic of "anointing" is seminally treated in 2:26-27.

John then develops these ideas. First, he reminds them that they know the truth, and so they should continue abiding in the truth they heard from the beginning. In particular, John is concerned about the truth of Jesus' identity as the Christ. These verses remind us of 1:1-4 because they draw upon a number of the same themes and theological points. The readers are encouraged to hold fast to the church's teaching about Jesus, and having done so, they *will abide in the Son and in the Father* (2:24).

The author's second point provides reassuring words. The validity of their *anointing* is demonstrated. He insists that those who have left the fellowship are deceivers, while his readers are abiding in an anointing from *him*. Therefore, they have no need to be taught by anyone who would deny Jesus Christ and so threaten the readers' "abiding" status with both Jesus and the Father.

OUTLINE

The Last Hour: Confusion and Schism, 2:18-20
Who Is the Liar? 2:21-25
Do Not Be Deceived: Be Confident, 2:26-27

EXPLANATORY NOTES

The Last Hour: Confusion and Schism 2:18-20

This unit begins in a fashion similar to 1:5-2:17. The author offers a simple theological statement that will be developed throughout the unit. This time, however, he adds *children*, a term of endearment similarly used in 2:1, 12, and 14. The opening word of affection hints at the tone that John wants to set: reassurance and affirmation. His readers need reassurance and affirmation because they are living in *the last hour*. As we will see, such a situation brings with it conflict and confusion.

The modern reader's challenge is to understand what the author means when asserting, *It is the last hour*; John is the only NT writer to use this specific phrase, and he only employs it here in 2:18. We find similar expressions elsewhere in the NT. In Acts 2:17, an example of early Christian preaching, Peter borrows the phrase "in those days" from Joel 2:28 and renders it, "In the last days." The same expression is found in 2 Peter 3:3; James 5:3; and 2 Timothy 3:1. In 1 Corinthians 10:11, Paul refers to the "ends of the ages"(cf. Heb 9:26; 1 Pet 1:20). John's Gospel repeatedly mentions "the last day" (6:39-40, 44, 54; 11:24). These verses tell us our author shares a common viewpoint with other early believers, but the question still remains: What is that view?

Many commentators recognize that this *last-hour* language arises from within an eschatological context. In the previous unit we have already seen that twice John refers to the *darkness . . . [as] passing away* (2:8) or the *world . . . [as] passing away* (2:17). Those two verses plus the repeated reference to *antichrist(s)* in this unit (2:18 [2x], 22; 4:3; 2 John 7) indicate that the author does have room in his theology for some type of eschatological thinking. But does he believe that he and his readers are living in a general period of the end? Or as F. F. Bruce (65) suggests, is it "11:55 p.m."?

John generally seems relaxed when making his observation that *it is the last hour.* He does not undertake any creative interpretation of the times in which he lives, unlike some of our contemporaries. He merely notes the presence of *antichrists* and asserts this is a sign of *the last hour.* Perhaps John's approach is due to his acceptance of the Johannine tradition's belief that "positive" eschatological events, such as the coming of Jesus the Messiah (1 John 1:1-4; John 1:1-18) and the anointing of believers with the Spirit (1 John 2:20, 27; John 14:16, 26; 16:7), have priority. Or he may share the fairly widespread early Christian view that the entire period between Jesus' incarnation and his second coming is the final period of time (cf. Acts 2:17; Heb 1:2; 1 Pet 1:20). And we should not rule out the possibility that John was taking seriously Jesus' own advice on the end times: it will be a time of turmoil and of attempts to lead believers astray, but his followers should not speculate on the details. Instead, they are called to be alert to the dangers at hand (Mark 13//Matt 24).

The manner in which the author employs *antichrists* shows that John views *the last hour* as a general time period. The actual words *antichrist* or *antichrists* are found only in 1 John and 2 John (1 John 2:18 (2x); 4:3; and 2 John 7), and because of this, many commentators assume that the author created the word. We should not conclude, however, that he alone is convinced of this teaching's validity. In fact, his phrase *as you have heard* (2:18) suggests that his readers are already well aware of this teaching.

Not only that, but 1 John and 2 John share this teaching with other early believers, as is evidenced by 2 Thessalonians 2; Matthew 24//Mark 13; and Revelation 12–13. Colin Kruse (99-102) has succinctly surveyed these passages and has come to five conclusions. First, the coming of some "antichrist" figure was part of early Christian doctrine. Second, there is a distinction between the "great antichrist figure" and "lesser antichrist figures whose influence is already being felt" (101). Third, these figures' primary agenda is to deceive believers. Fourth, all sources, except the Johannine epistles, view these antichrists as working from outside the church. And finally, John alone identifies them as "erstwhile members of a Christian community" (101).

It seems as though the early believers inherited this concept from Jewish apocalyptic thought found in writings such as Daniel. But as Roy Yates (42-50) and others have argued, the early Christians altered the mythical imagery by envisioning human figures who embody an adversarial role and are opposed to God's work. John, who may not have ruled out a future antichrist figure, was certainly aware of the present danger posed by a group's challenging accepted Christian doctrine and wounding the church by dividing it. Additionally, the author recognizes that already *many antichrists have come* (1 John 2:18). In 4:3 he generally describes it: *this is the spirit of the antichrist, of which you have heard that it is coming; and now it is already in the world.* John is the first to admit—as Kruse reminds us and as we will see in verse 19—that the antichrists can work within the church as well as attack it from outside. All of this leads to the conclusion that John viewed his era as a time of general opposition to God's work and not a five-minutes-to-midnight crisis situation.

First John 2:19 is foundational for any understanding of the historical situation that gave rise to the letter's writing. The statement *They went out from us* makes it clear that there has been a schism in the author's faith community, and the verb's past (aorist) tense makes it equally clear that the division happened at a specific point in the past. A few scholars argue that John's community "excommunicated" the secessionists, but the verb used in the opening of verse 19 does not really seem to carry with it a sense of coercion. The next phrase, *for if they had belonged to us, they would have remained with us*, suggests the possibility of the separatists' staying if they had agreed with the Johannine community's theology and ethic.

Equally unlikely is Bultmann's suggestion that the secessionists still claim to belong to John's group (1973: 36). Not only does the aorist verb counter this, but it is unlikely that these opponents would have sensed any welcome in the community or wanted to be welcomed. The language and images employed by John are certainly not inclusive and welcoming. Those who have left are *antichrists*. Earlier the author implies that they love the world more than God (2:15-16) and they have proved that they are in the dark because they hate other believers (2:9-11). Later John calls them *children of the devil* (3:10) and *false prophets [who] have gone out into the world* (4:1). In 4:4 he uses a war image: *Little children, you are from God, and have conquered them.* Indeed, one suspects that the division has occurred and neither side holds out hope for reconciliation.

Houlden (78) claims 1 John is unique on this matter because it is the first early Christian document to specifically report a schism within the Christian ranks. There is evidence of serious doctrinal disagreements in Pauline congregations (cf. 1 Cor 15 on resurrection, or Galatians on law observances), but we have no evidence that these doctrinal differences resulted in division. Yet Houlden (78) is not as helpful when he writes, "This development is all the more striking in that on many matters (such as their negative attitude to the world) no more than a hair's breadth can have divided the parties." On the contrary, the points under dispute here are not small: they strike at the core of the Christian faith. Hence the somewhat vitriolic language in the author's response is significant.

John's community and the separatists disagree on both doctrinal and ethical issues. They do not agree on "tradition" (1:1-4), the nature of and remedy for sin (1:5–2:2), or Jesus' identity as the Messiah (2:22, 24; 5:5). Apparently they also disagree over Jesus' central ethical teaching to "love one another" (2:3-6; 3:14; etc.), and the secessionists probably were considerably more open to "the good life" than was John's community. Related to these two charges is another serious one: they do not share their wealth with the poor (3:17). The secessionists' leaving was the final straw in the doctrinal/ethical controversy. Christian communities are "to remain together and maintain the unity of the group. The destruction of church unity makes the nature of the false teachers as antichrists evident" (Strecker: 64). M. M. Thompson (75-76), not without justification, writes, "This sin is as bad as, if not worse than, the actual doctrinal error, because in leaving the fellowship these secessionists have disregarded the cardinal and foundational command of Jesus to 'love each other.'"

Given all of this, Hans-Josef Klauck (55-65) puts forward a plausible scenario surrounding the schism. Arguments over both doctrine and ethical practice have led to this split, and there seems to be no hope of reconciliation. John's group was possibly the group that lacked positive social standing in the larger community where the two congregations existed. There was no "excommunication" because the smaller group of John's community lacked the means to do this. The secessionists continued to believe that they represented the true Johannine community and assumed they could bring our author and his community into their camp (cf. 1 John 4:1 and 2 John 7-11, which suggest that the secessionists were involved in some type of missionary work with John's group).

The conflict was intensified by social factors. First John 2:15-17 leads Klauck to conclude that the separatists were relatively wealthy, and 3:17 suggests that they were hesitant to share their wealth with the poor, likely John's community. At least the schism created economic material hardships for the author's community. In Klauck's words (57), "The author of the epistle and his supporters suddenly find themselves confronted with financial problems they had not dreamed of. They feel themselves to be 'betrayed and sold.'" While this amount of detail is admittedly speculative, the fact that there has been a split is not. And in John's opinion, the secessionists' decision to leave is simply more proof that *none of them belong to us*.

On arriving at the final verse of this subunit, we confront two challenges. First, the author uses a word that is rare in the NT: *anointed* (*chrisma*). Second, there is the identity of *the Holy One* who anoints the believers. Despite these two issues having provided sufficient fodder for scholars, it is clear that the author is referring "to a teaching or power that comes from beyond the believer" (M. M. Thompson: 77), and this source provides them with a "correct standard for critical examination" of their situation (Bultmann 1973: 37).

The two challenges are related and must be resolved as one because John writes that his readers *have been anointed by the Holy One*. The word for *anointing* (as noun) is used only three times in the entire NT, all of which are found in this unit. The word's verb form appears five times in the NT; and four of those occurrences refer to Jesus' anointing (Luke 4:18; Acts 4:27; 10:38; Heb 1:9). These four verses depict the anointing as a metaphorical action that gave Jesus his authority to act as the Messiah. Two verses mention the Holy Spirit as the anointing "substance" with which Jesus was anointed (Luke 4:18; Acts 10:38). This metaphorical anointing for authority no doubt draws upon the OT imagery of anointing Israel's kings. In the LXX the word is used around sixty times in the context of symbolic ritual (e.g., 1 Kings 1:39; 1 Sam 10:1; 16:1, 13).

But who is *the Holy One* who does the *anointing*? In the OT this phrase refers only to "the LORD." But in the NT, God is never referred to by this title. On two occasions, however, Jesus is called "the Holy One" (Rev 3:7; Mark 1:24). Considering this subunit's larger context, we should probably conclude *the Holy One* is Jesus. In 1 John 2:25 we read, *And this is what he has promised us, eternal life*. There *he* no doubt refers to Jesus and his promise preserved in John's Gospel. Additionally, we have two parallel statements—*the anointing that you received from him* (2:27), and *his anointing teaches you about all things* (2:27)—which encourage us to see Jesus as *the Holy One* who *anoints* believers. All of this brings to mind John 14 and 16, where we read of the Spirit's coming. John 14:16 and 26 tells us that the Spirit will be given by the Father, but at Jesus' prayerful request (14:16). In 16:7 we are told that Jesus will send the Spirit. We may be seeing, yet again, the author's tendency to identify Jesus with God the Father. Clarity over who does the anointing is not as important to our author as the end result of that anointing. Because of this anointing, his readers authoritatively know the truth in this situation of theological conflict. They *do not need anyone to teach* them (1 John 2:27) because *his anointing teaches you about all things, and is true* (2:27). Again, this connects to the Gospel of John, chapters 14 and 16. In 14:26 we read, "But the Advocate, the Holy Spirit, whom the Father will send in my name, will teach you everything, and remind you of all that I have said to you." Similarly, in 16:13 we read, "When the Spirit of truth comes, he will guide you into all truth." Our author introduces the anointing theme as an image designed to bolster his readers' confidence in troubled times. Ultimately all believers *have been anointed*, and so they all have sufficient knowledge. As we will see in 1 John 2:21-25, this knowledge is what they have been taught from the beginning.

Who Is the Liar? 2:21-25

In these five verses the author mixes assurance and argumentation. Verse 21 begins with words of assurance and closes by introducing the theme of "a lie." This theme is picked up and developed in verses 22-23, which for the first time partially reveal (see 5:5-12 for the detailed explanation of the error) the separatists' core error and the end result of their flawed thinking. In these verses John tries to make a case against their viewpoint. In 2:24 he returns to an encouraging tone, assuring his readers that if they hold to *what you have heard from the beginning* they will *abide in the Son and in the Father.* And the subunit closes with verse 25 and its promise of eternal life.

I begin a new subunit with verse 21 because of the opening line, *I write to you . . . because . . . .* The Greek wording is similar to 2:12-13 and exactly like *I write to you because* in 2:14. In those earlier verses, it was argued that that subsection set out to encourage John's audience, and that same agenda dominates this subunit. As in 2:12-14, in 2:21 the author uses three *hoti* clauses to communicate his encouragement. A translator must decide if this small Greek word should be translated "because" or "that." Most recent translation committees have opted for *because* in the first two *hoti* clauses and *that* in the third (see NRSV, RSV, REB; but NIV uses *because* for all three).

Regardless of the translation of the Greek word, the thrust is clear. After stressing their anointing by the *Holy One* and the fact that they all have knowledge in verse 20, John now underscores the crucial by-products of that anointing. First, they are not ignorant of *the truth*, for the anointing results in an awareness of what is truth amid this controversy. This stating of the idea in a negative form and then in a positive fashion is done so as to stress the point that they *know the truth*. The author liberally employs this technique as in 1 John 1:6, 8; 2:4, 7, 16, 23, 27b; 4:18; 3 John 11.

The positive statement of knowing the truth allows John to make a specific point that supports the argument against the secessionists in verses 22-23: no lie comes from the truth. As Johnson (58) observes, the author is not so much concerned about his readers' knowledge. They are probably aware that the false teachers' doctrine does not agree with the "historic teaching of the Johannine community." John's agenda is to affirm the knowledge they already have, and its correctness.

Up to this point we have seen hints that obliquely reveal aspects of the secessionists' thinking. In verse 22 John uses a rhetorical question to lay bare their fundamental error: *Who is the liar but the one who denies that Jesus is the Christ?* But what is meant by denial? John is probably not suggesting that the separatists have denied that Jesus is the OT-predicted Messiah. In other words, his opponents are not like "the Jews" in the Gospel of John who refuse to accept Jesus in this role. The secessionists' error lies elsewhere.

Numerous tantalizing verses help us reconstruct a plausible understanding of the false doctrine his opponents were advocating. In 1 John 4:2 we read a backhand accusation against the secessionists: *Every spirit that confesses that Jesus Christ has come in the flesh is from God.* In 1 John's final chapter, the author writes, *This is the one who came by water and blood, Jesus Christ, not with the water only but with the water and the blood* (v. 6). And 2 John 7 reads, *Many deceivers have gone out into the world, those who do not confess that Jesus Christ has come in the flesh; any such person is the deceiver and the antichrist!* These three verses are vital evidence that the disputed issue focused on the incarnation. The secessionists were denying the humanity of Jesus, especially as it related to his crucifixion (see comments on 1 John 5:5-12).

The epistle's opening takes us further. There the reader is encouraged to remember what was declared *from the beginning.* John uses sensory language to talk about *the word of life—this life was revealed, and we declare to you the eternal life that was with the Father and was revealed to us.* Elsewhere in 1 John we catch glimpses of the secessionists' claims of their own experiences that resulted in a relationship with God (1:6, 8, 10; 2:6, 9), but Jesus Christ in his humanity was apparently not central to these claims. Probably their "denial" was a refusal to accept the fundamental Johannine belief that Jesus of Nazareth was one with God the Father, thus revealing the Father (cf. the Gospel's words in 10:30, "the Father and I are one" (see also 5:17-20; 8:28; 14:9-14).

This plausible context helps make sense of 1 John 2:22b, *This is the antichrist, the one who denies the Father and the Son.* John easily jumps from denying that *Jesus is the Christ* to denying *the Father and the Son* because he and his readers know their opponents deny that Jesus in his incarnation and humanity revealed the Father and is the mediator to the Father. As John 14:6 ("I am the way, and the truth, and the life. No one comes to the Father except through me") shows, this was a central Johannine community tenet.

It is the secessionists' denial that triggers the author's strong words: *liar* and *antichrist.* The separatists have opted for a belief that runs counter to what John and other Christian leaders have taught about God's work. They suggest that there are other alternatives to knowing God than through Jesus and what God has done in his life and death. John views this as anti-God, and so he calls these people both *antichrists* and *liars.* The comments on 2:15 explain that *antichrist* figures embody an adversarial role, as opposed to God's work, and the same can be said for the concept of *liar.* As Becker and Link (470-74) state, the OT stresses that truthfulness is a key attribute of God, and when humans dissociate themselves from God, they oppose God and become liars (Pss 58:3; 116:11). The members of the Qumran community liberally used *liar* to identify those who opposed their understanding of God. While the Qumran faithful are called "sons of truth," their opponents are marked by lies. One historical opponent is known as "liar" or "spouter of lies" in both the Damascus Document (CD 8.13; "preaches lies" in Martínez: 38; "spewer of lies" in Wise, et al.: 59-60) and the commentary on Habakkuk (1QpHab 2.1-2; Martínez: 198). In this respect John is simply, albeit aggressively, employing a common cultural descriptor.

First John 2:23 continues the argument of verse 22 and reveals why the author resorts to such aggressive language. To follow the separatists' line of thinking is to cut oneself off from not only the Son, but also the Father. Thus one is without hope of knowing God. This is because John does not believe that there are alternative ways of salvation. The Johannine tradition is built upon an idea summarized in John 20:31: if you "believe that Jesus is the Messiah, the Son of God, . . . you . . . have life in his name." If one rejects this idea and replaces it with alternatives, then one turns one's back on both the Son who reveals and the Father who is revealed by the Son.

To stress this point, the author couches it in his "negative/positive" format by using the key words *deny* and *confess*. The essence of both words involves more than a person's saying or not saying something. They both touch upon behavioral matters. In classical Greek, *deny* carries with it a sense of refusal or rejection; in late Hellenistic literature and the NT, it "has the further meaning of disown, renounce" (Link and Tiedtke: 454). Conversely, the NT usage of *confess* carries with it the sense that "a man indicates that he stands by the fact of Christ and submits his life to it" (Fürst: 347). This sense probably goes back to the word's classical Greek use and its legal connotation. There, a confession was a promise associated with legal contracts. When the word was used in a religious context, it described a person's oath given to a deity when entering into a "treaty relationship" with that God (Fürst: 344). As Marianne Meye Thompson (81) observes, this denial touches not only on doctrinal matters: a "denial of Jesus is also a 'failure of allegiance' to him."

With verse 24 the author shifts back to assuring and encouraging his followers. We know this is the case because the first word of the verse is *hymeis*, or *as for you*. Unfortunately, most translations overlook the word. John shifts focus so as to offer his followers a simple remedy to ward off being led astray: *Let what you heard from the beginning abide in you. If what you heard from the beginning abides in you, then you will abide in the Son and in the Father.* The NRSV, RSV, and REB try to faithfully stress John's repeating of the phrase *what you heard from the beginning*, while the NIV does not. Through this repetition John wants his readers to know beyond a shadow of a doubt that the Johannine tradition (cf. 1 John 1:1-4) can facilitate a relationship with both the Son and the Father. John has appealed to the power of the tradition before (2:7, 13, 14) and will do so again (3:11; 2 John 5-6). This formula for faithfulness is not unique to John, as indicated by 1 Timothy 6:3; 2 Timothy 1:13; 4:3-5; Titus 1:9; 2 Peter 3:2; and Jude 17 and 20. When the author writes of accepting the message, for it to *abide in you*, he has more in mind than simply affirming abstract doctrine or preaching. This abiding is more dynamic. The message abides in the believer (John 5:38; 15:7; 1 John 2:14; 2 John 2) and the believer abides in it (2 John 9), thus enabling one to adhere faithfully to the Father and the Son (Bruce 1970: 74-75). On the dynamic nature of the abiding message, Brown is quite correct to note that the message *heard from the beginning* coexists with the Spirit's anointing. In Johannine thought the Spirit "contemporizes" the gospel message, as John 16:12-13 suggests (Brown 1982: 372).

The author's final encouraging word for this subunit occurs in 2:25. Abiding in the Son and the Father is not the final benefit. The ultimate benefit of confessing the Son and the Father is *eternal life*, which has been promised. The emphasis in the Greek text is on the promise, for the author literally writes, "the promise he promised." However, the content of the promise, *eternal life*, is easier to grasp than the time when the author thinks the promise is fulfilled. Most likely, when he identifies *eternal life* as the believer's hope, he has in mind John 17:3: "This is eternal life, that they may know you, the only true God, and Jesus Christ whom you have sent."

So, when does the author envision the promise being fulfilled? Evidence in both 1 John and the fourth Gospel indicates that this is a future event. First John 3:2 makes it clear that not all God's blessings are fulfilled in the present. And the Gospel of John has a fairly strong sense of future "life" blessings, as 5:28-29 and 12:25 show. Yet, as Marshall (161) argues, John also thinks that the blessing is available in the present. Thus the author writes, *We know that we have passed from death to life* (1 John 3:14), and *Whoever has the Son has life* (5:12). Moreover, the Gospel of John also asserts this in 3:36; 6:40, 47. Therefore we do best to view *eternal life* as available, in part, to the believer now, with its ultimate fulfillment in the future. This is because when the Johannine tradition refers to *eternal life*, it is not primarily addressing an issue of time or duration. Rather, quality is foremost in the writer's mind. As Brown points out, "Indeed, it [eternal life] is the life of God Himself" (1982: 168).

Do Not Be Deceived: Be Confident 2:26-27

With these final two verses we come to John's unit summary (v. 26), a final encouraging word about anointing and an imperative. Though the content here is generally straightforward, the final words of verse 27— *but as his anointing teaches you about all things, and is true and is not a lie, and just as it has taught you, abide in him*—exhibit 1 John's "frustratingly obscure syntax" (Rensberger: 82). The syntax here is similar to the grammatical complexity of 1 John 1:1-4. Helpful exposition of this complexity is found in either Brown (1982: 360-61) or Smalley (125-28).

When John begins 2:26 with *I write these things to you*, he is referring to what he has just penned in verses 18-25, and he is signaling his intention to draw this portion of the letter to a close. With that in mind, he makes one more specific reference to the secessionists, *concerning those who would deceive you*. Unfortunately, the NRSV translation of the participle, *tōn planōntōn*, with *those who would deceive you*, does not quite communicate the word's essence.

The Greek *planaō*, as used here, carries with it a sense of leading astray or causing to wander as well as deceive. The separatists are not simply disseminating misinformation: their goal is to have John's followers "move camps" or switch allegiance. And the verb's form shows why John is so agitated. *Planōntōn* is a present-tense participle that could be translated *those who are trying to lead . . . astray*, as in the NIV. In other words, we are led to believe that at the time of the letter's writing, the secessionists are actively attempting to "convert" members of John's community. John sees this as a serious threat.

Verse 27 again shifts the focus back to John's followers through the words *as for you* (NRSV, NIV, NEB) or *hymeis* (see comments on v. 24, above). Again the point is to draw a contrast between the *deceivers* and their views (NRSV) on the one hand, and the hope that the Johannine community possesses on the other hand. To this end John returns to the theme of *anointing* that was introduced in verse 20. In this closing verse, the author makes four comments about their anointing, all of which are designed to bolster the readers' confidence. First, Jesus is the source of the anointing (*that you received from him*). Second, it consistently remains with them like an endowment (it *abides in you*). Third, the anointing informs them about all the pertinent issues (it *teaches you about all things*). And finally, their anointing is genuine, unlike the teachings of the secessionists (it *is true and is not a lie*).

The third and fourth affirmations, which are the heart of the complex syntax, lead to a final exhortation: *Abide in him*. These three simple words have provoked discussion. The first issue focuses on the verb *abide* (NRSV) or *remain* (NIV). It can be either an imperative (*you should remain*) or an indicative (*you do remain*). Although the indicative may fit better with the reassuring tone of these verses, I think the author intends it to be understood as an imperative. Because people are trying to lead his followers astray, John sees the situation as warranting the instructional imperative. Therefore, he tells them to *remain*.

The second issue revolves around the identity of *him*. Though it is possible to see this as a reference to the Holy Spirit, the larger context makes it clear that the pronoun *him* means Jesus. Above we argued that *the anointing that you received from him* (v. 27) was a reference to Jesus. Therefore, *his anointing* must also refer to Jesus. Additionally, verse 28 encourages the readers to *abide in him*, using exactly the same three Greek words. In that verse there can be no doubt that *him* refers to Jesus because the verse reads *abide in him, so that when he is revealed we may have confidence and not be put to shame before him at his coming.* This verse can only be read as a reference to Jesus' second coming. In the final analysis the author's last word to his audience is to tell them to *remain/abide* in Jesus. While his words of warning about the separatists' erroneous theology and endeavors to lead them astray are useful, only by relying on their *anointing* and *remain[ing] in him* will the readers gain the confidence and wherewithal to resist their opponents' overtures.

SUMMARY

These ten verses are crucial for at least two reasons. First, they provide key evidence that helps the modern reader re-create a plausible historical theory for why the letter was written. There has been a schism within the Johannine community (2:19), and as noted above, this is the first written evidence of such an event within Christian circles. So far as we can tell, the divisive issue was Christological or doctrinal in nature. Specifically, it seems as though the secessionists denied some aspect of the incarnation (2:22) and may well have argued against the Johannine belief that Jesus alone has revealed God. Finally, 2:26 leads us to believe that the separatists were actively "evangelizing" the remaining members of John's community.

A natural response to such a situation would be self-doubt and temptation to join the separatists, especially if, as has been suggested above, the division left John's group as perhaps the minority party. In light of this perceived danger, John vigorously replies with words of accusation, reassurance, and encouragement. It is the secessionists who are in doctrinal error. And their error is so grave that they show themselves to be anti-God and thus warrant the labels *antichrist* (2:18, 22) and *liar* (2:22). Conversely, John's followers should take comfort in the fact that they are *anointed* with the Holy Spirit by Jesus himself. It is the Spirit who makes known afresh the message they heard from the beginning, which the separatists are denying. Between their anointing and holding fast to the message from the beginning, they abide in the Son and the Father and thereby gain eternal life.

THE TEXT IN BIBLICAL CONTEXT

The "Last Hour" and Deception

As mentioned in the Preview, this unit's use of the phrase *the last hour* indicates that John's main concern is of an eschatological or apocalyptic nature. There can be no doubt that this concept hails from such a context, but it is also clear that John's interest in *the last hour* is due to one narrow but serious related subject: deception of the faithful.

Long before believers penned the word *antichrist*, Jewish writers warned readers about people who would try to lead the faithful astray. Two early passages are in Deuteronomy 13:1-5 and 18:20. Both units prescribe the death penalty for any "false prophet," and 13:2 specifically identifies the crime's core as telling Israel, " 'Let us follow other gods' (whom you have not known) 'and let us serve them.' " That Israel occasionally took this injunction seriously is evidenced in the well-known confrontation between Elijah and the prophets of Baal (1 Kings 18). It is not only the prophet Elijah who is depicted as viewing the false prophets' deception as a serious threat. Isaiah also explains part of Israel's judgment as a result of false prophets who "teach lies, . . . who led this people . . . astray, and those who were led by them were left in confusion" (Isa 9:15-16). Jeremiah also speaks of deceivers in his day: "I am against those who prophesy lying dreams, says the LORD, and who tell them, and who lead my people astray by their lies and their recklessness" (23:32). Finally, late in the prophetic tradition we see Zechariah affirming the Deuteronomy 13 tradition:

> On that day says the LORD of hosts, I will cut off the names of the idols from the land, so that they shall be remembered no more; and also I will remove from the land the prophets and the unclean spirit. And if any prophets appear again, their fathers and mothers who bore them will say to them, "You shall not live, for you speak lies in the name of the LORD."(Zech 13:2-3)

The book of Daniel, probably written in the second century before Christ, depicts a figure that aggressively challenged Israel's faithful. This character is probably modeled on the Syrian king Antiochus IV Epiphanes. Among other blasphemies, the Syrian king dedicated a statue to Zeus in the Jerusalem temple and began sacrificing swine to Zeus on the high altar (1 Macc 1:54, 59; 2 Macc 6:3-5, 18-21; cf. 2 Macc 7:15-26). These actions could only be viewed as an attempt to turn the pious away from God, "the Ancient One," and Daniel's writer sums up Antiochus IV Epiphanes' undertakings with these words, "The king shall act as he pleases. He shall exalt himself and consider himself greater than any god, and shall speak horrendous things against the God of gods" (11:36).

From the time of Daniel through the end of the NT period, we see numerous references to deceptions and lies in what we might call minority Jewish groups, such as the Qumran community and developing Christianity. The Qumran community often labeled their opponents as liars and false prophets. Deceit was considered to be a trait of those opposing the faithful. Vermès (54) recounts one phase of Qumran's history when a group broke away from the main community. The separatists were led by a person who was variously known to the Qumran covenanters as the "Scoffer," the "Liar," and the "Spouter of Lies." Elsewhere we read, "Teachers of lies [have smoothed] Thy people [with words], and [false prophets] have led them astray, . . . and they, teachers of lies and seers of falsehood, have schemed against me a devilish scheme" (1QH 12 [formerly 4].7-12; Vermès, 1997: 57pb; 1995: 31hb). And in 1QS 4.9-10a we read, "But the ways of the spirit of falsehood are these: greed, and slackness in the search for righteousness, wickedness and lies, haughtiness and pride, falsehood and deceit" (Vermès, 1997: 102pb; 1995, 74hb).

That Jesus shared this general outlook is evidenced by his warning to his followers recorded in Mark 13:5-6: "Beware that no one leads you astray. Many will come in my name and say, 'I am he!' and they will lead many astray" (cf. Matt 24:4-5; Luke 21:8). As early as AD 50 or 51 Paul adopts this theme when he writes a second letter to the Thessalonians, addressing the issue of the day of the Lord and a figure he labels as the "lawless one" (2 Thess 2:8-9). Among other things, this figure employs both "lying wonders" and "wicked deception" as he "exalts himself above every so-called god, . . . declaring himself to be God" (2 Thess 2:4, 9-10). Similarly the author of Ephesians twice warns his readers to be on their guard against deceivers. Ephesians 4:14 warns about false doctrines propounded by the "deceitful scheming" of some people, and 5:6 addresses dubious moral teachings.

Additionally, the Pauline letters to Timothy show a decidedly stark parallel to this concern in 1 John: "Now the Spirit expressly says that in later times some will renounce the faith by paying attention to deceitful spirits and teachings of demons, through the hypocrisy of liars whose consciences are seared with a hot iron" (1 Tim 4:1-2). This touches upon the themes of the last days, deceit, liars, and apostasy. Second Timothy 3:12-15 draws the reader's attention to deceivers and "sacred writings" as a bulwark against opponents' challenges.

Finally, we should not overlook Revelation (16:13; 19:20; 20:10), which introduces a false prophet "who leads men to oppose God and the church" (Becker and Link: 474). Additionally, the congregation at Thyatira is criticized because it tolerates "that woman Jezebel, who calls herself a prophet and is teaching and beguiling [deceiving] my servants to practice fornication and to eat food sacrificed to idols" (2:20). And Satan is described as the ultimate deceiver (12:9; 20:2-3, 8, 10).

The Uniqueness of Jesus

First John 2:22 focuses on a question relevant to the faith in every age: How should one view Jesus? The author is aware of some who deny the historic Christian affirmation that Jesus was unique. In this verse the author asserts that denying Jesus' role as the *Christ* in his incarnate humanity (John 1:14) and his unique relationship with God is to move one away from *the* central Christian tenet. What is new is the fact that this discussion now takes place within the church. John and other believers would defend their position against pagan Greeks and nonmessianic Jews, who doubted either the need for salvation or the belief that Jesus of Nazareth was the Messiah. But since the schism, the author must remind his readers that Jesus the incarnate Son of God, through his death, is the solution to human sin and unrighteousness (1:5–2:2). Not only that, but he must also affirm that *the Father has sent his Son as the Savior of the world* (1 John 4:14; cf. John 4:42). Schnackenburg identifies a simple issue at stake: "It is the question of the One who brought redemption, nothing more and nothing less" (1992: 145).

Our author's position is not his alone. He stands firmly within the Johannine tradition. From the beginning of John's Gospel, the case for Jesus' redemptive uniqueness is articulated. In the opening verses we read of grand, even cosmic, claims about the Word. The Word was not only with God, but also is God (1:1). The Word is responsible for the creation of the world (1:2). The act of incarnation made God the Father known, whereas previously no one had ever seen the Father (1:18). And not only that: Jesus, the incarnate Word, also empowers believers "to become children of God" (1:12).

John 3:17-18 stresses this sweeping point:

> Indeed, God did not send the Son into the world to condemn the world, but in order that the world might be saved through him. Those who believe in him are not condemned; but those who do not believe are condemned already, because they have not believed in the name of the only Son of God.

To this end, John makes a point of introducing representative people who recognize Jesus' unique role. In a verse dripping with irony, Caiaphas, a Jew, tells the council, "You do not understand that it is better for you to have one man die for the people than to have the whole nation destroyed" (11:50). Martha confesses, "Lord, I believe that you are the Messiah, the Son of God, the one coming into the world" (11:27). Thomas's climatic acclamation, "My Lord and my God" (20:28), clinches her confession as does Mary Magdalene's, "I have seen the Lord" (20:18). Earlier a group of Samaritans came to a similar conclusion, that Jesus is "the Savior of the world" (4:42). Further, as perhaps a fulfillment of Jesus' earlier words referring to "other sheep" in 10:16, we read of a group of Greeks who seek out Jesus (12:20-26).

In the Pauline letters this idea of Jesus' uniqueness is widespread and viewed on a more personal level. Whereas the Johannine tradition thinks of Christ's work as touching groups or even the world, Paul often personalizes this uniqueness, often seemingly limiting it to Christians. We see this in passages such as Galatians 1:3-4; 2:20; 1 Thessalonians 5:9-10; and Romans 5:6-9: "God proves his love for us in that while we still were sinners Christ died for us. Much more surely then . . . will we be saved through him from the wrath of God." In a section addressing the issue of why he is an evangelist, Paul writes,

> So if anyone is in Christ, there is a new creation: everything old has passed away; see, everything has become new! All this is from God, who reconciled us to himself through Christ, and has given us the ministry of reconciliation; that is, in Christ God was reconciling the world to himself. (2 Cor 5:17-19)

One final Pauline passage leads us further back into the developing Christian tradition and speaks of the breadth of the church's teaching on this subject. Paul writes, "I handed on to you as of first importance what I in turn had received: that Christ died for our sins in accordance with the scriptures (1 Cor 15:3).

Acts reveals tantalizing snippets of that developing tradition, especially the early Christian proclamation regarding Jesus' role as the Messiah. We have two summary verses that depict Paul's using Scripture to "prove" Jesus' messiahship to Jewish synagogue members in Damascus (9:22) and Thessalonica (17:3). In 18:24-28 we read of Apollos, who "had been instructed in the Way of the Lord," and how his eloquence and knowledge of Scripture helped the Ephesian Christians, "show[ing] by the scripture that the Messiah is Jesus." These examples from the Diaspora align with the earliest Christian preaching in Jerusalem shortly after the resurrection: "Every day in the temple and at home they did not cease to teach and proclaim Jesus as the Messiah" (5:42). Thus, from the beginning to the end of the first century and beyond, the first Christians asserted that Jesus, the incarnate *Logos* (Word) of God, fulfilled a unique role in revealing and mediating God to humanity.

THE TEXT IN THE LIFE OF THE CHURCH

Schism and Doctrinal Truth

This unit raises numerous issues for modern Christians, but the two most important are schisms and commitment to doctrinal truth. In many ways what we have experienced in the twentieth and twenty-first centuries parallels John's experience. In John's case an intense discussion regarding Jesus' unique incarnational role as Savior, mediator, or revealer of God led to a congregational split. The more progressive (2 John 9) separatists seemingly taught that God could be known without accepting the incarnational humanity of Jesus Christ. I have heard fellow church attenders assert other but equally divergent theological ideas; however, I do not personally know of any congregational splits due to diverse theological reflection on Jesus as truly human and truly divine.

Embarrassingly, contemporary congregational splits often revolve around nontheological issues. In the past twenty years I know of one schism over the color of the new church carpet and a second regarding the type of windows selected for a church addition. Other splits or threatened splits focus on more obvious behavioral issues: worship style, the charismatic movement, the ordination of women, or discussions on homosexuality, to name a few. Why are Christians inclined to resolve differences by parting ways? Surely, in principle, this should not be a common solution for Christians facing group conflict. Yet it has been occurring since the first century. And if we are fully honest with ourselves, our spiritual ancestors were schismatics to one degree or another. Wesley's followers left the Church of England, the Anabaptists left the late medieval church, and the German Pietists left staid Lutheran congregations. Ironically, these splits often occurred despite first-generation leaders' pleas for tolerance and unity.

Walter Klaassen points out that early Anabaptist leaders espoused "religious tolerance," which is a crucial concept for church unity (290-91). Their own persecution influenced much of their thinking; and yet they advocated patience and tolerance with non-Christians and heretics. Balthasar Hubmaier argues that slaying heretics is the worst heresy of all because this is "contrary to Christ's teaching and practice" (Klaassen: 292). Hubmaier, drawing upon the wheat-and-weeds imagery in Jesus' teaching (Matt 13:24-30), seems to advocate unity even at the risk of impurity. But as we see in Dirk Philips's *The Church of God* (1562), the early Anabaptists did not advocate tolerance and unity at the risk of the church's destruction. Dirk also argues against persecuting a person due to his faith or lack of faith, but he also maintains that the church has been given the power of the ban to be exercised over "contentious and heretical people" (Klaassen: 299). Even so, many Anabaptist writers point to Matthew 18:15-20 and its patient due process before anyone is placed under the ban; such is the importance of church unity.

Although the Methodist Societies founded by John Wesley broke from the Church of England after Wesley's death, it was not because Wesley himself had condoned such action. Wesley was ordained as an Anglican minister and died as a member and minister in good standing. As early as 1762 he warned his followers about the dangers and unacceptability of church divisions. In that year he published a tract titled "Cautions and Directions Given to the Greatest Professors in the Methodist Societies," which was later incorporated into editions of *A Plain Account of Christian Perfection*. The sixth direction begins: "Beware of schism, of making a rent in the Church of Christ" (Wesley: 94). He warns against a "party" spirit that values one preacher over another, failing to attend class meetings, differences of opinion, and giving people a reason to leave the society (94-96).

We easily affirm that schisms are generally unacceptable. A congregational split certainly is no solution to differences of opinion regarding the color of the sanctuary carpet. And it is not the best way to resolve issues like the ordination of women. In part, we can see the danger of church splits because we live in an era that promotes tolerance as one of the highest virtues. When we disagree, we are to tolerate divergent views, and having done so, we can then coexist. But coexistence is not the same as unity. An even more urgent question is, Should everything be tolerated? Should Christians accept the popular view summed up as "It doesn't matter what you believe so long as you believe it sincerely"? Probably not. Sincerity of one's convictions does not make a conviction true. Hitler and his henchmen sincerely believed that the Jews, Slavic peoples, Gypsies, and homosexuals were a threat to their superior civilization. They sincerely believed that these groups must be destroyed. The Nazis, however sincere, were wrong. Sincerity and tolerance may not be the most important virtues for a sane society. And while being laudable secondary goals, they are not the highest Christian goals.

Earlier 1 John made a case for adhering to the church's moral standards, and here he strongly argues for a doctrinal tenet that is nonnegotiable. One cannot deny that *Jesus is the Christ* and still be a follower of Jesus Christ. Later our author will defend the incarnational humanity of Jesus (see comments on 1 John 5:5-12 below). One cannot deny that Jesus alone reveals and paves the way to God and still be a Christian. But even here we must admit that we are entering a complex area. What is meant by "deny"? One brief passage from the Venerable Bede (d. 735) shows that Christians have been aware of the complexity for some time:

> Denial of Christ is the supreme lie, a lie so great that it is hard to think of anything that can be compared with it. It is a lie that is evident among the Jews, of course, but the heretics, who do not believe in Christ in the right way, are guilty of it as well. It is also the case that orthodox people who do not follow Christ's commands are guilty of denying that Jesus is the Christ, not because they refuse to give Christ the love and devotion that is his due as the Son of God but because they treat him as if he were a man of no account and are not afraid to contradict what he says. (Bray: 189)

While Bede adds the third and ethical dimension of "denial," which is worth considering, John here focuses on the second. What are we to think and do when self-avowed believers deny historic affirmations about Jesus Christ?

Klaassen (23) suggests, "For Anabaptists, as for other Christians, Jesus constituted the heart of the Christian faith." Generally, early Anabaptists affirmed Jesus' divine nature and stressed his role as the believer's model. While Dutch Anabaptist writers "have agreed totally with emphasizing both the humanity and divinity of Jesus" (23), they did lean toward a docetic Christology, claiming that Jesus had a "heavenly flesh." In other words, the early Anabaptists tried to adhere to the historic faith's central tenets, but their detailed explanations occasionally moved into areas not affirmed by most believers. Yet the motivation behind stressing the divine over the human was the defense of Jesus' role as a perfect sacrifice for sin; they defended Jesus' uniqueness. Three illustrative quotes will suffice.

Around 1526-27 Balthasar Hubmaier wrote *The Twelve Articles*. In one article he puts forth this confessional paragraph:

> I believe also in Jesus Christ, your only Son, our Lord. I believe that he has made atonement to you, my Father, for the fall; that he has made peace between you and me, who am a poor sinner, and has won, through his obedience, an inheritance for me. He has now given me strength through the Holy Word that he has sent, so that I may become your child through faith. I hope and trust in him entirely. He will not allow the healing and comforting name of Jesus to be lost to me . . . but rather will save me from all my sins. For I believe that he is Christ, true God and true man. (Klaassen: 25)

In 1532 the Dutch writer Bernhard Rothmann published his *Confession of Faith*, which reads,

We also believe that almighty God allowed the eternal Word, his Son, . . . to become flesh, Jn 3, [16]. This happened after man fell into death out of that Word through the poison of wickedness of the old serpent so that death embraced the whole human race through one man. The Son was given for man into death in order that those who believe on the Son should not perish but have eternal life, Jn 3, [16]. Thus we believe in Jesus Christ the Son of the living God who for us poor sinners became man and suffered death on the tree of the cross for us and the whole world, in order that we, free from sin, should . . . walk in purity and without spot as befits our calling. (Klaassen: 35)

Finally, in 1556 Menno Simons wrote *Epistle to Martin Micron*. This was the second of two documents in which Menno defends himself from public accusations made by Micron regarding Menno's "flawed" view of the incarnation. In his defense Menno writes,

Neither partisan agitation nor disputing will prevail against God and His Word. . . . If you do not believe that Jesus Christ is the Son of God, that His testimony and Word are true, and that His ordinances are the true ordinances; if you are not born of God, do not become of divine disposition and nature; are not urged and possessed of the Holy Spirit, do not sincerely repent; if you are not in Christ, nor Christ in you, then according to the doctrine of John, you are one of those who have no God. I John 2:22.

But if you have Christ, if you actually believe that He is the true Son of God, then you have both the Father and the Son (I John 2:24); and you will walk as He walked and you will deceive none. (Wenger: 937-38)

These quotes are representative of sixteenth-century Anabaptism. They affirm historic Christian doctrine and do so in a Johannine vein. The early Anabaptists affirmed historic teachings about Jesus' uniqueness, in part, because it was viewed as enabling the believer to model one's life after Jesus' own life. As in 1 John, doctrine and ethics are intertwined.

Still, the question remains for the contemporary situation: What are we to do when church members call into question key historic Christian affirmations? Two evangelical writers may help us here. Recently Robert Gundry published *Jesus the Word According to John the Sectarian*. Gundry wrote this book because of his perception of evangelicalism's increasing accommodation to the broader American culture and his concern that many evangelicals, especially those associated with the "academy," are turning away from core Christian doctrines and principles. Although the volume is occasionally aggressive in tone, it is an honest attempt to begin dialogue on this subject. Surely it is better to agree to discuss our diverse viewpoints than to prematurely concede that all viewpoints are of equal value or accept schism without thoroughly and honestly discussing our perception of doctrinal truth. Perhaps we will learn that we were simply stressing different aspects of the same truth.

At the same time, we should not be naive. There will be people who refuse to accept historic Christian doctrine in affirming *both* the divine and human nature of Jesus. They, like the secessionists in 1 John, will be in error. What then? Here Gary Burge makes a few helpful points. As Burge reads 1 John, he sees the author dealing with the situation differently than does Paul in 1 Corinthians 5, where he advocates excommunication. The separatists voluntarily left John's church, and Burge asks, "Is this John's pastoral strategy?" (137). Burge believes that "John stood firm and would not compromise on the essentials of belief and experience and permitted the secessionists to discover their own discomfort alone. And after a while, they departed" (137). There is merit in this approach, if that is what happened. The pastor and congregation can be both affirming of the church's tradition and welcoming of people who disagree with that tradition. It is, however, the dissenters' responsibility to exclude themselves from the group that holds fast to the core tenets. There is no need for heresy trials.

Not all conflicts, doctrinal or otherwise, will be amicably resolved. In John's case, even after the separatists left, they apparently caused considerable confusion for John's community. As Burge states, in that situation the author did not passively sit back or gently encourage "everyone to find a middle ground" (138). The tone of 1 John makes it clear that the author went on the offensive when he saw the community under serious threat, and he firmly advocated holding to the truth taught from the beginning. Likewise, there may well be contemporary occasions when church leaders will need to adopt a similar firm position. Such a posture, however, should be taken only as a last resort in the face of impending doom and after discussion and gentle, patient advocacy of the church's historic faith.

1 John 2:28–3:10

Abiding and Doing Right

PREVIEW

"Wait till your father gets home" are the six worst words I ever heard my mother say to me. This was not because she deferred to my father to apply discipline. She usually did that very well herself. On this day, however, a friend who spent his summers with our family and I had been throwing a ball in the living room, and we knocked his prize deer antlers off the wall. In one fluid and inaccurate motion, we had violated two of my dad's basic rules: Don't throw balls in the house. Don't touch the antlers. By our behavior we had shown that we did not respect his views: we had done what we wanted to do. The day passed slowly, and we were not hopeful that things would turn out okay when he did arrive. We were correct.

Throughout this unit, John stresses the importance of imitating Jesus. The reason for this emphasis on behavior has to do with John's expectation that Christ will return. When this occurs, individuals will either have confidence or shame, depending upon their basic orientation. John approaches this issue with a simple dualist outlook. Either people abide in Christ, avoid sin, and do right or they commit sin, do not do right, and fail to love their brothers and sisters. The former establishes a basic orientation toward God and confirms one's status as a child of God. The latter depicts a fundamental orientation toward the devil, God's adversary, and confirms one's status as a child of the devil.

The previous unit's central issue focuses on Jesus' identity. Is he the Christ? John argues affirmatively. The incarnation reveals Jesus' unique role. But John also speaks of a future revealing: Jesus will return (2:28). Therefore believers stand between two points of revelation. How they (and we) live between these points will result in either confidence or shame when Christ returns. This is so because our lives reveal our basic orientation. In response to God's ultimate revelation, we move toward either God or the devil, depending upon our acceptance or rejection of Jesus and his way of living. These verses may be organized with the "revealing" theme in the center and the two response options set out in left or right columns (see below). Moreover, 1 John 2:18-27 introduced motivational evidence for the letter's writing: a doctrinal schism. In particular, the community has taken sides regarding Jesus' messianic role. Thus here John writes to reassure his readers. It is the secessionists who are in error. His readers are to be encouraged by the church's teaching and the Spirit, who confirms the message that they have heard from the beginning.

In 2:28–3:10 John takes up the challenge in another way. He argues that a person's life reveals to what degree one comprehends God's revelation. Does she do right in an attempt to reflect God's revealed righteousness? If so, she is a child of God. Does he sin and hate his brothers and sisters? Then he is the devil's child. In John's typical dualist approach to life, it is that simple: one's ethics reveal one's theological understanding and religious commitments. For John, theology and ethics are inextricably intertwined.

Doing Right   **Sinning**

Little Children (Part One) 2:28–3:6
2:28 And now, little children, abide in him, so that when he is <u>revealed</u> we may have confidence and not be put to shame before him at his coming.

2:29 If you know that he is righteous, you may be sure that everyone who [pas ho] does right has been born of him.

3:1-2 Parenthetical Explanation
See what love the Father has given us, that we should be called children of God; and that is what we are. The reason the world does not know us is that it did not know him. Beloved, we are God's children now; what we will be has not yet been <u>revealed</u>. What we do

know is this: when he is <u>revealed</u>, we
will be like him, for we will see him as he is.

3:3 And all who [pas ho] have this hope
in him purify themselves; just as he
is pure.

versus

                3:4 Everyone who [pas ho] commits sin
                       is guilty of lawlessness;
                           sin is lawlessness.

        3:5 Parenthetical Explanation
        You know that he was <u>revealed</u> to take
        away sins, and in him there is no sin.

3:6a No one who [pas ho] abides
in him sins; . . .

versus

                3:6b no one who [pas ho] sins has
                      either seen him or known him.

        Little Children (Part Two) 3:7-8
        3:7a Little children, let no one
        deceive you.

3:7b Everyone who does what is right is
righteous, just as he is righteous.

versus

                3:8a-b Everyone who commits sin is a
                  child of the devil; for the devil has been
                      sinning from the beginning.

        3:8c The Son of God was <u>revealed</u> for
        this purpose, to destroy the works
        of the devil.

3:9 Those who [*pas ho*] have been born
of God do not sin, because God's seed
abides in them; they cannot sin, because
they have been born of God.

> *3:10a* The children of God and the
> children of the devil are <u>revealed</u>
> in this way: . . .

> *3:10b-c* all who [*pas ho*] do not do what
> is right are not from God, nor are those
> who do not love their brothers and sisters.

OUTLINE

Little Children (Part One), 2:28–3:6
Little Children (Part Two), 3:7-10

EXPLANATORY NOTES

General Comments

At this point we may think that the author begins to repeat himself.
He drones on about some concepts and returns to earlier ideas. He
continues to address eschatological issues, sin is reintroduced, and
the theme of loving the brothers and sisters is again stressed in 3:10.
We sense that John is spinning his thematic wheels.

However, that is not the case. There is development of thought
and refinement. He does not simply continue to argue for the
world's *passing away* (2:8, 17) or for blindly following the love commandment (2:7-11). He envisions a specific event as the finale of the
passing away: Christ's return (2:28). Moreover, this event triggers
thoughts about how we can know, with *confidence* (2:28), that we will
be ready. Whether we are prepared or not for Christ's coming will
depend on what our lives now reveal about our fundamental orientation. Are we God's or the devil's children? Specifically, are we
aware of our status as God's children and, thus, do what is right, just
as Jesus is right(eous)? Or are we still caught up in sin, which is now
defined as *lawlessness* (3:4) and refusing to *love* (3:10)?

As noted in the Preview, *revealing* is a central theme in 2:28–3:10.
Here the Greek verb is used five times (2:28; 3:2 [2x], 5, 8 and the
related adjective once in 3:10), all essentially communicating a
sense of something being clearly shown or made visible. Four times
the verb is used in connection with Jesus Christ: his return (2:28; 3:2)

and his incarnation (3:5, 8). While the nature of the future *revealing* is unspecified, the purpose of the earlier *revealing* is clear: he appeared to *take away sins* (3:5) and *destroy the works of the devil* (3:8).

Furthermore, *reveal* is twice associated with believers (3:2, 10). The first usage is vague and future oriented: *What we will be has not yet been revealed*. But in this present time not everything is veiled. In 3:10 we read that one's true identity is *revealed* by how we live. The period between Jesus' incarnation and Christ's return is a crucial time of revelation: by our lives and deeds we display to whom we belong. Moreover, this orientation impacts our future (3:2).

The unit's other recurring feature is John's repeated use of the words *pas ho*, which the NRSV translates variously as *everyone who* (2:29; 3:4), *all who* (3:3, 10b), *no one who* (twice in 3:6), and *those who* (3:9). Its use is evenly divided between those who are shown to be God's and those who are revealed as the devil's own. Additionally, one's deeds place him into one of two groups. He either does right or sins. To strengthen this concept, John uses family language (3:1, 2, 8, 10) and birth imagery (2:29; 3:9).

This unit highlights numerous critical issues and familiar concepts. What does John mean when referring to *confidence*, and how does that relate to the well-known words of 3:1? What is meant by further defining sin as *lawlessness*? Who or what is *the devil* in John's worldview? Finally, many cite a conflict between the understanding of sin in 3:6 and 9 and that in 1:8 and 10. We turn our attention to these topics.

Little Children (Part One) 2:28-3:6

The theme of imitation runs throughout this entire section, and this initial subunit establishes two crucial points in John's case for imitating Christ. First, he argues Christ will be *revealed* (RSV *appear*) again (2:28; 3:2). Second, he assumes that his readers are *children of God* (3:1, 2; cf. 3:9, 10). These two themes further develop ideas already seen. Christ's appearance rounds out John's eschatology, which 2:8, 17, and 18 initially note. The idea of God's children moves our thinking forward on the theme of abiding and the source of the Christian life. The subunit begins with another call to *abide in him*, which closed the previous unit. In 2:27, however, the call *to abide* sums up a doctrinal unit. In 2:28-3:10 "abiding" relates to ethics. John encourages readers to *abide . . . so that when he is revealed we may have confidence and not be put to shame before him at his coming* (v. 28).

One word, *coming* (*parousia*), develops 1 John's eschatology. This word shows that our author does not simply adhere to realized eschatology [*Eschatology, p. 306*]. Although the term *parousia* appears only here in the Johannine literature, its usage indicates that he agrees to some degree with early Christian apocalyptic eschatology, which envisioned Jesus' second coming at the end of time. The NT authors use the term *parousia* twenty-four times in various passages (such as Matt 24:3, 27; 1 Thess 3:13; 5:23; James 5:7-8; 2 Pet 1:16; 3:4, 12). In secular literature, the word describes the arrival of a head of state or a divine being. This arrival was often associated with celebration and rejoicing, but the king or deity's advent might also result in judgment. The early believers, including our author, accepted this latter idea as well as the former.

The hope of Jesus' future revelation or *coming* rounds out John's eschatology. In these verses he uses the verb *phaneroō* (NRSV, *reveal*; RSV and NIV, *appear*) five times. Not only has Jesus been revealed in the past (3:5, 8) as the conqueror of sin and the devil's work, but he will also be revealed in the future (2:28; 3:2) as judge and ruler (Schnackenburg 1992: 152). But *reveal* is also associated with believers: *What we will be has not yet been revealed* (3:2). The assumption is if one *abides* and embodies her status as God's child, which involves doing right as Christ is righteous (2:29) and avoiding sin (3:6, 9), then she will be shown "officially" to *be like him* (3:2) when Christ comes again. The period between the incarnation and the second coming is crucial for humanity. Here we display our basic orientation. Either we overcome sinning and reveal ourselves to be children of God, or we continue to sin and reveal ourselves to be the devil's children (3:10).

Moreover, our present orientation has future implications: we will either have *confidence* or *be put to shame* at the second coming. The Greek word behind *confidence* translates literally as *saying all*. It is used nine times in John's Gospel, four times in 1 John, and a total of thirty-one times in the entire NT. Early in its usage it was employed to communicate the idea of freedom to speak openly in political matters. Though used infrequently in the LXX, first-century AD Jewish writers employ it to depict open communication with God (Brown 1982: 380). As Brown further notes (380), "In all 4 uses in I John it refers to one's having confidence before God or His Son as one makes petitions (5:14) or faces judgment (2:28; 4:17) or both (3:21-22)." The context here makes it clear that a believer's *confidence* rests on abiding in Christ, which includes both correct doctrine and endeavoring to live a life consistent with Jesus' own righteousness (2:29).

The alternative is *shame*. The core element of the Greek word for *shame* (*aischynomai*) is not psychological, as with the English word "shame." The Greek verb originates in and is associated with law-courts, thus referring to guilty convictions or condemnation (Schnackenburg 1992: 156), which can secondarily serve as a source of personal disgrace. The idea of shame at the final judgment appears in Revelation 6:15-17. Just as *confidence* at Christ's return is based on abiding faithfully, *shame* is a result of failing to abide (cf. Mark 8:38). As Howard Marshall (167) suggests, "Those who will be ashamed when he comes are the people who were merely nominal in their allegiance to him."

But our author does not view his readers as nominally committed. We see this when we read the well-known words of 1 John 3:1: *See what love the Father has given us, that we should be called children of God; and that is what we are.* The idea of being God's child is a central Johannine concept (cf. 3:2, 10; 5:2). At one level he tries to draw a parallel between the believer's relationship to God and Jesus' Father-Son relationship. This verse stresses love as the core element. But it is God's love for us that is important, because it is God's love that enables us to be *children of God.*

In 3:1 there is more in John's mind than communicating intimacy and love. In 2:29 John has already employed birth imagery when he writes, *born of him.* Some scholars believe the author repeatedly uses this expression (cf. 3:9 [2x]; 4:7; 5:1 [3x]; 5:18 [2x]) because the secessionists were also claiming to have been born of God. John attempts to clarify what being *born of God* or *children of God* means. The secessionists have probably assumed that this relationship absolves them from righteous living. Kenney (28) suggests that they may have focused on a teaching such as John 13:10 ("One who has bathed does not need to wash . . . but is entirely clean") or John 15:3 ("You have already been cleansed") to justify a sense of perfection that ignored ethical behavior. John, however, argues that a relationship with God has clear ethical implications. Each time he refers to being *born of God,* it is tied to some reminder that such a person does not sin, does act aright, or has overcome the world or the evil one. Similarly, the *children-of-God* image connects to a pro-God orientation that leads to right behavior (cf. 1 John 3:10; 5:2) *[Children of God / Born of God, p. 302].*

Some note the sudden shift from *abiding* (2:27, 28) to *born of him* and *children of God.* In reality, John probably viewed these terms as synonymous. Here and elsewhere, he intends to communicate the real possibility of an intimate relationship with God. Moreover, he wants to make the point that such a relationship finds its origin in God's love and not in our good deeds. We are to respond positively to God's prior action and love, however, by doing *right* (cf. 2:29; 3:7, 10) and avoiding sin (cf. 3:4, 6, 8, 9).

In 3:4 the author returns to the theme of *sin*, which has not been mentioned since 2:12. In the next five verses, he repeatedly refers to this word, and he begins with a simple definition: *sin is lawlessness.* Some writers, like Houlden (92), connect *lawlessness* with the reference to *purify* oneself in verse 3, concluding that the author's agenda has ritual overtones. Houlden further suggests that John thought sin was simply lawbreaking, specifically disobeying the command to love one another. Ultimately Houlden (92) argues that John is more concerned with rule breaking than with sin as a "cosmic force of evil."

Such a view ignores apocalyptic literature's use of *lawlessness*, as well as this specific context. As Strecker (94) observes, the word "appears frequently in apocalyptic writings" and is employed "to describe the activity of Satan against God immediately before the end." One specific quote from the Dead Sea Scrolls suffices to make this point:

> All the children of falsehood are ruled by the Angel of Darkness and walk in the ways of darkness. The Angel of Darkness leads all the children of righteousness astray, and until his end, all their sin, iniquities, wickedness, and all their unlawful deeds are caused by his dominion in accordance with the mysteries of God. Every one of their chastisements, and every one of the seasons of their distress, shall be under the sway of his persecution; for all his allotted spirits seek the overthrow of the Sons of Light. (1QS 3.20-24; cf. *Testament of Dan* 5:4-6; 6:1-6; 1QS 4.9, 17, 19; 5.2; Matt 24:12; Luke 13:27; 2 Cor 6:14; 2 Thess 2:3-4; 2:7-8; *Did.* 16.3-4; *Epistle of Barnabas* 4.1-4; 14.5; 15.7; 18.2)

Our author senses cosmic forces facing off in what he has already counted as the last days (cf. 2:8, 17-18). This dualist theme is developed in 3:7-10 by repeatedly using *child[ren] of the devil* and *children of God/born of God*. Moreover, if John uses *lawlessness* as other NT writers do, his view of sin moves beyond rule breaking. Within an apocalyptic worldview, *lawlessness* involves siding with God's opponents and the forces of evil. Behind every sinful action (cf. 5:16-19 for John's awareness of the complexity of sin) is an action against God. John attempts to communicate that humans have two options, God or the devil, and actions tell to which group one gravitates (Rensberger: 90).

Little Children (Part Two) 3:7-10

In part two it is clear that John's thought connects to and parallels that of 2:28–3:6. Brown tries to lay out a chiastic pattern but admits that a clean-cut chiasm is not easily achieved (1982: 419). M. M.

Thompson (95) is more helpful: "Although the basic structure of thought parallels that of 3:4-6, the imagery differs." John follows a basic threefold pattern, focusing on the character of sin (v. 8a), the work of God's Son (v. 8b), and the implications of Jesus' work for believers (vv. 9-10; M. M. Thompson: 95-96). The orientation, however, is decidedly negative in its focus on the devil and his children's behavior. In this sense 3:7-10 is antithetical to 2:28–3:6.

Apocalyptic thinking still dominates John's mind as he explores this threefold pattern. That is why the *devil* (*diabolos*) is used four times in verses 8 (3x) and 10 (once). Moreover, he repeatedly notes the theme of sin and siding with either God or the devil. In the OT the *devil* (*śaṭan*) is accuser (Ps 109 [108 in LXX]:6) or adversary (1 Chron 21:1; Job 1:6). The *devil* (*śaṭan* in Hebrew, or *diabolos* in Greek) appears even more frequently in Hellenistic Jewish thought in the two centuries before Christ (cf. *Apocalypse of Moses* 15-20 [*Life of Adam and Eve* 9-17]; *Jubilees* 1:20; 11:5; 48:15, 18; *1 Enoch* 40:7; *Apocalypse of Zephaniah* 4:2-7; 10:1-5). Within the Gospel traditions, being *of the devil* denotes opposition to Jesus Christ and his work (Matt 16:23//Mark 8:33//Luke 22:3//John 13:2, 27). John 8:44 is striking: in a dialogue between Jesus and unbelieving Jews, Jesus says,

> You are from your father the devil, and you chose to do your father's desires. He was a murderer from the beginning and does not stand in the truth, because there is no truth in him. When he lies, he speaks according to his own nature, for he is a liar and the father of lies.

Marshall (184) suggests that 1 John 3:7-10 casts additional light on the theme begun in 3:4-6: sin as rebellion against God. The new information is the rebellion's source: the devil, God's adversary. Again John asserts Jesus' role as destroyer of the devil's works (3:8; cf. 3:5). This destruction then facilitates one's positive response to God by the refusal to sin (3:9). However, John is not so naive as to assume that everyone responds positively to God and God's work in Christ. John argues that the secessionists have come under the devil's influence and decided to oppose the gospel that our author articulates. They "refuse to believe in Jesus because their lives are evil, and so by imitation they become like the devil" (Brown 1982: 405).

A final explanatory issue is the apparent contradiction between what is said in 3:6, 9 about not sinning and the statements in 1:8, 10 and 2:1-2 about forgiveness and cleansing. The same tension reappears between 5:16-17 and 5:18. It is an understatement to say our author has a complex view of sin [*Sin and Perfectionism, p. 311*]. So NT scholars try to resolve the dilemma by appealing to grammatical, theological, and situational arguments. Not all endeavors are convincing, and to some degree Rensberger (93) correctly suggests that we may be reading the words of "an author less concerned with clarity and consistency than we might wish." Still, at least two plausible solutions have been suggested.

One option is to recognize that John thinks on two different levels or writes in two distinct literary contexts (Brown 1982: 414-15). Some argue that 1:8, 10 and 2:1-2 take on a pastoral tone when he acknowledges both sin and forgiveness. But when writing in 3:6, 9 and 5:18 he holds up the ideal possibility that believers need not sin. A variation on this is Brown's choice to view these verses as having distinct literary contexts. Thus 1:8 and 1:10–2:2 encourage the readers to remember the proclamation of forgiveness that they originally heard. As the letter develops, the focus shifts to the current apocalyptic context, which involves wrestling with evil. A part of this mentality is the "expectation [that] the final period would be without sin on the part of those who were close to God" (Brown 1982: 415).

Another option is to assume, with Rensberger (93-94), that the claim behind 3:6, 9 and 5:18 can be traced back to the secessionists' views. To some degree, the thinking resembles that of 1:8 and 10. In this case, John may be agreeing with their basic point that, as "children of God," believers are transformed people. However, the point leads him to a different conclusion. The secessionists ask, "Who is sinless?" and reply, "The children of God." Our author, however, begins by asking, "Who are the children of God?" He answers, "Those who do not sin, . . . those who love one another." Rensberger (93) believes that John 8:39-47 underlies the author's thinking. One's actions are important because they reveal one's parentage. By focusing on behavior, especially the love command, John exposes his opponents as children of the devil.

THE TEXT IN BIBLICAL CONTEXT

Two Forces at Work and Our Choice

Due to this text's apocalyptic background, duality between God and evil is highlighted, and humans are, in a sense, caught between these two forces. Such thinking can be found elsewhere in the NT. In 2 Thessalonians 2:3-12 Paul warns his readers about the coming rebellion against God and the advent of "the lawless one," who "opposes and exalts himself above every so-called god, . . . declaring himself to be God." In 2 Corinthians 6:14–7:1 he reminds his readers that righteousness and lawlessness are two distinct categories, and Christ is opposed to Beliar. Matthew's depiction of the apocalyptic end (24:3-

14) includes false prophets leading people astray, an increase of law-lessness, and the possibility of remaining faithful (cf. 24:9-14).

But the NT's view of opposing spiritual forces is not limited to apocalyptic passages. A strong, if infrequent, theme throughout the NT focuses on "the devil" as a figure that opposes God and works to draw humans away from God's sphere of influence. We expect to see it in the larger Johannine tradition and are not disappointed. For example, John explains Judas's betrayal of Jesus as having been influenced by the devil (13:2; cf. John 6:70). As noted above, John 8:39-47 probably stands behind our author's thinking in this unit. There the discussion between Jesus and Jewish leaders revolves around the question of who can call themselves God's children. Because "the Jews"—but certainly not all Jews—have rejected Jesus, they are the devil's children and not God's (see Swartley's Essay on "The Jews," in *John*, forthcoming BCBC volume).

The Pauline tradition is aware of the diabolical pressure that believers face. In Ephesians 4:27, readers are given directives for living and admonished, "Do not make room for the devil." Later in that same book's famous passage on the armor of God, believers are told, "Be strong in the Lord and in the strength of his power. Put on the whole armor of God, so that you may be able to stand against the wiles of the devil" (Eph 6:10-11). According to 1 and 2 Timothy, even church leaders are not immune from the devil's negative influence (1 Tim 3:6-7; cf. 2 Tim 2:26).

Not surprisingly, letters traditionally associated with early Jewish Christianity exhibit an awareness of the tension as well. In James 4:7 we read, "Submit yourselves . . . to God. Resist the devil, and he will flee from you." The advice in 1 Peter 5:1-9 encourages church leaders to submit to God (5:2); all members are to "humble [themselves] under the mighty hand of God, so that he may exalt you in due time" (5:6); and they are warned: "Your adversary the devil prowls around, looking for someone to devour" (5:8). Finally, Matthew's parable of the sheep and goats depicts those who refused to act in Christ's name being relegated to "the eternal fire prepared for the devil and his angels" (25:41).

As one turns to the OT, the image of a single figure embodying opposition to God and tempting away the people of God is mostly absent. The obvious exceptions are the God-Satan dialogues in Job and Zechariah 3. However, the tension between God and opposing forces remains, as does the theme of humans caught between the two. Also present, and perhaps intensified, is the theme that people exercise their free will as they decide to align with anti-God forces. This is certainly the case in Deuteronomy, where we read,

Jacob ate his fill;
 Jeshurun grew fat, . . . bloated, and gorged!
 He abandoned God who made him,
 and scoffed at the Rock of his salvation.
 They made him jealous with strange gods,
 with abhorrent things they provoked him.
 They sacrificed to demons, not God,
 to deities they had never known. (Deut 32:15-17; cf. Ps 106:36-38)

A repeated refrain throughout Judges is the summary note that Israel "abandoned the LORD and worshiped Baal" (2:13; 10:6, 10; cf. 1 Sam 12:10). Ahab, who is depicted as the worst of Israel's kings, is primarily viewed this way because of his cavalier attitude toward sin, intermarriage with pagans, and worship of Baal (1 Kings 16:29–22:40). Prophet Elijah confronted Ahab. The famous confrontation in 1 Kings 18 occurs, in part, to clarify the source of trouble for Israel: Ahab or Elijah? Elijah's triumph over the prophets of Baal is offered as evidence that Ahab actually created Israel's difficulties because he had "forsaken the commandments of the LORD and followed the Baals" (1 Kings 18:18). Similarly, later prophets accuse Israel of abandoning God to follow other gods and idols (Jer 2:1–3:5; 7:8-15; 11:9-17; Hos 11:1-7; Isa 1:1-4; 2:5-8; 9:8–10:4).

A rich scriptural tradition recognizes both positive (God/the LORD) and negative (Baal/idols/the devil) influences upon humans. Humans choose to align with one or the other. A person's choices prove oneself to be either of God or of the forces opposing God. We are not puppet victims of the evil one. As Brown states, "Personal sins create an orientation toward darkness and away from light; then the orientation leads to more sin" (1982: 205).

We Shall See God and Be Like God

The possibility that the faithful will see God is present in the OT (Pss 11:7; 17:15; cf. 42:1-5). Moreover, intimate encounters with aspects of God are recorded in the Bible. Adam and Eve, as they hear God walking in the garden in the cool of the day, encounter God's presence (Gen 3:8). Enoch is also depicted as walking with God (5:21-24). Moses had a number of encounters with God (Exod 3; 19–20; Deut 34; etc.). Samuel heard the voice of God calling his name (1 Sam 3:1-18). Elijah stood at the cave's mouth, where he witnessed various manifestations of God (1 Kings 19:9-13). Isaiah saw "the LORD" in the temple (6:1-13).

In the NT this concept of intimate contact with God shifts slightly due in large measure to the incarnation. Before Jesus' birth God contacts humans like Zechariah and Mary (Luke 1:11; 1:26) through angel intermediaries. But with Jesus' birth there is a sense that people have seen God's clearest self-revelation. Simeon (2:25-35) and Anna (2:36-38) take note of Jesus' identity when his parents present him in the temple. John the Baptist recognizes Jesus as "the Lamb of God" (John 1:29-34). Similarly, Andrew and Philip quickly acknowledge Jesus' uniqueness (1:35-51). After Jesus' resurrection, various figures confess his unique status. Thomas, when confronted by the risen Christ, exclaims, "My Lord and my God!" (20:28). Peter has a vision and hears the Lord's voice telling him to eat "unclean" animals (Acts 10:9-16). Finally, Paul's famous meeting with the risen Christ leads to his conversion (9:3-9).

However, to see God as God really is and to be like God is reserved for the future. Even the writer of Revelation, who had clear visions of God, does not offer us a vision of God as God is. In the throne room, the seer observes only God's hand holding the scroll (Rev 5:1). Earlier he sees the throne, the surrounding rainbow and the glass sea before the throne, but God's being eludes him (Rev 4:1-11). Still, the seer holds out a great hope for the future. Someday God will make the divine home with mortals. God will personally live among us, and God will comfort us directly (Rev 21:1-4).

To see God and Christ fully remains beyond our grasp and comprehension for the present, but someday we will see, when God makes "all things new" (Rev 21:5). As our author promises, *We will be like him, for we will see him as he is* (1 John 3:2). This promise is based upon the intimate relationship that we can have with Jesus in this life. Such intimacy is articulated initially in John 14–17, and our author stands within that tradition. Just as God and Jesus had an intimate relationship, so also believers can have an intimate relationship with Jesus Christ and with God through Jesus Christ.

THE TEXT IN THE LIFE OF THE CHURCH

Holiness

This unit has particular importance for our churches. Especially significant is the theme of overcoming sin and living as God's children. Yet this emphasis on holy living is not the sole theological possession of Anabaptists. The Venerable Bede, an eighth-century English scholar and churchman, provides evidence of this:

> There are many who say they have faith in Christ but somehow seem to forget about this pure aspect of it. It is clear that anyone who has real faith will demonstrate that fact by living a life of good works, . . . by

rejecting ungodliness and worldly desires and by imitating Christ's sober, righteous and godly life. (Bray: 196)

Numerous early Anabaptist writers address this general topic. Hans Denck (or Denk), when accused of self-deception in claiming sinlessness according to 1 John 1:8, replied, "We are all fallen on account of sin. The less one acknowledges this, the more one sins: the more one bemoans it, the less one sins. He who once has bemoaned it in truth, is born of God and sins no more. Everyone who sins has neither seen nor known God. John and the truth affirm all this openly to him who has ears and eyes (1 John 3:6)" (Furcha: 225). Similarly, Michael Sattler, in his tract "On the Satisfaction of Christ," argues for taking seriously the NT witness regarding a righteous life. Among his numerous proof texts is 1 John 3:7 (Yoder: 110). Menno Simons, in his first "post-Roman Catholic" pamphlet, argues that in light of the new birth, God gives believers the "mind and disposition of Jesus," which brings forth fruit in the believer's life (Wenger: 52):

Then when they have conformed to the image of God and have been born of God, and also abide in God, they do not sin, for the seed of God remains in them, and they have overcome the world. They are crucified to the world, and the world unto them: they have mortified their flesh and have buried their sinful body with Christ in baptism, with its lusts and desires, and now no longer serve sin unto unrighteousness, but much more righteousness unto sanctification. For they put on Christ and are purified through the Holy Ghost in their consciences from dead works to serve the living God; bringing forth through the Spirit the fruits of the Spirit, whose end is eternal life. (Wenger: 56)

Concerns for holiness find expression after the first-generation Anabaptists as well. A well-known proponent of holy living was John Wesley (d. 1791). His preaching often focused on sin and sinlessness. Wesley taught that the ideal Christian life is one resulting in believers seeking holiness through faith in God's power. The goal is to allow love to rule all their conscious desires. The sanctification process begins when one accepts Christ's atonement for sin and Christ's resurrection power to overcome sin. In his book *A Plain Account of Christian Perfection*, Wesley puts forth his case that a believer can live a life of discipleship unhindered by sin's power.

In his book *Streams of Living Water*, Richard J. Foster describes six Christian spiritual traditions. At the beginning of each chapter, he identifies significant figures and movements associated with each tradition or "stream." Menno, the Anabaptists, John Wesley, and the eighteenth-century Holiness Movement are listed as represen-

"means the ability to do what needs to be done when it needs to be done. It means being 'response-able,' able to respond appropriately to the demands of life; . . . a holy life is simply a life that works." Our spiritual ancestors have stressed the value of living a Christlike life or "life that works." In these days, amid various definitions of what it means to be Christian, we do well to listen to the voices that call us to holiness of life. Perhaps one brief story will suffice. I once heard Duke University theologian Stanley Hauerwas tell the following tale. A Mennonite farmer went to town and was approached by a zealous evangelist. The man asked the farmer, "Are you saved?" The farmer wanted to know what that meant. "Is Jesus your Savior and Lord?" asked the man. The farmer took a pencil and piece of paper from his shirt pocket and began writing. Then he gave it to the evangelist. The puzzled man asked how this list of names answered his question. The farmer told him that the people on the paper were his neighbors, and they would have a better idea about his salvation than he did: they were able to observe how he lived his life.

1 John 3:11-24

Illustration, Encouragement, and Transition

PREVIEW

Several years ago I hired a locksmith to replace our home's front door locks. In the course of his visit, he tried to convince me that he was also an on-call special operations secret agent. He repeatedly and resolutely claimed a lot, but he did not provide any tangible evidence to back up his claim. I did not believe him that day, and I still do not believe his claim. I think he was a locksmith because that is what I saw him do. The harsh reality is that our actions often reveal much more about us than our claims or casual chatter.

This unit constitutes John's final argument regarding the schism facing his community. The split's divisive issue focused on the Johannine tradition's teaching that Jesus' messianic role was revealed in his crucifixion. The previous unit, 2:28–3:10, speaks to the topic of how well one understands the truth of God's revelation in Jesus Christ. By doing what is *right*, one displays a positive relationship to God. On the other hand, one who sins and hates his brothers and sisters is the devil's child.

Here our author argues that the central test of a person's faith is whether or not one loves other believers. This is so, in part, because this is the original Christian message. In typically dualist fashion, John now starkly illustrates this principle. He encourages his read-

ers to avoid Cain-like behavior (3:12-15). This OT figure highlights
the ultimate rejection of love. The alternative is to imitate the One
who laid down his life for us (3:16-18).

Finally, the author follows a pattern we have seen before: he
offers a pastoral parenthesis (3:19-22). John raises the issue of a
guilty conscience and assurance before God. The core concern is
one's obedience to divine commandments. John is aware that even
the faithful can wrestle with a sense of inadequacy, and he graciously addresses that topic before drawing this section to a close.

Introduction 3:11
*For this is the message you have heard from the
beginning, that we should love one another.*

Illustrations of Hate and Love 3:12-18
3:12-15 Hate
*We must not be like Cain who was from
the evil one and murdered his brother.
And why did he murder him? Because his
own deeds were evil and his brother's righteous.
Do not be astonished, brothers and sisters, that
the world hates you. We know that we have
passed from death to life because we love
one another. Whoever does not love abides
in death. All who hate a brother or sister are
murderers, and you know that murderers do
not have eternal life abiding in them.*

versus

3:16-18 Love
*We know love by this, that he laid down his life
for us—and we ought to lay down our lives for
one another. How does God's love abide in
anyone who has the world's goods and sees
a brother or sister in need and yet refuses help?
Little children, let us love, not in word or
speech, but in truth and action.*

A Pastoral Parenthesis 3:19-22
*And by this we will know that we are from the truth and will reassure
our hearts before him whenever our hearts condemn us; for God is*

*greater than our hearts, and he knows everything. Beloved, if our
hearts do not condemn us, we have boldness before God; and we
receive from him whatever we ask, because we obey his commandments
and do what pleases him.*

Summary and Transition 3:23-24
*And this is his commandment, that we should believe in the name
of his Son Jesus Christ and love one another, just as he has
commanded us. All who obey his commandments abide in him,
and he abides in them. And by this we know that he abides in us,
by the Spirit that he has given us.*

OUTLINE

Introduction, 3:11
Illustrations of Hate and Love, 3:12-18
A Pastoral Parenthesis, 3:19-22
Summary and Transition, 3:23-24

EXPLANATORY NOTES

General Comments

Some scholars believe the second half of the letter begins with 3:11.
They argue this, in large measure, because this verse's phrase *For
this is the message you have heard from the beginning* resembles 1:5.
Such a viewpoint overlooks the small but important word *hoti*,
which here can be translated *for* or *because*. Its presence makes a
clear connection to the previous subunit.

The view that this section continues John's previous argument is
not based on one small word, however. The negative illustration of
Cain, the archetype of an evil brother, serves as his argument's climax. Cain is *the* best-known OT figure who could be described as a
child *of the devil* (3:10). The alternative to Cain is Christ (3:16). Both
these figures are employed as concrete illustrations of the two alternatives given in 3:10.

Additionally, 3:11-24 fleshes out John's more general argument
found in the previous verses. In 2:28–3:10 the author makes a case
for practicing righteousness. Now he points to one particular practice that is righteous: loving one another. This is not a new literary
or argumentative device. In fact, 3:11 is the positive complement of
3:10bc, which holds that *those who do not love are not from God*. In 2:3-
10 John makes a general case that knowledge of God leads to obedience (2:3-6), and he specifically advocates adhering to the old/new

command of mutual *love* as evidence that one is in the light of God (2:7-11; cf. 1:5).

Finally, *confidence*, a theme found in the previous unit (2:28; 3:1), is addressed in the pastoral parenthetical statement (3:19-22). Even a cursory reading of 3:19-22 shows John's attempt to put forward a developed explanation of Christian confidence that grows out of one's obedience to divine commandments. Therefore we must conclude that this unit of 3:11-24 provides a climax for the argument begun in 2:28, if not as far back as 2:18.

These verses also have a transitional quality as well. Chapter 4 will repeat the expression *Love one another* three times (4:7, 11, 12). Large portions of that chapter and the initial verses of chapter 5 focus on the love theme. Additionally, 3:24 introduces a topic that will be found intertwined with the theme of love: the Spirit or the spirits, which is introduced in 3:24. These two themes will dominate chapters 4 and 5. In this sense 3:11-24 is a bridge between the previous section and the next.

Introduction 3:11

Have we heard this verse before? Yes, we read similar words in 1:5 and 2:7, where John writes, *Beloved, I am writing to you no new commandment, but an old commandment that you have had from the beginning.* We will see it again: *I ask you, not as though I were writing you a new commandment, but one we have had from the beginning, let us love one another* (2 John 5-6). While these verses show John's concern to remind his readers of a specific commandment regarding love that was handed down within the Christian community, this letter reveals his general concern for holding on to various traditional teachings.

The letter opens with an appeal to tradition, when the author writes, *We declare to you what was from the beginning* (1:1). He makes a doctrinal appeal by using tradition in 1:5 and saying, *This is the message we have heard from him and proclaim to you, that God is light and in him there is no darkness at all.* Even his attempts to reassure are, in part, based on an appeal to tradition: *Let what you heard from the beginning abide in you. If what you heard from the beginning abides in you, then you will abide in the Son and the Father* (2:24).

These uses of the phrase *from the beginning* lead to the conclusion that John relies heavily on specific elements of the larger early Christian tradition handed down from various church leaders. Moreover, these traditions are not limited to either doctrine or moral teaching or even pastoral care. In fact, as we have seen in the previous unit, the author and his community do not separate the Christian life into separate categories of theology, ethics, or pastoral care. All three intersect, and in John's view they have always done so in a tradition focusing on Christology and mutual love. He and his followers have inherited a traditional way of life, and he appeals to those core elements of the tradition in his defense against the secessionists.

In 3:11 the particular message to *love one another* probably refers to the same behavior called for in 2:10; 3:10, 14; 4:20-21. Moreover, it is likely that John assumes that this directive has originated not with the apostles, but with Jesus himself. After all, the Johannine tradition depicts Jesus as mentioning this commandment to love three times in its Last Supper depiction (John 13:34; 15:12, 17). In both this letter and John's Gospel, one's love for another believer is *the* distinguishing mark of the Christian life (cf. John 13:34-35; 1 John 3:10). Ultimately these references to love one another were viewed as sacred community tradition by the author and his followers. Additionally, their mutual love sets them apart from the secessionists.

These repeated references to *love one another* raise uncomfortable questions. Does John view the believer's obligation to love as narrowly as it seems? Is he sectarian? Or worse, is he implying that it is acceptable for believers to hate those outside the fellowship? Thomas Johnson (80) provides a useful approach to resolving these questions. In light of the circumstances of the Johannine community, we do well to read this injunction with empathy and sympathy. The Johannine community has faced persecution from the beginning. The Gospel of John reflects serious tension between nonmessianic Jews and the Johannine community. The tensions have continued and are perhaps heightened by the community split evidenced in this letter. As is apparent throughout the epistle, this schism had severe impact upon those who remained with the Johannine community.

Yet the author has just advocated rejecting sin and has never suggested that it is acceptable to hate the secessionists. Clearly their doctrine and behavior are rejected, but John does not suggest that hatred is an option for his followers. In fact, the following verses tell us that sin leads to murder and that the world hates, but believers are different in that they, like Christ, are life-givers and loving. Despite the fact that the separatists have aligned themselves with the world, John is probably aware of the complexity of love and hate, especially in this heated context. After all, he does remind his readers that Christ *is the atoning sacrifice for our sins, and not for ours only but also for the sins of the whole world* (2:2). In 4:14 he will remind them that *the Father sent his Son as the Savior of the world*, a message reminiscent of John 3:16 and 4:42.

What is John suggesting when he writes, *Love one another?* Strecker (108) reminds us that this document is fundamentally an "ecclesial writing." John is primarily writing a pastoral letter to a struggling and persecuted church. Among his concerns is how to ensure its survival. He believes the congregation's best hope is to take seriously Jesus' farewell commandment, *Love one another.* Through such expressions of love, the members will develop internal bonds of unity that will ultimately result in the group's long-term survival. If, however, they fall into sin, selfishness, and doctrinal error, as happened with the secessionists, they have no future as a Christian fellowship. The author is not implying that his readers are to hate either the world or the separatists. Ultimately, John is not "sectarian," as we and our contemporaries might understand the word, but his social context has created an environment in which his church must defend its identity and purpose. Thus he argues that their first and central agenda is to love one another. That is a challenge: it requires all their focus and spiritual energy.

Illustrations of Hate and Love 3:12-18

While Schnackenburg accurately labels this subunit as "a masterpiece dealing with the meaning, character, and rewards of practical Christian love" (1992: 178), such a glowing conclusion glosses over a number of challenges. Initially, there are grammatical points that are not easily interpreted. For example, we once again read the ambiguous phrase *God's love* in 3:17 (cf. 2:5 and comments there). We stumble across awkward Greek phrases behind *Murderers do not have eternal life abiding in them* (3:15), and we must decide between two interpretations of the phrase *We know that we have passed from death to life because we love one another* (3:14).

Additionally, both John and his readers accept traditions of which we are not immediately aware. For example, a sound case can be made that the author and his readers would accept this developing argument because it is based, in part, on the Johannine Gospel tradition found in John 8:37-47 (Dodd: 83). Also, a case can be made that John's assertions regarding loving one another are convincing to his readers because they also know of, and accept as authoritative, Jesus' Last Supper commandments to "love one another" (13:34; 15:12, 17). Finally, talk of Jesus' laying down his life for us, our duty to do likewise, and the importance of "abiding" probably is connected to the Gospel's Good Shepherd saying (10:1-18) and the Last Supper directives (15:1-17).

A final challenge worth mentioning is the fact that John writes as though his readers understand contemporary contextual assumptions that we have not yet been introduced to at this point. For example, Colin Kruse (135) identifies 1 John 3:13 and its reference to the world as a "digression." Indeed, as we will see, this verse is part of his masterpiece argument linking the secessionists to Cain and the evil one. It builds upon an assumption that he shares with his readers, but he has not specifically mentioned it and will not do so until 4:1 (cf. 2 John 7). These are a few of the challenges found in these verses. Still, the basic flow is clear: love separates believers from unbelievers.

After the introductory verse (1 John 3:11), John returns to the previous subunit's dualist theme. There he drew a distinction between *the children of God and the children of the devil* (3:10). God's children do what is right, and the devil's children *do not love their brothers and sisters*. Verse 12 introduces the epistles' only reference to the OT: Cain (Gen 4). Specifically, Cain is a negative role model, as the verse's opening words imply. The phrase *we must not be like* (*ou kathōs*) is rarely found in the NT; it is used only four times: John 6:58; 14:27; 2 Corinthians 8:5; and here. The usage in John 6:58 also introduces a "negative" OT model.

Cain was a popular focus of both Jewish and early Christian speculation in the centuries before and after Jesus' birth. We know of at least eight extrabiblical texts addressing Cain and his "evil" (see Kruse: 235-42). Both the *Apocalypse of Abraham* (24:3-5) and the *Testament of Benjamin* (7:1-5), for example, suggest that Cain's murderous act was inspired by the devil. Another Jewish legend explained Cain's action as the natural end product of his parentage. It was held in some Jewish circles that the devil had seduced Eve and that Cain was the result of that union. We cannot say whether or not the author of 1 John knew of this legend and accepted it; however, he does seem to be influenced by the Johannine tradition, especially in John 8:37-47, which revolves around parentage. The children of the devil do his works, which include murder (John 8:44).

The word behind *murdered* speaks of intense violence. In the NT it is found only in this letter and Revelation. There it is used to refer to Christ, the slain lamb (5:6, 9, 12; 13:8) and the death of Christian martyrs (6:9; in 6:4 and 13:3 the verb appears also but with an entirely different usage). In the LXX it is used in cultic (Gen 22:10; Isa 57:5) and profane (Num 14:16; Judg 12:6; 1 Kings 18:40) contexts. Perhaps John chooses this word to heighten the sense of intense hatred on the part of the devil's children as well as their victims' innocence.

This difference between Cain and his brother is reinforced in the final sentence of 3:12: *His [Cain] own deeds were evil and his brother's righteous*. Although this statement appears as merely an answer to

the earlier question *Why did he murder him?*, more is at stake. John's
statement regarding evil and righteousness reinforces the gaping
difference between unbelievers and believers described in the previous subunit. Unbelievers not only fail to love; ultimately they also
are driven by evil, and so their actions are of an ultimate and deadly
type. Unlike the positive illustration of Christ (in 3:16), the unbelievers are life-*takers* rather than life-*givers*. Verses 14-15 will argue that
this is evidence that they still *abide in death*.

Verse 13, far from being a digression, is the next and closely connected point in the argument. Our author has argued that a particular evil pattern is to be avoided by believers. If they do this, there
will be a response from unbelievers, those who have elected to follow the evil one. Believers will be hated by the world. Marianne
Meye Thompson (102) rightly advises us to be careful as to John's
meaning. John is not suggesting that "the *more* righteous we are, . . .
the *more* the world will hate us." The author is simply stating a fact.
There is hostility between the world and the believer.

Thus John begins the verse with the words *Do not be astonished*, a
phrase found only here and in John 3:7 and 5:28. Further evidence
of our author's reliance on the Johannine Gospel tradition is found
in this subunit. John mixes his admonitions, encouraging his followers to love one another and warning believers of the world's hatred.
The same thematic mix is found in John 15:9-17 and 18-25. The difference, as Kruse observes (134), is that here the hatred is a reality
and not just a warning of potential hatred. Moreover, the tension is
between two groups claiming to be Christian. As we have already
suggested (see comments on 2:19), John addresses a divided community; in 2:19 he writes, *They went out from us.* John views the
secessionists as embodying the antichrist movement. Here both he
and his readers assume that the expression *the world* can be applied
to the separatists. He does this explicitly in 4:1 and 2 John 7. This
hate/love and evil/righteousness dualism takes on a new element
in the next verses.

Verses 14 and 15 are words of reassurance, adding a new dimension to John's dualist argument. The author returns to the love theme
noted in verse 11. The community's mutual love is evidence of a crucial spiritual reality: *we have passed from death to life.* Again the writer
appeals to the Johannine tradition: the same words occur in John 5:24.
There Jesus tells his disciples that whoever "hears my words and
believes him who sent me has eternal life, and does not come under
judgment, but has passed from death to life." The dualism of hate/
love and evil/righteousness has a third component: death/life.

According to the Johannine tradition, the incarnation's goal was to offer life to humanity (cf. John 3:15-16, 36; 11:25-26; 12:44-50; 10:9-10; 14:6; 20:31). By accepting Jesus and obeying his commandments, especially to love, one is transferred from the realm of death to that of life. The perfect tense of the verb *we have passed* (*metabebēkamen*) shows that John accepts that this shift has already occurred and that the believer is no longer bound by or *abiding in death* [*"Abiding" in the Johannine Letters, p. 300*]. Moreover, this theological assertion ends with *true* believer's behavior. Mutual love within the faith community is the final evidence that one has been given *life* and is no longer in bondage to death. Ultimately John's dualist thinking in this subunit looks something like this:

Death → evil → hate (or life-taking; see Cain as the illustration)
Life → righteousness → love (or life-giving; see Christ as the illustration)

As before, John connects theology and ethics. John, however, does not wield the stick of theology and ethics so as to beat his readers. Rather, he begins with their ethical behavior, reads the thought process backward, and so offers words of reassurance. In other words, their *love* [for] *one another* is indicative of their righteousness or acceptance of Jesus Christ and his teachings. Finally, this acceptance is evidence that they have moved from the destructive realm of death to the constructive realm of life. Conversely, as verse 14c succinctly notes, the opposite is also true: *Whoever does not love abides in death.* There can be little doubt this is a reference to the secessionists and John's view of their spiritual status.

Verse 15 simply reinforces v. 14c. Numerous commentators note the similarity between this verse's thought and that of Matthew 5:21-24. In Matthew, anger with a brother or sister is equated with murder. Here, John returns to the theme of hating a brother or sister and connects it to murder. Typical of his mindset, John envisions an extreme reward for such behavior: *Murderers do not have eternal life abiding in them.* For John, to live hatefully within the faith community or to fracture its common life through heretical teachings and hateful behavior can only logically result in the forfeiture of *eternal life.*

As we come to this subunit's closing verses, John provides the readers with a positive image of love: *He* [*Christ*] *laid down his life for us.* Again he relies on the Johannine tradition, for while Christ's death is a key part of the early Christian creed, the phrase "to lay down one's life" is found only here and in John 10:11-18; 15:13. In fact, 1 John 3:16 communicates the core idea of John 15:12-13 in

similar form. We should also note that John's use of Christ intentionally contrasts to Cain's behavior. While Cain was a "life-taker,"
the verb *laid down* (*ethēken*) stresses that Jesus voluntarily gave up
his life (cf. the Gospel of John's trial and crucifixion that stresses the
same). Moreover, the Greek sentence structure puts *for us* (*hyper
hēmōn*) at the beginning of the phrase *He laid down his life for us*, thus
emphasizing that we benefited from his death.

Additionally, this concrete example of Christ dying to benefit others is an act of revelation: *We know love by this* . . . We learn that "true"
love is more than an emotional rush of warm feelings. It is a matter of
self-sacrifice for others. Moreover, we know the depth and essence of
God's love for us. Our author reminds his readers of the Johannine
tradition that God paid the ultimate price in order that we might live
and live abundantly.

Interestingly, John does not take time here to explain how Jesus'
death benefits us (see comments on 1 John 2:1-2). Instead he moves
on to an unnerving assertion: . . . *And we ought to lay down our lives for
one another*. The author is not so much interested in speculative
theology as in functional ethics. Despite some scholars' assertion,
the early believers took Jesus as a role model (see TBC below). John
shares that view. He affirms and emphasizes the Johannine Gospel's
assertion that Jesus loves his disciples so intensely that he gave his
life for them; and, likewise, he calls them to love one another (John
15:12-13). Again John's theology leads to ethical action. As David
Rensberger notes, "The believers' long-held knowledge is thus not
just a comforting doctrine. It is knowledge with a point, the point
being the imitation of Jesus' love" (1997: 100).

In verse 17 our author focuses on one aspect of sacrificial love.
He argues there is no reason why believers who know God should
refuse to care financially for needy brothers and sisters. This particular illustration may have been selected because it was a burning
reality for his community. Already in 2:16 he refers to *pride in riches*,
which suggests he knows people who take pride in their wealth. It
is not difficult to imagine the separatists were economically "better
off" than John's community, and since the schism they have ignored
the remaining members' material needs.

The language he employs here is intentionally strong. He talks
of seeing, beholding, or "staring" (*theōrē*) at a person in need while
refusing to help. The NRSV's translation *yet refuse to help* is rather
weak. The Greek expression, literally "closes one's intestines," sig-
nifies callous indifference. In the ancient world the intestines were
thought of as the locus of compassion. North Americans would say

the attitude addressed here was "heartlessness." There can be no
question that behind this verse is a painful reality.

The NRSV's opening question *How does God's love abide in anyone*
actually comes at the end of the Greek verse; it contains a mysteri-
ous expression that we have already seen in 2:5 (see comments
there). While *God's love* can be interpreted three ways, the question's
basic thrust is clear. How can anyone claim to know God or God's
love if they ignore the economic needs of other community members? Equally clear is how John expects this question to be answered.
The Greek phrasing of the question calls for a negative response. In
other words, anyone who sees need and has the where-with-all to
help but refuses to do so does *not* know God's love.

The subunit closes with an affectionate encouragement to love in
tangible ways. It begins *little children*, an expression first used in 1 John
2:1 (see comments there). The readers are encouraged to love *not in
word or speech, but in truth and action*. The first pairing readily makes
sense. John does not want his followers to only talk about love, hence
the use of *word* and *speech*. Both nouns connote the same idea. But what
is the point of the words *truth* and *action*? They do not seem to focus on
the same thought. Johnson (85) offers a reasonable explanation, " . . . In
the letter of John, *in truth* usually means 'within the sphere of God's
truth,' i.e. God's revelation of the way things really are in Christ, who is
the truth (John 14:6)." By encouraging his readers to love *in truth*, John
is asking his readers to love self-sacrificially as Jesus Christ loved. In this
way, both *in truth* and *action* focus on the same thought.

A Pastoral Parenthesis 3:19-22

In the next four verses we confront a relatively controversial and
puzzling portion of the letter. Rensberger describes 1 John 3:19-20
as "one of the most obscure sentences in the New Testament" (103).
While we cannot focus on the challenges in detail, we must address
the truly controversial subject: do verses 19-20 address the topic of
God's harshness or mercy? The early church fathers, Augustine,
John Calvin, and the Counter-Reformation Catholics argued these
verses point to God's severity. Luther and most modern commentators hold that John assures us of God's mercy.

In large measure the controversy results from the confusing
Greek grammar. Johnson provides the following literal English translation of verses 19-20, which consists of one Greek sentence:

> (19) *And by this we shall know that we are of the truth, and before him we shall
> assure [persuade?] our heart, (20) that [for?] if [when?] our heart condemns
> us, that [for?] God is greater than our heart and knows everything.*

The key grammatical questions are these: (1) to what does *by this* refer? (2) Does the verb *peisomen* mean *assure* or *persuade*?

In my judgment, *and by this* in 3:19 is a thematic reference to 3:16-18, which is also continued in verses 23-24. In verse 19 John addresses a crucial question: How do we know we are from the truth or belong to God? In verses 16-18 he argues that practical expressions of love, first in Christ's death and then in one's economic sharing, are evidence of belonging to God. He takes up this theme again in verses 23-24, when he reminds the readers of two key Johannine commands: *Believe in the name of . . . Jesus Christ and love one another.* He then stresses the importance of obeying these commands. Verses 19-20 are a pastoral parenthesis in this disputation with the separatists, whereby he reminds his shaken followers that there are tangible ways of knowing who belongs to God. There can be no doubt that John's followers are wrestling with *confidence* because he raises this topic repeatedly (cf. 2:1, 28; 4:17; 5:14-15).

The controversial issue of how to translate *peisomen* seems a little overdrawn to me. Some argue for *persuade* or *convince* because generally the verb's other usages in the NT (42 of 51 occurrences) bear this meaning. The argument then runs this way: John highlights the believer's need to change. In essence, the believer is at fault before God, and a change of heart is needed to avoid God's judgment, implied in verse 20: *For God is greater than our hearts, and he knows everything.* Alternatively, others would translate *peisomen* as *reassure*, as does the NRSV, or *set . . . at rest*, as in the NIV. These translators highlight not a warning, but words of assurance, which (as noted above) are a recurring theme in the letter.

As Marianne Meye Thompson (106) states, "*Peisomen* can mean persuade or reassure. The difference is not great, since the point of 'persuading' our hearts is to reassure ourselves in the presence of God." Here John is trying to convince and reassure his readers that they are acceptable to God so long as they obey the commandments. They were probably wrestling with questions relating to their acceptability before God in light of the community split. After all, they were not wealthy or powerful. They did not adhere to the secessionists' new and creative teachings. Were they acceptable to God? Would they be able to stand before God at the last judgment (cf. 2:28; 4:17)? Does their sin separate them from God (2:1)? Does God hear their prayers (5:14-15)? So 3:19-20 is best taken as John's attempt to reassure the fearful and convince the doubters that what they have heard from the beginning (cf. 1:1-4) is true, and that they are in good standing before God despite their misgivings.

Verse 20 continues onward, not striking fear into the readers' hearts, but reminding them that God's viewpoint is more important than their feelings. There are times when believers sense that they have failed at being a Christian. Indeed, *our hearts condemn us*. In essence, John encourages his readers to trust God, not their guilty feelings. What has John already said about their relationship with God? *If we confess our sins, he who is faithful and just will forgive our sins* (1:9), and *Whoever obeys his word, truly in this person the love of God has reached perfection. By this we may be sure that we are in him* (2:5). *But you have been anointed by the Holy One, and all of you have knowledge* (2:20). *See what love the Father has given us, that we should be called children of God; and that is what we are* (3:1). Or as he will soon write, *In this is love, not that we loved God but that he loved us and sent his Son to be the atoning sacrifice for our sins* (4:10). Far from being words of warning about God's severity, 1 John 3:19-20 are additional reassuring words.

In verses 21-22 our author addresses one implication arising from his words of assurance: prayer. To be sure, what John suggests is rather stunning to many modern readers: *We have boldness before God; and we receive from him whatever we ask.* By now we should be aware that John makes extreme assertions (see 2:5; 3:6, 9; 4:17). Yet upon further inspection, this claim has an important qualification, and John's logic is reasonable.

He begins simply enough: *Beloved, if our hearts do not condemn us, we have boldness before God.* If we have misgivings, we will lack confidence while approaching God in prayer. But the author has argued that just the opposite is the believer's actual situation: God is merciful to those who endeavor to be faithful. Therefore, they can approach God with *boldness (parrēsia)*. We must not confuse this word with overtones of arrogance or demand. Demosthenes (in *Orations* 3.3-4) uses the word to describe the citizen's right to speak freely. John uses this word to refer to the second coming (2:28). He will use it again in 4:17 in connection with the day of judgment and in 5:14 with regard to prayer.

More puzzling are the words in 3:22a: *And we receive from him whatever we ask.* Is John suggesting that we can ask for anything and receive it? We cannot deny that such thinking is at home within the Johannine community. In addition to 3:22 and 1 John 5:14, this is a frequently recurring theme in John's Gospel (cf. 11:22; 14:13-14; 15:7, 16; 16:23-24). Moreover, other early Christian communities express similar thoughts on prayer, as is evident in Ephesians 3:20; James 1:5-8; and Matthew 7:7-11; 18:19-20; and 21:22. In fact, this teaching finds its origin in Jesus himself. In John's Gospel, Jesus says, "If you ask anything of the Father in my name, he will give it to you"

(16:23), and Matthew reports that Jesus told his disciples, "Ask, and it will be given.... For everyone who asks receives" (Matt 7:7-8).

But before we begin praying for a luxury automobile, we must note John's qualifier: *because we obey his commandments and do what pleases him.* While our author encourages us to freely ask and tells us God freely gives, there are parameters. In this case, we are told to obey and please God. In 5:14 John will also qualify how we are to pray: *If we ask anything according to his will, he hears us.* It is clear John's understanding of prayer differs significantly from that of the advocates of a health-and-wealth gospel. John assumes that the one who prays shares an intimate and filial relationship with God (cf. 3:1 and John 1:12). Therefore such a person prays while being fully aware of God's nature. Additionally, they desire to obey and please God; therefore their prayers are in line with God's desires, not selfish agendas. To such a person, God can freely give.

Summary and Transition 3:23-24

The final verses serve both as a unit summary and a bridge to the closing chapters. Verse 23 connects directly to *We obey his commandments* (22b) in that it specifies the content of the commandments: *We should believe in the name of his Son Jesus Christ and love one another.* The opening and closing phrases of the verse form an *inclusio* highlighting the importance of Jesus' double commandment.

John now uses the singular *his commandment* (3:23, with God as referent from vv. 20-22), indicating that the essence of the faith can be summed up in one directive or agenda. But this command has two elements: belief and love. He stresses both points separately: Jesus as an object of faith (as in 1 John 5:1, 5, 10, 13; cf. John 1:12; 2:11, 22-23; 3:15-16, 18, 36; 4:39; 6:29, 35; etc.) and love for other community members (as in 1 John 2:10; 3:10-11, 14, 16-18; and later in 4:7-8, 11-12; 5:1-2). The author directly and specifically ties the two together. They are two sides of the same coin (see Swartley on John 15 for the Gospel's use of singular and plural for commandment(s): forthcoming). Moreover, as we saw in the last subunit, John connects a theological statement to an ethical imperative.

To *believe in the name of his Son Jesus Christ* relies on a common oriental concept that makes a theological statement against the separatists. The expression *in the name of* was an idiomatic statement in the ancient world. It was shorthand for a person's character and authority. For the first time John uses the verb *believe* in relation to Jesus, although this idea is implied earlier in the letter. But it will not be the last time. John reminds his followers that they are to believe or "trust" Jesus and his unique role as the Son of God. Jesus' particular identity as God's Son is a favorite, primary, and creedal idea in Johannine literature (see 1 John 1:3, 7; 2:23-24; 3:8, 23; 4:9-10, 14-15; 5:9-13, 20; 2 John 3, 9; John 1:49; 3:18; 5:20, 23, 25; 10:36; 11:4, 27; 20:30; Rev 2:18). This element of the commandment is probably a subtle strike against the separatists' teaching, minimizing the significance of Jesus, as we will see in 1 John 4:1-6.

However, belief in an abstract theological concept, even Jesus as God's Son, is not the believers' only defining mark. They also *love one another*. John has already argued for loving others in this unit (3:11, 14, 16-17) and earlier in the letter (2:10). It will also become a major theme in the closing chapters (4:7-8, 11-12, 19-21; 5:2). John's repeated emphasis on love shows that he does not understand Christianity as a merely intellectual exercise. Faith in Christ leads to action. Conversely, simply "loving" is not the only mark of a believer either. Christians also have faith in Jesus Christ as God's Son, trusting him and submitting to his authority by following the divine command to love that he revealed.

Then 3:24 serves the dual function of summarizing the thrust of 3:11-24 and transitioning to the next unit. One could also argue that these words address a key agenda of the letter. The clauses *All who obey his commands abide in him, and he abides in them* sum up both this subunit and a general theme of the letter (cf. 2:3-6). The closing reference to *the Spirit which he has given us* moves our thinking to the next unit's theme, where John will warn against blindly accepting false prophets and their teachings. But more than this, the reference to the Spirit is a component in John's attempt to reassure his readers, which is a driving agenda behind his writing of this letter.

John's concern is not simply obedience to divine commands. This is evident in verse 24, where he notes that there is a distinct benefit to obedience. Obedient ones *abide in him [God], and he abides in them*. This concept of *abiding* (*menō*) is a recurring and crucial one for this letter *["Abiding" in the Johannine Letters, p. 300]*. It is first mentioned in 2:6 and finally noted in 4:16 (cf. 2 John 2 and 9). In 1–2 John the word is used twenty-six times. Here in 1 John 3:24 the emphasis is on mutual abiding between God and the believer; and as Strecker (129) observes, it is an appropriate expression, coming from an author who believes that we can be God's children (cf. 3:1-2 and John 1:12). Verse 24a, in essence, assures the readers that their obedience results in an intimate relationship with God.

Finally, John points to a specific factor supporting his claim that God *abides in us: the Spirit that he has given us*. We are left with the firm impression that the Spirit's presence in the believers' lives is evidence of divine/human fellowship; but as numerous scholars remark, John does not specifically inform us as to how this assurance is manifested. Does the Spirit simply provide one with confidence? Is there an "inner consciousness of being loved by God" (Marshall: 202)? Is he referring to some ecstatic manifestations? Does our author have all these ideas and more in mind? We simply do not know, but we do know that he firmly believes this point. He mentions it again in 4:13, using similar words. Ultimately the topic of the Spirit becomes the focus of the next unit, where John advises discernment of various spirit influences, and it will reappear in 5:6 and 8.

SUMMARY

In this subunit John draws to a climatic close his line of argument begun in 2:28. Although the unit presents the reader with numerous interpretative challenges, the thrust is clear: loving one another and believing in Jesus Christ distinguishes believers from unbelievers. Moreover, in his attempt to reassure his readers, John provides a simple formula for discerning one's basic orientation. "To hate" is evidence of one's evil disposition and residence in the realm of death. Conversely, "to love" marks one righteous, that one has passed from death to life. Further reassurance is found in 2:19-20, where John reminds the reader of God's mercy, which is greater than human doubt. Last, he introduces the Spirit as a final comforting theme, and one that takes center stage in the next unit.

THE TEXT IN BIBLICAL CONTEXT

The Role of "Religion"

Since the Enlightenment, a common approach to religion has been to analyze it rationally and objectively. In some circles the general topic was (and is) a field that should be approached dispassionately. Furthermore, religion is a broad area and has been classified into individual categories as diverse as biblical studies, spirituality, or world religions. This modern tendency to isolate and dispassionately examine religion is not part of the biblical worldview. The Bible's integrative and "subjective" tendency is especially clear in this section regarding theological belief and ethics. John is keenly aware that our theology, or understanding of God, impacts our ethics. The divine nature, once revealed, calls forth human behavior that reflects or approximates God's being. Specifically, those who abide in God, who is love, are to behave lovingly as well.

John is not alone. When "the Lord" first reveals the divine name and
nature to Moses (Exod 3:1-17), we are told that God hears Israel's cries
and is moved to redeem them from oppression. The plan to reverse
centuries of injustice involves Moses' catching God's vision for Israel's
liberation. More specifically, once the nation is delivered, "the Lord"
descends to Mt. Sinai and meets with Moses, Israel's representative
(19:3-6). The key event in this rendezvous is the giving of the Ten
Commandments and the law (Exod 20; 24; 34). The tendency in
Christian circles is to begin "counting" the commandments with 20:3,
"You shall have no other gods before me." But in Jewish circles, 20:2 is
central to the first commandment: that verse reminds us that God's
concern for justice, compassion, and grace led to Israel's liberation. The
ethical commands designed to guide Israel's social interactions are
rooted in a compassionate, just, and gracious God's liberating actions.
Furthermore, Israel is called to be a holy nation because the Lord is holy
(Lev 11:44; 19:2; 20:7; cf. 1 Pet 1:13-16; 2:9c).

When their peers rejected the Lord and the law, Jeremiah and Micah
refer to the exodus and the ensuing covenantal relationship (Jer 2; 11;
34:8-21; Mic 6:1-8). Like many of the prophets, these two men proclaim
judgment because the people rejected the Lord and the law. Frequently
this rejection is manifested as worshipping foreign gods, making alli-
ances with militarily stronger states, and oppressing the weak and poor
within the Promised Land. In short, the Israelites' sinful behavior was a
rejection of both the Lord and social mores based on the Lord's divine
nature. The well-known words of Micah 6:8 sum up the fundamental
attributes expected of Israel, "What does the Lord require of you but to do
justice and to love kindness?" (cf. Isa 56:1). Moreover, Amos invokes the
exodus imagery before promising punishment for such immoral behavior as oppression, violence, and robbery (3:1-15). Furthermore, Hosea
accuses Israel of forgetting God, which resulted in immoral behavior such
as lying, murder, stealing, and adultery (4:1-3). Finally, Zephaniah warns
Judah of a coming divine judgment because the people are idolatrous,
violent, and fraudulent (1:4-9) and the residents of Jerusalem oppress
others while refusing to trust the Lord (3:1-2).

There is a strong tradition in the NT that "knowing" Jesus involves
personal sacrifice and following him. Repeatedly the synoptic Gospel
tradition depicts Jesus as calling people: "Follow me" (Mark 2:14//
Matt 9:9//Luke 5:27; Matt 4:19; 8:22). Frequently this call involves
divesting oneself of wealth and giving it to the poor. At other times it
involves assuming the role of a servant or slave. Mark, in particular,
makes a case for imitating Jesus' servant attitude in chapters 8–10. In
8:34-38 Jesus challenges would-be followers to "deny themselves and

take up their cross and follow me." Martin Hengel (51) has made a convincing case that crucifixion was commonly viewed as "slaves' punishment." In other words, when Jesus uses this metaphor, he is probably calling people to a life of total servanthood. Mark 9:33-37 further encourages disciples to assume the role of "servant of all." In 10:35-45, Jesus equates greatness with the role of a servant. Not only that but a truly great person also is "slave of all," following Jesus' own role as one who "came not to be served but to serve" (10:44-45).

This tradition of imitating Jesus as servant continues in Paul, as seen in Philippians 2:1-8. The irony is that although many scholars argue that Paul did not rely on traditions about Jesus, his advice regarding the "taking the form of a slave" clearly falls in line with the synoptic tradition. Moreover, Paul certainly viewed himself in this role for he repeatedly identifies himself as a slave of Christ (NRSV mg.: Rom 1:1; Phil 1:1; Titus 1:1). Nor is Paul the only early Christian writer who has this same self-understanding. Evidence of this appears in James (1:1), 1 Peter (2:16), and 2 Peter (1:1).

Finally, the basic structure of Luke-Acts reveals Luke's conviction that to know Jesus truly is to imitate his behavior. While some first-century religions promoted abstract intellectual knowledge as the path to salvation, Luke organizes his two books so as to focus on Jesus Christ's ministry and his disciples' imitation of that ministry. The key elements of the Gospel are reiterated in Acts. The Spirit is given and ministry is conducted in the power of the Spirit, the good news is proclaimed, evil spirits are cast out, people are healed, persecution and rejection occur, and people are martyred for the cause. There is even a geographical parallel between Jesus' work, which begins in a backwater area and ends in a capital city, and the progression of the disciples' work. There is no question that for Luke to "know" Jesus' theological identity impacts the way his followers lived their lives.

Having and Helping

First John's blunt rhetorical question in 3:17, *How does God's love abide in anyone who has the world's goods and sees a brother or sister in need and yet refuses help?* is not the author's unique view of material wealth. The NT provides abundant evidence that the early church was firmly committed to Jesus' call to give to the poor (see Matt 19:21; Mark 10:21; Luke 18:22; Matt 25:34-40; cf. Matt 6:19). We are familiar with the twice-noted communalism passages in Acts (2:43-47; 4:32-37). The first believers are depicted not only as pious, praying converts, but also as materially generous to the point that "there was not a needy person among them" (Acts 4:34; cf. 2:45; cf. 11:27-30; 20:35; 2 Cor 8–9). And who is not aware of James's version of the Johannine question, assuming faith that does not result in sharing of one's wealth in the face of need is dead and useless (2:14-15)? Less well known, perhaps, are Paul's attempts to rally his mission congregations to provide material relief for famine-stricken believers in Judea (Acts 11:29-30; Rom 15:25-29; 1 Cor 16:1-4; 2 Cor 9:1-15; cf. Gal 2:10).

Jesus' teaching and the church's behavior are not innovations in the biblical context. The OT reflects Judaism's long-standing compassionate convictions regarding the poor. Ronald J. Sider claims, "Hundreds of biblical verses show that God is especially attentive to the poor and needy" (1999: 56). The ancient Jews understood "the Lord" as a God who actively worked to elevate the poor and oppressed (Exod 3:7-8; 6:5-7). This divine compassion becomes a central concern for Israel's corporate life. Laws regulate how orphans, widows, and foreigners are to be treated (Exod 22:21-24; 23:9; Lev 19:33-34; Deut 10:12-20; 14:28-29). The sabbatical year and the year of Jubilee are designed so that people might be freed from their debt (Lev 25; Deut 15), and Leviticus 25:39-55 forbids enslaving fellow Israelites who have fallen on hard times. The prophets rail against exploiting the weak of society and predict divine judgment on such behavior (Isa 3:14-25; 10:1-3; Jer 5:25-29; 22:22-29; Amos 5:11-12; Mic 2:1-3). Even Israel's folk wisdom equated kindness extended to the poor as being equal to treating the Lord kindly (Prov 14:31; 19:17).

THE TEXT IN THE LIFE OF THE CHURCH

Imitating Christ

Not surprisingly, John continues his emphasis on love and refusing to sin. What becomes clear, however, is his belief that victory over sin and evil is more than an abstract notion. One must be able to point to evidence of this transformation, this passing *from death to life* (1 John 3:14). Here he argues that the clearest evidence is our love for one another, which manifests itself in sharing our material goods with the poor. We should not, however, assume that this is the only way to demonstrate our spiritual reorientation. First John 3:18 contains the foundational principle that has innumerable applications: *Let us love, not [only] in word or speech, but [especially] in truth and action.* John sees the true motivation behind such concrete acts of love as the believers' attempt to be faithful to Jesus and his ways.

In the midst of troubled human affairs, God has always raised up leaders and empowered people to imitate Jesus in kingdom building. Before the beginning of the Anabaptist movement, the obvious figure is Francis of Assisi, who died in 1226. Francis lived in a time riddled with fear of Others, such as lepers; a time of the free exercise of violence against one's Italian neighbors, German overlords, and Muslim expansionists; and a time of passion for accumulating wealth. As a young man he benefited from his father's thriving cloth business. He robustly participated in war against the neighboring town of Perugia, and he dreamed of becoming a knight. Finally, he was horrified by and feared the numerous lepers living near his town. And then he was changed.

His frustrated father dragged him before the local bishop, who told him that if he wanted to serve God, he must return the wealth his father had given him. Francis agreed, disappeared into the next room, returned completely naked, and handed his clothing and money to his father, saying, "Please listen, everyone. Because I want to serve God from now on, I am giving back to my father the money about which he is so distressed and also my clothes" (via House: 69). For the rest of his life he owned nothing but a rough cloth robe and rope belt, ministering to the poor and working with lepers. Moreover, he traveled all over Europe, preaching the gospel to anyone willing to listen. He even preached to al-Kamil, the Egyptian sultan, in the hope of converting him and ending the violence of the fifth Crusade (209-13). For his unwavering commitment to living the gospel, he faced rejection and persecution throughout much of his life, and still he lived by his well-known motto: "Preach the gospel always. If necessary, use words."

Some early Anabaptists, such as Dirk Philips and Leonhard Schiemer, knew of Francis and were influenced by his core convictions (Davis: 232-43). While imprisoned in 1528, Balthasar Hubmaier wrote his *Apologia* to King Ferdinand of Hungary and Bohemia. His first subpoint, "In the Name of Jesus, Amen," addresses the topic of "mere faith." Hubmaier decries his contemporaries who claim to have faith yet evidence growing vices such as "violent dominion . . . and wantonness" (Pipkin and Yoder: 527). Such people are "mere mouth-Christians, boasting and saying, 'Look! we believe that Jesus Christ suffered torture and death for us'" (526). Hubmaier responds by using 1 John 3:18-19 for biblical support: "We must also exercise our faith in works of love toward God and our neighbors."

Seventeen years later Pilgram Marpeck echoed Hubmaier's beliefs when he wrote his letter "On the Inner Church" (Klassen and Klaassen: 418-26). In this essay Marpeck tries to explain the life of faith as a connection between both inner and outer manifestations of the Holy Spirit. In other words, the Christian life is more than either a merely spiritual inner experience or a mechanical external action. Early in the document he points to the belief that Christ abides in the believer and the believer in Christ. This mutual abiding, echoing Johannine theology, results in specific external manifestations, as Marpeck explains: "These are the ones who love the Father and the Son, and keep the words in unity. . . . Furthermore, we must also recognize that we love one another, as He loved us. . . . The true revelation of Christ Jesus is to feel and recognize that the will, work, and good pleasure of the Father is, through Christ, performed in us" (420). Various elements of the sixteenth-century Anabaptist movement endeavored to embody many of the ideals noted in 1 John 3:11-24, including mutual love for one another (v. 11), laying down one's life for a brother (v. 16), sharing with a sister in need (v. 17), seeking to obey God (v. 22), and abiding in God (v. 24).

This aspect of the five-hundred-year-old Anabaptist tradition still finds expression in today's world. For example, the Hutterian Brethren, heirs of Jacob Hutter, live "communally," stressing mutual giving and sharing. Robert Friedmann (82-83) identifies three key motives behind their communal life: (1) "brotherly love in action"; (2) heart dedication, which stresses "*forsaking all selfishness* and one's own will"; and (3) "obedience to the divine commandments." Additionally, thousands support American Friends Service Committee, Brethren Church Services, and Mennonite Central Committee, which carry on worldwide missions of relief and development. One congregation, when told of the gravity of the AIDS epidemic in Africa, raised over $25,000 in one Sunday morning worship service. No doubt many individuals take seriously this Johannine mandate, and they give sacrificially to those in need, motivated by a firm conviction that Jesus Christ is the central figure of human history and by a desire to express his love in a fragmented and suffering world.

In addition to church tradition and human need as motivators for taking seriously John's assumption that theology and ethics go hand in hand is the fact that the people of God are moving into a new era of human affairs. Much is written about ministry and faith in postmodernity, especially from people described as evangelicals. This phenomenon has been referred to as the Emergent Church movement, and one of its leading voices is Brian D. McLaren. He and others advocate a Christianity that is gracious and seeks to embody the risen Christ for the good of the world. Recently McLaren (121) wrote: "Bear fruit now—don't just talk or say the right things, but live out the teachings of the Kingdom of God, especially in the area of compassion for the weak and needy and vulnerable. Have confidence in Jesus so that you will actually do what he says." No doubt these "emergent" believers would make excellent dialogue partners and perhaps even allies in the wider church. Now is not the time to take lightly the intertwining of theology and ethics.

Section 3: 1 John 4:1–5:12

The Work of the Spirit

OVERVIEW

The previous subunit concludes with the dual command to *believe in the name . . . of Jesus Christ* and *love one another* (3:23). The readers are further reminded that *all who obey his commandments* will benefit from a mutual abiding, and the supporting evidence for this abiding is *the Spirit* (v. 24).

This is 1 John's penultimate section (4:1–5:12). It reaffirms much of what we have seen before; superficially, then, it looks as though the author is simply repeating themes. In reality, mention of the Spirit in 3:24 is this unit's key underlying motif, and John employs it to move his argument forward. Abstract theological reflection is not his only concern. The *spirit* theme serves a dual purpose of theological argumentation and pastoral affirmation.

Commentators note that these verses are an expansion of 3:23-24. In particular, 4:1-6 develops 3:23b (*believe in the name of his Son Jesus Christ*), and 4:7–5:4a expands upon 3:23c (*Love one another*). Finally, 5:4b-12 brings the argument back to the foundational Christological issue of Jesus' role as Son of God. With these verses, the author brings his argument and encouragement to a close.

OUTLINE

Belief and the Spirit, 4:1-6
Love and the Spirit, 4:7–5:4a
Testimony of the Spirit, 5:4b-12

1 John 4:1-6

Belief and the Spirit

PREVIEW

When facing significant challenges, it is all too easy to offer stock answers and glib advice. Perhaps this letter's original readers think that our author has done just that up to this point. He quickly encourages them to trust tradition (1:5 and 2:7), obey commandments (2:3-6; 3:22-24), and love each other (2:10; 3:11-18). The words *trust, obey,* and *love* are small but challenging in difficult times.

In a situation like the one behind this epistle, how does one know what to trust? There are at least two appealing options. How does one know which is to be obeyed? It is tempting to follow the path of least resistance. And where does the strength come from to love in the midst of conflict? This larger unit (4:1–5:12) provides John's answer to these questions. The Spirit's presence in the believers' lives makes obeying the commandments to believe and love possible. The previous unit's closing words of assurance introduce this theme: *By this we know that he abides in us, by the Spirit that he has given us* (3:24).

In 4:1-6 the author applies his spirit theology to the commandment to *believe in the name of . . . Jesus Christ* (3:23a). Given the two options—apostolic tradition (noted in the opening verses of the first chapter) versus the secessionists' innovative theology—how does one determine what to believe about Jesus? Discernment is John's reply in 4:1-3. Confession *that Jesus Christ has come in the flesh* confirms the Spirit's presence. Denying such confession of Jesus comes from *the spirit of the antichrist.*

In the last three verses of this unit, the author returns to his earlier pattern of offering pastoral encouragement. Beginning with

one of his terms of endearment, *little children* (4:4), he reminds the
readers that they are *from God* and have overcome their opponents.
This victory is based not on their superior intellect or morality.
Rather, it is a result of *the one who is in you* (4:4). Furthermore, they
should not be discouraged because the secessionists' message is
received by *the world*. In John's mind, this is expected because the
separatists are *from the world* (4:5).

From God   *Not from God*

       Testing Spirits 4:1-3

         4:1a Command to Test
         Beloved, do not believe every spirit, but
         test the spirits to see whether they are
         from God;

         4:1b Reason for Testing
         for many false prophets have gone
         out into the world.

         4:2-3 The Test
         Introduction 4:2a
         By this you know the Spirit of God:

4:2b Confessing   ⟶   **4:3 Not Confessing**
every spirit that confesses   *and every spirit that does not*
that Jesus Christ has come   *confess Jesus is not from God. And*
in the flesh is from God,   *this is the spirit of the antichrist,*
                                of which you have heard that it is
                                coming; and now it is already in
                                the world.

         Words of Encouragement 4:4-6
         4:4a Words of Affirmation/Criticism
         Little children, you are from God,
         and have conquered them;

4:4b Reason for Your Affirmation ⟶ *4:5a Their Deception*
for the one who is in you is greater   They are from the world; therefore
than the one who is in the world.   what they say is from the world,

4:5b World Listens to Them
and the world listens to them.

4:6a Further Affirmation
We are from God.

4:6b The Godly Listen to Us
Whoever knows God listens to us,
and whoever is not from God does
not listen to us.

4:6c Conclusion
From this we know the spirit of truth
and the spirit of error.

OUTLINE

Testing Spirits, 4:1-3
Words of Encouragement, 4:4-6

EXPLANATORY NOTES

Testing Spirits 4:1-3

In the previous unit John stresses the importance of conforming to
the message to love one another. As part of that argument the
author affirms that his readers have *passed from death to life because
[they] love one another* (3:14). The unit closed with the statement that
all who obey his commandments abide in him (3:24), and evidence of his
abiding is *the Spirit that he has given us* (3:24). Here (in 4:1-6) John
begins unpacking that closing comment by addressing the commandment to *believe in the name of his Son Jesus Christ* (3:23) and
explaining how the Spirit facilitates such belief.

John begins with a term of endearment, *beloved*, which he used
previously (2:7; 3:2, 21) and which we will see again (4:7, 11; 3 John
2, 5, 11). The repeated use of this term leads us to conclude that the

author has a positive relationship with his readers, and what is about to be addressed comes as encouragement rather than rebuke. Specifically, the readers are told, *Do not believe every spirit, but test the spirits to see whether they are from God.*

The author, and presumably his readers, believed that a variety of "spirits" were at work in the world. Such a conviction was common during this time in both Christian and Jewish circles. Some NT evidence is found in the Pauline concept of "principalities and powers" (cf. KJV: Rom 8:38; Eph 1:21; 3:10; 6:12; Col 1:16; 2:15; Heb 1:4, 14; see Swartley 2006: 222-45) and in John's Gospel as Satan or "the ruler of this world" (8:44; 12:31; 13:27; 14:30; 16:11). Many, if not all, of these verses assume that these spiritual forces exert influence over humans.

The notion of spiritual forces was accepted in the post-NT period as well. Ignatius, the third bishop of Antioch, twice makes reference to this in his letters. Before his martyrdom during Trajan's reign (AD 98-117), he wrote to a number of churches, including those at Ephesus and Philadelphia. In *To the Ephesians* he writes, "Be not anointed with the evil odor of the doctrine of the Prince of this world, lest he lead you away captive from the life which is set before you" (17.1). Ignatius, in *To the Philadelphians* 6.2 says, "Flee then from the wicked arts and snares of the prince of this world, less you be afflicted by his device, and grow weak in love."

The widespread notion that spiritual forces influenced human life was inherited from Jewish theology from before Jesus' birth. The second-century BC *Testament of the Twelve Patriarchs* contains a quote that neatly parallels 1 John 4:1-6: "So understand, my children, that two spirits await an opportunity with humanity: the spirit of truth and the spirit of error. In between is the conscience of the mind which inclines as it will" (*Testament of Judah* 20:1-2). Additionally, the Qumran community also inherited and adhered to this belief, as is evidenced by *The Community Rule* (1QS 3.13-15).

Given such a worldview, it is entirely sensible that John encourages the community to *test the spirits to see whether they are from God.* The verb *test* (*dokimazete*) is in the present imperative form and carries with it a sense of discerning or experimenting with something. For example, some ancient sources use this word to describe the process of testing a metal's quality. In other words, John tells his readers to critique the messages they are hearing because not all teachings are from God.

Just as the idea of competing spirits was common in the ancient world, so is the concept of testing those spirits and those who may be under their influence. In 1 Thessalonians 5:19-22, a close parallel to our verse, we read, "Do not quench the Spirit. Do not despise the words of prophets, but test [*dokimazete*] everything; hold fast to what is good; abstain from every form of evil" (cf. Rev 2:2). Sometimes the test was based on conduct (Matt 7:15-23), and at other times, as here, doctrine is the standard of measure (cf. 1 Cor 12:3).

The early believers and some first-century Jews also practiced "testing." The *Didache* 11.1-12 provides a detailed testing process to be applied to itinerant prophets, and 12.1 reads, "Let everyone who 'comes in the Name of the Lord' be received; but when you have tested him you shall know him, for you shall have understanding of true and false" (Lake 1926: 329). Similarly, the Shepherd of Hermas, in *Mandate* 11.7-16, encourages the testing of prophets (Lake 1926: 119-23). Also, *The Community Rule* at Qumran tells us that new members were to be "tested" upon entrance, and all members were periodically to be tested (1QS 3.13-14; 5.20-21).

One final observation regarding the call to *test the spirits* is noteworthy. Both verbs (*do not believe* and *test*) are in the plural form. Additionally, *beloved*, is also plural. It is likely, then, that the author envisions the act of discernment or testing as a corporate process. The individual is not the determining factor in establishing what the community believes with respect to doctrine. Traditional doctrine has been transmitted by a group (cf. 1:1-4), and the faith community is responsible for the ongoing "testing" of doctrinal issues.

In the last portion of 4:1 John provides the reason for testing: *Many false prophets have gone out into the world*. This is the only place in 1 John (cf. Rev. 16:13; 19:20; 20:10) that uses *false prophets* (*pseudoprophētai*), although it is a relatively common category in early Christianity. Often the word is associated with the end times and with misleading the faithful, as we see in Jesus' warning in Mark 13:22, "False messiahs and false prophets will appear and produce signs and omens, to lead astray, if possible, the elect" (cf. Rev 16:13; 19:20; 20:10; *Did.* 11.4-12; Shepherd of Hermas, *Mandate* 11.1-4, 7). Raymond Brown correctly warns us not to assume that these *false prophets* were primarily distinguished as charismatics (1982: 490). While they may have been, the author's primary concern is their false teachings, as evidenced by 1 John 4:2, 5-6; 2:18-28; 2 John 7. Brown states that the "office" of prophet was frequently associated with teaching, as in Acts 13:1; 1 Corinthians 12:28; 2 Peter 2:1; 2 Thessalonians 2:3; *Didache* 11.3-12. By describing them as having *gone out into the world*, he labels them as anti-God. He develops this theme in 4:3, 5.

No doubt John is concerned about a situation in which *false prophets* propose and articulate dubious doctrine. Such a scenario calls for testing spirits. While believers are commanded to love, they are not to be naive. As John Stott (152) writes, "Neither Christian faith nor Christian love is indiscriminate." John is convinced that in order to adhere to correct doctrine regarding Jesus Christ his readers must discriminate between true and false teachings. But the question remains: What is an appropriate test?

Verses 2 and 3 provide a dual test. The affirmative aspect is addressed in verse 2, and then verse 3 uses a negative counterpoint. Together these verses are critical for understanding the secessionists' theology. Unfortunately, both verses present challenges to the contemporary reader. The language of verse 2 is ambiguous, with a significant textual variant in verse 3.

The process of discerning *the Spirit of God* has an interesting parallel in Deuteronomy 13:1-5 (cf. 18:20-22). There the Israelites are encouraged to test the advice of prophets who tell Israel, "Let us follow other gods" (13:2). These false prophets' teachings are to be tested against the Lord's commandments (13:4). While God's commands are the measure in Deuteronomy, one's view of Jesus Christ is the test in 1 John 4:2. Anyone who *confesses that Jesus Christ has come in the flesh is from God.* John has already employed the word *confess* in 1:9 (see commentary on 1:8-9). Similarly, *No one who denies the Son has the Father; everyone who confesses the Son has the Father also* (see commentary on 2:23). The word carries with it a sense of "acknowledging" or "declaring publicly." The challenge associated with the verse is the positive confession's content. What is to be acknowledged about Jesus Christ?

Unfortunately, the original Greek, which literally says *Jesus Christ in flesh having come*, is ambiguous. Commentators argue for one of three nuanced options. First, the confession may be this: *Confess Jesus Christ come in the flesh*, where the confession affirms the entire phrase. Second, it could read, *Confess Jesus Christ as come in the flesh*, where the confession affirms both Jesus Christ and his coming in the flesh. Finally, the Greek may be translated as *Confess Jesus as the Christ come in the flesh*. Here again are two affirmations: Jesus is the Christ, and he came in the flesh. The arguments based on grammar are detailed and highly nuanced. The confession affirms both Jesus' messianic role and the incarnation.

As Brown points out, the first option stresses that there is no separation between "Jesus" and "Christ" (1982: 493). The historical Jesus must be viewed as the Messiah, and vice versa. Furthermore, the confession affirms that Jesus the messianic figure took on human flesh. This is not surprising. The author began the letter with such an affirmation (1:1-4) and will affirm it again in 5:6-12 and 2 John 7. So the question is, Were the secessionists denying the general idea that Jesus was the incarnation of God? Probably not.

We suspect their error was more nuanced. One hint may be the verb form of *has come* (*elēlythota*), which is a perfect active participle. This form carries with it the sense of having come (completed action) plus an enduring nature of his incarnation. It may be that the opponents were proto-Gnostics who believed that the "divine Christ" descended on Jesus at his baptism and departed before his death. Thus they affirmed part of his life, while denying the value of his death. Or it may be that the secessionists questioned the continuing significance of Jesus Christ for salvation. Either way, we suspect that John is arguing that Jesus of Nazareth was *the* revelation of God, and that his life *and* death have resolved the issue of sin and salvation for humanity (cf. 1:5–2:2). Not only that, but the author also believes, perhaps unlike his opponents, that Jesus Christ's life provided a model of love that is a key element of the ongoing salvation of the world—hence the letter's emphasis on the love commandment. As David Rensberger (115) writes, "If the messiahship of Jesus was a material human event, 'in the flesh,' then it provides both a basis and a mandate for Christians' lives to be meaningful in material human reality, both individual and social." The positive aspect of the test then is to acknowledge the broad significance of the incarnation.

Verse 3 clearly has a relationship of "antithetical parallelism" to verse 2 (Brown 1982: 494). In essence, it restates the positive test of verse 2 in a negative way: *Every spirit that does not confess Jesus is not from God.* Despite the parallelism, there are differences between the two verses. Most obvious is the long closing sentence regarding *the spirit of the antichrist.* The parallel is the short prepositional phrase *from God* in 4:2 and *not from God* in 4:3. In verse 3 John then provides a detailed explanation of what is meant by *not from God.* Verse 3 also contains an important textual variant that needs attention, but first we address the difference between *Jesus* (v. 3) and *Jesus Christ* (v. 2).

Some commentators view the shift from *confesses . . . Jesus Christ* to *confess Jesus* simply as the author's attempt at stylistic variation or shorthand. To use the personal name *Jesus*, however, without the theological title *Christ* may be an important hint as to John and his opponents' views. D. Moody Smith (98-99) asks if it is possible that the secessionists affirmed Christ without adequately affirming the human Jesus. Smith is inclined to see the opponents' failure as having something to do with Jesus' humanity. Why else, he asks, would the author stress the physical, auditory, and tactile aspects of the *word of life* in the letter's opening verses? The use of *Jesus* alone may be significant if the above suggestion that the separatists were proto-Gnostics is probable. In this case, they denied or at least downplayed the salvific nature of his death. As we have already seen, however, this salvific death is crucial for John. Jesus' death *cleanses us from all sin* (1:7), and he is *the atoning sacrifice for our sins, and not for ours only but also for the sins of the whole world* (2:2; cf. 4:10). This theme emerges again in 5:6-12. The use of *Jesus*, instead of *Jesus Christ*, is probably more than a matter of style or shorthand.

This brings us to the textual variant, which may well be related to the use of *Jesus* alone. All modern translations follow the Greek manuscripts that unanimously read *mē homologei* (*does not confess* or *does not acknowledge*). To their credit they have faithfully followed a fundamental translation principle: assume that the original wording is what appears in the oldest and most reliable Greek texts. This principle conflicts with another principle: the more difficult wording is probably original. The idea is that easier or more sensible texts are later alterations and clarifications of the difficult readings.

Such a case arises in verse 3. The Latin Vulgate uses the word *solvere* ("annuls" or "dissolves") instead of a verb meaning "confess," as in the Greek text. Additionally, Mount Athos Codex 1739, a tenth-century copy of a sixth-century Greek manuscript, has an important marginal note. It has the word *lyei*, or "destroys," "annuls," or "does away with"— and an explanatory note reading, "Thus Irenaeus in Book 3 of *Adversus haereses* [*Against Heresies*]; Origen clearly in Book 8 of his *Commentary on Romans*; and Clement the Stromateus [of Alexandria] in his *About the Pasch*" (Brown 1982: 494). In other words, three patristic writers from the second and third centuries believed that the original text read something like every *spirit that annuls* (*lyei* instead of *mē homologei*, "does not confess") *Jesus is not from God.* If we take this note seriously, that would mean that the verb probably was changed to *homolegeō* in order to improve the parallel thought between verses 2 and 3.

While I hesitate to retranslate this verse using the verb *annuls*, we can make the point that if *lyei* was original, it would make sense of the situation facing John and his community. Clearly the opponents challenge the traditions about Jesus that the Johannine elders handed down. They probably have doubts about some aspects of the incarnation, and they question Jesus' role as Savior. Moreover, they seemingly question his key teaching on love. In short, it must have looked as though they were intent on setting aside Jesus and his significance.

In light of such a stance toward Jesus, John concludes that such a person is *not from God.* Instead, this attitude is motivated by *the spirit of the antichrist.* We initially saw *antichrist* in 2:18-25 (see commentary thereon), and as noted there the expression is associated with the "end times." Both in 2:18 and here the author makes reference to the community's awareness of this figure (*of which you have heard* in 4:3 and *as you have heard* in 2:18), and so it is not unreasonable to assume that teachings about the *antichrist* were part of the Johannine tradition. In the NT the word is used only in 1 and 2 John.

There is one significant difference between the use in 2:18 and 4:3. In the previous verse, the author assumes that while *the antichrist* is still to come, many antichrists *have come.* In 4:3, John writes that those who refuse to confess Jesus are influenced by *the spirit of the antichrist,* but he stops short of identifying them as *antichrists.* Moreover, he writes, *you have heard that it* [the spirit of the antichrist] *is coming; and now it is already in the world.* One is tempted to ask, "Is it here or is it not here?" We suspect that John's answer would be "Yes." The conflictive situation and presence of false prophets is clear evidence of *the spirit of the antichrist* being present. And since these false prophets are aligning themselves with *the* antichrist that will come, they appear as *many antichrists.* Although we noted above that a theology of the antichrist may well be part of the traditional community teachings behind 1 and 2 John, we must also recognize that this theoretical teaching may be in the process of development in light of the real-life dilemma facing the community.

Words of Encouragement 4:4-6

As we transition to the next subunit, the first word and sentence indicate that the author's attention shifts from a focus on spirits to a primary focus on people influenced by those spirits: *Little children, you are from God.* The word *teknia* (*little children*) was first used in 2:1 (see comments there) and is a term of endearment that the author uses to describe his readers. The point of these verses is to affirm these *little children* by continuing the dualist-spirit argument begun in 4:1-3.

This theme continues with the use of emphatic personal pronouns at the start of each verse: *you* (*hymeis* in v. 4), *they* (*autoi* in v. 5), and *we* (*hēmeis* in v. 6). Additionally, the author reemphasizes the *God-* and-*world* duality (v. 4), which is explained in verses 5 and 6 and concludes with a reference to *the spirit of truth* and *the spirit of error* in verse 6. The gist of these verses is to reassure his readers that they are aligned with God.

Again John assures them that they are *from God,* which is similar to, if not the same as, what we have seen in 3:1 and 9 and will see again in 4:7; 5:1, 4, 18. In addition to the affirmation of God as their source, the author believes that his hearers *have conquered them*. The verb *conquer* (*nikaō*) was first used in 2:13-14, which speaks of conquering *the evil one*. In fact, when John employs this verb, it refers to overcoming the evil one, the antichrists, or the world. In this context, however, those who are conquered (*them*) are probably the *false prophets* mentioned in 4:1, who are under the influence of the *spirit of the antichrist* (4:3). Given this understanding of *them*, the Johannine believers' victory is probably doctrinal in nature. They have rejected the false teachings and remained faithful to Jesus Christ and the Johannine community's traditional understanding of him.

John, however, does not want his readers to assume that their victory is their own doing. In reality, it results because *the one who is in you is greater than the one who is in the world*. The *one who is in the world* is probably the evil one. Already in 2:13 the readers receive affirmation because they *have conquered the evil one*. More challenging is the identity of *the one who is in you*. The Greek word for *the one* is a masculine definite article, thus leading us to conclude that John means the term "God," a masculine noun, and not "the Spirit," a neuter noun.

There is, however, significant support to conclude that the author ultimately envisions the Spirit's role in making God present in the believers' lives. The immediate context's emphasis on the spirits' influence over humans must be acknowledged. In 4:1-3 we have seen the idea that various spirits exert influence for good or evil. And in 4:6 John assumes that there are two spirits vying for influence. The broader context of Johannine literature, especially the Gospel of John, has a theology of the Spirit (Paraclete) that views the Holy Spirit as a self-giving gift of the Father. The Paraclete is described as "the Spirit of truth" (John 14:17; 15:26-27; 16:13) and functions in such a way as to facilitate God's and Jesus Christ's abiding in the believer (John 14:16-17). First John has assumed this abiding role, as we have seen in 3:24 (*And by this we know that we abide him and he in us, by the Spirit that he has given us*) and will see it again in 4:13 (*By this we know that he abides in us, because he has given us of his Spirit*). Ultimately, while John may see the victory as resulting from God's and Jesus Christ's presence in the believers' lives, he would also acknowledge that the divine presence and power is due to the *Spirit*, which God has given.

Verse 5 continues this encouragement by addressing the issue of the secessionists' apparently successful teaching. While this verse certainly does not provide an image of overwhelming success, a degree of their success is implied by the closing expression: *The world listens to them*. The Greek construction (*autōn akouei*) suggests that the world has not only heard the message but also accepted it (Brown 1982: 498). Often missiological success is used to argue for the essential correctness of the message. No doubt the separatists used this line of argumentation against the Johannine community. The author counters that some "success" is to be expected because the secessionists *are from the world* or under the antichrist's influence, as is the world. They, the secessionists, speak the world's language and share the world's outlook. The faithful are encouraged to view their opponents' success not as a sign of their essential correctness, but as evidence of their erroneous orientation toward the forces opposing God.

Verse 6 complements verse 5. If the separatists are from the world and the world accepts their message, then *whoever knows God listens to us*. This is because *we are from God*. For the modern reader, the question is, Who is envisioned by the verse's references to *we are from God, listens to us, does not listen to us*, and *from this we know*? Some think these plural pronouns are referring to a third party, specifically the elders or bearers of the tradition. In that case three groups are assumed in 4:4-6. More likely, however, only two basic groups are in view. When labeling the secessionists as a single group in 4:1, John treats them as *false prophets*, and 4:5 further collectively identifies them as *they*. There is no attempt to distinguish a group of leaders and a group of followers within the opponents' camp. Similarly, John's community may have functional groups within the larger group, but the entire Johannine community is in view in 4:6. This is supported by the parallelism of verses 5 and 6, where the focus is on audiences' listening to the two groups' messages: the world listens to them, and anyone who knows God listens to us. Using the collective term *we* (*hēmeis*) in 4:6 provides the readers with the additional encouragement of being included with the broader traditional group to which the author belongs.

The final sentence, *From this we know the spirit of truth and the spirit of error*, presents two puzzles. What is meant by *the spirit of truth and the spirit of error*? And what is the evidence or process by which *we know* the difference? The easier challenge is the first. Within the Johannine tradition, *the Spirit of truth* is a synonym for the Holy Spirit or Paraclete (John 14:17; 15:26; 16:13). Similarly, in 1 John 5:6 we read, *The Spirit is the one that testifies, for the Spirit is the truth*. *The spirit of error*, however, is used only here in the entire NT. The repeated duality of these verses certainly leads us to conclude that this spirit is the opposite of the Holy Spirit. The phrase uses *planē* (*error* or *deception*). In Revelation 12:9 the related participle is used to describe the devil as the "deceiver [*planōn*] of the whole world." First Timothy 4:1 also talks about "deceitful spirits [*pneumasin planois*] and teachings of demons" that lead some to renounce the faith. *The spirit of error* in 1 John 4:3, therefore, is likely a synonym for *the spirit of the antichrists*.

The final question is to what does John refer when he writes, *From this* [*ek toutou*] *we know*? The Greek expression *ek toutou* unambiguously refers to something that precedes the phrase, but what is it? Commentators point to one of three options: (1) 1 John 4:6abc (*We are from God. Whoever knows God listens to us*); (2) the encouraging words in 4:4-6; or (3) the entire unit of 4:1-6. The evidence seems to support the third option best. The use of *ek toutou* in 4:6 has a parallel expression in the use of *en toutō* in 3:24 (*By this we know that he abides in us, by the Spirit that he has given us*). Additionally, the phrase *know the Spirit of truth and the spirit of error* in 4:6 returns to the theme of 4:1 on *testing* the spirits. These two points suggest that John has created an *inclusio* (bookends/brackets) in these verses. In other words, these six verses are meant to stand together. The testing of spirits that affirm or denounce a particular Christology and listening to their respective messages indicates whether one is influenced by *the spirit of truth* or *the spirit of error*. These elements also reveal who is aligned with God and who follows the forces opposing God. Those who are faithful are commended, and those who follow a false path are judged negatively.

THE TEXT IN BIBLICAL CONTEXT

Spiritual Influences

Although it may be an overstatement, many Westerners probably struggle with this unit's assumption that spiritual forces influence human behavior. As heirs of the Enlightenment and the scientific method, we cannot readily accept John's view without some reservations. People from developing nations, however, tend to face no such challenges. Mental and physical illnesses are often explained as a result of demonic activities. Blessings come because God or the gods make them come. Good deeds are accomplished because of the Holy Spirit's presence. Their views are close to the biblical text.

In the OT spiritual influence is seen as overwhelmingly positive. Even on occasions mentioning the presence of an evil spirit, that spirit is sent by "the LORD" (cf. Judg 9:22-57; 1 Sam 16:14-23; 16:15; 18:10). The tendency to trace all spiritual activity to the Lord is due to the Jewish theological conviction that their God is the sovereign Lord. Therefore, all spiritual activity comes under the Lord's control, and it tends to be good just as the Lord is a good God. This goodness is seen at the outset when the world is created through the presence of the divine spirit (Gen 1:2). And the spirit's creative aspect is later employed to explain artistic creativity (Exod 31:3; 35:31).

More common is the motif associating good leadership with a spiritual presence. In Numbers 11 the complaining people become a heavy burden to Moses. The solution is depicted as a distribution of responsibility to the seventy elders. The spirit that Moses bore was "put . . . on them" so that "they shall bear the burden of the people along with you [Moses]" (Num 11:17). Similarly, before his death, Moses laid hands on Joshua, who was then full of "the spirit of wisdom" (Deut 34:9).

In Judges "the spirit of the LORD" repeatedly influences designated judges. The classic and well-known spirit-led judges are Gideon, who was possessed (6:34) as he battled the Midianites and Amalekites, and Samson (13:25; 14:6, 19; 15:14, 19). But the spirit also inspired Othniel (3:10) and Jephthah (11:29). Even when Israel rejected the role of judges in favor of kingship, the Lord gave his spirit to both Saul (1 Sam 10:9-13) and David (1 Sam 16:13).

Eventually Israel's prophets are viewed as the main recipients of the Spirit. In 2 Chronicles 15:1, Azariah, under the influence of God's spirit, warns Asa to not abandon the Lord. And in 2 Chronicles 24:20-22, "the spirit of God took possession of Zechariah, son of the priest Jehoiada," who challenged Israel for their forsaking the Lord and transgressing the commandments. Isaiah 42:1-9 envisions a servant figure that under spiritual influence will bring justice to the nations, and Isaiah 61:1-11 offers an image of a spirit-led figure who is commissioned to bring salvation to the oppressed. In Ezekiel the spirit is the medium through which the prophet learns of the Lord's plans to deliver the exiles (2:2–3:12, 14, 24; 11:5-12). Ezekiel, however, also holds out hope that the renewed nation will receive the spirit of the Lord so that they may "follow my statutes and be careful to observe my ordinances" (36:27). The well-known passage from Joel echoes this by promising "I will pour out my spirit on all flesh" (2:28-29).

Turning to the NT, the positive theme of spiritual influence continues and broadens, in line with the expectancy of Joel and Ezekiel. But there is a clearer awareness and acceptance of negative spiritual influences. This development takes place in the intertestamental period, when apocalyptic thinking gains a strong foothold within Judaism [Apocalypticism, p. 301].

All four Gospel writers testify that from the beginning of his ministry Jesus is imbued by the Holy Spirit. This occurs at his baptism

(Mark 1:9-11//Matt 3:13-17//Luke 3:21-22//John 1:29-34). The synoptic writers develop this imagery further by depicting Jesus' wilderness testing of the Spirit's empowerment for his ministry (Mark 1:12-13//Matt 4:1-11//Luke 4:1-13). Luke, who has a strong sense of the Spirit's role, tells us that in his "inaugural address" Jesus quoted, with some modification, Isaiah 61:1-2a. Further evidence of Luke's conviction regarding the Spirit's influence occurs before Jesus is fully grown. Simeon, who longs for the "consolation of Israel," is told by the Spirit that he would see this (Luke 2:25-26), and the same Spirit "guided" him to the temple to observe Jesus' dedication (2:27).

Not surprisingly, since Jesus' ministry is carried out in the Spirit's power, he is repeatedly depicted as confronting "unclean spirits." Mark reports Jesus' first miracle as a confrontation with an "unclean spirit" possessing a man whom Jesus meets in a synagogue (Mark 1:21-28; Luke 4:31-37). After his transfiguration he cures a young man who is tormented by a spirit (Mark 9:14-29). Additionally, Luke includes summary statements leading us to conclude that Jesus regularly confronted and overcame evil spirits that plagued people (4:36; 6:18; 7:21; 8:1-3).

Both Johannine and Lucan theology envision the Spirit's work continuing after Jesus' death and as a key element of the church's success. Jesus' farewell discourse (John 13–17) makes repeated reference to the coming of the Paraclete and its role in believers' lives. These functions include teaching and reminding believers what Jesus taught (14:25-31), testifying to the world (15:26), proving the world wrong (16:7-11), and guiding believers into all truth (16:12-14).

Luke constructs Acts as an intentional parallel to his Gospel. In Acts 1:8 Jesus promises the believers they "will receive power when the Holy Spirit has come upon you; and you will be my witnesses in Jerusalem, in all Judea and Samaria, and to the ends of the earth." As promised, at Pentecost, the early believers were filled with the Spirit (2:1) and began to speak as the Spirit led them (2:4). Most believers cooperated with the Spirit's leading. Stephen, who is described as "a man full of faith and the Holy Spirit," becomes the first martyr (6:1–8:1a). Philip proclaims the gospel and cures people afflicted by evil spirits and, through the Spirit's leadership, witnesses to the Ethiopian eunuch (8:4-40, esp. vv. 29-39). Peter, led by the Spirit, approaches the Gentile Cornelius with the gospel (10:1–11:18, esp. 10:19; 11:12). In Acts 16:6-10 the Holy Spirit directs Paul's travels by obstructing his desire to go into Asia and instead sends him to Macedonia. And believers in Tyre, acting under the Spirit's influence, ask Paul to not travel to Jerusalem because they see danger awaiting him there (21:1-6).

We should not conclude that the first Christians experienced only the positive ministry of the Holy Spirit. They knew it was possible to resist the Spirit and align with anti-God forces. According to Acts such behavior manifested itself during the church's early days. In Acts 5 Ananias and Sapphira "agreed together to put the Spirit of the Lord to the test" (v. 9). Under the influence of Satan, they conspired to withhold and lie about financial proceeds from the sale of property. Additionally, as noted above, letters in the Pauline tradition accept a realm of spiritual powers that negatively impact human lives (Eph 1:21; 3:10; 6:12; Col 1:16; 2:15; 1 Tim 4:1-2). In fact, in Romans 8 Paul develops a detailed argument regarding the spiritual life with the opposition between "flesh" and "spirit" (cf. 1 Cor 2:6-16 and his similar arguments in Gal 3:1-5; 5:16-26).

Particularly problematic for Paul was the congregation at Corinth. In his first letter to the Corinthians, he seeks to clarify a Christian understanding of "spiritual gifts" (12:1-31). Apparently some members under the influence of a spirit other than the Holy Spirit had been uttering confessions that directly opposed those given by the Holy Spirit (12:3). He returns to this theme in his second letter to them: "But I am afraid that as the serpent deceived Eve, . . . your thoughts will be led astray from a sincere and pure devotion to Christ. For if someone comes and proclaims another Jesus than the one we proclaimed, or if you receive a different spirit from the one you received, . . . you submit to it readily enough" (2 Cor 11:3-4).

THE TEXT IN THE LIFE OF THE CHURCH

Christology

From the church's beginning, Christians have believed Jesus was and is the *pivotal* figure for human salvation. It is relatively easy to make broad statements and affirm "mystery" on some points. The challenge comes when we attempt to be more specific or when we undertake the task of communicating the gospel to a new culture. Thus it should not be surprising that Christians have wrestled with how to understand who Jesus was, what he did, and what he is for us today. Frequently the church decided that some views were unacceptable.

Often the fault lines related to his human and divine nature. Gnostic sects argued that Jesus was one of the many lesser gods (see Martin: 289-90), and Docetics believed that Jesus only appeared to be human. The Ebionites, on the other hand, argued that Jesus was simply a human being who benefited from the Spirit's presence that came upon him at his baptism. These christological issues were not resolved in the first century. For example, Augustine (354-430), who was a Manichaean before his conversion, wrote against the Manichaeans, a serious fourth-century threat to the Christian faith. Mani had grown up in a Jewish-Christian sect, but he began his own group after receiving revelations about releasing the soul from bondage to the body. Although Mani called himself an apostle of Jesus Christ, his Christology was unacceptable to many mainstream Christians, including Augustine.

With these and numerous other christological and theological issues articulated during the first few centuries, it is understandable that eventually the church decided to standardize its doctrine. Two important councils were convened and included christological agendas. In AD 325, the Council of Nicaea affirmed God's presence in Jesus. Jesus was not a subordinate divine being; rather, he was "the only-begotten Son of God, begotten of his Father before all worlds, God of Gods, Light of Light, God of God, begotten, not made, being of one substance with the Father" (Nicene Creed, in Church of England: 213). This council affirmed Jesus' divine nature. Then in 451 the Council of Chalcedon declared Jesus to be both God and human, "consisting of a reasonable soul and body; of one substance with the Father as regards his Godhead, of one substance with us as regards his manhood," with two natures but "without confusion, without change, without division, or without separation; the distinction of natures being in no way abolished because of the union" (via Dowley: 175). These "official" pronouncements, however, did not put an end to the divergent views. For example, in the twelfth and thirteenth centuries a group called the Cathars, or Albigensians, taught that Jesus was the son of the good god who created the spiritual world. He was a living spirit that only appeared to be human; while they accepted some NT doctrines, they rejected the incarnation.

The early Anabaptists tended to affirm traditional Christology. Hubmaier, in the preface to *A Christian Catechism*, writes, "Grace and peace in Christ Jesus, our only Savior, to whom be praise, thanks, honor, and glory forever and ever, that he so graciously, without any merit on our part, entered our tossing boat with us poor miserable and powerless humans" (Pipkin and Yoder: 340). The catechism itself further affirms that we know God's mercy by God's "sending his only-begotten Son, our Lord Jesus Christ, into this world that it may not be lost because of sin, but through him attain to eternal life" (345).

Menno Simons repeatedly addressed the issue of Christology. He generally shows himself to be doctrinally "sound" and usually biblical in his argumentation. This is true whether he is writing a pastoral letter regarding christological error ("Doctrinal Letter to the Church in Groningen," 1550) or responding to his opponents' accusations (*The Incarnation of Our Lord*, 1554). In his *Reply to Martin Micron* (1556), he writes,

> Our position is . . . that the whole Christ Jesus . . . is the first- and only-begotten Son of God, as . . . all the Scriptures confess him to be; that He is the incomprehensible, eternal Word by which all things are created, supernaturally come from heaven. We hold that by the power of the Holy Ghost He became man in the Virgin Mary, . . . a true man, like unto us poor children of Adam in all things, sin excepted. He hungered and ate, thirsted and drank, became tired and rested. He was fashioned in the likeness of men. . . . At the last He died the bitter death innocently for us who are guilty. . . . He has purchased, sanctified, and cleansed us by His own blood and not by the blood of another; He has reconciled us with God. . . . He was delivered and raised from the bonds of death and ascended to His Father where he was before." (Wenger: 884)

As Gertrude Roten says, the life and death of Jesus is at the heart of 1 John 4:1-6. The incarnation is of crucial significance for John and other NT writers. As God in human form, Jesus reveals God's love for humankind and divine expectations for us: "Jesus lifted our sights, compelling us to obey and follow him" (Roten: 139). Furthermore, his human existence encourages us to attempt a way of life that we might otherwise conclude is impossible. Through his death salvation is extended to us. Despite his innocence he died the death that we all must die. In that death God and humankind met and were reconciled. This is a glorious mystery that theologians must try to explain and writers of confessions desire to affirm. Ultimately the incarnation is an incomprehensible mystery. It is a matter of faith, which only the Spirit can move us to embrace.

Discerning Spiritual Claims

For some this passage may trigger recollections of painful church arguments over spiritual issues. For thirty or more years the church has experienced what can be described as Pentecostal or charismatic renewal. There has been an interest in the Holy Spirit's work not only in traditional Pentecostal denominations, such as the Assemblies of God, but also in hierarchical groups, such as the Roman Catholic and Episcopal churches, as well as among free-church groups, including Mennonites and other groups of Anabaptist descent. In reality this modern emphasis on the Spirit is much older than three or four decades. James Dunn traces the development through the American Holiness movement and back to John Wesley, whom he describes as "the great-grand father of Pentecostalism" (via Dowley: 618). A key

Pentecostal turning point was the Azusa Street Revival, which began in Los Angeles. The revival lasted three years (1906-09), and eventually people from around the globe visited the meetings and then took the experience and teachings home. Today Pentecostalism's influence can be seen around the world, but it is especially widespread in Africa and Latin America.

The movement stresses the Holy Spirit's present activity in the believer's life through spiritual gifts, such as speaking in tongues, healings, prophetic utterances, and ecstatic forms of worship. There can be no doubt that generally these brothers and sisters are a genuine gift to the church. Every movement, however, has a fringe that can be described as bizarre or even dangerous. I know of one Pentecostal person who makes "unusual" prophetic utterances, saying that God wants church members to replace major kitchen appliances. At the other extreme, many of us have seen news reports of children dying because their Pentecostal parents refuse medical treatment, believing that the child has been healed of a serious disease. How does one wisely discern between the good, the bad, and the silly that is attributed to the Spirit's work?

This challenge is not new. Late in the second century a group called the Montanists arose within the church. A Phrygian named Montanus claimed to speak for the Paraclete. Assisted by Prisca and Maximilla, two prophetesses, they claimed to offer Christians a "New Prophecy" through visions, speaking in tongues, and intense religious experiences. Their teachings included advocating boldness in faith matters, extreme asceticism, and seeking out persecution, even to the point of martyrdom. They initially enjoyed a high degree of success, and among their converts was a respected early church leader named Tertullian. Eventually the larger church determined that their ministry was not a valid expression of the Spirit.

Beyond the historical dimension of dubious claims to the Spirit's influence is belief in the actual existence of spirits *of error*, as John describes them (1 John 4:6). During the 1970s Hollywood made the devil a source of entertainment with the production of films like *Rosemary's Baby*, *Omen*, and *The Exorcist*. Not everyone assumed that these films merely entertained. A 1989 survey of Anabaptist groups revealed that 90 percent of those interviewed believed in "an active personal devil" (Kauffman and Drieger: 69). When the same survey was administered again in 2006, that belief had dropped to 82 percent (email report by John Eby 2010; data not included in Kanagy's book). In the Western world there is a growing interest in the occult, as anyone can see by entering a major bookstore. The chains have well-stocked sections on the subject. In 1987 a consultation on "Bondage and Deliverance" was held at Associated Mennonite Biblical Seminaries, where scholars, pastors, laity, and mental health professionals discussed the subject. One of the Findings Committee's general observations is telling:

> We note high interest and concern in relation to this subject. This is reflected in the unexpected number of participants in this consultation. In the paganized society of North America we increasingly find ourselves in a missionary context, including the spread of the occult, which may call for a "crisis intervention" type of deliverance ministry. With the Charismatic movement's reemphasis on the Holy Spirit has come a greater awareness of the spirit world, including evil spirits. The inadequacy of the modern scientific models and of traditional understandings of the demonic push us to seek new models of understanding that integrate the material, social, and spiritual dimensions of life. We have noted that an existential hunger for that which transcends our mechanistic existence is being expressed both inside and outside of the church. (Swartley 1988: 211)

A follow-up consultation, "Hard Cases: Confronting the Spirit World," was sponsored by The Institute of Mennonite Studies in April 2004. The papers and case studies from that gathering can be found in *Even the Demons Submit* (Johns and Krabill 2006).

Even if we are hesitant to accept the Johannine perspective including the existence of spirits seeking to influence humans, we should thoughtfully consider the influence and perhaps even the *spirit of error* that we face from society. Some of these influences can be described as anti-God. All one needs do is watch television for one evening. We are repeatedly bombarded by commercials selling us products to make us look good, alter our moods, increase our social status or sexual satisfaction, and simply help us fit in with social expectations. Often the selling point is nothing better than "you deserve it." Can we not conclude that such conspicuous consumption and self-centeredness is anti-gospel?

Regardless of how we understand the influences we face, we need to recognize that there are forces that run counter to the life and teachings of Jesus Christ. To submit to these influences is to annul the Lord's validity. Given this reality, the church needs to take seriously John's advice to *test the spirits* and to use Jesus as the standard by which we determine the value of those other voices. John envisions this as a realistic possibility for any community that is sensitive to the Holy Spirit's promptings. We should not assume, however, that such undertakings of discernment are easy. We live in a complex world, and we are not infallible. In our zeal to be faithful to Christ, we may make grievous errors of judgment. Perhaps this is why the next unit (4:7–5:4a) focuses on another crucial benefit of being influenced by the Holy Spirit: the power to *love one another*.

1 John 4:7–5:4a

Love and the Spirit

PREVIEW

In 1992-93 my family lived in Nairobi, Kenya, while I taught at a Christian college in the city. I regularly attended chapel and quickly noticed that songs were sung with great conviction. They were also repeated—a lot! The same stanzas and choruses would be repeated over and over. I asked why this was so. The answer: "Repeating is good." I was not in tune with this aspect of the culture.

This unit once again addresses the subject of love. Like a Westerner in an African worship service, we are tempted to say, "Again!" This topic was a crucial element in 2:7-11 and 3:11-24. We must recognize, however, the centrality of *love* in this passage: the verb *to love* (*agapaō*) is used twenty-eight times in 1 John, and eighteen of those occurrences are in this unit. Additionally, the noun *love* (*agapē*) is employed thirteen times here, with an additional five occurrences in the rest of the letter. Clearly, *love* is a central theme in these verses. The question then becomes: what is "new" that warrants such a concentrated focus on *love*, despite John's having already addressed the subject twice?

Love, however, is not the only subject in this unit that occurred before. In 4:10 Jesus is *the atoning sacrifice for our sins*, reaffirming what we read in 2:2. The themes of *knowing* and *abiding* have already appeared in 2:3-14, 18-21; 2:24-27, and they reappear in 4:13-16. The idea of confidence or boldness on the judgment day is found in 2:28 and 4:17. While the commandment to love is addressed in 4:21, it has also been mentioned in 2:7-11 and 3:23. Additionally, this unit makes polemical arguments against the secessionists, calling them *liars*, just as in 2:4. Finally, doing *right*—loving one's brothers and sisters—is evidence of being God's child (2:29–3:10 and 5:1-4a).

Numerous scholars observe that what is new in this unit is John's attempt to tie together his christological and ethical concerns in an even more intentional fashion. There is no doubt that this is the case. As he nears the letter's end, he offers one more exposition of how theology and ethics are drawn together. Thus in one sense this unit might be viewed as the author's argumentative climax.

There is, however, more than renewed and intensified effort to wed these themes. The unit's argument falls into three stages: the author identifies love's source and purpose (4:7-11), he then further explores the theme of love and draws implications from it (4:12-19), and finally love is identified as a context for his polemic against the secessionists (4:20–5:4a). In this first subunit, John points to God as the source of love (4:7a and 8b) and rather typically declares that having or not having love (4:7b-8a) presents us with a duality:

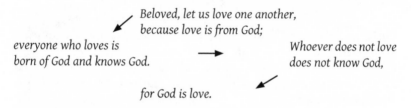

He also argues that the incarnation reveals God's love for us and ought to spur us on to love one another.

In the second subunit, John explicitly (4:13) introduces the theme of the *Spirit*. This idea was hinted at in 4:7 and will be addressed in 5:1 by his use of the phrase *born of God*. This subunit is organized around two assumptions. First, it is the Spirit that keeps the believer connected to (*abiding in*) God (4:13-16). The second assumption is that the Spirit's empowerment to love results in the believer's confidence on the day of judgment (4:17-19). Finally, he closes the unit with a strong polemic against the secessionists' using love as the ironic measure of one's faithfulness (4:20–5:4).

OUTLINE

The Source and Purpose of Love, 4:7-11
Further Exploration and Implications of This Love, 4:12-19
Polemic Against the Separatists in Light of Love, 4:20–5:4a

EXPLANATORY NOTES

The Source and Purpose of Love 4:7-11

This first subunit puts forth the basic concepts that will be explored in the larger unit: God is the source of love, and believers are to love one another. In fact, this segment begins and ends with these two points (vv. 7a, 11). Additionally, both verses begin with the word *beloved*. It is a term that the author uses six times, initially in 2:7, when he offers pastoral encouragement.

As one reads 4:7–5:4a, one notes much theological development and exploration, and there is even development within the opening verses, as we see when comparing 4:7a and 4:11:

Beloved, let us love one another, because love is from God. (v. 7a)
Beloved, since God loved us so much, we also ought to love one another. (v. 11)

The first line simply encourages love within the fellowship since love is from God. There has been some thought development, however. By the time we read the second line, John concludes that in light of the magnitude of God's love, believers *ought* to love one another. The point is not a matter of obligation to love or merely following rules. The sense behind the word *ought* (*opheilomen*) is that this love should naturally manifest itself within the fellowship. Such love is a natural response to God's example. He uses this expression in 1 John 3:16, and it is employed in John 13:14 as well. In these instances the believer is encouraged to imitate Jesus' behavior.

We must, however, be quite careful when talking about love and how it "naturally" manifests itself. There are different types of love. Even the world loves, but its love is not the love that the author has in mind here. In John 15:19 we read, "If you belonged to the world, the world would love you as its own." The Greek verb describing the world's love is *phileō* (extending general friendship). John, on the other hand, uses the verb *agapaō* and the related noun *agapē* to describe God's love and the love Christians are to embody (though in the Gospel *phileō* and *agapaō* overlap; both describe similar relationships). Clearly John envisions different kinds of love, and this raises two questions: How do flawed humans begin to manifest God's type of love? What is the nature of this divine love? Both questions are answered in 4:7b-10.

John's dualist worldview is apparent in 4:7b-8a. Some people love and know God, and others do not love or know God. This is duality in the moral sense, but here it is rooted in being, an ontological sense of a special sort (see "Duality" in the Introduction and [Duality in the Epistles, p. 304]). The difference, according to 4:7b, is whether or not one is born of God. Those who love and know God are born of God. This expression is found in the letter at six places (twice in 3:9; 4:7; 5:1, 4, 18) in two similar forms. Additionally, in 2:29 we have already seen the expression everyone who does right has been born of him. In 5:18 we will read, But the one who was born of God protects them [believers].

The unwritten assumption behind born of God is found in the Johannine tradition. In John 1:12-13 we read, "But to all who received him, who believed in his name, he gave power to become children of God, who were born, not of blood or of the will of the flesh or of the will of man, but of God." This assertion is further clarified by the conversation between Jesus and Nicodemus in John 3. The birth that the Johannine community expects is a spiritual birth "from above" (3:3). In fact, membership in God's kingdom comes through "being born of water and Spirit" (3:5), and "what is born of the Spirit is spirit" (3:6). In 1 John the author concludes that this birth results in both loving and knowing God. Conversely, the author makes a not-so-subtle jab at the secessionists in 4:8a when he suggests that anyone who does not love, as the author understands it, shows that they do not know God. Ultimately the separatists cannot know God, whose primary essence is love (4:8b), because they do not love as God loves. Rather, they love as the world loves because they have not been born of God.

In 4:9-10 John qualifies the nature of this love and how it is that humans can love as God does. Our author believes that this divine love is revealed in the incarnation. John recognizes the utter uniqueness of this event when he describes Jesus as God's only Son (monogenēs). While the incarnation of God's only Son is unique, at some level the author assumes that all believers share child-of-God status with God's only Son (cf. 3:1). In fact, the true nature of God's love was revealed (see comments on 1:2 above) in that he sent his Son so that we might live through him. In Johannine theology, God's love moves God to send his Son in order that humanity might have life through Christ by being born of God. This birth is the foundation and source of this unique love that believers are to embody. God acts lovingly in accordance with the divine nature, and humans are born to new life, which naturally results in both love and knowing God. This love is concretely manifested when believers love one another, which is love's logical conclusion.

Finally, 4:10 provides a crucial qualifier regarding this love that is the focus of the segment. The author does not envision just any manifestation of human love. The love he has in mind is not a generic love that the average human can muster for God. Rather, this love begins with God's love for humanity: *In this is love, not that we loved God but that he loved us.* The author points to a specific event that displays God's love: *[God] sent his Son to be the atoning sacrifice for our sins.* (On John's understanding of Jesus as *atoning sacrifice for our sins,* see comments on 2:1-2 above.) It is the sacrificial death of Christ that reveals the depth and breadth of God's love (4:11).

These verses set out the basic assumptions behind the entire unit. God's basic attribute is love. That love was graciously directed toward humanity in the incarnation and specifically in Jesus' death on the cross. Through this unique event, God offers new life and release from sins. All who accept this love and new life are born of God (through the Spirit) and become God's children. They in turn, as God's children, are to respond to God's action by loving others, just as God loves.

Further Exploration and Implications of This Love 4:12-19

This subunit begins and ends with comments about this love and its source: *God.* Verse 12 serves as a transition to this unit because it moves forward the author's thought in verse 11. The core of the subunit is organized around the twice-repeated expression *by this* (*en toutō*) in verses 13 and 17. The first theme focuses on the believers' abiding in God via the Spirit and the second theme is the believers' confidence in light of the love they embody. This subunit builds upon the assumption that being born of God results in both loving and knowing God, and it further builds upon the incarnational motif in 4:9-10.

We ended the previous subunit with the conclusion *Beloved, since God loved us so much, we also ought to love one another* (4:11). While that affirmation provides a clean closure to the unit which began with the encouragement to love because love is from God, some may ask, "Why? What will this love reveal?" The author is firmly committed to a theology that relies on imitation or embodiment of the divine nature. We have seen this in 1:5-7 and 2:28–3:10, and just a few verses earlier we are told that God's love was revealed through the incarnation of his only Son (4:9-10).

As John points out, God is invisible and has never been seen. Moreover, the *only Son* is no longer on earth. God, however, is not without a witness. If those who are *born of God* (4:7) *love one another* (4:12), God is present and *his love is perfected in us.* In other words, when believers love one another, God's love is tangibly evident; therefore, God can be seen in the midst of human interactions. When the author talks about divine love's being perfected among believers, he is not suggesting that God's love is imperfect without us. Rather, the word used in verse 12 is *teleioō*. It does not refer to imperfection: instead, it suggests a sense of direction, completion, or achieving a goal. As Howard Marshall (217) states, "When we love others, God's love for us has reached its full effect in creating the same kind of love as his in us." John advocates a practical faith, not an abstraction, as do the secessionists. John's faith recognizes God as the source of love revealed through Jesus Christ, and this love is expressed in the loving acts of Christ's followers for each other. This embodiment has two specific implications for believers.

First, the author reintroduces themes that we have already seen in 3:23-24: belief in Jesus Christ, love for one another, and divine/human unity via the Spirit. In chapter 4, however, the order differs, with verse 13 addressing the Spirit, verses 14-15 focusing on the Christian confession of Christ, and verse 16 highlighting love. The author is trying to provide a linear connection among the three topics suggested in the opening line: *By this [en toutō] we know that we abide in him and he in us* (v. 13). Thus this subunit is designed to provide the reader with three assurances of mutual divine/human indwelling (Rensberger: 119).

To be sure, 4:13 is virtually identical to 3:24b; but the differences, although slight, are significant. In 3:24b we read *that he abides in us*; here in 4:13 John envisions mutual indwelling between God and the believing community: *We abide in him and he in us*. We assume that God is the one who is abiding in believers because this verse naturally flows from verse 12, where God is clearly identified. Second, in 3:24b the verb *give* is in the past (aorist) tense, meaning that the Spirit was given at a particular point. Here the perfect tense occurs, suggesting that the giving of the Spirit, once given, has an enduring effect, for both abiding and loving. Finally, here the Spirit is more specifically identified as *his Spirit* rather than simply *the Spirit* in 3:24b. Thus 4:13 is a further refinement of the author's thinking in 3:24b. The first evidence that John's community not only knows God, but also abides in God, is that God has given them *his Spirit*, and that presence is continuous.

The presence of the Spirit gives rise to a second evidence of the community's true faith: confession and testimony, noted in verses 14-15. This second point begins with the emphatic *kai hēmeis*, which the NRSV understates as *And we*. A more accurate nuance might be *As for us, we . . . ,*" indicating distinction of *we* from others (AT). This same expression is used in verse 16, where the author emphasizes the community's awareness of the love that God has for them. The presence of this emphatic expression likely is intentionally employed to remind the readers how they differ from the separatists.

John's community certainly has a different view of Jesus than do the secessionists. They have accepted the traditional teaching initially referenced in 1:1-4, and here we are told, *The Father has sent his Son as the Savior of the world*. In the entire NT, Jesus is described as *the Savior of the world* only here and in John 4:42, even though Luke is the Gospel that most often ascribes to Jesus the title "Savior." This specific note in 4:14 is probably John's attempt to add a particular element to his assertion in 3:23, where he does not specify what one is to believe when reminding his audience that *we should believe in the name of his Son Jesus Christ*.

Although verse 15 is a follow-up conclusion to verse 14, it actually appeals to an argument that the author makes in 4:1-2. There John encouraged his readers to *test the spirits to see whether they are from God* (4:1). Any *spirit that confesses that Jesus Christ has come in the flesh is from God* (4:2). Verses 14 and 15 build on this simple test. The Spirit mentioned in 4:13 enables believers to both testify to the incarnation (1:1-4; 4:14) as well as confess that Jesus is the Son of God (4:15). To do so is the second piece of evidence supporting the mutual indwelling between God and John's faith community. Additionally, this particular confession sets them apart from the secessionists.

The final evidence of the community's separation from the secessionists and their error is found in verse 16: believers *have known and believe the love that God has for us*. As noted above, this verse begins with the emphatic *kai hēmeis*, or *As for us, <u>we</u>*, thus implying that their opponents do not know or believe. John's use of verb tense for *know* and *believe* is perfect, and the expression should be translated, *We have come to know and believe and still know and believe*. Likely this is a subtle jab at their opponents, who have stopped believing. What the community still knows and believes is *the love that God has for us*. The verb *has* is in the present tense, which communicates duration (Haas, de Jonge, and Swellengrebel: 127). What is more difficult to determine is John's intention when he writes *for us (en hēmin)*. The NRSV translation gives the impression that God has love *toward* us, but the literal translation is *in us*. David Rensberger (121) rightly suggests that John is probably trying to highlight the love that is "in our midst." Verse 16a then would read, *As for us, we have known and believe and still know and believe the love that God has in our midst*.

Verse 16b is a parallel to verse 15. John concludes this third argument by reaffirming a point from 4:8: *God is love*. Anyone who abides in love, as do his readers who have God's love in their midst (16a), logically therefore abide in God and God in them. The reasoning is simple and straightforward. With verse 16 the first implication draws to a close. Between verses 13 and 16 the author offers three evidences that his community *abide[s] in him and he in us* (v. 13). Foundationally, they have been given the Spirit, which enables them to testify and confess that Jesus is the Son of God and manifests God's love in their midst.

The author's pastoral concerns move to the foreground in the next three verses (4:17-19), when he addresses the second implication of this love: believers have confidence. In the Greek the second and final thought of this subunit is signaled by the expression *in this* (*en toutō*). His argument moves one step further. All that is mentioned in 4:13-16 functions as the foundation for his belief that believers have *boldness on the day of judgment* (4:17).

Verse 17 puts forth the claim that admittedly is couched in a rather awkward fashion, but the point is clear. The love that the community expresses is the divine love that Christ expressed on earth. Thus they are in the world the same way *he* (*ekeinos, that one*) was in the world. In 1 John *ekeinos* always refers to Jesus (see comments on 2:4-6). The end result of their imitating Jesus Christ at this point is *boldness* or complete confidence on the *day of judgment.* If they have aligned themselves with Jesus in their daily affairs by loving as he loved, there is no reason to be concerned when he returns. John believed that Jesus would return for a day of reckoning, as already mentioned in 2:28-29 (cf. John 5:22, 27). The source of confidence is not that the believers' love is *perfect,* as in "flawless." Rather, as said in 4:12, when the author uses the word *teleioō,* he envisions a love that has arrived at its final destination: the lives of believers. Their complete confidence will be because they embrace Jesus Christ's love and give it a home in their community. Furthermore, their *perfect* love parallels the love between God and Jesus (cf. John 14:10; 15:9-10; 17:11, 15-16, 21-23).

In this kind of life there can be no fear or, more specifically, fear of judgment that results in punishment. The Greek wording behind *Fear has to do with punishment* (1 John 4:18) is another example of the author's obscure use of Greek. Literally, it reads, *Fear has punishment.* He is saying that fear is the sign of one's awareness of failure, and failure results in punishment. This was a theme in early Christian eschatological thought (cf. Matt 25:1-46; 2 Pet 2:9). John's community, however, has not failed to love; rather, they have embodied and imitated Jesus on this point. Hence there are neither grounds for punishment nor reason to fear.

Ultimately, 1 John 4:18 argues that the love given the community is a powerful antidote to self-doubt and uncertainty regarding their standing before God. In fact, the author strongly makes this point in the opening phrase, *Perfect love casts out fear*. The Greek phrasing emphatically stresses the nature of the casting out. He assumes that their love has utterly and totally removed the grounds for fear, and that is why he can close the verse with the words *Whoever fears has not reached perfection in love*. He knows that they have *reached* this *perfection*; therefore they have no reason to fear.

Numerous commentators point out that verse 19 looks back to or repeats the theme of previous verses, such as 4:7 and 11. It does, in fact, build upon a previous verse: 4:12. These two verses complement each other. Verse 12 begins the line of argumentation with a conditional clause: *If we love one another, God lives in us*. Then, in 4:19, after the author's long argumentation, he concludes, *We love*.

Granted, in 4:19 the Greek verb *agapōmen* could be either indicative (*We love*) or subjunctive (*We ought to love*). We best view it as the former, as do the translators of the NRSV, NIV, and RSV. Given all that the author has said to this point, including his pastoral encouragement on the correctness of his readers' understanding of the faith, it is difficult to imagine that he would intentionally call into question the validity of the community's love. Instead, he probably wants to affirm that they do love; and therefore they abide in God and God in them (4:13). Moreover, he tells them that the love they have is a response to God, who initiated this love *because he first loved us*. This affirmation probably harks back to his argument in 4:9-10, which cites the sending of Christ into the world and the affirmation of God's love shown in sending *his Son as an atoning sacrifice*.

This verse may also serve as a transition to the next unit. It seems to contain an initial punch at the community's theological opponents, who clearly become the focus of the next subunit (4:20–5:4a). John views his theology and ethics as having a divine source; but as we have repeatedly seen, he expresses serious doubts about the secessionists' theology and ethics. This contrast is highlighted when we compare *We* (*hēmeis*) *love* in verse 19 with *Those who say, "I love God" and hate their brothers or sisters* (v. 20). One group successfully embodies God's love; the other group merely claims to love God. We turn now to John's polemic in 4:20–5:4a.

Polemic Against the Separatists in Light of Love 4:20–5:4a

In this third and final subunit of this section, John returns his attention to the separatists. His polemic is both ethical and theological.

In 4:20-21 he offers an ethical argument based on love, and in 5:1-4a his polemic is a theologically informed love ethic. Additionally, the author is probably citing the separatists' argument and behavior when he writes, *Those who say, "I love God," and hate their brothers or sisters*. . . . He has used a similar polemical approach in 1:5–2:17. In 4:20-21 the charge of lying while disobeying the commandment to love echoes 2:4.

The author's closing polemic is more precise than his earlier argument. For 4:20 employs an ancient argumentation moving from the "lesser to greater" elements (Rensberger: 126). It is difficult to assess one's love for God, who is unseen. But we can observe how one interacts with one's fellow human beings. If one does not love a brother or sister, who can be seen, it is unlikely that person can love God, whom they cannot see.

This line of argumentation is augmented by the citation of the commandment in 4:21: *Those who love God must love their brothers and sisters also*. Although John may simply be citing the Johannine Last Supper tradition (John 13:34; 14:15; 15:12, 17), the specific connection of love for God and love for brother and sister is more likely a reference to Jesus' teaching on the greatest commandment (Mark 12:28-34; Matt 22:34-40; Luke 10:25-28). Love for God cannot be separated from love for other humans, as the secessionists are apparently doing. What John has done in this closing polemic is to clearly identify the vague commandment referenced earlier in 2:3-4.

Thus in 4:20-21 John sets up the separatists for his final polemic in 5:1-4a. He has specifically declared that, despite their claims to love God, they follow a flawed love ethic. Their flaw is their failure to love other Christians as well as loving God. In 4:21, however, John introduces their fundamental error: they have ignored the teaching of the tradition and God's commandment in Christ. As John will argue in 5:1-4a, this failure to follow Christ's commandment goes back to the secessionists' erroneous Christology.

John's argument in 5:1-4a, however, presents the reader with challenges. There is much debate regarding what John has in mind when he writes, <u>By this</u> we know that we love the children of God (5:2). Is he referring to a previous thought or to one that follows the phrase *by this*? Colin Kruse (172) believes that here the author's thinking "appears to go in a circle." In a sense Kruse is correct; but the author is not employing circular reasoning. Rather, he is returning to a number of the fundamental points that he has already made in the letter. Among these are the importance of our status as God's children once we have been *born of God* (5:1, 4a), the importance of obeying the com-

mandments we have been given (5:2-3), and, above all, believing *that Jesus is the Christ* (5:1), which is foundational to the other two points. Perhaps John intends ambiguity by writing *By this* in 5:2. He has already asserted and reasserted his basic points. In 5:1-4 his concern for correct Christology, Christ's commandment to love, and moral evidence of one's status as God's children blend together. These points occur throughout these four verses. So does *By this* refer to concepts before or after 5:2? The answer is "both before and after."

From the beginning (1:1-4) and various points along the way (1:7; 2:2, 22-24; 3:8; 4:9-10, 15), John has argued for a particular Christology: *Jesus is the Christ* (5:1) who has come in the flesh, and how one responds to this theology determines one's relational status with God. Whoever believes this Christology is then aligned with God, has been born of the Spirit, and *know[s] the spirit of truth* (4:6). Whoever denies the incarnation and its revelation does not love God and instead has *the spirit of the antichrist* (4:3-4). That sound incarnational Christology is important to John is evident by the fact that he will explore this theme in detail in 5:5-12.

John, however, is not willing to stress only abstract orthodox Christology. This is primarily due to the fact that his Christology draws upon actual historical events and impacts anyone who accepts that Christology. Initially, to accept traditional Johannine Christology alters one's status before God. Whoever believes that *Jesus is the Christ* then is *born of God* (5:1b) and becomes one with God's many children. If one moves into the family of God, one accepts the basic two-pronged commandment that Christ taught: love God and love the children of God (5:1c). Loving God, which the separatists are willing to do, also involves accepting Jesus Christ, God's Son, and his demand to love others (5:1c), which John believes the separatists are unwilling to do. As John says in 5:3, authentic love for God involves obedience to his commandments, in particular, the love command as revealed by Jesus, the incarnate Son.

Finally, in 5:3b, John may be challenging a common assumption held in the separatists' camp, that the commandments of Jesus are burdensome. John counters this opinion: viewing the commands as a burden is simply untrue. Back in 2:17 he wrote that the world is *passing away*, but anyone who does God's will lives forever. Thus one's obeying the commandments results in one's overcoming the world. That conviction is reiterated in another fashion when the author writes, *For whatever is born of God conquers the world* (5:4a). Specifically, it is *our faith* (5:4b) that provides the victory. In the next unit, John describes the content of this conquering faith, but he has already hinted at its substance in 5:1.

THE TEXT IN BIBLICAL CONTEXT

Theology, Experience, and Daily Living

One of John's fundamental assumptions moves front and center in his argument found in 4:7–5:4a. The events of our daily living are to be shaped and informed by our theology and religious experience. In John's worldview there is no place for separating our theological reflection from our personal or social ethics. Additionally, if one has experienced divine grace, one's life will reflect this in interactions with others. Our author is not alone in this belief. He has certainly inherited this from the larger Johannine tradition, though the apostle Paul also accepts this basic conviction, as does Israel's earliest experience.

Early in the Gospel of John, religious experience is stressed. In the opening chapter we read, "But to all who received him, who believed in his name, he gave power to become children of God, who were born, not of blood or of the will of the flesh or of the will of man, but of God" (1:12-13). John's core conviction of the importance of religious experience in forming and re-forming us is encapsulated in the third chapter. There Jesus forthrightly declares to Nicodemus, "I tell you, no one can see the kingdom of God without being born from above" (3:3).

John, however, is not solely concerned about religious experience. The two passages cited above are found in the larger context of his argument for a particular theology. The Gospel's first chapter is rife with incarnational Christology. The Word that was with God from eternity (1:1-2) is the source of life that is the light of all people (1:4). Moreover, that Word was incarnate in the midst of humans (1:10, 14). In his prologue, John organizes his Gospel in such a way as to highlight Jesus, the incarnate Word, distinguishing him from another important first-century Jewish religious figure: John the Baptist. The Gospel writer does not want his readers to confuse Jesus' and John's significance. Jesus, the Word, is much more important than John the Baptist, who is unworthy to untie Jesus' sandals (1:27). The Baptist identifies Jesus as "the Lamb of God" in 1:29, 36. In 3:27-30 John is portrayed as "friend of the bridegroom," standing at Jesus' side for the wedding that the Gospel announces—and because of this, John's "joy" is "fulfilled." In 5:33 John's witness is adduced as confirming Jesus' claims about himself. John's important role as witness is reaffirmed in 10:40-41, near the end of Jesus' public ministry.

In the rest of the book, Jesus is repeatedly contrasted with the Jewish teachers and traditions. Whereas Moses gave the law, Jesus is the source of "grace and truth" (1:17) and reveals God (1:18). He is contrasted with various festivals and is depicted as the true embodiment of these traditions (2:12-23; 6:4-14; 7:2-24, 37-38; 8:12; 10:22-39); he claims to be greater than Abraham (8:48-59); and he is Israel's true king (12:12-19). Additionally, he is the source of abundant life as the thirst-quenching water (4:9-10; 7:37-38; 19:34), the bread of life (6:1-14, 35, 51-58), and the resurrection and the life (11:25). Finally, John's Gospel depicts Jesus as dying when the Passover lambs are slaughtered and casts his death as fulfilling regulations governing this ritual (19:28-37).

As important as religious experience and sound theology are to John, he is also concerned about how his disciples live. Whereas, the synoptic Gospels briefly depict the Last Supper, John devotes five chapters (John 13–17) to this event, distinct with a lengthy farewell address. In these chapters Jesus essentially focuses on instructing his followers how to live once he departs. He models that they are to serve one another as the footwashing scene implies (John 13:1-17). They are commanded to love one another (13:34-35; 15:12-17). He promises to send the Holy Spirit to teach them and empower their lives for the gospel (14:16-31; 16:5-15). Finally, he prays that the Christian community may be unified (17:6-25). Indeed, in John's thinking, religious experience, theology, and ethics are interconnected.

Clearly, the apostle Paul's writings reflect a similar commitment to wedding religious experience and ethics. This should not come as a surprise to anyone familiar with his dramatic conversion experience (Acts 9), his missionary travels (Acts 13–28), and his works of theological and ethical reflection and argumentation, such as Romans and Galatians. In this limited space we focus on 1 Corinthians only, where all three themes interact.

Even a cursory reading of the themes in 1 Corinthians reveals Paul's concerns. In 1:10–4:21 he focuses on divisions within the congregation. A recurring appeal here is that the Corinthians are *in Christ* (1:30) and the Spirit is actively moving within the life of the church (2:4-5, 10-16; 3:16). The work of the Spirit, which is the source of Paul's preaching power and the Corinthians' conversion, is the basis for Paul's ethical teaching (5:1–7:40). In the midst of his teaching on ethical matters Paul writes, "But you were washed, you were sanctified, you were justified in the name of the Lord Jesus Christ and in the Spirit of our God" (6:11). The Corinthians are encouraged to avoid sexual immorality, and Paul asks, "Do you not know that your body is a temple of the Holy Spirit within you, which you have from God and that you are not your own?" (6:19).

When addressing the issue of worship and religious experience (11:1–14:40), which the Corinthians relish, Paul again appeals to the Holy Spirit as a source of wisdom, right doctrine, and unity (12:1-11). Paul does not tell the Corinthians to forsake their religious experiences, but he reminds them in the famous words of chapter 13 that love is the greatest gift of all (13:13), implying it is the remedy to their shameful divisions between rich and poor at the Lord's Supper (11:17-22) and arguments over spiritual gifts (1 Cor 12). In 12:12-13 he writes, "For just as the body is one and has many members, and all the members of the body, though many, are one body, so it is with Christ. For in the one Spirit we were all baptized into one body, . . . and we were all made to drink of one Spirit."

Though Paul's attempt to employ theology to resolve the issues facing the Corinthians can be seen throughout his first letter to them, his commitment to such a use of theology reaches its climax in chapter 15. There Paul defends and argues for his view of the resurrection. His arguments do not focus on theological abstractions; instead, he is concerned with practical implications of this key theological point. His religious experience is based on the resurrection (15:7), as is the Corinthians' faith (15:11). If Christ has not been raised, the Corinthians are adhering to a futile faith (15:17). The Christian faith, however, is not futile because we live between Christ's resurrection, which vindicates Jesus' proclamation of the kingdom of God, and the final resurrection, when Christ "hands over the kingdom to God" (15:24). Amazingly, in the middle of this argument "for" the resurrection, Paul writes, "Come to a sober and right mind, and sin no more" (15:34). Ultimately the resurrection is our victory over sin and death, enabling us to inherit the kingdom of God (15:50-57), and the future resurrection is our sustaining hope as we are "steadfast, immovable, always excelling in the work of the Lord, because you know that in the Lord your labor is not in vain" (15:58).

Even Israel's ethic is deeply rooted in theology and its landmark experience of "the LORD." In his burning-bush experience, Moses, and eventually all of Israel, is informed that "the LORD" hears and acts upon the people's cries and brings good out of evil (Exod 3:7-12). Repeatedly we read that worship of the Lord is to be the result of this reversal of grave injustice that Israel faced in Egypt (3:12, 18; 4:31; 5:1, 3). Additionally, their experience of bondage in Egypt and the LORD's deliverance is the preamble—"I am the LORD your God, who brought you out of the land of Egypt, out of the house of slavery" (20:2)—to the Ten Commandments, Israel's core ethical directives.

The first elaboration on these commandments (in Exod 20:22-26) deals with worshipping "the LORD." The second regulates the keeping of slaves (21:1-11). Reversing Israel's past experience, permanent bondage is forbidden. After six years of service, a male Hebrew slave is to be set free "without debt" (21:2) and receives "some of the bounty with which the LORD your God has blessed you (Deut 15:13-14). Families that entered into bondage together are set free together (Exod 21:3). Female Hebrew slaves cannot be sold to foreigners, but rather have the right to be "redeemed" (21:8). If a female slave is married to a master's son, she is to be treated as a daughter (21:9). Clearly the experience of slavery in Egypt and the Lord's redemption of Israel had an ameliorating impact on Israel's legal and ethical code.

THE TEXT IN THE LIFE OF THE CHURCH

The New Birth and Believers Churches

The last thirty or forty years have presented members of the believers churches with a serious theological challenge: What do we think about the "new birth"? The particular challenge I refer to is the rise of evangelicalism and its central emphasis on being "born again." Frequently, but not always, this process of being "born again" revolves around intellectual and emotional assent to a set of theological propositions, such as (1) I am a sinner, (2) Christ has died for my sins, (3) I accept his gift of salvation, and (4) I will spend eternity with God. Unfortunately, as Ronald J. Sider says in his book *The Scandal of the Evangelical Conscience: Why are Christians Living Just Like the Rest of the World?* and as public polls indicate, this act of "being born again" has little or no influence upon how the new Christian lives.

Members of believers churches often respond to evangelicalism in one of two ways. First, we can see the social acceptability and influence that evangelicalism has, and we throw our hats into their ring. We then use the same evangelistic arguments, our faith becomes a private affair, and we invest time, money, and energy into building evangelical congregational outposts. Or we can reject this influence by arguing that it ignores Jesus' radical teachings on discipleship. We then avidly hold to our traditions and his words and know the "joy" of being countercultural, but we may not know the joy of salvation.

At least one other option also beckons, which is John's argument. Experience, theology, and ethics are woven together into a faith that *overcomes the world* (5:4 NIV, RSV). This has been a fundamental marker for believers churches. In his classic pamphlet *The Anabaptist Vision*, Harold S. Bender (13), drawing upon Max Goebel (1811-57), argues that the Anabaptists are primarily distinguished from major Protestant Reformers by their "great emphasis upon the actual personal conversion and regeneration of every Christian through the Holy Spirit." So what is meant by "actual personal conversion"? The Anabaptists, argues Bender, insisted upon a "true Christian life" resulting from that conversion experience (16). The markers of this life are "first a new conception of the essence of Christianity as discipleship; second, a new conception of the church as a brotherhood [family of faith]; and third, a new ethic of love and nonresistance" (20). Similar to John, Anabaptism intertwines religious experience, theology, and ethics.

Bender's description of the evidence for this new life in Christ is readily documented from sixteenth-century Anabaptist sources. The writings of first-generation Anabaptist leaders support Bender's theses. I cite two, Menno Simons and Dirk Philips.

In the introduction to Menno's *The New Birth* (1537), J. C. Wenger (88) writes, "The booklet is pervaded with a strong ethical flavor and an evangelistic zeal. . . . Menno . . . warns that unless men [and women] are born again, their portion eternally will be the lake of fire and brimstone. What people need is to die and rise with Christ, to be spiritually circumcised, to receive the baptism of the Holy Spirit, to put on Christ." Menno himself writes,

> You see worthy reader, all those who are thus born of God with Christ, who thus conform their weak life to the Gospel, thus convert themselves to follow the example of Christ, hear and believe His holy word, follow His commandments which He in plain words commanded us in the holy Scriptures, these are . . . the true children of God, brothers and sisters of Christ. . . . These regenerated people have a spiritual king over them who rules them by the unbroken sceptre of His mouth, namely, with His Holy Spirit and Word. (in Wenger: 93-94)

Menno's convictions are echoed by his contemporary Dirk Philips, who wrote *The New Birth and the New Creature* (1556). Dirk begins his pamphlet with an admonition with these thoughts:

> Dear brothers and sisters in the Lord: there are many persons at this time who pride themselves of the new birth; they chatter much about the new creature. . . . But the true new birth and character [nature] of the new creature is found in few people. . . . Therefore, I was compelled out of Christian love to warn you of all such false Christians . . . and through God's grace to write to you a little about the new birth and the new creature, and then to show how not everyone who boasts of the new birth . . . is therefore a new person who is born of God. But whoever has become a partaker of the divine character, the being of Jesus Christ and the power and character of the Holy Spirit, conforms him-

self to the image of Jesus Christ [and] in all submission, obedience, and righteousness serves God, in summary is a right-believing Christian; that one is a new person and a new creature in Christ Jesus. (Dyck, Keeney, and Beachy: 293-94)

For further documentation of Anabaptist appeal to Scripture for the essential fruit of personal transformation in discipleship, love, and nonresistance, see Swartley's citations of how Anabaptists used John 18:11, "Put your sword back into its sheath," and 18:36, "My kingdom is not of this world" (TLC on John 18–19, forthcoming). For the Anabaptists' practice of mutual aid, a foundational expression of brotherhood/sisterhood, see the three essays by Umble, Sprunger, and Roth. For Anabaptists the basis for these distinctive moral practices was the transformed life through Jesus Christ.

Roughly one hundred years later a German Pietist, Philipp Jakob Spener, wrote *Pia desideria* (1675). Spener and the earliest Pietists were concerned that Christianity was supposed to be practical. His book, in part, is a strong criticism of his contemporary Lutheran Church, which had focused on intellectual theology used to counter and combat the theological views of other Christians. The Pietists wanted a reformed church in which the clergy's theological training was geared toward "the practical concerns of the churches" (Erb: ix), in which "righteousness must express itself in conduct eventuated in a decided pressure to 'do good'" (x). *Pia desideria* became "the" treatise of the early movement, and it influenced German speakers everywhere as it set out a number of key proposals for "improving" the church.

Spener's third proposal is this: "The people must have impressed upon them and must accustom themselves to believing that it is by no means enough to have knowledge of the Christian faith, for Christianity consists rather of practice. Our dear Savior repeatedly enjoined love as the real mark of his disciples (John 13:34-35; 15:12; 1 John 3:10, 18; 4:7-8, 11-13, 21) (Erb: 36). Two years later Spener confirms this conviction in *The Spiritual Priesthood*, which is a pamphlet of seventy questions and answers. Question 38 and its answer reads thus:

> Is it necessary to a saving and living knowledge of the Scriptures to desire to be made better by them?
> Yes, indeed. Otherwise we will read them not as the Word of the great God, . . . our regard for whom must effect in us not only deep reverence, but also *obedience* to do what we hear from his Word and mouth. . . . He who does not read the Scripture in this way does not read them as God's Word. He deprives himself of their power, and, therefore, will not come to the true spiritual knowledge of them. (Erb: 57-58)

Given these voices from the past, we must be careful in how we respond to other Christians who use language similar to our own, but define the content differently than we do. It seems dangerous, if not foolish, to overreact and abandon one or two aspects of biblical faithfulness. Is it not better to listen to earlier believers who argued that the new birth must result in the new life? More important, 1 John reminds us that sound theology, conversion experience, and righteous ethics work together to produce a faith that is not only a benefit to its adherents, but also to people waiting for and needing redemption.

1 John 5:4b-12

Testimony of the Spirit

PREVIEW

In this penultimate unit, we encounter both more of the same and new developments. The author continues to rely on the Johannine Gospel tradition, especially the purpose statement in John 20:31, and he continues to write with his opponents in mind. Once again he accuses them of making God *a liar* (cf. 1:10). Additionally, he continues to address the issue of belief, but this unit discloses new information on the subject. In particular, John finally brings to a conclusion his central disagreement with his opponents. This core issue is Christological, and the insistence on the water and the blood in 5:6 reveals that the two groups have affirmed Jesus as the Son of God, but for different reasons. For John the opponents' explanation of Jesus' sonship is inadequate. It is not, however, merely inadequate and, therefore, a mild point of disagreement. Rather, his opponents' failure to grasp Jesus' true sonship puts at risk the believer's eternal life and, therefore, one's potential to conquer the world.

Unfortunately, we also face "utter obscurity" (Brown 1982: 595) in the author's writing. In particular, we are not well informed as to what he means by expressions such as *the water, the blood, human testimony,* and *testimony of God,* and so we are left to weigh numerous options. Additionally, this section contains one of the best-known textual variants in the entire NT. The KJV reads, *For there are three that bear record in heaven, the Father, the Word, and the Holy Ghost: and these three are one* (v. 7). However, the Greek textual support for this reading is virtually nonexistent. Most modern translations of verse 7, therefore, omit the reference to *Father, Word,* and *Spirit.* Moreover, the language in verses 6-8 is so obscure at places that translators, struggling to communicate the meaning of the Greek in English, have resorted to various verse arrangements. This is apparent by comparing the RSV and NRSV:

> RSV: [6]This is he who came by water and blood, Jesus Christ, not with the water only but with the water and the blood. [7]And the Spirit is the witness, because the Spirit is the truth. [8]There are three witnesses, the Spirit, the water, and the blood; and these three agree.

> NRSV: [6]This is the one who came by water and blood, Jesus Christ, not with the water only but with the water and the blood. And the Spirit is the one that testifies, for the Spirit is truth. [7]There are three that testify: [8]the Spirit and the water and the blood, and these three agree.

Clearly the author is trying to communicate core theological content regarding Jesus' status as God's Son and the implications of that Christology. The progression of the argument appears in the following textual re-creation with a question that follows from the preceding verses. While the RSV and NRSV put verse 5 with the preceding paragraph, as its conclusion, I suggest that it introduces the exposition to follow.

A Rhetorical Question, Answer, and Testimonial Support 5:5-8 (in 4b context)

5:5 The Question and Answer
Who is it that conquers the world
but the one who believes that Jesus is the Son of God?

5:6a-b The Answer Clarified
This is the one who came by water and blood, Jesus Christ,
not with water only
but with the water and the blood.

5:6c-8 The Testimonial Support
And the Spirit is the one that testifies,
for the Spirit is the truth.
There are three that testify:
the Spirit and the water and the blood,
and these three agree.

The Result of Accepting or Rejecting the Testimony 5:9-12
5:9 God's Testimony Is Greater
If we receive human testimony,

> the testimony of God is greater;
> for this is the testimony of God
> that he has testified to his Son.

5:10 Believing and Not Believing

Believing 5:10a

Those who believe in the Son of God
have the testimony in their hearts.

Not Believing 5:10b

Those who do not believe in God
have made him a liar by not believing
in the testimony that God has given
concerning his Son.

5:11 Summary of the Testimony

And this is the testimony:
God gave us eternal life,
and this life is in his Son.

5:12 The Result Reiterated

Having Life 5:12a

Whoever has the Son has life;

Not Having Life 5:12b

whoever does not have the Son of God
does not have life.

OUTLINE

A Rhetorical Question, Answer, and Testimonial Support, 5:4b-8
The Result of Accepting or Rejecting the Testimony, 5:9-12

EXPLANATORY NOTES

A Rhetorical Question, Answer, and Testimonial Support 5:4b-8

This initial subunit clarifies and fleshes out the final statement of the previous subunit: *And this is the victory that conquers the world, our faith.* From the outset *faith* has been a key issue. More specifically, the faith issue has focused on Jesus as the Son of God. We have seen this assertion previously in 4:15, and 3:8 subtly makes a similar point. Further, 3:8 helps us understand the author's point in 5:6. Here in 5:5, however, John is primarily concerned to establish that the believer's ability to conquer the world is directly tied to one's belief about Jesus as God's Son.

Verse 6 carries this specific argument forward and at the same time finally reveals the real christological bone of contention between John and the secessionists. Thus 5:6a—*This is the one who came by water and blood, Jesus Christ, not with the water only but the water and the blood—*

asserts that Jesus' true identity is revealed in both *the water* and *the blood*. This is John's view, while the separatists' view hinges on just *the water*. The point is that faith in Jesus' true and full identity is what enables and empowers the believers' victory over the world.

Yet the problem is, What does John mean by these two elements? We begin to find a solution by observing that John used the verb *come* earlier in the letter, in 4:2, where we read, *every spirit that confesses that Jesus Christ has come in the flesh is from God*. This word occurs again in 2 John 7, denouncing "*those who do not confess that Jesus Christ has come in the flesh*." In all probability 1 John 5:6 is also intended as a christological confession: *came by water and blood* thus tries to clarify the precise nature of the incarnation of Jesus. The secessionists seemingly are willing to settle for a truncated water-only revelation of Jesus' incarnation, while John encourages his readers to adhere to a fuller revelation displayed in *the water* and *the blood*.

Still, we are left to wonder about the exact references to *water* and *blood*. The significance of *the water* is generally accepted to be a reference to Jesus' baptism. John 1:29-34 contains the Johannine tradition that Jesus' baptism was a revelation of his divine sonship status, and it points to the descending Spirit, which remained on Jesus, as evidence of his sonship. The secessionists no doubt valued "the Spirit" in their religious experience (see the argument in 4:1-6), and they probably also held tenaciously to that part of John's tradition that witnessed to the coming of the Spirit upon Jesus at his baptism. For them that was all they needed as proof that Jesus was the Son of God.

What the separatists ignored, and what John insists upon, is that the Gospel of John's version of Jesus' baptism also identifies him as "the Lamb of God who takes away the sin of the world" (John 1:29-36). In the Johannine Gospel tradition, much is made of Jesus' "hour," referring to his death. References to this appear early in the Gospel, when Jesus' mother asks Jesus to turn water into wine and he responds, "My hour has not yet come" (2:4). As the tension between Jesus and the authorities increases, there is a failed attempt to arrest him "because his hour had not yet come" (7:30; cf. a similar line in 8:20). As the story moves into the last week of his life, Jesus exclaims, "The hour has come for the Son of Man to be glorified" (12:23). Four verses later we read, "Now my soul is troubled. And what should I say—'Father, save me from this hour'?" (12:27). Then in 13:1 the narrator discloses the clue: "Now before the festival of the Passover, Jesus knew that his hour had come to depart from this world and go to the Father." Finally, as Jesus begins his high-priestly prayer, he says, "Father, the hour has come; glorify your Son so that the Son may glorify you" (17:1).

The "hour" to which the tradition refers is Jesus' death on the cross. The Johannine tradition tells of Jesus' death in such a way as to highlight Jesus as the sacrificial lamb. John's chronology has Jesus dying on the cross at the same time the Passover lambs are slaughtered [*John's Cross Chronology, p. 309*]. Additionally, we are specifically told that Jesus' legs were not broken (John 19:33) just as the bones of the Passover lambs were not to be broken (Num 9:12). John's crucifixion has the soldiers offering Jesus wine in a sponge lifted up on a hyssop branch, which was also the plant used at the exodus Passover to paint the Israelites' doorposts (Exod 12:22). Clearly the Johannine tradition stresses the significance of Jesus' death and the sacrificial nature of that event. For John, *the blood* is a symbolic expression of that crucial event.

The author is committed to upholding the entire tradition, not just the Spirit/baptismal element. On this matter, the writer places himself squarely within the Johannine tradition. In the opening verses he says he has declared what was from the beginning (1 John 1:1) and what was revealed (1:2). He immediately launches into his argument regarding how Jesus has cleansed us from sin by his blood (1:7) and is our atoning sacrifice (2:2). Anyone who follows Jesus' commandments is in the light and not in the darkness, which is passing away (2:8; cf. 2:17). Further, those whose sins have been forgiven have conquered the evil one (2:12-13). John probably believed that Jesus, the Son of God, was revealed most clearly in his death on the cross, where his purpose was specifically *to destroy the works of the devil* (3:8). He certainly believes that anyone who has accepted the tradition's explanation of the centrality of the cross as the revelation of God's Son and the offer of life would conquer the world (5:4-5). In this respect the author probably held to a *Christus Victor* model of the atonement as the foundation for Christian salvation and living, rather than simply relying on the Spirit and baptism alone, as did his opponents (see TLC below).

The author, however, does not disregard the Spirit. The Johannine tradition ascribed a confirming role to the Spirit when it descended and remained upon Jesus at his baptism (John 1:29-34). Within the tradition the Spirit is linked to truth (Rensberger: 132). In the Gospel of John we read that worship is to take place in "spirit and truth" (4:24), the disciples are promised "the Spirit of truth" if they keep Jesus' commandments (14:17), and this Spirit "will guide you into all the truth" (16:13). Additionally, in 15:26 this Spirit of truth witnesses to Jesus. Rensberger (132-33) even suggests that the testimony to the blood and water at Jesus' crucifixion (19:34) is that of the Spirit, and that these verses stand behind the mention of the Spirit's testimony and its truthfulness in 1 John 5:6.

While some may regard Rensberger's suggestion debatable, what is clear is the idea that our author points to the tradition's use of the Spirit as a way of reinforcing his position over against that of the separatists. Within the Johannine tradition, the Spirit is a source of truth and clarifies Jesus' role and nature. Here also, in 1 John 5:6-8, the Spirit along with the water and the blood form a threefold witness to Jesus Christ. It is not any of these elements alone that fully testify to his role as the Son of God, but all three work together. There can be little doubt this threefold witness is John's attempt to provide an unshakable testimony supporting his holistic Christology. This judicial model goes back to the biblical motif of requiring multiple witnesses to provide true testimony (Deut 17:6; 19:15; Matt 18:16; John 8:17; 2 Cor 13:1; 1 Tim 5:19; Heb 10:28). The Greek in 1 John 5:7 stresses the word *three*, and 8b emphasizes the unity of their witness.

Finally, the famous textual issue in 5:7 merits attention. As mentioned in the Preview, the KJV reads, *For there are three that bear record in heaven, the Father, the Word, and the Holy Ghost: and these three are one. And there are three that bear witness in earth....* These words are found in many Latin Vulgate manuscripts and a few late Greek manuscripts, dating mostly from after AD 1400. Textual experts generally agree that these words first found their way into the Latin texts in or around the fourth century. The Johannine Comma, as these words have come to be known, "is quoted by none of the Greek Fathers.... Its first appearance in Greek is in a Greek version of the (Latin) Acts of the Lateran Council in 1215" (Metzger: 717). It appears in four late Greek manuscripts, which were translated from "a late recension of the Latin Vulgate": manuscripts 61 (16th c.), 88 (12th c.), 629 (14th or 15th c.), and 635 (11th c.), "which has the passage written in the margin by a seventeenth-century hand" (716-17). The Comma does not appear in any Syriac, Coptic, Armenian, Arabic, or Slavonic NT translations before AD 1500. Copyists, aware of the Vulgate version, likely added these words to the later Greek manuscripts that then were frequently reproduced and used for the KJV. Because of the lack of support from the earliest and most reliable Greek manuscripts, modern translators omit these words [*The Johannine Comma, p. 309*].

The Result of Accepting or Rejecting the Testimony 5:9-12

In this second section we move from the previous focus on unified testimony to the end result of accepting or rejecting that testimony. While verse 9 is a transitional statement, verses 10-12 address the significance of accepting the testimony. Again John at least assumes the authority of the Johannine tradition, especially John 5:31-47 and 20:31, even if he is not working directly with a text before him. Additionally, he is reverting to his opening argument of 1 John 1:2: *This life was revealed, and we have seen it and testify to it, and declare to you the eternal life that was with the Father and was revealed to us.*

Verse 9 opens with a simple comparison between human and divine testimony. Although the Greek behind the opening phrase is somewhat obscure, the thrust is something like this: *If we accept human testimony, then we should accept God's testimony.* The question is, What human testimony does John have in mind? It probably is John the Baptist's testimony at Jesus' baptism, which the separatists are willing to embrace in a limited way. But the verse makes it clear that the Baptist's testimony, as the secessionists understood it, is insufficient. Instead, God's testimony, argued for in verses 6-8, is greater (*meizōn*). Here again we see the author aligning himself with the Johannine tradition. In 1:2 he testified to what was *with the Father and was revealed to us*, and his testimony probably harks back to John 5:31-47, which also highlights the comparative tension between human and divine testimony to Jesus. That passage accepts the importance of the Baptist's witness, but stresses God's testimonial support for Jesus' work. Verse 36 is particularly relevant, "But I have a testimony greater than John's. The works that the Father has given me to complete, the very works that I am doing, testify on my behalf that the Father has sent me." Furthermore, we must recall that "the works that the Father has given me to complete" were not complete, according to the Johannine tradition, until the hour of Jesus' death.

The second part of 1 John 5:9, *for this is the testimony of God that he has testified to his Son*, is the final transitional element to verses 10-12, which spell out the implications of accepting or rejecting the testimony of God. Verse 10 is typically dualist, as we have repeatedly seen in this letter. Those who accept the Johannine tradition about Jesus, as handed down by our author, have internalized the testimony; they *have the testimony in their hearts*. We must be careful that the NRSV's expression, *in their hearts*, does not mislead us. These words may encourage us to conclude that this is an emotional reassurance. In fact, the Greek simply reads *has the witness in himself*, leaving us with the impression that sound theological testimony has been internalized by the believer who accepts the Johannine witness. This may result in some emotional aspect of the reassurance, but emotionalism is not the key; rather, sound Christological reflection is the driving point.

The theological nature of the internalized message is further developed by the second sentence in 5:10: *Those who do not believe in God have made him a liar by not believing in the testimony that God has given concerning his Son.* This is the fifth time John accuses his opponents of some aspect of lying. We saw it initially in 1:10, when he wrote, *If we say that we have not sinned, we make him a liar, and his word is not in us.* Then in chapter 2 he twice accuses his opponents of being liars (2:4, 22) when they ignore the commandments and deny that Jesus is the Christ. In 4:20 the liar is one who says that he loves God but hates his brother or sister. For John, to deny the full testimony about Jesus, God's Son, makes both the one who denies and God himself into liars. Ultimately, not to believe God's testimony about Jesus is *not [to] believe in God* (10a).

What particular testimony does John have in mind? That question is specifically answered in verse 11: *And this is the testimony: God gave us eternal life, and this life is in his Son.* These words are probably an allusion to the Gospel of John's summary "These are written so that you may come to believe that Jesus is the Messiah, the Son of God, and that through believing you may have life in his name" (20:30-31). Jesus, God's Son, is the source of life for those who believe in him and his messianic role. Verse 12 then draws out the final dualist implication of the argument. Whoever believes in the Son, meaning whoever has internalized the theological Johannine tradition regarding Jesus (v. 10), has this life. Thus those who do not accept the Johannine tradition, as argued for in 5:6-8 and the entire letter, do not possess life. By implication, when considering where this line of argument began, nonbelievers cannot conquer the world, while believers can (5:5).

In this penultimate subunit, John brings his entire argument to a climactic conclusion. His initial question in 5:5 reveals why he argues so firmly against the secessionists: what one believes about Jesus has an impact on one's survival in the world. To believe God's testimony, which John believes he has faithfully handed down, results in eternal life. While the separatists are willing to hold to an abbreviated Christology, John, drawing upon the Johannine tradition embodied in the Gospel of John, insists upon a fuller understanding of Jesus' sonship, which includes both his baptism and his death.

THE TEXT IN BIBLICAL CONTEXT

Jesus' Victory on the Cross

The writers of the NT employ numerous words, images, and metaphors when trying to explain the rich complexities of what was accomplished on the cross. Joel Green and Mark Baker (97) identify five key cultural contexts and concepts: court of law (justification), commercial dealings (redemption), personal relationships (reconciliation), worship (sacrifice), and battleground (triumph over evil). Often these images are fused together in a given section of Scripture (see TLC below). Many early believers preferred the view that in the cross God conquered evil and set humans free from their bondage to the evil one. These early Christians evidently used the NT as the basis for this view.

In 1 John the affirmation recurs that *the darkness is passing away* (2:8), and *the world and its desire are passing away, but those who do the will of God live forever* (2:17). These assertions are brackets (*inclusio*) for a pastoral section about overcoming sin and remind the readers that they *have conquered the evil one* (2:13; cf. 2:14). In fact, 3:8 reads, *The Son of God was revealed for this purpose, to destroy the works of the devil*, and in 5:6-8 that purpose was revealed most clearly on the cross. The author reminded his readers that *our faith* provides the victory over the world (5:4b). In chapter 4 John wrote, *Little children, you are from God, and have conquered them [false prophets and spirits of the antichrist]; for the one in you is greater than the one who is in the world"* (4:4). Finally, the letter closes with this reassurance: *The one who was born of God protects them [the faithful], and the evil one does not touch them. We know that we are God's children, and that the whole world lies under the power of the evil one* (5:18-19).

The notion of Jesus Christ's conquering evil appears in Revelation as well. In the well-known throne-room scene we read of the dramatic opening of the scroll. The one seated on the throne holds a scroll, and an angel asks, "Who is worthy to open the scroll?" (5:2). The seer is distressed because apparently no one is worthy, until the Lion of the tribe of Judah appears. Ironically, the lion appears as a lamb, and not just a lamb, but a lamb that looks as though "it had been slaughtered" (5:6). As the scene develops, the reader is told why the lamb was slaughtered and why it is worthy:

> You are worthy to take the scroll and open its seals,
> for you were slaughtered and by your blood you ransomed for God
>   saints from every tribe and language and people and nation;
> you have made them to be a kingdom and priests serving our God,
>   and they will reign on earth. (Rev 5:9-10)

This imagery of Christ's death ransoming, or setting people free from bondage, appears also in Mark 10:45. In the midst of a heated debate about greatness, Jesus tells his disciples that true greatness

involves service. He is depicted as illustrating this service by pointing to his own impending death: "For the Son of Man came not to be
served but to serve, and to give his life as a ransom for many." This
image of ransom is adapted by the early church fathers, especially
Irenaeus, to argue that God has overcome the evil one in the cross,
thus setting humanity free from bondage to evil.

The same imagery occurs in the Pauline corpus as well. Paul
begins his letter to the Galatians with a greeting that highlights the
believers' freedom from evil: "Grace to you and peace from God our
Father and the Lord Jesus Christ, who gave himself for our sins to
set us free from the present evil age, according to the will of our God
and Father" (1:3-4). Paul returns to this theme in the closing chapter. This is just after the well-known postscript that Paul claims to
have written himself (6:11). After arguing that the Galatians should
not resubmit to the law and tradition, Paul writes, "May I never
boast of anything except the cross of my Lord Jesus Christ, by which
the world has been crucified to me, and I to the world" (6:14).

The clearest illustration of this imagery is found in Colossians. As
the author is arguing for the superiority of Christ over other philoso-
phies and human traditions as well as encouraging his readers to
avoid bondage to "elemental spirits of the universe" (2:8), he says that
Christ is "the head of every ruler and authority" (2:10). Believers have
their freedom and new life through Christ and "faith in the power of
God" (2:12). This and more is the result of the cross, where "he [God
or Christ; see Martin: 114] disarmed the rulers and authorities and
made a public example of them, triumphing over them in it" (2:15).

Clearly the early Christian understanding of the cross includes
this significant theme. Not only are sinners justified, personal relationships renewed through reconciliation, and worship enabled
through sacrifice, but also the evil force(s) that have held humanity
and all of creation (Rom 8:18-21) in bondage are overcome. This
triumph and freedom cleared the way for God's children to participate freely in the coming new order, in which God alone rules. The
author of 1 John encourages those who have been set free to live
freely and faithfully (5:3-5, 18-20).

THE TEXT IN THE LIFE OF THE CHURCH

Christus Victor in the Early Church

In his *Baker's Dictionary of Theology* article on "Atonement," Baptist
scholar Vernon C. Grounds (72) says that the *Christus Victor* understanding of the cross dominated Christian thinking for a thousand

years. While the suggestion of its millennial reign may be a little optimistic, this general motif certainly did dominate from the second through the fourth centuries.

The basic idea was first formulated by Irenaeus, bishop of Lyon, who died around AD 202. Drawing upon the NT and writing within a social context of conflict with both the Roman Empire and heretical teachers, Irenaeus suggested that Christ was a "second Adam," and in his death humanity was set free from bondage to evil. Through the cross "God recapitulated in Himself the ancient formation of man and woman, that he might kill sin, deprive death of its power and vivify humanity" (*Against Heresies* 3.18.7; quoted in Green and Baker: 119). All the great early Christian thinkers worked within this theological framework when addressing the significance of the cross, including Tertullian (d. ca. 228), Clement of Alexandria (d. ca. 215), Origen (d. ca. 254), Athanasius (d. ca. 373), and Gregory of Nyssa (d. ca. 395). Even Augustine (354-430), who relied heavily on a satisfaction theory of the cross, made room for the *Christus Victor* model, going so far as to describe "the cross as a mousetrap baited with the Savior's blood" (quoted in Grounds: 72).

Though Augustine's imagery may make modern Christians shudder or laugh nervously, this understanding of the cross made perfect sense to the Christians who lived on the margins of society. They faced both persecution from the state and theological challenges from people who shared some theology with them, but adhered to other nontraditional points of view that threatened the core of the faith, as we have seen in 1 John. No doubt the great temptation was to think that they were alone against a hostile world and the forces of evil at work in the world. But John insists that authentic faith *conquers the world*, and authentic faith is one that *believes that Jesus is the Son of God* (5:4-5). Furthermore, he argues that Jesus Christ was most clearly revealed in both his baptism *and* his death (5:6). Both baptism and death are key elements of our faith that overcomes opposition from the world.

Most North American Christians are aware of significant cultural shifts that are taking place. In particular, we are moving away from a Constantinian social world, where Christianity stands at the heart of society, to a post-Christian social world, where Christians and their beliefs are marginalized. Some Christians, like conservative evangelicals, want to fight to keep Christianity at the center of society. Other Christians, like those in the Emergent Church movement, welcome the move to the edges, contending that since this is where Christianity began, this is where it should be now.

Whether Christians are on the edges of society, where most believers-church members have been in the past, or at the heart of society, where numerous believers-church members seem to be now, the fact remains: evil is everywhere. What are we to think and do about the manifestations of *the world* around us? Do we believe that *our faith* in Jesus Christ *conquers the world*? Do we even believe that *the world* needs to be conquered?

The evening news seems to suggest that a faith that *conquers the world* may still be useful. There is evidence all around us that although *the world* and the evil one are passing away, they have not gracefully abandoned human affairs. International, national, state, and local news reports regularly mention poverty, acts of bigotry, violence, and exploitation. Not only do humans yield to specific evil behavior, we also seem to be incapable of finding the right priorities on which to focus our attention. For example, television commercials compete to sell us various drugs to cure erectile dysfunction, but no drug company has found a cure for malaria, which kills an estimated ten thousand children daily. We need a faith that conquers.

I am not thinking of a faith that sponsors Crusades and Inquisitions. We are not looking for a faith that misuses power for self-promotion. Rather, I am hoping for a conquering faith that does not give in to hopelessness and then willingly settle for business as usual according to the world's standards. If the death of Christ has conquered the forces of evil entrapping us, is that not a reason for hope? Can we not hope that since we have been set free from sin and death, we, through our faith in Jesus Christ, can begin working with and following God's lead in living toward God's kingdom gift (Matt 6:33)? At the least, are we not free to live lives to foreshadow what God will do in the future? For the good of the world and the glory of God, we need a faith that both sets us free and gives us hope: freedom and hope to encourage international pharmaceutical corporations to work at stopping killer diseases, freedom and hope to build safe communities for their residents, freedom and hope to work for just societies, and a host of other concerns, both local and international. Most of all, we need freedom and hope to witness to the One who offers both that freedom and hope.

1 John 5:13-21

Concluding Words

PREVIEW

The final minutes of a pastoral visit are crucial. This is especially true if the meeting has resulted from some type of crisis. In this time the pastor will take the opportunity to reiterate concern for the parishioner, summarize counsel given, and offer final words of reassurance. In these final nine verses, John tries to draw to a conclusion his various concerns and to leave his readers with a general sense of confidence.

The author's primary agenda seems to be pastoral. This pastoral concern to bolster the readers' confidence is seen throughout the letter. Verse 13, which is a transition between the previous subunit and the two subunits in this conclusion, begins with words (*I write these things to you*) similar to those in 2:1 and 2:12-14, which also have pastoral overtones. At the same time, scholars have noted similarities between 5:13 and John 20:31.

John's pastoral assurances fall into two categories. First, the author addresses concerns about sin and prayer in verses 14-17. These verses present the modern reader with John's notion that there are different categories of sin, which have varying degrees of gravity. Second, he continues his closing assurances by reminding the readers that they *know* that they do not sin and that they are protected (v. 18), they *know* that they are God's children (v. 19), and they *know* that God's Son has come, having given them understanding to *know him who is true* (v. 20). Thus verses 18-20 create a subunit that three times employs the expression *we know*. Additionally, many have observed that these three verses present themes already

253

addressed in the letter. For example, 5:18a is almost identical to
3:9a. Then 5:19 echoes 2:15-17; 4:4-6; and 5:4-5. And christological
concerns in 5:20 occur in earlier verses: 1:3, 5; 3:23; 4:8-10, 14-16; 5:1,
10-11. Nor should we overlook the author's words *We are in him who
is true* (5:20c), an idea appearing in 2:5-6, 24, 28; 3:6, 24; 4:13, 15-16;
and so forth.

Finally, the letter closes with *Little children, keep yourselves from
idols*. While certainly an abrupt ending to the letter, these words are
not unrelated to the closing unit. They thematically connect to verse
20, and they remind us that pastoral concern can be both encouraging
and cautionary.

Believing in the Name, Having Eternal Life 5:13
*I write these things to you who believe in the name of the Son of God,
So that you may know that you have eternal life.*

Confidence in Prayer in the Face of Sin 5:14-17

5:14-15 Confidence in Prayer
*And this is the boldness we have in him,
that if we ask anything according to his will, he hears us.
And if we know that he hears us in whatever we ask,
we know that we have obtained the requests made of him.*

5:16-17 Prayer and Sins

Not Mortal Sin 5:16a
*If you see your brother or sister committing
what is not a mortal sin, you will ask,
and God will give life to such a one—
to those whose sin is not mortal.*

Mortal Sin 5:16b
*There is sin that is mortal;
I do not say that you should
pray about that.*

Complexity of Sin 5:17
*All wrongdoing is sin,
but there is sin that is not mortal.*

5:18-20 Foundational Knowledge
The First Foundation 5:18
*We know that those who are born of God do not sin,
but the one who was born of God protects them,
and the evil one does not touch them.*

The Second Foundation 5:19
We know that we are God's children,
and that the whole world lies under the power of the evil one.
The Third Foundation 5:20
And we know that the Son of God has come
and has given us understanding
so that we may know him who is true;
and we are in him who is true,
in his Son Jesus Christ.
He is the true God and eternal life.

5:21 Final Admonition
Little children, keep yourselves from idols.

OUTLINE

Believing in the Name, Having Eternal Life, 5:13
Confidence in Prayer in the Face of Sin, 5:14-17
Foundational Knowledge, 5:18-20
Final Admonition, 5:21

EXPLANATORY NOTES

Believing in the Name, Having Eternal Life 5:13

There is some discussion among scholars as to whether or not verse 13 is a part of the previous section or this closing unit. The verse does share themes of *believe, eternal life,* and *Son of God* with the preceding verses. Verse 20, however, references the specific concepts of *eternal life* and *Son of God* and affirms that the Son of God is our source of understanding. For this reason Rensberger (137) argues that verses 13 and 20 form an *inclusio,* or self-contained unit. Additionally, the theme of *know* in verse 13 figures prominently in 5:15, 18-20, as do the words *eternal life* in 5:11, 13, and 20. Considering these facts, it is best to view 5:13 as both a transitional and introductory verse.

Also, the wording of 5:13 is similar to that of John 20:31, and it functions in much (if not exactly) the same way. John 20:31 serves as a concluding purpose statement, as does 1 John 5:13: *I write these things to you who believe in the name of the Son of God, so that you may know that you have eternal life.* The demonstrative word *tauta* (*these things*) is probably a reference to the entire letter. Our author uses expressions similar to *I write these things to you* when either offering words of assurance (cf. 2:12-14, 21) or warning (cf. 2:1, 26). These closing verses contain both assurance and warning as the author seeks one last time to exercise his pastoral role in a summary fashion.

Finally, this verse's construction in the NRSV, RSV, and NIV is the opposite of the original Greek's construction. A literal translation might read, *I write these things to you so that you know you have life eternal, [to you who are] the ones believing in the name of the Son of God.* The Greek phrasing stresses belief in the Son of God's name. It is this belief that makes *eternal life* possible. This observation will help us resolve the author's notion of mortal and nonmortal sin below, and it seems that this believing *in the name* was a part of the Johannine tradition (cf. 1 John 3:23; John 1:12; 3:18).

Confidence in Prayer in the Face of Sin 5:14-17

Throughout this letter the author tries to reassure his readers amid the conflict they were facing with the secessionists. Given the competing claims, surely John's audience must have asked numerous questions: Who has the accurate understanding of who Jesus was? What is the significance of his life and death? What does it mean to be obedient? What are the crucial markers of the Christian life? And who really belongs to God? Verse 13 begins this closing section by reminding the readers that anyone who believes *in the name of the Son of God*, as the author set it out in 5:4-12 and elsewhere in the letter, has *eternal life*.

That reminder is the foundation for the assurance that John establishes in verses 14-15. This belief *in the name* is not a vague theological affirmation, nor is this the first time we have seen this *assurance* (NIV), *confidence* (RSV), or *boldness* (NRSV) before God in prayer. The notion appeared earlier in 3:21-24. After reminding his readers that they are *children of God* (3:1; cf. 3:10), he also tells them that they can have *confidence* (3:21 NIV, RSV) because they *believe in the name of his Son Jesus Christ* (3:23) and they *obey his commandments* (3:24), specifically that they *love one another, just as he has commanded us* (3:23). This obedience results in mutual abiding or intimacy between God and the believer (3:24).

Verses 14-15 are a shorthand version of 3:21-24. Prayer, in this instance, is not a pious activity designed for personal advancement or benefit. Neither is it separated from ethical considerations. Prayers must be offered in accordance with God's will. As 3:22 points out, *We receive from him whatever we ask, because we obey his commandments and do what pleases him.* The author is not suggesting that we obey simply to be heard. Rather, he assumes that the children of God are so aware of God's agenda that they naturally pray in accordance with the divine will, thus guaranteeing a positive hearing. This idea of praying with confidence is a recurring theme within the Johannine literature, as we see in John 14:13; 15:7; 16:23-24.

The general words of assurance in verses 14-15 serve as the background for one specific form of prayer: intercession for a sinning brother or sister. Verses 16-17, which deal with sin and prayer, present two challenges to the contemporary reader. The easier dilemma is the verse's Greek phrase *aitēsei kai dōsei autō zōēn*, which literally says, *He will ask, and he will give him life* (AT; cf. RSV). The question is, Who *will give* life: the praying believer or God? Since the strong tendency within Johannine literature is to view God or Jesus as the source of life (1 John 5:11; John 5:21; 6:33, 63; 10:28; 17:2), most scholars conclude that *He will give . . . life* refers to God's acting. The NRSV, NIV, and RSV follow this conclusion when they translate the phrase as *God will give*.

The greater challenge is the author's advice to pray for a brother or sister who continues to commit (present active indicative) what is *not a mortal sin*, and his acknowledgement and direction that *There is sin that is mortal; I do not say that you should pray about that*. On a first glance, it certainly looks as though the author has at least two categories of sin: one that results in death and one that does not. One class is grave, and the other is not. Before we quickly accept the notion that John is ranking *sin*, we need to take seriously the words *All wrongdoing is sin, but there is sin that is not mortal* (5:17). In other words, John realizes that all sin is a problem for people, but some sin is more easily dealt with once it occurs.

In fact, he has already addressed the *not-mortal* sin in 1:5–2:2. Even believers sin (1:8; cf. 1:10), and to deny this is naive. Once believers recognize their sins, they are to confess them (1:9) and receive the forgiveness and cleansing available to them through Jesus (1:7; cf. 1:9). The author closes this section by encouraging his readers *not to sin* (2:1) and to remember that Jesus Christ is their advocate before the Father if they do sin (2:1-2). In other words, those who trust Jesus Christ to deal with their sins are not in danger of sinning irredeemably. The advice of 5:16 probably fleshes out the community-oriented process for dealing with sin within the community of faith. When an individual community member sins, the members of the community are encouraged to pray for that person, who will, hopefully, confess the sin and turn to Christ, the advocate before the Father. If this process is followed, John assures his readers that forgiveness and life will be granted. Thus there is sin that is not mortal, although it is wrong.

If that is the case, what could possibly be a *mortal sin*? Both 1 John 1:5–2:2 and 5:13 provide crucial information for resolving this mystery. The beginning of this subunit (5:13) makes it clear that belief in the name of Jesus Christ results in eternal life. In the comments above, I pointed out that this belief was defined in 5:4-12, which argued for a Christology that takes seriously both Jesus' life and his death and so results in *eternal life*. Additionally, 1:5–2:2 argues that Jesus' *atoning sacrifice for our sins*, meaning his death, is central to resolving sin. The problem is that John's opponents do not accept Jesus' death as significant. Therefore, having rejected the traditional Johannine understanding of Jesus' death, they cannot benefit from that death and thus receive life. Therefore they have committed a *mortal sin*: they reject the Johannine tradition's view of who Jesus was—the Son of God. The reason John advises against praying about this type of sin probably arises out of the intense conflictive situation giving rise to the letter. The secessionists have created significant problems for John's community, and he views this behavior as evidence of their commitment to the world and rejection of Jesus Christ.

Foundational Knowledge 5:18-20

Numerous commentators note the summary nature of 5:18-20. These verses touch upon themes we have already seen, such as the new birth, victory over evil and the world, belonging to God, and sin in the believer's life. Surely the three *we know* clauses were designed to reassure the original readers, just as the earlier use of *we* or *you know* clauses (2:20, 21; 3:2, 5, 14, 15; 5:13) gave reassurance in light of the theological conflict in which they found themselves. Like the rest of the letter, these verses are either expressly or implicitly dualist, and they attempt one last time to highlight the benefit of being in Jesus Christ.

Verse 18 affirms that *those who are born of God do not sin*, and they are protected from *the evil one*. This verse seems to make a claim that modern readers find puzzling: believers do not sin. This assertion is not new to the letter: 5:18 echoes 3:9, leading us to believe that Christians can move beyond sinning. Unfortunately, such a notion conflicts with the author's assertion in 1:5–2:2, where he writes, *If we say that we have no sin, we deceive ourselves*. And just two verses earlier we are told that we are to pray for those who commit nonmortal sins. The apparent dilemma would move to resolution if English translators tried to communicate the sense of the Greek verb *sin*, which is in the third-person singular, present active indicative. Therefore, a helpful translation might be thus: *Those who are born of God do not continue sinning*. The author is arguing that the believer's life is not characterized as continually sinning: they do not continue to live a sinful lifestyle that characterizes their life. Rather, sin is the exception, given the new birth the believer has experienced. And as the letter has earlier argued, these occurrences of sin must be dealt with by confession (2:9) and prayer (5:16).

The reason the believers' life is not typified by sin is the fact that they are protected from the evil one's influence by *the one who was born of God*. The meaning of this phrase divides scholars. Most think it is a reference to Jesus Christ, despite the fact he is never referred to in this way elsewhere in the Johannine corpus. The reasons for this conclusion include the following. First, Johannine documents never suggest believers can protect themselves. Rather, they overcome the evil one by God's word abiding in them (2:14) and their abiding in God if they love God and keep 1 John's dual commandment (4:16; 3:24). Second, John 17:11-15 clearly depicts Jesus as protecting his followers and asking God to continue protecting them after his death. Third, 1 John 3:5, 8 affirm that Jesus *was revealed to take away sins* and *to destroy the works of the devil*. Finally, the assurances in 5:19-20 are squarely based on divine actions and not on the believers' self-defense (see Rensberger: 142).

Verses 18 and 19 work together to create a strong sense of the believer's identity, orientation, and safety because *we know that we are God's children* (19a), which amplifies 18a. Further, *the whole world lies under the power of the evil one* (19b) builds upon 18c. The author strongly makes the point that believers belong to the realm of God, not the world's realm, and they are not subject to the *power of the evil one*. The subtle implication, given the rest of the letter, is that some, such as the secessionists, who have gone out into the world (cf. 1 John 4:1), are *under the power of the evil one*. This point of belonging is emphatically stressed not only by the obvious dualist statement, but also the phrases *of God* (5:19 RSV; *God's* in NRSV) and *of the evil one* (RSV, NRSV), are found in the emphatic position in the Greek sentence construction. This sense of belonging to either God or the world has been observed already in 1 John 2:15-17 and 5:4-5. This conflict between God and the world with its ruler appears also in the Gospel of John (cf. 12:31; 14:30; 16:11). At the same time it needs to be pointed out that this strong sense of belonging to God is not simply an arrogant conviction on the author's part. Ultimately he sides with the Johannine tradition's hope that the *world* might be *saved* (John 3:17; cf. 1 John 2:2; 4:14) from the evil one, who is the enemy.

The final words of assurance relate to the work of Christ: *the Son of God has come and has given us understanding so that we may know him who is true* (5:20). The advent of the Son's revealing God the Father is a pervasive theme in Johannine literature (cf. John 1:18; 15:19-23; 10:30, 37-38; 14:7-11; 1 John 1:5; 4:8-10, 14-16). In this letter the Son reveals God's nature as light and reveals God's love. In a recent mediation on 1 John, Nicholas Wolterstorff explores this relationship of divine light and love. Wolterstorff (9) notes that Calvin pointed to "light" as the key metaphor for God because it highlights God's infinite nature. Wolterstorff (10) suggests, however, that 1 John stresses God's love as the essence of the divine being's infinity, since "out of love God has given us a commandment that illumines our way. And that commandment itself speaks of love. We are to love one another." "But even more fundamental," argues Wolterstorff (26), "light radiates out from the sun to nourish us, to provide the energy without which there could be no life. How better to describe God as love—love radiating out from God onto and into us and from us to the neighbor—than to say that God is light?"

God's love is especially important for it not only reveals God's light to the world and believers (1 John 4:14); it also reveals the importance of love as *the* element that radiates light and facilitates mutual abiding between God and the believer (4:16; cf. the repeated commandment to love in 3:23-24 and 5:1-4). Our author assures his readers that they, and by implication not their opponents, *are in him who is true, in his Son Jesus Christ.* This expression *his Son Jesus Christ* calls to mind previous christological statements such as those found in 1:3; 3:23; 5:1, 10-11.

While 1 John has shown that our author has a "high" Christology, making strong claims to Jesus' divinity, the closing words of this verse, *He is the true God and eternal life,* makes a profound theological statement. Although some scholars believe this is a reference to God and not Jesus, there are good reasons to conclude John is making a statement about Jesus. Grammatically, the closest antecedent to the Greek demonstrative pronoun is Jesus Christ. Within the tradition Jesus is referred to as divine or having divine qualities. We see this in the Gospel of John's prologue (1:1), where the "Word was with God, and the Word was God." Thomas's confession, before the risen Christ, which can be seen as the climax of the Gospel narrative, reads, "My Lord and my God!" (20:28). Both in this epistle and the Gospel of John, Jesus is the source of life (1 John 1:2; John 11:25; 14:6). Making this exalted christological statement at the end of the letter makes sense in light of the earlier, but slightly less exalted, christological affirmations. In fact, the entire verse makes revelatory sense if John understood Jesus to be divine. However, we should not equate John's view of Jesus' divinity with the even more highly developed christological statements found in later church confessions and councils.

Final Admonition 5:21

The final six words seem to bring the letter to an abrupt close, and they almost seem disconnected from the previous verses. Yet the initial term, *Little children* (*teknia*), shows that our author is rounding out his final pastoral segment with an admonition. He has used this word, *teknia*, in earlier pastoral segments (cf. 2:1, 12, 28; 3:7, 18; 4:4) when encouraging his readers. What he warns his followers about, idolatry, is grave, and so the verb tense he employs is the past (aorist) imperative, which in Greek communicates a strict prohibition. The question is, What idolatry does John envision?

Despite the tendency for English translations to leave us with the impression that John is making a general statement about idols, the Greek contains a definite article, and so it literally reads, *Keep yourselves from the idols.* John has a particular concern in mind. Given this verse's specific context, which has identified Jesus as divine in verse 20 and the letter's recurring concern that the secessionists have abandoned the Johannine tradition regarding Jesus' role (1:1-4; 2:1-2; 5:6-12), we best conclude that John probably has his opponents and their teachings in mind. They are the *antichrists* who *went out from us* (cf. 2:19; 4:1-6), rejecting the theological tradition that John taught and replacing it with a stripped-down Christology and dubious ethic that does not view love and obedience to Jesus' commandments as central to the Christian life. As such, these words are a fitting, albeit sudden, end to the letter.

THE TEXT IN BIBLICAL TEXT

The Complexity of Sin

A common notion in some Christian circles is that "sin is sin." That is to say, all sins are of equal gravity; all sin separates us from God. And to be separated from God is surely a serious dilemma. Sins are also grave because they rupture human relationships. Are all such offenses of equal weight? Does God view tax evasion as equally grave as murder? Even more significant is this question: Is there any sin that can permanently separate us from God? Typically the sin-is-sin approach argues that since all sins are equal, God's solution of sending Christ covers all sin. Nevertheless, this epistle of 1 John does not agree. John and other biblical writers have a much more nuanced view of sin.

An interesting beginning point is Numbers 15:27-31, which clearly distinguishes between sins that are "unintentionally" committed (15:27) and those committed "high-handedly" (15:30). For the former a year-old female goat is to be sacrificed by a priest. On the other hand, the person who intentionally sins "shall be cut off from among the people" because his sin "affronts the LORD" (15:30). This idea of unintentional and deliberate sin seems to serve as the foundation to the sacrificial system. The preface to the Leviticus code for "sin offerings" reflects this: "The LORD spoke to Moses saying, Speak to the people of Israel, saying: When anyone sins unintentionally in any of the LORD's commandments about things not to be done, and anyone does any of them . . ." (4:1-2; cf. Lev 4:13, 22, 27; 15:15-18; Deut 17:12; Ps 19:13).

In the OT, some sins are beyond atonement or prayer. Eli's sons sinned against the Lord by having sexual relations "with the women who served at the entrance to the tent of meeting" (1 Sam 2:22-25). When Israel refused to heed calls to repentance and instead celebrated, the Lord tells Isaiah, "Surely this iniquity will not be forgiven you until you die" (22:12-14). The Lord tells Jeremiah to refrain from interceding for the idolatrous nation (7:16-20; cf. 14:7-12).

A classic example of the OT's viewing sins as more or less grave is found in Deuteronomy 22:22-29, which focuses on "sexual sins." "Sexual sins" are in quotation marks because clearly both rape and consensual sex are covered in this section. Today we would make a distinction between these acts, but the OT does not. There is, however, a distinction in gravity made in this section of Scripture. The end result for adultery is death for both people (22:22). If a young engaged virgin has sex with a man in town and does not call out for help, both people are to be stoned (22:23-24). If a man rapes an engaged woman "in the open country," he is to die (22:25-27). Yet when a man rapes an unengaged virgin, the man has to marry her and give her father fifty shekels (22:28-29). Clearly in the OT not all sins are equal, given the prescribed punishments noted above.

We observe a similar diverse view of sin when turning to the NT, and at least one verse in addition to 1 John 5:16-17 distinguishes between forgivable and unforgivable sins. Mark 3:19b-30 records a conflict story between Jesus and the Jerusalem scribes. The scribes attribute Jesus' ministry to Beelzebul and demonic influences. Jesus responds, "Truly I tell you, people will be forgiven for their sins and whatever blasphemies they utter; but whoever blasphemes against the Holy Spirit can never have forgiveness, but is guilty of an eternal sin" (3:28-29; cf. Matt 12:31-32 and Luke 12:10, where speaking against the Holy Spirit is unforgivable, but speaking against the Son of Man is forgivable).

At the same time what we might label as a redemptive view of sin is strongly attested in the NT. Matthew 18:15-20 offers a community model for dealing with sin within the church. If one is sinned against, the believer is to "point out the fault" to the one who sins. If that person "listens to you, you have regained that one." If, however, the sinner does not accept the reproof after two further attempts, that person is to be viewed "as a Gentile and a tax collector." In his second letter to the Corinthians, Paul advises a gracious approach to those who have "caused pain"; he encourages the Corinthians to forgive so as to not overwhelm the offender. He reminds them to do so "that we may not be outwitted by Satan" (2:5-11). Similarly, in Galatians 6:1-2, Paul counsels his readers to deal with transgressors "in a spirit of gentleness." Second Thessalonians 3:14-15 suggests a firmer yet still hopeful tact and tack when dealing with disobedience, "Take note of those who do not obey what we say in this letter; have nothing to do with them, so that they may be ashamed. Do not regard them as enemies, but warn them as believers." Finally, James 5:13-20, assuming sickness is a result of sin, advises anointing with oil, confessing their sins to one another and praying for each other, "so that you may be healed" (5:16). The letter closes with the hope that those who wander from the truth can be brought back, thus saving "the sinner's soul from death" and covering "a multitude of sin" (5:19-20).

The NT writers, however, are clearly aware that graver sins exist. As in the OT, these sins often relate to willful disobedience to divine imperatives or rejecting God's work. The Gospel of John warns that those who refuse to "believe" in Jesus "will die in your sins" (8:24; 9:39-41). Acts 5:1-11 recounts the story of Ananias and Sapphira's sudden deaths, which are depicted as divine retribution for lying to the Holy Spirit. Paul takes a hard line on a case of incest in the Corinthian congregation, telling them "to hand this man over to Satan for the destruction of the flesh, so that his spirit may be saved in the day of the Lord" (1 Cor 5:1-5). These are the words of the same person who advised the same congregation to act graciously in 2 Corinthians 2:5-11. The opening chapter of 1 Timothy warns against false teachers and lists sins that are contrary to "sound teaching" (1:10; also 4:2); it closes by reporting that "certain persons have suffered shipwreck in the faith" (1:19), and in particular Hymenaeus and Alexander were "turned over to Satan, so that they may learn not to blaspheme" (1:20). Finally, Hebrews takes a dim view of apostasy, committed by one who rejects God's grace. The author offers this stern warning: "Anyone who has violated the law of

Moses dies without mercy 'on the testimony of two or three witnesses.'
How much worse punishment do you think will be deserved by those
who have spurned the Son of God, profaned the blood of the covenant
by which they were sanctified, and outraged the Spirit of grace?"
(10:28-29; cf. 6:4-6; 12:16-17).

Intercessory Prayer

These verses raise the issue of intercessory prayer and, in particular, prayers offered on behalf of people caught up in sin. While we
are quite familiar with intercession for family and friends who are
facing illness, grief, and decisions, the Bible contains a fairly strong
tradition of praying for people who are facing sin.

In the OT it is primarily people of some significant religious stature who intercede for others. As far back as the patriarchal period,
we read of intercessory prayer and prayers offered even on behalf
of nonbelievers. Genesis 18:23-33 depicts Abraham's conversation
with God over Sodom's fate. Abraham initially asks God to spare
Sodom's sinners if "fifty righteous within the city" can be found
(18:24). Eventually Abraham bargains the number to ten righteous,
and the Lord agrees. Two chapters later King Abimelech of Gerar
takes Sarah; upon learning that she is already married to Abraham,
the king learns he is to die for this. Despite Abraham's own dubious
involvement in the situation, God tells King Abimelech, "Return the
man's wife; for he is a prophet, and he will pray for you and you
shall live" (20:7).

More familiar is Moses' repeated intercession on behalf of sinful
and rebellious Israel. Perhaps the best-known story is the golden-calf
incident. Moses convinces God to refrain from destroying Israel for
this act of idolatry. The next day Moses approaches God a second time
to ask God to "forgive their sin" (Exod 32:32), but the ultimate
response is that the sinners in this instance will be punished for their
sins (32:11-34). Similarly, upon receiving the Ten Commandments a
second time, Moses prays, "O Lord, I pray, let the Lord go with us.
Although this is a stiff-necked people, pardon our iniquity and our
sin, and take us for your inheritance" (34:9). Finally, on the verge of
entering Canaan, when the Israelites rebel and want to return to
Egypt, Moses intercedes for the people: "Forgive the iniquity of this
people according to the greatness of your steadfast love, just as you
have pardoned this people, from Egypt even until now" (Num 14:19;
cf. intercessory prayers in Ezra 9; Neh 9; Dan 9).

The concept of intercessory prayer continues into the NT, but
there is a significant development. It is no longer only the religious

elite, such as the prophets, who can effectively intercede for people. Nor are intercessory prayers offered only after sins have been committed. In the era of the kingdom of God, begun by Jesus, all believers can exercise intercessory prayers for others, and these prayers are both preventative and restorative. Evidence for this is in Paul's writings, James, and 1 John as well, as we have seen.

In his closing words of 1 Thessalonians, Paul asks the congregation to pray for him and his fellow missionaries (5:25; cf. Heb 13:18). He later writes to the same congregation saying, "Finally, brothers and sisters, pray for us, so that the word of the Lord may spread rapidly and be glorified everywhere, just as it is among you, and that we may be rescued from wicked and evil people; for not all have faith" (2 Thess 3:1-2). Earlier in this epistle, Paul reminds the readers that "we always pray for you, asking that our God will make you worthy of his call and will fulfill by his power every good resolve and work of faith" (1:11). The Thessalonians are not the only people for whom Paul prays such a preventive intercessory prayer. In Colossians 1:9-10 we read, "Since the day we heard it, we have not ceased praying for you and asking that you may be filled with the knowledge of God's will in all spiritual wisdom and understanding, so that you may lead lives worthy of the Lord" (cf. Eph 1:15-16).

While Paul's view of mutually exercised intercessory prayer tends to be proactive when dealing with sin and potential moral failure, James's use of intercession aligns more with 1 John. James's closing advice encourages prayer if one suffers (5:13), but more specifically church elders are to be called by those who are sick, probably resulting from sin. The elders will both anoint the ill person and offer a "prayer of faith" (5:15). Seemingly these intercessory prayers of faith will result in the forgiveness of sins as well (5:15). Praying for the sick sinner is not just the responsibility of the elders. James 5:16 reads, "Therefore confess your sins to one another, and pray for one another, so that you may be healed. The prayer of the righteous is powerful and effective." Thus James's understanding of how intercessory prayer is to function tends to agree with that found in 1 John and the rest of the Bible.

THE TEXT IN THE LIFE OF THE CHURCH

Sin and Church Life

This portion of the letter introduces a topic with which the church has been wrestling since the beginning. What should we think about sin in the believer's life? And how should we respond to such sin?

We have seen the tension even in this small letter. On the one hand, obedience is reasonably expected from the believer (1 John 2:3-6; 3:4-10; 5:18). On the other hand, it is naive to claim that we do not sin (1:8; cf. 5:16-17). What is a Christian to think and do about sin within the community of faith?

As early as the middle of the second century, Christians struggled to find their way between this rock and a hard place. The Shepherd of Hermas is a fine example of the tension. In a vision a "man of glory," dressed as a shepherd, appears to the writer. Among the questions the author asks the visitor is this: "I have heard, sir, from some teachers that there is no second repentance beyond the one given when we went down into the water and received remission for our former sins" (*Mandate* 4.31.1; Lake 1926: 83). The visitor responds, "You have heard correctly. . . . For he who has received remission of sin ought never to sin again, but to live in purity" (*Mandate* 4.31.2). Just a few sentences later, however, we are told there is one chance for "conversion" after baptism because God "being merciful, had mercy on his creation, and established this repentance." The visitor quickly adds, however, that this mercy is not to be abused because the Christian "has one repentance, but if he sin and repent repeatedly, it is unprofitable for such a man, for scarcely shall he live" (*Mandate* 4.31.5-6).

Less than one hundred years later, a famous Christian had serious doubts about this advice. Tertullian (d. ca. 220), a North African leader, argued for taking a hard line on sin after conversion and baptism. He advocated strict church discipline and ascetic behavior. In the end he left the larger church to join the Montanist movement, which believed, among other things, that to fall from grace made one unredeemable.

By the beginning of the fifth century, the church had become quite aware of the complexity of sin even in the believer's life. This is evident in Augustine's sermon on Matthew 5:44. Augustine, who after the Apostle Paul is clearly the most influential Christian thinker before the Reformation, if not throughout the entire scope of the church's history, addresses 1 John 5:16 in a tangential comment in this sermon. He acknowledges, "There are some sins among the brethren which are more grievous than persecution by enemies" (Kavanagh: 99). For Augustine, a "sin unto death" is committed when a believer "assails the brotherhood . . . and is inflamed by the fire of envy against the grace by which he was reconciled to God" (100). A "sin not unto death" is failure "to perform the required duties of the brotherhood" (99). These people can and should be prayed for.

Augustine continues on and introduces the idea of different types of repentance for sin. "Judas the betrayer" acknowledged his sin but refused to "humble himself and ask for pardon" (101). Apparently even the most grave sin will be forgiven if sinners "put away their pride in order to render their hearts humble and contrite, and thus to implore forgiveness" (101).

By the time of the Reformation, the Catholic Church had developed a complex system of venial and mortal sins. John Calvin, for one, did not accept this distinction, which he viewed as "altogether foolish" (Calvin and Henry: 100). For him, "whatever is contrary to God's law is sin and in its nature leads to death" (100-101). When facing sin, Christians are not to "forsake God and wholly surrender themselves to Satan to be his slaves" (101). People who are involved in this grave type of sinning "have no fear of God [and] must be reprobate and given up to destruction" (101). While that sounds harsh, Calvin takes a surprisingly gentle and gracious line earlier when dealing with sin that does not lead to death. In fact, he argues that the community of faith has a responsibility to the sinning brother or sister. It is biblical "to care for each other's salvation; and he [John] would also have us regard our brother's falls as stimuli to prayer" (100). Furthermore, Calvin writes, "He [John] also reminds us how much we ought to avoid the cruelty of condemning our brothers or an extreme severity in despairing of their salvation" (100).

The Anabaptists were also concerned about sin in the believer's life, and so early in the movement they instituted "the ban" in some circles. In 1527 a gathering of Swiss Anabaptists met at Schleitheim and agreed to a document titled *Brotherly Union of a Number of Children of God Concerning Seven Articles*. The second article addresses the ban, which clearly assumes the process set out in Matthew 18 for dealing with a sinning brother or sister. If anyone who claims to be a Christian will "slip and fall into error and sin, being inadvertently overtaken," they are to be warned twice privately and once publicly before the entire church (Yoder: 37). The third article makes it clear that the concern is to keep communion pure, excluding those who "follow the devil and the world" (37). The redemption of the sinner is not in view here.

Ironically, this document reflects a much sterner approach than Calvin. Not all Anabaptists, however, viewed sinning believers so rigorously. In his essay *A Kind Admonition on Church Discipline* (1541), Menno Simons stresses the constructive side of church discipline: "If his fall be curable, from that moment endeavor to raise him up by gentle admonition and brotherly instruction, before you eat, drink, sleep or do anything else, as one who ardently desires his salvation" (Wenger: 412). If the admonition is successful, Menno advises the readers "no matter how he has transgressed, receive him as a returning, beloved brother or sister" (412).

Dirk Philips offers an even more "gracious" approach. In his essay *True Knowledge of God* (1558), Dirk writes, "We must love the brethren and the Scripture. . . . This love is not only found in supplying the bodily needs of our poor brothers, but one [also] remembers the brothers and sisters in every prayer, prays to the Lord for them, cares for their souls, and if one sees anyone falling from the way of truth, we should instruct him with God's Word and with a gentle spirit, so that we may uphold his soul and win it from destruction" (Dyck, Keeney, and Beachy: 261-62). Dirk reaffirms this other-focused and gracious approach in his article, "The Congregation of God" (ca. 1560-62): "But true brotherly love is that we seek first of all one another's salvation . . . with our fervent prayers to God, . . . with scriptural instruction, admonition, and discipline. . . . By this way we may instruct those who are overtaken in a fall to win their soul and seek it with Christian patience, by which we carry the weak and do not become well pleased with ourselves" (370-71).

Given the complexity and seriousness of sin, the biblical injunctions to pray for those caught up in sin, and the diverse voices from church history, what should we think and do today? Some of us may conclude that our congregations and Christian thinking have been unduly influenced by the permissive and laissez-faire thinking of our culture. Others will recall the harsh methods of church discipline from the not-so-good old days, when countercultural church values were equated with the teachings of Christ. We are, indeed, between the proverbial rock and a hard place. What is the way forward?

First, we must recognize that sin is a serious threat to both the individual believer's spiritual well-being and the general spiritual health of the community of faith. As 1 John repeatedly insists, we are called to obey the commandments of the Lord, if we are children of God and abiding in the truth. We cannot assume a laissez-faire approach to personal ethics. Second, we need to be clear about what is and is not biblically identified as sin. There may be inherited mores that have little or nothing to do with genuine sin. Even then there may be degrees of gravity or complex situations in which a fellow believer becomes caught up in a sin. When facing these scenarios, our responses and decisions need to be liberally infused with humility, patience, and prayer. Third, I suggest that our motivation for dealing with sin should primarily be a desire for the sinner's return and not to maintain the purity of the fellowship. No fellowship is pure, and if purity is the driving force, it becomes easy to identify scapegoats. If, however, the safe return of a sinner is our goal, we hopefully will work creatively, prayerfully, and proactively to accomplish this.

One story from the 1940s will suffice. In October 1941, a Brethren in Christ young man, John Zercher, was willingly inducted into the U.S. Army, rather than claim CO status. He violated the denomination's rule and should have been automatically disfellowshipped by his bishop, C. N. Hostetter Jr., who was a staunch pacifist. Hostetter was also wise, pious, and humble. Although he respected and supported the church rule, he did not rush to implement it; instead, he opted for a more redemptive and patient approach. Upon Zercher's return from Europe, the two men entered into a series of conversations lasting roughly a year and a half, while Zercher was on church probation (Sider and Hostetter: 17). Hostetter also gave him books to read on nonresistance and the church's peace position. Before returning to full fellowship, Zercher was to write a "confession of error" (17). The initial drafts did not meet Hostetter's standard, but eventually the two men agreed, and Zercher was received back into full fellowship in early 1949. In the course of the next thirty-plus years, Zercher became one of the most influential leaders in the denomination and a vocal advocate for peace.

I often wonder how many valuable brothers and sisters are lost to the kingdom of God because we either fail to take sin seriously or deal with sinners harshly and without prayer. Perhaps we need to act more like C. N. Hostetter Jr. and others who exercise grace, firmness, patience, and prayer in the face of sin.

2 John

PREVIEW

One of life's challenges is to know how to respond in a situation involving conflict. Does one withdraw and hope that the situation simply "goes away"? Or is one driven by a "need to win," thus entering the fray with relish? What resources and tools are at hand to be implemented? In this second letter, John continues to face the conflict laid out in the previous letter. Now, however, it appears that the separatists have taken to sending out missionaries to proclaim their message. How should the Johannine Christians respond?

With its thirteen verses, 2 John is one of the shortest documents in the NT and was probably written on one sheet of papyrus. This should not be surprising because its form clearly resembles thousands of similar documents from the ancient Near East. Unlike 1 John, this document is an ancient letter; as such, 2 John consists of an introduction, body, and conclusion. We must acknowledge, however, that ancient letter forms were more complex than this (see Brown 1982: 788-95), and there were variations in form.

The presence of such a short work with specific concerns raises at least two questions. First, what is the reason for this letter? The letter's body addresses two topics. Initially, the readers are encouraged to love one another, a theme that repeatedly appears in 1 John. Second, and probably the driving agenda, they are informed about how to deal with *deceivers* (7). We have also seen the theme of false teachers in 1 John. Below I will approach this letter as if it is another literary attempt to deal with this situation giving rise to 1 John. It seems clear to me that this letter's author addresses the same situation as in 1 John.

The second question relates to authorship of 2 John. Were 1 John and 2 John penned by the same person? At the least the author is well versed in and accepting of the Johannine traditions and theology. He knows the importance of the commandment to love one another (5-6) and is aware of the christological split facing his church. Additionally, the letter's body makes it clear that John also sees a strong connection between orthopraxis and orthodoxy, as we will see when examining verse 7. If these observations are not enough to lead us to conclude these documents were written by the same person, we have the matter of syntax and vocabulary. Raymond Brown writes, "They [the authors of 1 and 2 John] have much the same vocabulary and lack of concern about syntax" (Brown 1982: 683). Like 1 John so also 2 John presents significant interpretative challenges to us because of the author's writing style. On occasion similar or exactly the same poor wording is used in both letters. Therefore, I lean strongly toward supporting a single author for both documents.

OUTLINE

Greetings, 1-3
Body, 4-11
    4-6   Rejoicing and Encouragement
    7-11   Directions Regarding Deceivers
Closing, 12-13

EXPLANATORY NOTES

Greetings 1-3

The letter begins in a fashion common in ancient letters: both the sender and recipient(s) are identified, and a greeting is offered. Usually the sender's personal name is given, and the writer is also identified by a role. This occurs in the opening verse of Romans, 1 Corinthians, James, and 1 Peter. Occasionally the sender or senders are identified without referencing their role, as in the opening verses of 1 and 2 Thessalonians and Philemon. In 2 John no personal name appears. Rather, the sender is only identified as *the elder*. The word *presbyteros* could either be a reference to the writer's age or his role within the church. We know from other NT passages that a class of church leaders was known as "elders" (Acts 14:23; 15:2-6, 22-23; 20:17; 1 Tim 5:17-19; James 5:14). Some scholars observe that in the NT "elders" is a collective term, and we do not see one elder acting alone. They therefore conclude that the term here should be understood as a reference to the sender's age. This letter's body, however, makes it quite clear that the sender has some authority over the recipients, and he is probably writing as a church authority. Third John begins in the same fashion, and there the sender is, in part, defending his authority.

The identity of the recipients is also debated. A few commentators believe the document was sent to a woman named Electa. This is unlikely. In the Bible it is not uncommon to apply feminine metaphorical language to a collective group. In Isaiah 54:1-8, Jerusalem is seen as the mother of Israel (cf. Gal 4:25). First Peter 5:13 refers to the church in Rome as "your sister church in Babylon," and Revelation 12:17 identifies the church as "the woman." Additionally, 2 John 13 would run counter to the nonmetaphorical reading of *the elect lady*. There *the children of your elect sister* are identified as sending their greetings. Is it unlikely that there were two sisters named Electa. Thus our author is simply using a metaphorical image to describe the congregations with which he works. This is reinforced by the numerous plural pronouns throughout the letter (6, 8, 10, 12).

Before the official greeting in verse 3, the elder makes a statement about love and truth. He professes his love for the readers, and it is a genuine and deep love. Literally, he writes, *whom I love in truth* (*egō agapō en alētheia*). Because there is no definite article here, we should translate this initial use of truth as "I truly love" or "I genuinely love." The next two uses of *truth* do use definite articles, and they (vv. 1b and 2a) are probably referring to theological truth that the Johannine faithful have in common. The author assures his readers that this truth not only binds them together and serves as the foundation for their love, but it also *will be with us forever* (v. 2). Because the Johannine believers are facing deception, the elder begins with this affirmation of love and reassurance that they are found in the truth. This is similar to the pastoral affirmation we have seen in 1 John.

Because of the truth (v. 2), the elder writes a somewhat unusual greeting (v. 3). The tendency of ancient greetings was to express a wish or desire for the reader. For example, 1 Peter 1:2 reads, "May grace and peace be yours in abundance" (cf. 2 Pet 1:2; Jude 2). Here the elder simply states a fact. Because of the Johannine believers' commitment to the truth, *Grace, mercy, and peace will be with us*. Again, this statement of fact was probably chosen to provide reassurance to the readers. Additionally, the writer stresses his readers' possession of *grace, mercy, and peace* by placing *will be with us* at the beginning of the original Greek sentence. These blessings come directly *from God the Father and from Jesus Christ, the Father's Son*. This assurance is theirs because they have accepted and adhere to the truth revealed in Jesus Christ and handed down within the Johannine tradition (1 John 1:1-4; 2:23; 4:15; 5:10).

Finally, some have noted that the sender's greeting differs from the content of Paul's traditional greeting ("grace and peace"; cf. Rom 1:7; 1 Cor 1:3; 2 Cor 1:2; Gal 1:3; Phil 1:2; Philem 3). The greeting in 2 John 3 is similar to the one in 1 Timothy 1:2 and 2 Timothy 1:2. We can only speculate as to why the elder added *mercy* to the more common greeting of *grace and peace*. The use of the word here is its only use in the whole of the Johannine literature. One could argue, however, that mercy is not totally foreign to Johannine thought. After all, one of the opening arguments in 1 John focuses on sin and how it is understood within Johannine theology (1 John 1:5–2:2). Although mercy is never specifically cited in those verses, it would hardly be an unknown concept in the writer's mind.

Body 4-11

4-6 Rejoicing and Encouragement
This subunit addresses the first of two crucial points made in the letter. Unfortunately, it also shows the elder's casual approach to syntax in verse 6. The second part of the verse has been described as "well-nigh incomprehensible" (Rensberger: 150). Although there are challenges to grasping particular elements of it, the overall concern is evident. Additionally, we can approach this as one unit because of the similar thrusts in verse 4 (*walking in the truth, just as we have been commanded*) and verse 6 (*this is the commandment just as you have heard it from the beginning—you must walk in it*).

In ancient letters it is not uncommon to find a word of thanksgiving after the formal greeting (cf. Rom 1:8-15 or 2 Macc 1:11), and that is what we find in verse 4. The elder *was overjoyed to find some of your children walking in the truth*. These words trigger speculation on the part of modern commentators. It is probably safe to conclude that the author has had some contact with members of this church who reported on its internal affairs. Though certain types of postal service existed in the ancient world [*Letters in the Ancient World, p. 310*], it is likely that these letters were carried personally to the congregations by fellow believers—the "Holy Internet" as Michael Thompson describes it.

The source of the elder's joy is the fact that some are *walking in the truth, just as we have been commanded by the Father*. We have already seen the use of *walking* imagery in 1 John. It is used in 1 John 1:6-7: *If we say that we have fellowship with him while we are walking in darkness, we lie and do not do what is true; but if we walk in the light as he himself is in the light . . .* (cf. 1 John 2:6, 11). The context there makes it clear that the author uses this expression as shorthand for one's behavioral patterns. The same applies here. The elder is overjoyed to learn that there are people in this church who live out *the truth.*

The obvious question is, What is this truth? It has something to do with what *we have been commanded by the Father.* First John absolutely stresses obedience to the commandments. Evidence of knowing God is revealed in obeying the commandments (1 John 2:3-6). If believers internalize what they have *heard from the beginning,* they *will abide in the Son and in the Father* (1 John 2:24). The fundamental dual focus of the commandment in Johannine theology is found in 1 John 3:23: *This is his commandment, that we should believe in the name of his Son Jesus Christ and love one another, just as he has commanded us.* It is tempting to narrow the commandment in 2 John 4 to love alone because verse 5 takes up that theme. But we should probably view verse 4 as an overall introduction to the letter's dual truth concerns of mutual love and orthodox Christology that are found in the letter's body.

In verse 5, the elder turns his attention to the first of his concerns: *But now, dear lady, I ask you.* What he asks about is not a *new commandment, but one we have had from the beginning, let us love one another.* We have seen a similar concern expressed in 1 John 2:7: *Beloved, I am writing you no new commandment, but an old commandment that you have had from the beginning.* Here in 2 John 5 the elder is simply reminding his readers of the long-standing tradition, in particular the tradition about mutual love, which serves as a marker for the Johannine communities. This is the sixth and final reference to the explicit and important command to love one another in these letters (cf. 1 John 3:11, 23; 4:7, 11, 12; see also John 13:34-35; 15:12-13, 17). We also know from 1 John that the love envisioned and encouraged here is a tangible love (cf. 1 John 3:17): it is not merely emotion. It is a love manifested in daily living. It shows that the revelation of God in Jesus Christ is relevant to the concerns of this world.

As the opening of verse 6 says, the believers' submission to the commandment to love one another reveals another love: *And this is love, that we walk according to his commandments.* By loving others we also show our love for God by obeying God's commandments. What is not so clear is the closing part of the verse. Literally, it reads, *This the commandment is, just as we have heard from the beginning, that in it you should walk.* Having taken a slight detour to highlight the importance of keeping all of God's commandments (esp. the command to love in 6a), the elder returns to his primary concern: the commandment to love one another. The NRSV translation is rather obscure, and at this point one ought to consult either the RSV: *This is the commandment, as you have heard from the beginning, that you follow love*; or the NIV: *As you have heard from the beginning, his command is that you walk in love.*

7-11 Directions Regarding Deceivers

In verses 7-11 the elder shifts his attention to the driving agenda behind the letter: how to deal with theological deceivers. Nevertheless, these verses are not unrelated to verses 4-6. That is evident by the presence of the word *hoti* at the beginning of verse 7. *Hoti* can be translated *because*, and only the RSV reflects this sense and connection to the previous unit in its translation, <u>For</u> *many deceivers have gone out into the world.* These false teachers are the reason the elder wants his readers to walk in love, which is one aspect of the truth. The other aspect is doctrinal orthodoxy. It is not difficult to imagine that a new teaching about Jesus has caused a breakdown in the community's unity and a failure to obey the commandment to love one another. Thus the elder holds the *deceivers* responsible for people violating the dual command to *believe in the name of his Son Jesus Christ and love one another* in 1 John 3:23.

The more significant issue in verse 8 is the textual variant in the phrase *what <u>we</u> have worked for.* The vast majority of ancient texts read *what <u>you</u> have worked for*, and this is reflected in the NIV and RSV. One of the two oldest existing manuscripts (Vaticanus) and a few others read *we*. To determine the original text, readings in older texts are regarded as more reliable than readings in many later texts. Thus preference should be given to *we*. Additionally, whichever reading is more difficult to explain should be viewed as more likely to be the original. Again, *we* would qualify. Why would a copyist shift from "you-you-you" to "you-we-you"? A scribe would not make such a shift, so *we* points back to the author. The NRSV provides the best translation: *Do not lose what we have worked for.*

The next obvious question is, To whom does *we* refer? There are two common answers. Some see the elder drawing upon his role and authority as a tradition bearer (cf. 1 John 1:1-4). He and others have worked hard to pass on a reliable and life-giving tradition about Jesus Christ. Others argue that the elder is simply including himself among those who have taken the Johannine tradition seriously, and to follow these deceivers would be to risk losing their reward: eternal life. I am not convinced that we must decide between the two options. Clearly the tradition bearers are a part of the Christian community. There is no evidence to show that they formed a separate group claiming a special salvation. Neither do we have evidence that the tradition bearers are somehow safe from being led astray. They, like other believers, must be on their guard against the deceivers and continue their *work* to abide (cf. 1 John 2:18-27, esp. vv. 23-25).

Verse 9 provides the explanation for how one loses one's reward: *Everyone who does not abide in the teaching of Christ . . . does not have God.* Conversely, *whoever abides in the teaching has both the Father and the Son.* A parallel is found in 1 John 2:22-25. There John argues that whoever denies Jesus' role as the Christ also denies the Father. In particular, they are denying the revelation that God gave through Jesus Christ. Without this revelation, which is the source of eternal life, no one can understand or relate to God. In fact, any conduct or doctrine that *goes beyond* the *teaching of Christ* leads people astray from the truth and does not encourage their *walking in the truth* (2 John 4, 6).

The verse makes it abundantly clear that it is crucial to remain in *the teaching of Christ.* A quick survey of translations also makes it clear that it is difficult to know how to interpret the original Greek *didachē tou Christou.* The RSV reads *the doctrine of Christ*, the NRSV and NIV say *the teaching of Christ*, and the REB has *the teaching about Christ.* The expression *didachē tou Christou* could be either a subjective genitive, meaning Christ's teaching, or an objective genitive, meaning teaching about Christ. The context is our best approach to resolve this dilemma. Second John 7-10 makes it clear that teaching is the chief bone of contention. Verse 7 specifically points to the secessionists' refusal to *confess that Jesus Christ has come in the flesh.* They and the elder disagree about the incarnation or a teaching about Jesus. It is the incarnational revelation of Jesus that makes abiding in God possible (1 John 2:22-25; cf. 5:6-12). If one does not have a clear grasp of who Jesus is, then one also has a warped view of God. Therefore, we probably should translate *didachē tou Christou* as *teaching about Christ.* We should also acknowledge a subtheme of the *teaching about* Christ, to include Christ's teaching as well. By now it is obvious that the Johannine tradition values Jesus' teaching, especially the love commandment, as much as it values the teaching about Jesus. The two cannot be separated.

Verses 7-9 are a preface to the directive in verse 10, which gives the reason for writing the letter. If anyone, such as the deceivers, brings a *teaching* different from the Johannine tradition, they are not to be received or even greeted. At first glance such advice seems to run counter to both 1 and 2 John's affirmation of the love commandment. However, the elder knows that another issue is at work here. In the ancient world traveling teachers and missionaries depended upon private hospitality to carry out their mission (cf. 3 John 5-8; Acts 16:4-15; Rom 12:13; 15:23-24; Titus 3:13). There were few safe and reputable inns. Most congregations met in private homes (Rom 16:5; 1 Cor 16:19; Col 4:15; 1 Tim 3:15; Philem 2; cf. *Did.* 12). The elder sees the real danger of materially supporting and housing false teachers in homes that may serve as venues for house churches. If such a teacher were there, it would only be natural to give that person opportunity to present false teachings that would threaten the church's well-being.

Verse 11 adds a specific reason for refusing hospitality to false teachers: *To welcome is to participate in the evil deeds of such a person.* While we may not give credence to the "birds of a feather flock together" philosophy, it was an element of ancient hospitality mores. Colin Kruse (213) makes the point that strangers in a new town had no social or legal standing, and they needed a patron to vouch for them. If you were to welcome an unsavory person into your community, you were responsible for him and his actions (cf. Malina: 181-83). Thus the elder directs his readers to avoid contact with false teachers and refuse to give them hospitality. In an age of tolerance such advice makes us uncomfortable. Robert Kysar, however, asks a crucial question at this point, "How flexible can the perimeters of Christian belief be without sacrificing the integrity of faith itself?" (1986a: 132).

Closing 12-13

The letter closes succinctly and in a fashion much like 3 John. The two letters are verbatim on one point: their use of *face to face* (which literally reads *mouth to mouth*, occurring also in Num 12:8 in the Hebrew). Like many letters from the ancient world, the elder indicates that he has other points to communicate, and his preference is to do this in person and not via a written document. Therefore his hope is to visit in person: *face to face, so that our joy may be complete.* Some commentators, who see an eschatological concern in this letter, assume this "complete joy" is another eschatological reference. This is probably not the case. Instead, the elder is simply pointing out that to visit these believers would be quite a pleasant experience. His final sentence, *The children of your elect sister send you their greetings,* is simply a metaphorical expression designed to pass on a greeting from the members of his congregation to the members of the recipient congregation.

THE TEXT IN BIBLICAL CONTEXT

Hospitality

We must acknowledge that 2 John's advice to withhold hospitality from the separatist teachers runs counter to the majority view in both the Bible and the ancient world. Even the obvious exception to this assertion differs slightly from the situation in 2 John. In Mark 6:7-13 Jesus sends out the twelve on a preaching mission and instructs them to accept the hospitality at one home. If, however, people will not receive them and refuse to hear their message, the twelve are to reject them, and as a symbolic act they are to "shake off the dust that is on your feet as a testimony against them." The twelve are to respond thus when others refuse to extend hospitality to them.

Mark 6:7-13 is instructive regarding the pervasiveness of the hospitality ideal in the ancient world. Travelers could expect to be received within Jewish and Christian circles. Jesus' instructions reveal that to be refused hospitality was a grave offense. Whereas Greeks and Romans tended to use hospitality as a means for upward mobility, Jews and Christians were motivated by theological concepts to reach out to all people, especially the marginalized and aliens (Pohl: 16-35). In the OT the notion of the covenant and Israel's alien status served as the larger framework for hospitality, and in the NT the kingdom of God serves the same capacity.

Genesis 15:1-21 establishes Israel's covenant relationship with "the LORD" and lays out its primary identity. Despite the nation's unique status before God, their formative experience will include four hundred years of oppression and slavery, and they "shall be aliens in a land that is not theirs" (15:13). Once freed from slavery, the core of the law, which is to guide their behavior as the Lord's faithful people, begins with a reminder of this oppression and alien status: "I am the LORD your God, who brought you out of the land of Egypt, out of the house of slavery" (Exod 20:2). This formative experience is reflected in the law code that requires them to respect and care for the alien and marginalized. The essence of the law is summed up in Deuteronomy 10:12-22. In addition to fearing, loving, serving and walking humbly with God (10:12), Israel is to love the stranger, "providing them food and clothing" (10:18) because God loved Israel's ancestors (10:15) and because the Israelites "were [once] strangers in the land of Egypt" (10:19). The poor, both Israelite and alien, are to be protected (24:14-15; Exod 22:21-27). Moreover, aliens are to be included in Israel's religious life (Deut 29:10-14), even the Passover celebration (Num 9:14; cf. Exod 12:43-49). Thus Israel's law codes clearly reflect the assumption that strangers are to be welcomed and respected.

Christine Pohl (24-27) makes the point that it is not only the law codes that stress openness to "the other." The OT has reinforced the importance of hospitality by incorporating four key stories. In Genesis 18:1-15 Abraham and Sarah offer hospitality to three travelers. The couple gives them water to wash their feet, a shady place to rest, and a large meal. In return the leader predicts that Sarah and Abraham will have a child. The negative side of this story immediately follows in Genesis 19. The three travelers go to Sodom and stay with Lot, who tries to protect them from the residents who, instead of welcoming them, try to sexually assault the strangers (19:1-29). Hence Sodom is destroyed. Further, one of Israel's greatest prophets, Elijah, benefits from the hospitable kindness of an alien woman (1 Kings 17:1-24).

Just as the covenant and Egyptian experience is formative for Jews, the hope for the kingdom of God sets the standard for Christians. In Matthew 22 Jesus tells a parable to describe the kingdom, which he likens to a wedding banquet. The original guests refuse to attend, and so the king sends his servants out to "invite everyone you find to the wedding banquet" (22:9). Three chapters later, Matthew records Jesus' parable of the sheep and goats. The kingdom is given to "the sheep," who gladly show hospitality to the hungry, the thirsty, the naked, the sick, and the stranger (Matt 25:34-36). Eternal punishment, on the other hand, is the reward for those who refuse to extend hospitality to the marginalized.

Paul, who some scholars believe was not heavily influenced by the Jesus tradition, seems to be firmly in touch with this hospitality motif. In Romans 12:9-21 he lists the marks of a devout believer. Among these traits are one's willingness to "contribute to the needs of the saints [and] extend hospitality to strangers" (12:13). A few verses later he warns against vengeance and recommends that believers ought to feed their enemies if they are hungry and give them something to drink if they are thirsty (12:20). This epistle is not alone on this matter. The pastoral epistles list hospitality as a key quality for a bishop (1 Tim 3:2; Titus 1:8). First Peter 4:9 encourages Christians to "be hospitable to one another without complaining," and Hebrews 13:2 offers similar advice regarding outsiders: "Do not neglect to show hospitality to strangers, for by doing that some have entertained angels without knowing it."

THE TEXT IN THE LIFE OF THE CHURCH

Hospitality and Divergent Views

This small letter's apparent motivation, which advocates withholding of hospitality, presents the contemporary reader with at least two challenges. The first is the larger issue of hospitality as a spiritual practice that, for the most part, is a lost tradition within Christian circles. Second John advocates a minority view within the Scriptures and speaks to a narrow situation. Most of Scripture assumes that hospitality is a spiritual and ethical practice carried out by the faithful. Thus contemporary Christians face a dilemma. We hear a variety of biblical voices on the topic of hospitality, and confusion may well ensue. Generally speaking, I believe that we must listen to the majority view that was not influenced by the unique context surrounding the Johannine letters. This challenging situation is created by a second and difficult issue facing the writer of 2 John: How should we interact with people who teach a theology that moves away from accepted Christian thoughts and ideas? This is certainly an important topic, given the religious pluralism we now face as well as the need to communicate the gospel afresh to each new generation.

Initially we must acknowledge that we probably cannot recover the early church's positive hospitality practices exactly, as even a brief survey of the church's practice will reveal. We can, however, do better than we are doing. The main reason it would be difficult, if not impossible, to recapture the practice of hospitality as it was carried out by the early church is the shift to an institutional model of the church's life together. The early church met in private homes and dwellings. Most spiritual practices, including hospitality, primarily took place in people's homes. Today few of us do this. We have separated our private dwellings from our church buildings. There are exceptions, but for the most part when we "go to church," most of us go to a church building and not to another Christian family's home.

This shift toward institutionalization has a long and ironic history, as Christine Pohl notes in her book *Making Room*. It began as early as the fourth or fifth century, when the institutional church assumed the duties and practices once associated with various spiritual practices carried out by individual laypeople. The church established hostels for traveling strangers, hospitals for the sick and poor, and monasteries, which housed pilgrims (43). At least one early church leader noticed the shift and commented on it. John Chrysostom, according to Pohl, insisted "that hospitality remained a personal, individual responsibility as well," and he urged Christians to keep a guest room in their homes (45).

Pohl argues that by the late medieval period, care for the marginalized had become impersonal and separated from the church. The exception is that the wealthy were welcomed guests in monasteries, a practice that reinforced social boundaries (48). I think of a classic illustration of this trend. On visiting Durham, England, one could walk to the highest point in the town to visit Palace Green. At one end of the green is Durham Castle, and at the other end is the magnificent Durham Cathedral, begun in 1096. The third oldest building on Palace Green is the Almshouse, built in the fifteenth century to care for the poor. This small simple building is roughly one hundred yards from the cathedral's main entrance. By the late medieval period, care for the poor no longer took place within the walls of the church. It had been "outsourced," as the almshouse's location reveals. The sixteenth-century reformer John Calvin (340), commenting on Hebrews 13:2, wrote, "This office of humanity has . . . nearly ceased to be properly observed among men; for the ancient hospitality celebrated in histories, is unknown to us."

John Wesley and the early Methodists are a notable exception to this trend, and this is largely due to their initial reliance on cell groups. Wesley, who was familiar with early church writings, employed small groups for discipleship purposes. These groups regularly met in the homes of church members, and as Pohl says, this pattern reintegrated "church and household" (54). A key element of Methodism's cell-group structure was the sharing of simple meals, called "love feasts." Wesley also encouraged his followers to visit and care for the sick in their homes; yet while this personal approach was encouraged, the early Methodists also established institutional homes for widows and orphans. This attempt to respond to the desperate social needs of eighteenth-century England undercut Wesley's desire to reinstitute a "home church" based hospitality. Additionally, he never clearly identified these works and practices as "hospitality," and so the practice as a spiritual act was never fully recovered (54-55).

Our own time period is not without groups witnessing to the importance of hospitality as a component of the faith. The Catholic Worker Movement, begun in the 1930s by Dorothy Day and Peter Maurin, operates 185 communities providing hospitality and services to North America's poor. Servants to Asia's Urban Poor (www.servantsasia.org) works with urban poor in both Asia and the West. The rescue-mission movement, begun in the late nineteenth century, continues to reach out to the homeless and needy.

There will always be a need for hospitality, opportunities for people to connect, and care to be extended to those on the margins of society. The question is, Do the Christians of our time have a heart and vision for such work? Have we applied our best creative thinking to the subject? In 1981 a group of concerned and visionary believers decided to do something to help the marginalized in Central Pennsylvania. In faith they applied for a loan to purchase a rundown multistory brick building on Paxton Street in Harrisburg. Their goal was to provide "a home for the poor, the disadvantaged, the mentally challenged, and the downcast" (www.paxtonmin.org). Twenty-eight years later, eighty-five residents plus staff members and their families live on site at the original location. The ministry has expanded to the Hudson Street Apartments, which house an additional five residents and a staff family, and the Boas Street House, which is home to five other independent residents. Thirty full-time and seven part-time staffers and a host of volunteers help provide a home for people needing a stable environment. Paxton Ministries is but one example of contemporary Christians trying to creatively provide hospitality in the name of Christ.

John's advice to withhold hospitality and even greetings from false teachers (*deceivers*, 2 John 7, 9-11) may present an even more complex scenario for contemporary Christians. One should not confuse this advice, which focuses on an internal theological dispute within Christianity, with a refusal to have interfaith dialogue. At the same time, we must recognize that Christian theology has always been somewhat diverse, but not without boundaries.

Given the increasing globalization of our world and pluralism of both U.S. and Canadian culture, it strikes me as essentially wise, if not necessary, for Christians to enter into dialogue with people from other faith traditions. Every day at school my youngest son eats lunch with a Muslim boy. I can drive approximately one hour from my home and visit a Buddhist monastery. At the least we would benefit from learning what values and truth we share. Open dialogue would also help us recognize the points where our thinking diverges.

Yet in order to have such an interfaith dialogue, we need to possess a fairly clear idea as to what we believe. This observation moves us directly back to both 1 and 2 John. We must not let the larger reality of our pluralistic world distract or muddle our thinking about the fact that Christianity holds to and advocates a particular set of theological beliefs. In my opinion, we do not want to approach faith issues in the same fashion as a senior high Sunday school teacher who approached his pastor to test a curriculum idea. He suggested he spend a quarter introducing the basic beliefs of the major world religions and then "let the students decide for themselves" which one was best. The pastor rejected this suggestion because as a Christian church, it was their responsibility "to advocate for Christianity." The elder knew this when he wrote 2 John, even if his solution of withholding hospitality was extreme.

The problem is that two thousand years has left us with a wealth of diverse thinking about the faith. This diversity of thought did not develop since the Reformation. Rather, it was there from the beginning, as James D. G. Dunn has shown. In his essay "Earliest Christianity: One Church or Warring Sects?" (1985: 79-100), Dunn makes the point that earliest Christianity consisted of diverse groups and understandings of the faith. There were, for example, Jewish and Gentile Christians. There was diversity within Jewish Christian circles as well. Despite the rich diversity, the early Christians had unity on a number of theological points. In particular, Dunn points to their "belief in Jesus—in Jesus as the climax of God's ongoing purpose for [hu]man's redemption, the one whom God had raised from the dead and exalted as Lord, the man who demonstrated most clearly what God is like" (99). This was a nonnegotiable truth for the early believers. Dunn also identifies a number of other points upon which Christians agreed "in essence": God and Jesus as one, salvation resulting from faith in Christ, "experience of the Spirit," the OT and traditions of Jesus as "authoritative for faith and life," "Christianity's continuity with Israel," baptism in Jesus' name and the Lord's Supper as a remembrance of Jesus, and "the need for an ethical outworking of faith through love" (99). Our challenge is to find ways to faithfully articulate these core beliefs, remain devoted to the faith without going *beyond it* (in the elder's words in 2 John 9), and be relevant to the world around us.

Perhaps there is a way forward between these two concerns for hospitality and theology that departs from the tradition(s). Is it not wise to know what we believe about Christ and why we believe these ideas? And if one of our convictions about Jesus Christ is that he is the pivotal figure in human affairs, should we not know how to articulate this in reasonable and inviting ways? Perhaps we must admit that for now the era of polemics must give way to apologetics. If apologetics is the order of the day, then hospitality becomes a crucial aspect of our lives as believers, as we seek to help others understand and know Jesus and the Scriptures in their witness to him. When people experience a gracious welcome in our homes and faith communities, they may graciously welcome and hear the message that we will eventually offer when asked why we believe and live the way we do. If the people we welcome use our hospitality to advocate teachings contrary to the gospel and the faith we have received from Scripture, then John's teaching may lead us to refuse hospitality.

3 John

PREVIEW

When we are facing a crisis, it often is not easy to formulate a plan for the way forward. This is certainly true for groups. Different members highlight and propose alternative action plans. Sometimes these strategies lead to conflict, and tensions rise. The scenario becomes quite complex when we add issues of power and authority. That is what we face in this third epistle.

This letter, the shortest in the NT, contains many puzzles. Initially it appears to be both personal and rather secular in form. More than any other NT letter, 3 John follows the classic Greco-Roman letter style. Additionally, God is only mentioned three times, and each time (in v. 6 and twice in v. 11) the name appears in a formulaic fashion. The names Jesus and Christ are not specifically used although the Greek expression *for the sake of the name* (*hyper gar tou onomatos*) in verse 7 probably is a reference to Jesus. Therefore the NRSV translates the phrase *for the sake of Christ*. Some scholars view the letter as so personal that they see little or no theological significance in the text. Rather, it merely provides a window into the early church's developing polity and church structure.

Additionally, it mentions four individuals and makes passing reference to a personal conflict between two of them. The elder, who has no further specific identity, is writing to an equally unknown but faithful Gaius to enlist his help, having been rebuffed by a person named Diotrephes. Not only has Diotrephes ignored the elder; he has also gossiped about him; and if the elder is to be believed, Diotrephes takes a little too much pleasure in being in charge. If that is not enough, Diotrephes refuses hospitality to *the brothers*, who are traveling missionaries, and wants to expel any church member who would provide such hospitality. Finally, a man named Demetrius is highly recommended to Gaius by the writer.

Such scant information has not hindered speculation about the situation that prompted the letter. Although we cannot fully explore all the nuanced theories, the basic arguments fall into two general categories: doctrine and polity. Often the theoretical contexts are rather simplistic, revolving around orthodoxy and heresy (the elder represents one camp, and Diotrephes falls into the other), or traditional church structure and developing polity. Raymond Brown, who provides a brief summary of six hypothetical contexts (1982: 733-39), wisely suggests that both issues may be at work. Clearly this letter is concerned about traveling missionaries, as in 2 John. Some of those individuals were advocating false doctrines. Equally obvious is the fact that the elder believes Diotrephes has ignored his (the writer's) authority at some level and is assuming a leadership role that the elder finds difficult to accept. Brown suggests that both the elder and Diotrephes want to stop false teachers, but they disagree on tactics to do so. The elder wants believers to apply the "spiritual test" set out in 1 John 4:1-6. Diotrephes follows a more radical approach: *no* traveling missionaries are to be welcomed. Though Brown's theory is appealing, it too is mere speculation about the reason this enigmatic letter was written.

A clearer case, however, can be made for the connection between 3 John and the Johannine literary tradition. The letter repeatedly employs words that we have frequently read in 1 and 2 John, such as *children, love, truth,* and *testimony* (3 John 1, 3-4, 6, 8, 12). The author uses two expressions that also occur in the previous letter. *I rejoice greatly* (AT) occurs in both 2 John 4 and 3 John 3, and even more important is the reason for the author's great joy: in both instances believers *walk in the truth*, which is the second expression (2 John 4; 3 John 3, cf. 1 John 1:6-7). The same verb (*exerchomai*) is used in both 2 John 7 (*have gone out*) and 3 John 7 (*began their journey*) to describe the travels of roaming teachers, both faithful and unfaithful. Also, the opening verses of both 2 and 3 John share a verbatim expression (*I love in truth*). The conclusions of each, privileging a visit over more writing (2 John 12 and 3 John 13-14), are also similar. Nor should we forget that both letters are written by *the elder*, who is addressing the same core issue of hospitality for traveling missionaries. Clearly 3 John is somehow related to 2 John and in turn to the entirety of the Johannine corpus. John's dual pattern of response comes into play on this topic as well, as illustrated here for verses 11-12:

11-12 Another Opportunity for Hospitality

Beloved, do not imitate what is evil	but imitate what is good.
Whoever does good is from God;	whoever does evil
	has not seen God.

Everyone has testified favorably about Demetrius,
and so has the truth itself.
We also testify for him,
and you know that our testimony is true.

OUTLINE

Prescript, 1
Prayer and Author's Joy, 2-4
Body of the Letter, 5-12

5-8   Affirming Gaius's Support for Missionaries
9-10   Criticizing Diotrephes' Refusal to Support Missionaries
11-12   Another Opportunity for Hospitality

Closing, 13-15

EXPLANATORY NOTES

Prescript 1

As with 2 John, this letter begins in a form common to ancient letters: it initially and succinctly identifies both the sender and the recipient. Here, as in 2 John, the sender is simply known as *the elder*. For further details on the elder's role, see comments on 2 John. It seems clear that 3 John, like 2 John, is in part concerned about the sender's authority. Here the exact situation that calls into question his authority is both vague and complex, as noted in the Preview.

We know nothing about the recipient apart from what is revealed in this letter. His name is Gaius, he is loved by the elder, he is faithful *to the truth* (3), he supports *the friends* (5-8), who are probably traveling missionaries aligned with the elder, and the elder trusts Gaius enough to recommend another person, Demetrius, to him (11-12). *Gaius* was a common name in the Roman Empire, and we should not conclude this Gaius is the same as any of the men with the same name mentioned in Acts 19:29; 20:4; Romans 16:23; or 1 Corinthians 1:14. Though Gaius is essentially unknown to us, he seemingly is well known to the sender, for he is described as *beloved* and one whom the elder *love[s] in truth*. In 2 John we concluded that the expression *in truth* (*en alētheia*) should be translated *truly*. Therefore, the opening verse stresses the sender's positive regard and affection for Gaius. This should not be surprising although it may be redundant to call him *beloved* and to affirm that he is truly loved. We must remember that ultimately the elder needs Gaius's support, and a positive opening cannot hurt his cause.

Prayer and Author's Joy 2-4

More than any other letter in the NT, 3 John closely follows the classic letter form found widely in the ancient Greco-Roman world. This is especially true of verses 2-4, which form an *exordium*. This epistolary device followed the greetings and was designed to create a bond between the sender and receiver in that it expresses a desire or prayer for the recipient's good health and makes positive affirmations about the receiver (see Kruse: 220-21). After beginning with a term of endearment, *beloved*, which we will see two more times (in 5 and 11) and have repeatedly seen in 1 John (2:7; 3:2, 21; 4:1, 7, 11), the elder cites his prayer. His desire is that *all may go well with you and that you may be in good health, just as it is well with your soul* (2). This prayer expresses a desire that Gaius's entire being or existence, not simply his spiritual being, is in good order. We see this especially from the author's use of the word *psychē*, translated as *soul* in the NRSV. In John 10:15, 17-18 Jesus gives up his *psychē*, or entire being (cf. 1 John 3:16).

Verses 3 and 4 focus on the reason for the elder's affirming Gaius: he is faithful *to the truth* (3). Evidently the elder has received positive reports from believers to whom Gaius has shown hospitality (cf. 5-8). We cannot be totally certain that these *friends* (*brothers* in the original Greek) were missionaries, but given the letter's concerns, this is certainly a probability. The verb tense in verse 3 leads us to believe that there was not simply one good report; rather, it seems that there were numerous and consistent reports regarding Gaius's *faithfulness to the truth*. The author's use of the expression *walk in the truth* reminds us of similar terms in the other two letters (2 John 4, 6; 1 John 1:6-7, 10-11; 2:6, 11). The expression is probably shorthand for the Johannine community's understanding of the gospel. Gaius, according to verses 3-4 and the reports referred to there, is a model of the Johannine tradition's stressing both correct doctrine and correct behavior. The greatest joy that the elder knows is that church members, even those at a distance, are faithful.

Body of the Letter 5-12

5-8 Affirming Gaius's Support for Missionaries

While verses 3-4 generically affirm Gaius's commitment to the truth, verses 5-8 address one specific aspect of his commitment. He

loves, which as we have seen in 1 John, is at the heart of the
Johannine tradition. Verse 5 tells us that Gaius's love is consistent
(*You do faithfully whatever you do for the friends*) and without reservation (*even though they are strangers to you*). Verse 6 leads us to believe
that it was the recipients of this practical Christian love who made
the positive reports to the elder and his church: *They have testified to
your love before the church.* Numerous scholars conclude, reasonably
so, that Gaius had generously and graciously extended hospitality to
the people who made the positive reports to the elder and his congregation.

Verses 6 and 7 explain why these strangers needed Gaius's assis-
tance: they were traveling missionaries. These verses provide three
phrases that lead us to this conclusion:

1. *You do well to send them on in a manner worthy of God.*
2. *They began their journey for the sake of Christ,*
3. *accepting no support from non-believers.*

The first expression, especially *you do well*, is one that occurs in
later letters of recommendation for traveling Christian missionaries.
For example, Ignatius's letter *To the Smyrnaeans* (10.1) reads, "You do
well to receive as deacons of God, Philo and Rheus Agathepous, who
followed me into the cause of God" (Lake 1912: 263). Additionally, this
initial expression uses the verb "send on" (*propempō*) that is used in
the NT to describe the act of supporting and aiding traveling missionaries (cf. Acts 15:3; 20:38; 21:5; Rom 15:24; 1 Cor 16:6; 2 Cor 1:16; Titus
3:13), and it implies offering material aid to the travelers. The second
expression specifically provides the reason for their travels: *the sake of
Christ.* Literally, the Greek text reads *for the name,* but we know this is
a Christological expression from such texts as Acts 4:12, 17, 30; 8:12;
9:21, 28; 10:43; 16:18; 22:16; 26:9. Repeatedly the early believers did
and said things "in the name" of Christ Jesus, and in this instance they
were traveling so as to share the gospel of Christ. Finally, the expression *accepting no support from non-believers* clarifies why Gaius's support is so invaluable. In this respect Gaius is the embodiment of the
hospitable individuals who made missionary activity possible in the
early church.

Even the final verse of this subsection hints at *the friends'* role as
missionaries. They work *with the truth,* which for the author is probably a reference to his community's traditional understanding of the
gospel. More than this, however, is suggested by verse 8. In this verse
the elder reinforces the essential importance of people like Gaius in

supporting these traveling missionaries. To offer such material aid not only helps the missionaries carry out their task; it also establishes the donor as a *co-worker* in spreading the gospel.

9-10 Criticizing Diotrephes' Refusal to Support Missionaries

Having affirmed Gaius's commitment to the truth and in particular his love displayed in his hospitality extended to traveling missionaries who are personally unknown to him, the elder now turns his attention to a negative role model: Diotrephes. Unfortunately, we know nothing about him apart from the information given in this letter. On the positive side, we can say that Diotrephes had some degree of authority in his congregation. He believes he has a right to ignore a letter the elder sent to the church (9). While there are numerous theories as to the identity of this letter, including the belief that it was 2 John, we simply cannot identify it. There is a good chance that it is lost, having been destroyed because Diotrephes disagreed with it. Not only does he think he has the authority to ignore the elder, but he also exercises authority over other believers who want to side with the elder on the issue of welcoming missionaries. Diotrephes *expels*, or excommunicates, people who ignore him and follow the elder's advice on this matter (10).

Diotrephes' refusal to follow the elder's specific *authority* regarding missionaries lies at the heart of this conflict, but it is not the only point of tension between the two men. The elder levels two other charges: he *likes to put himself first*, and he spreads *false charges against us*. The word used to describe Diotrephes' attempts to *put himself first* (*philoprōtenō*) is extremely rare and used only here in the NT. It does not occur in the LXX or in Greek writings of the early church period (Kruse: 226, n16). A similar noun (*philoprōteia*) and an adjective (*philoprōtos*), however, are used in classical Greek writings. Brown theorizes that the elder created this word, which hints at ambition, so as to avoid Diotrephes' actual ecclesiastical title (1982: 717). The elder's other charge is that Diotrephes is, literally, *babbling against us with evil words* (v. 10). Seemingly the elder's opponent had engaged in a verbal campaign to discredit him in the congregation. It may well be a result of these *false charges* that the elder resorts to contacting Gaius as a potential supporter for the elder and his community's missionary endeavors. If this is the case, Gaius was probably the leader of a Christian congregation in Diotrephes' general vicinity, but not under his direct control.

One final point is to be made on these verses. The use of the personal plural pronouns in the phrases *does not acknowledge our authority* and *spreading false charges against us* has fostered a fair amount of debate. While some scholars view the shift from the dominant first-person singular to these plural forms as simply stylistic, others assume that their presence is evidence that the elder is part of the group of tradition bearers of which 1 John 1:1-5 speaks. These tradition bearers have stressed correct behavior (love) and correct doctrine (Jesus is the Christ), and these two themes are the basis for salvation and church unity. As Brown notes, to reject the elder's letter and advice is more than a personal affront: it threatens the fellowship with other believers who hold to the Johannine tradition (1982: 745).

11-12 Another Opportunity for Hospitality

The final subsection of the letter's body begins with *beloved*, which we have seen twice previously in this epistle. This closing section serves at least two purposes. First, it reminds Gaius of a foundational Johannine duality, focusing on evil and good. This duality can be depicted in a fashion similar to much of John's argument in the first letter, here in chiastic structure (A, A': evil; B, B': good):

> Beloved, do not imitate what is evil   but imitate what is good.
> Whoever does good is from God;   whoever does evil has
>   not seen God.

The unit's second goal is to introduce a new person, Demetrius, to the letter's recipient.

In verse 11 the elder highlights Johannine traditional duality between good and evil. Those who are *from God* do good, and those who have *not seen God* do evil. We have already seen this theology articulated in 1 John 2:29; 3:6, 10; 4:7. In fact, given the opening emphasis on Gaius's love and hospitality, the elder may have in mind a verse like 1 John 3:10: *The children of God and the children of the devil are revealed in this way: all who do not do what is right are not from God, nor are those who do not love their brothers and sisters.* The Gospel of John (5:29) employs the same "do good/do evil" language. Such thinking was not, however, unique to the elder and the Johannine tradition (see Rom 12:21; 1 Cor 10:1-13; 2 Thess 3:6-13; 1 Pet 3:9-14).

The second concern is the introduction of a man named Demetrius, who probably delivered this letter to Gaius. Like Gaius and Diotrephes, the only information we have about him is found in the letter. We know even less about Demetrius because we are only told that *everyone has testified favorably about Demetrius.* The elder goes out of his way to emphasize this point. Not only does *everyone* have a positive testimony about him, but also *the truth itself has testified*, and *we* confirm this. It is difficult to know what is meant by *so has the truth itself*. It could simply mean that because Demetrius supports the elder and is thus aligned with *truth*. More likely Demetrius's lifestyle, much like Gaius's own lifestyle, reveals his commitment to the truth. The final testimony comes from a group that the author simply identifies as *we*, but he does assert *that our testimony is true* (12). This is probably a reference to the Johannine tradition bearers, as noted above in the comments on verses 9-10. Some scholars have concluded that Demetrius was an official missionary from the Johannine school, and this may well be the case. We do not, however, have any supporting evidence for this assertion. Assuming that Demetrius is the bearer of this letter, it is clear that he would probably need at least overnight lodging and food before returning to the elder, and so the elder, as sender of the letter, vouches for him.

Closing 13-15

As many scholars notice, the closing resembles other first-century epistolary closings and the closing of 2 John. It is succinct and clear. Like a typical ancient letter, the elder asserts his preference to converse in person rather than through the mail. Second John and 3 John share both similar and exact wording at points, for example, the desire to speak *face to face* (*mouth to mouth*, as the Greek literally puts it; 2 John 12; 3 John 14).

The exception to this formulaic custom is the inclusion of a wish for peace. Often this appears at the beginning of an ancient letter. What we see here may be the start of a Christianized conclusion because both Ephesians 6:23 and 1 Peter 5:14 also contain a reference to peace. Additionally, Ignatius's letter *To the Smyrnaeans* (12.2) reads, "Grace be to you, mercy, peace, and endurance forever." The influence to close this way may have come from the Gospel of John, where the risen Christ says to his disciples "peace be with you" (20:19, 21, 26).

THE TEXT IN BIBLICAL CONTEXT

Imitation

Such a personal letter presents a challenge when we are seeking to identify themes that appear elsewhere in the Bible. The notable exception is 3 John 11: *Do not imitate what is evil but imitate what is good*. The idea of imitation is a recurring theme in early Christianity, even if the verb *mimeomai*, "to imitate," is found only four times in the entire NT (here; 2 Thess 3:7, 9; Heb 13:7). In 2 Thessalonians, Paul is arguing that the recipients ought to imitate him and his peers' commitment to hard work, rather than lapsing into idleness. Hebrews encourages its readers to imitate the positive role models given by the leaders who have shared the Gospel.

The noun *imitator(s)* is found six times (1 Cor 4:16; 11:1; Eph 5:1; 1 Thess 1:6; 2:14; 1 Pet 3:13; Heb 6:12). In 1 Corinthians 11:1, Paul encourages the wayward Corinthians to be "imitators of me" (cf. 4:16). The Ephesians are told to be "imitators of God, as beloved children" (5:1), and Paul reminds the Thessalonians, "You became imitators of us and of the Lord" (1 Thess 1:6; cf. 2:14, which also commends the recipients for imitating other churches facing persecution). Hebrews 6:12 encourages the imitation "of those who through faith and patience inherit the promises" (cf. 13:7). Although believers are encouraged to imitate both church leaders and Christ, Christ is the ultimate role model. This notion of imitation within early Christian writings may well be based upon Jesus' own teaching that believers must imitate God's perfection (Matt 5:48; for further analysis of "imitation in the NT and its relation to discipleship," see Swartley 2006: 360-76).

Jesus may also be the source of emphasis on imitating *good* and not imitating *evil*. John 5 expresses Jesus' teaching about resurrection events. Verse 29 tells us Jesus taught that in the resurrection "those who have done good" will be raised and given "the resurrection of life," while "those who have done evil" will be given "the resurrection of condemnation." I am inclined to believe that this traditional teaching has influenced the Johannine letters at places like 1 John 2:29; 3:6, 10; 4:7, 12; and 3 John 11, as well as the letters' firm dualist moral worldview. It is not only the Johannine letters that stress imitating good and avoiding evil; we see this in 1 Peter as well. When giving advice on Christian behavior in the presence of Gentiles, Peter advises his readers to keep the day of the resurrection and judgment in mind, and so they are to perform "honorable deeds" (1 Pet 2:12). Believers thus silence the foolish "by doing right" (2:15), but their freedom is not "a pretext for evil" (2:16; cf. 1 Pet 3:17).

THE TEXT IN THE LIFE OF THE CHURCH

Supporting Missionaries

The central issue behind this personal letter, supporting traveling missionaries, is a topic worth reflecting upon in our contemporary situation. Admittedly, the first-century scenario radically differs from contemporary internationalized and denominationally organized missions work. The positive encouragement of verse 8, *We ought to support such people, so that we may become co-workers with the truth,* raises questions: How might we support aid workers and missionaries? How might that support be a benefit to us who stay at home? The importance of supporting those who work for the gospel is, perhaps, easier to grasp. Here I am thinking well beyond financial support. Something more personal is in mind. As someone who has lived internationally, I assure you that letters (and now emails) from home are positive morale boosters. Nor can I begin to explain the excitement my wife had when friends were passing through the United Kingdom and decided to go out of their way to visit us. Even more important may be how we provide for missionaries when they are on furlough. Where will they live for this temporary time? What will they do for an automobile? Who will be their friends here while they are missing their friends there? Who is going to offer fashion hints to their teenage mission kids? Although that may not be important to you or me, I suspect that this is rather important to many adolescents who are entering a new culture. How can we go out of our way to support our missionaries and provide welcoming church communities for them?

More challenging is the question: How does our providing such support make us *co-workers with the truth*? At both the emotional and material level, our support for missionaries is a valuable work for the gospel. During these short furloughs, missionaries should be focusing on agendas other than trying to cope with all the stressors of everyday life associated with reentry into another culture. Thus our support makes their home assignments easier. To have a mechanically sound vehicle makes their deputation travels to various congregations possible. Once at these congregations, they are then able to share and report on their work. This personal contact facilitates connectedness and encourages wise prayer support for the missionaries' undertakings. Finally, if we make good use of our time with missionaries, we will learn of the successes and struggles of brothers and sisters around the world. Such awareness can only move the thoughtful Christian to thankfulness, prayer, and support for the many good missionaries and aid workers from our denominations. Indeed, extending hospitality to those who work for the gospel still has numerous benefits and is a source of positive kingdom building.

Church Conflicts

As the letter reveals, conflict in the church is not a new phenomenon. Christians have disagreed with one another since the church's beginning. What else can we expect when people from different cultural backgrounds, holding differing values and worldviews, come together?

Add variations of personality and emotional flaws, and the conditions for conflict are perfect. Is there any Christian who has not experienced or heard of conflicts within the church? This reality becomes even more discouraging when we realize that we have been called to a life of peace, and the church is to be a model of the coming kingdom. Although 3 John is too brief for us to even begin thinking about who was right and wrong, it does offer a few helpful insights as to what to avoid or how to proceed when facing potentially conflictive situations.

First, when in the midst of conflict, it is not helpful to give in to our selfish natures. We can only begin to guess why Diotrephes needed to be *first* and why the elder needed to state that he had this problem (9). Either way it seems as though we have two people at odds over personality issues. Important congregational issues should be decided without dragging personal matters into the discussion. This will only complicate the situation. If a congregational decision goes in a direction other than the way I prefer, I should not conclude that it is a "vote against me." It may be a bad choice, but it is not necessarily one designed to slight me. And if the votes always go in a direction that I do not think wise, perhaps I should wonder about my perspective. Humility goes a long way toward diffusing potentially explosive situations.

Second, we must be careful to avoid gossiping about those with whom we disagree. Not only should we not spread false rumors, as Diotrephes apparently did; we also should be careful about what we say and to whom we speak when talking about conflict. I realize that we often need to talk to a third party when in the midst of intense disagreement, but we must also ask ourselves, "Will this person keep this discussion confidential?" Additionally, we need to be fair to the other party when reporting conversations to the third party. Always ask yourself if the story is told as fairly and accurately as possible. We must avoid the temptation to lapse into passive-aggressive behavior, especially the temptation to gossip about the other person. And we should never tell the story in such a way as to attract people to our side.

Finally, the elder is on the right track when he expresses an interest in dealing with the conflict in person (vv. 10, 14). While face-to-face conversations involving conflict are threatening and potentially painful, they are better than unresolved conflict, miscommunication, and misunderstanding. The anxiety associated with such conversations is worth investing in, especially if the conflict can be better understood and possibly resolved. Perhaps that is why Jesus gave us specific instructions for handling interpersonal conflict (see Matt 18:15-20). We should be hesitant to ignore the teachings of our Lord.

Outline of 1, 2, 3 John

1 John

Introduction	**1:1-4**
The Content of Our Proclamation	1:1a-d
The Content of Our Writing	1:1e-2
The Reason We Proclaim	1:3
The Reason We Write	1:4
Knowing *and* Doing	**1:5–2:17**
Our Claims and Reality	1:5–2:2
Theological Introduction	1:5
Claiming Fellowship, Walking in Darkness	1:6-7
Claiming Sinlessness, Deceiving Ourselves	1:8-9
Claiming Not to Have Sinned, Making Him a Liar	1:10–2:2
To Know Is to Obey	2:3-11
Introduction of a General Principle	2:3
A General Test of the Principle	2:4-6
A Parenthetical Clarification on the Principle's Origin	2:7-8
A Specific Test of the Principle	2:9-11
Why I Write to You	2:12-14
Triplet One	2:12-13
Triplet Two	2:14
Do Not Love the World	2:15-17
An Exhortation and First Reason	2:15
Behavior Revealing One's Orientation to the World	2:16
A Second Reason for the Exhortation	2:17

The Present Situation: Confidence Amid
   Conflict and Confusion   **2:18–3:24**
The Last Hour and Confusion   2:18-27
   The Last Hour: Confusion and Schism   2:18-20
   Who Is the Liar?   2:21-25
   Do Not Be Deceived: Be Confident   2:26-27

Abiding and Doing Right   2:28–3:10
   Little Children (Part One)   2:28–3:6
   Little Children (Part Two)   3:7-10

Illustration, Encouragement, and Transition   3:11-24
   Introduction   3:11
   Illustrations of Hate and Love   3:12-18
   A Pastoral Parenthesis   3:19-22
   Summary and Transition   3:23-24

The Work of the Spirit   **4:1–5:12**
Belief and the Spirit   4:1-6
   Testing Spirits   4:1-3
   Words of Encouragement   4:4-6

Love and the Spirit   4:7–5:4a
   The Source and Purpose of Love   4:7-11
   Further Exploration and Implications of This Love   4:12-19
   Polemic Against the Separatists in Light of Love   4:20–5:4a

Testimony of the Spirit   5:4b-12
   A Rhetorical Question, Answer, and Testimonial Support 5:4b-8
   The Result of Accepting or Rejecting the Testimony   5:9-12

Concluding Words   **5:13-21**
Believing in the Name, Having Eternal Life   5:13
Confidence in Prayer in the Face of Sin   5:14-17
Foundational Knowledge   5:18-20
Final Admonition   5:21

2 John
Greetings   1-3
Body   4-11
   Rejoicing and Encouragement   4-6
   Directions Regarding Deceivers   7-11
Closing   12-13

3 John

Prescript   1
Prayer and Author's Joy   2-4
Body of the Letter   5-12
    Affirming Gaius's Support for Missionaries   5-8
    Criticizing Diotrephes' Refusal to Support Missionaries   9-10
    Another Opportunity for Hospitality   11-12
Closing   13-15

Essays

"ABIDING" IN THE JOHANNINE LETTERS Given the larger social context of conflicting theologies and church schism in which these letters were written, it should not be surprising that the theme of "abiding" or remaining is a significant topic in 1 John. Those who decided to remain within the Johannine tradition likely had some passing doubt of the correctness of their decision. The concept of "abiding" is not a new theological category created by our author. In the larger Johannine tradition, it is a central theme, denoted by the verb *menō* ("abide" or "remain"), which is used forty times in the Gospel of John, twenty-four times in 1 John, and three times in 2 John. These sixty-seven uses account for 55 percent of the word's employment in the NT. The significance of the concept increases when one considers that the Johannine tradition also uses the expression *einai en* ("to be in") in an almost interchangeable fashion (Brown 1982: 259).

In the Johannine tradition "abide" is "almost exclusively" a term applied to "*divine* indwelling" (261). It is a concept from the OT that addresses God's eternal existence (Pss 9:7; 102:12; Dan 6:26 in the LXX; cf. similar thoughts without the use of *menō* in Pss 90:1-2; 99:1; Mic 5:2; Hab 1:12). God, however, is not only eternal or merely enthroned above the earth in the heavens. The OT also has a sense of God's immanence or presence with Israel. Predominantly this Presence is fulfilled in the cultic context. In the temple the Lord chooses to dwell with his people. At the dedication of the temple, Solomon is aware that this building cannot contain the Lord's glory and being, but it was built as God's "exalted house, a place for you [God] to reside in forever" (2 Chron 6:2; cf. Ezek 48:35; Zech 2:10-11; Joel 3:21). The concept continued into the intertestamental period, as Jubilees 1:17, 26; Sirach 24:3, 8; Wisdom 7:25 and 27 show (Brown 1982: 284).

In the Johannine tradition this sense of divine immanence is taken one step further, and at some level this is a radical leap forward. God no longer merely dwells *with* his people; rather, God and his people dwell *within* each other. For example, 1 John 3:24 reads, *All who obey his command abide in him, and he abides in them. And by this we know that he abides in us, by the Spirit that he has given us* (cf. 1 John 2:6; 4:12-13, 15-16). Thus some scholars use the expression "mutuality" to describe the nature of the Johannine sense of "abiding" (Brown 1982: 284; Smalley: 210; Painter: 101).

This sense of mutual abiding probably goes back to the Johannine traditional teaching. The divine Word took up residence in the midst of humanity, revealing his "glory as of a father's only son, full of grace and truth" (John 1:14). The relationship between the divine Father and the Son (God and Jesus) was perceived as one of mutual indwelling or abiding (14:10-11; cf. 10:38). Furthermore, the ideal relationship between the Word and the believer is described with the vine and branches imagery in John 15. There Jesus encourages his followers to "abide in me as I abide in you" (15:4). Having made these two separate identifications of mutual indwelling, it becomes easy for our author to conclude, *If what you heard from the beginning abides in you, then you will abide in the Son and in the Father* (1 John 2:24). Elsewhere, he affirms that believers abide in God (2:6; 3:24; 4:13, 15-16) and in Jesus (2:27-28; 3:6; cf. John 6:56; 15:4-7), and also God abides in the believer (1 John 3:24; 4:12-13, 15-16).

Finally, this divine/human indwelling has implications for the corporate gathering of believers. When John writes, *You will abide in the Son and in the Father* (1 John 2:24), he uses the plural form of *you* (cf. 3:24; 4:12-13). Each individual believer abides in the Father and the Son and is not alone. Other believers are also abiding in God and Jesus. Thus there is a mutuality among those who are faithful to the things they have heard from the beginning (1 John 1:1-4); unlike the secessionists, they *believe in the name of his Son Jesus Christ and love one another* (3:23). Their common life is found in what God has done in the person of Jesus and they endeavor to order their lives according to his teachings. As 1 John 4:12 says, *If we love one another, God lives in us, and his love is perfected in us.* Thus Painter concludes, "Believers are described in terms of the community of mutual love, which is grounded in God's love" (101). This may well explain why the command to "love one another" appears only in the Gospel of John and the Johannine letters (John 13:34-35; 15:12, 17; 1 John 3:11, 23; 4:7, 11-12; 2 John 5; cf. though Rom 12:10; 13:8; 1 Pet 1:22).

APOCALYPTICISM The word *apocalypticism* comes from the Greek word *apokalypsis*, meaning "revelation" or "unveiling." Though in the past there was disagreement among scholars regarding the origin of apocalyptic thought within Judaism and just how widespread it was within Jewish circles before Christ, currently there is growing agreement on these subjects. For example, we are aware that apocalyptic thinking was not limited to Judaism. Canaanite religion has left relics of an apocalyptic mythology (Rowland 2006: 191), and volume 1 of *The Encyclopedia of Apocalypticism* (Collins; see Rowland: 2005) contains three initial articles regarding apocalypticism in Near Eastern mythology, Persian thought, and Greek and Roman antiquity. Thus Rowland can conclude, "The world of late antiquity was one characterized by the quest for divine wisdom, which came through dreams and other forms of revelation" (2006: 191).

Apocalyptic thinking was widespread within Second Temple Judaism with evidence that it had influenced priests, Pharisees, Essenes, and others

(190). At some level this should not be surprising in light of the fact that apocalyptic elements are found in both OT prophetic and wisdom literature (191). Additionally, apocalyptic literature from late Jewish and Christian antiquity points to the general popularity of this genre. These texts include *1, 2, and 3 Enoch*; *2 Esdras* (*4 Ezra*); *The Apocalypse of Abraham*; *The Ascension of Isaiah*; and the works of the Shepherd of Hermas. Moreover, two apocalyptic books were finally included in the Christian Bible: Daniel and Revelation. Rowland identifies six "well-defined characteristics" within Jewish apocalypticism (2006: 190). There is a hope that a better world will arrive when God's kingdom appears in human history. The thinking tends to be "dualist," with a tension between this evil present time and the future. "Eschatological expectation" anticipates a radical transformation of this age (190). Because of the contrast between evil and good in the present age, there is a tendency to embrace sectarian thought within the communities that embrace apocalyptic categories. Their eschatological hope includes a belief that the end of the world is imminent. Finally, human history is viewed deterministically. Essentially apocalypticism is a hopeful theological movement because its adherents believe these truths are divinely revealed through various types of revelations including "visions, epiphanies, otherworldly journeys, angel interpreters, and secret books" (Yeatts: 440). The divine source of these revelations is the foundation for that hope. Moreover, the receiving community is encouraged to believe that they will be vindicated when God's kingdom breaks into their history.

CHILDREN OF GOD / BORN OF GOD As R. Alan Culpepper notes (2006: 590), the idea of using familial language to describe the divine/human relationship is quite old and not limited to biblical writings. In the Bible, however, expressions like "child of God" or "son of God" denote a unique relation between God and those who are faithful to God. Though not widespread, the OT uses this familial imagery and assumes or highlights the covenant between the Lord and Israel. This is particularly true of the crucial event in Israel's early history. In the exodus, the Lord claims Israel as "my firstborn son" (Exod 4:22; cf. Hos 11:1). The parental imagery appears in other literary genres as well, such as Psalm 103:13: "As a father has compassion for his children, so the LORD has compassion for those who fear him" (cf. Prov 3:12). This theme of "fearing" or respecting the Lord highlights another aspect of Israel's identity as God's child or son: as a member of the Lord's family, Israel is expected to be obedient to the Lord. Because they are "children of the LORD," they are to refrain from pagan behavior (Deut 14:1-2; cf. Ps 82; Hos 1:1–2:1). When Israel disregards its relationship with the Lord, the nation is described as "degenerate children" who deal "falsely with him [the LORD]" (Deut 32:4-6; cf. Isa 1:2, 4; 30:1).

In the NT the notion of covenant as the basis for familial imagery gives way to incarnation. This is especially true in Pauline thought, but it also appears elsewhere. Paul uses the expression "children of God" (Rom 8:16, 21; 9:8, 26; Gal 3:26; Phil 2:15) as well as "sons of God" (Rom 8:14, 19 RSV; "children of God" NRSV) and "children of the promise" (Rom 9:8; Gal 4:28; cf. the expression "heirs according to the promise" in Gal 3:29 and the use of "heir" in Gal 4:7; Titus 3:7). Romans 8:1-17 is of particular interest. In these verses Paul addresses the tension between life in "the flesh" and life in "the Spirit." Those who are "in Christ" (8:1-2) have been set free and are no longer "in the flesh." Rather, they are "in the Spirit since the Spirit of God dwells in you" (8:9). Paul argues further, "If the Spirit of him who raised Jesus from the dead dwells in you, he who raised Christ from the dead will give life to your mortal bodies also through his Spirit that dwells in you" (8:11). Paul later concludes, "All who are led by the Spirit of God are children of God" (8:14), and this status as children of God means that believers are "heirs of God and joint heirs with Christ" (8:17). While the early Christians came to view Jesus as the "unique" Son of God (Matt 14:33; Mark 1:11; 3:11; 9:7; 15:39; John 1:34; 3:17-18; 5:25; 10:36; 11:4; Acts 9:20; Rom 1:4; 2 Cor 1:19; Gal 2:20; Eph 4:13; Heb 4:14; 1 John 3:8; 4:15; 5:5, 10, 13, 20), they also came to see themselves as his "siblings" and by extension "children of God."

The fact that the metaphor continued to be used is probably due to Jesus' own thinking and teachings. He taught his followers that they should think of God as "Father" (Matt 5:48; Luke 6:35-36) and address God as "Father" when they pray (Matt 6:9; Luke 11:2). One of his best-known parables depicts God as the patient and loving father of two difficult sons (Luke 15:11-32). Moreover, it is clear that he accepted the OT idea that the children of God are faithful to God's ethical expectations. Matthew 5:48 identifies God, the Father, as the standard for Jesus' follower's behavior. In this same chapter (5:9, 45) we read that those who are peacemakers and love their enemies will be known as "children of God." And those who pray to their "Father" (Matt 6:9) are to forgive others if they desire forgiveness.

"Children of God" is used only twice in the Gospel of John (1:12; 11:52) and four times in 1 John (3:1, 2, 10; 5:2), and yet it is an important self-descriptor in the tradition (cf. Culpepper 2006: 592). The initial use of the term in the Gospel's prologue is found at the structural turning point (592). The Gospel's introduction makes the point that a key result of the incarnation of the Word is that to all "who believed in his name, he gave power to become children of God" (1:12). The next verse makes it clear that this act of becoming a child of God is due to divine action. The concept is clarified in the dialogue between Jesus and Nicodemus (John 3). Only those who are "born from above" can see the kingdom of God (3:3), and this rebirth is the result of "being born of water and Spirit" (3:5), which is made possible by the crucifixion (3:14-15; 7:37-39; 19:34). Belief in the incarnation and death of Jesus Christ is the factor that contributes to one's status as a child of God (3:16-18). As the comments above point out (esp. on 1 John 4:7–5:4a and 5:4b-12), this is a crucial theological point, which 1 John defends.

The letter accepts this foundational idea that belief or knowledge of what God did in Jesus Christ is crucial to the believer's self-understanding, but there is more. First John 3:1 makes the dual point that becoming a child of God is a result of God's love (*See what love the Father has given us, that we should be called children of God*) and the trait distinguishing the *children of God* from *the world* is knowledge or lack of knowledge of God. Additionally, 1 John 3:2 makes the point that child-of-God status has an eschatological element. The author expects a future revelation at Jesus' return (2:28), and at that time the children of God will be shown to *be like him, for we will see him as he is* (3:2).

DOCETISM In the church's earliest days, believers explored numerous theological categories to explain what they perceived God as doing in their midst. Not surprisingly, christological reflection was a central concern. Docetism is one christological line of thought that the early church ultimately refused to accept. Docetism takes its name from the Greek word *dokeō*, or "seem," because the Docetics argued that Jesus only appeared or seemed to be human.

From surviving first- and second-century documents, we learn that this movement was both diverse and perhaps relatively widespread. The core issue was the relationship of Jesus' humanity (his flesh or physical body) and his divine nature (his spiritual essence). In this respect, docetic thought overlaps with Gnosticism *[Gnosticism, p. 308]*. People adhering to a docetic Christology resolved the tension between the physical and spiritual in different ways. Some argued that Jesus was the Christ, but he only appeared to have a physical body. Others affirmed that the human Jesus received the spiritual Christ at his baptism in the form of a dove (cf. Mark 1:9-11). They further argued that the Christ left the human Jesus before his death on the cross. As we have seen in the commentary above (cf. comments on 1 John 1:1-4; 2:22; 4:2-3, 14-15; 5:6-12; 2 John 7), our author is countering some manifestation of docetic thought, as did the writer of the Gospel of John (cf. 1:14-18).

The diversity of docetic thought can be observed by comparing 1–2 John with the writings of Ignatius of Antioch and early Christian references to Cerinthus. What little we know about Cerinthus comes from various early church fathers. He lived sometime between AD 85 and 100, and according to tradition he was from Alexandria, Egypt. Cerinthus, an early Gnostic, denied the incarnation, believing instead that the Christ descended upon the human Jesus, whom he viewed as a righteous man, at his baptism. Schnackenburg argues that the Docetists with whom Ignatius was familiar, on the other hand, were motivated by soteriological concerns and advocated their unique Christology in Asia Minor, where Ignatius had his ministry (1992: 18-23). They refused to take seriously Jesus' humanity. For them, Jesus Christ only appeared to be human (22). Thus Ignatius insisted that Jesus was genuinely born of a virgin, suffered on the cross, and was resurrected (cf. *To the Smyrnaeans* 1–3; *To the Trallians* 9–10).

DUALITY IN THE EPISTLES "Dualism" in the Johannine literature is not to be confused with philosophical dualism or religious dualism, such as in Zoroastrianism, which posits two ultimate coequal forces, good and evil, as Miroslav Volf has clarified (Bauckham: 19-50; cf. Swartley 2006: 292-94). Volf points out that according to John 1:3, God is a creating divinity who has "created everything that is not divine" (in Bauckham and Mosser: 23), thus implying that the whole world is God's, whether it loves or hates the one God who created and loves it. Not only did God create the world (cosmos), but God also intends to redeem it and "overcome oppositional dualities—

darkness versus light, below versus above, falsehood versus truth" (23). While the world opposes God, God still loves the world. Volf argues that the Johannine tradition points to God's desire to overcome the duality and create communion between God and the followers of Christ (24). In light of the work of Christ, God's agent, all other dualities are also being transformed. However, the resolution of these dualities lies in the future, for as Volf admits, "Even if John is not ultimately dualistic, he makes some of the most rigid oppositional dualities of any New Testament writer" (25). Hence the term *duality* is frequently employed in this commentary to remind us of this fine distinction, clarifying what John hopes for in the future but is not a present reality in his experience.

One of the dualities of which our author is fond relates to the separatists. If one decides to leave the church, or the children of God, there is only one place to go: the world, which does not embody God's love (1 John 2:15); rather, it lives out *the desire of the flesh, the desire of the eyes, the pride in riches* (2:16). This is where the false prophets teach (4:1) and the spirits refuse to confess Jesus has come in the flesh (4:2-3). On the other hand, the children of God know that Jesus was revealed to take away sin, and they abide in him and in God; therefore they do what is right and possess eternal life (3:5-7; cf. 3:9; 2:20-25). Not only do the children of God clearly understand Jesus, they also follow his commandment to love one another (2:3-6, 10; 3:10-19; 4:7-12 and 5:2). This two-pronged theme of thinking correctly about Jesus and obeying his commandment to love is foundational to John's duality, as 1 John 3:23 and 5:1-3 show.

Moreover, the theme of obedience helps us grasp the Johannine and, in general, the early Christian, understanding of duality. N.T. Wright argues that the early Christian sense of evil was not attributed to coequal forces, but to oppositional ones. Evil is in the cosmos because humans are "in rebellious idolatry by which humans worship and honor elements of the natural world rather than the God who made them. The result is that the cosmos is out of joint" (2008: 95). This ignoring of God, grasping for power and pleasure, results in death for humans and the whole of the created order. The early Christians, including John, recognized God's plan for the transformation of the world, and the resolution of these dualities included a new and significant development in the person of Jesus Christ (see Wright 2008: 93-108, chap. 6, "What the Whole World's Waiting For").

While some scholars, such as Bultmann (1927: 138-58), believe that our author was influenced by early Gnosticism—which was truly dualistic, stressing opposing good and evil forces—I do not believe this is the case; rather, the influence comes from a stream of thought that preceded even the Christian movement: Jewish apocalypticism. We know that apocalyptic thinking influenced early Christians, as Revelation shows. Additionally, Mark 13 and other Gospel passages would lead us to believe that Jesus himself reflects this way of thinking. What did it involve? This is certainly not the place for a detailed exploration, but we identify the following elements [*Apocalypticism, p. 301*].

In the last centuries before Jesus was born, apocalyptic thinking became important to Judaism as a way of making sense of their long history of persecution at the hands of the Gentile world. It recalled the covenant and placed its hope firmly on God's promises of faithfulness. Often this hope focused on the belief that at some point in time, God would intervene in human affairs to vindicate the faithful and vanquish the unfaithful anti-Godly forces in the world. While the events fueling this thinking were real-world political and social actions, often the Jews described their apocalyptic hopes in vivid and lurid images, as we see in Daniel 7–12, for example. N.T. Wright argues that "Jesus inherited this tradition and made it his own in one way in particular. He told stories whose many dimensions cracked open the worldview of his hearers and forced them to come to terms with God's reality breaking in to their midst" (1999: 38). When Jesus preached and told parables about the present and coming kingdom of God, he was speaking and thinking "apocalyptically." He held out the hope that the way the world was is not the way the world will always be because God is faithful and has promised to remake the world, overcoming those forces bent on its destruction and degradation.

This hope of overcoming *the world* is a key element of the duality that John accepts. It is a promise that he holds before his readers. The schism surely created doubts in their minds as to which party was "correct." We do not know, but perhaps the group accepting the new interpretation of the tradition and leaving the church was the larger group. John, in his unique pastoral fashion, goes out of his way to reassure the remaining minority. He promises that their acceptance of the traditional teaching on Christology and the command to love makes them members of the group that will be victorious over the world (1 John 5:4-5; cf. 5:10-12; 2:15-17, esp. 17). The author reminds the readers that the faithful will confidently face the judgment day (1 John 2:28; 4:17-18; 5:1-5, esp. 4-5; cf. 3:21-22).

ESCHATOLOGY The theological word *eschatology* comes from the Greek adjective *eschatos*, meaning "last." The term is applied to thoughts about the end of time, which in the biblical text includes concepts such as the day of judgment, the resurrection of the dead, the second coming (or *parousia*) of Christ, rewards and punishments, and the final victory of God. There are eschatological elements in the OT, and it seems as though such thinking expanded to incorporate new ideas in the intertestamental period, with the ultimate development appearing in the NT writings. The early Christians came to see Jesus Christ as the focus of their eschatological hopes.

Stephen Cook (300) makes the point that early OT traditions attribute eschatological overtones to human events in light of their belief that "God is about the business of perfecting humanity and the cosmos as a whole." Therefore, Psalm 137:7 refers to the destruction of Jerusalem in 586 BC as an eschatological event. Amos warns Israel of its impending doom or "end" (8:1-3, 11-14). Of particular importance, Cook notes, is the notion of "the Day of Yahweh," on which God and the divine plan will be vindicated as the Lord dramatically intervenes in human affairs. This idea is particularly evident within the prophetic tradition (see, e.g., Isa 25:9; Amos 5:18-20; Zeph 1:14-18; specific references to "the Day of the LORD" include Isa 2:12; 13:6, 9; 34:8; Jer 46:10; Ezek 13:5; 30:3; Joel 2:1; 3:14; Amos 5:18; Zeph 1:7-8; 2:2-3;

Mal 4:5; cf. 1 Cor 5:5; 2 Cor 1:14; 1 Thess 5:2; 2 Peter 3:10). The prophetic hope is that God will intervene to bring justice to the righteous and set right the affairs of the nations.

In the eschatological thought of later OT writings, the idea of the resurrection becomes an important theological belief (see Cook: 307). Ezekiel 37 and Daniel 12 are probably the best-known OT texts in this respect. Daniel 12:2 reads, "Many of those who sleep in the dust of the earth shall awake, some to everlasting life, and some to shame and everlasting contempt" (cf. Isa 26:19; Ps 22:29). Daniel 12:2 makes it clear that already in the OT the resurrection is associated with some form of reward and judgment.

The early Christians inherited this general eschatological framework, but their convictions about Jesus Christ had a major impact upon their thinking. As Dale Allison states, Jesus was viewed as the person who embodied and fulfilled Judaism's eschatological hope (via Cook: 294). Thus the early Christians' eschatological future expectation fully focused on his return or second coming. However, the incarnation's most significant impact is that the early Christians came to believe that the rule of God had already begun in the work of Christ. The NT scholar C. H. Dodd coined the expression "realized eschatology" to identify this thinking. Jesus, as the Messiah, came preaching the arrival of the kingdom of God in the midst of the nations, and his resurrection was a foretaste of the resurrections to come (cf. 1 Cor 15, esp. vv. 20, 23). According to Allison, some NT writers show evidence of the belief that "God has already judged the world" (via Cook: 295). This is especially true in the Gospel of John. John 12:31-32 depicts the crucifixion as the moment when all people are drawn to Christ and the world is judged. Earlier in the Gospel (5:24), we read, "Very truly, I tell you, anyone who hears my word and believes him who sent me has eternal life, and does not come under judgment, but has passed from death to life." Paul speaks of the old things passing away and a new creation arriving (2 Cor 5:17; Gal 6:15).

At the same time, the NT writers are clearly aware that the ultimate consummation is a future event. Like some OT writers, the early Christians anticipated a future series of traumatic events. These events would precede the final intervention by God in the second coming of Christ. The classic evidence of this is found in Mark 13 (cf. 1 Cor 7:26; Rev 7:14; 1 Pet 4:7-19). At some level the ministry, death, and resurrection of Jesus initiated this last phase before the final consummation. Therefore, believers are living in these troubled "last days" between the beginning and the end. This turbulence will cease with the return of Jesus Christ, the *parousia* (cf. Matt 24:30-31; 1 Cor 15:23; 1 Thess 2:19; 2 Thess 2:1, 9; James 5:7-8; 2 Peter 1:16; 1 John 2:28). His return will precipitate the anticipated resurrection of the dead (Mark 12:18-27; John 5:25-29; 1 Cor 15; Rev 20:4-5) and judgment (Rev 20:11-15). Both heaven and earth will be transformed and redeemed (Rev 21–22). Ultimately the early Christians accepted a tension between the "already" nature of the kingdom of God and the "not yet" of its full completion.

Although it is certainly probable that the author of 1 John accepted the "realized eschatology" of the Gospel of John, it is also obvious that he believed in a future consummation as well. Because he is aware of the *pass-*

ing away of the darkness and the world (1 John 2:8, 17), he encourages his readers to be prepared for Christ's return (3:2), which is to be preceded by the arrival of antichrists (2:18-27; 4:3). In fact, this time of trouble, or the *last hour*, is already upon them (2:18; 4:3). A significant reason for his emphasis on obeying the commands is the hope that his readers will be prepared for Christ's return and therefore will not be put to shame when that occurs (2:28).

However, the author of 1 John is also aware of the present sense of the kingdom, which impacts his eschatological thinking. First John 4:13-21 clearly makes the point that the Spirit has already been given to believers, thus enabling them to *abide in him and he in us* (4:13). The end result of this abiding is the confession that *the Father has sent his Son as the Savior of the world. God abides in those who confess that Jesus is the Son of God, and they abide in God* (4:14-15) and they love one another (4:16b-21). It is their current communal love that will enable them to *have boldness on the day of judgment* (4:17), a reference to the second coming of Jesus. Ultimately 1 John's eschatology is broad enough to incorporate a sense of the past, the present, and the future. We should not, however, confuse 1 John's complex eschatology with the modern eschatological thought known as dispensationalism. For a summary of this line of thinking, see Elias's essay on eschatology (1995: 355-57).

GNOSTICISM "Gnosticism" is a broad categorical term for a diverse collection of religious movements existing throughout the Roman Empire between the second and fifth centuries AD. The term is based on the Greek word *gnōsis*, or "knowledge," which plays an important role in all manifestations of Gnosticism. The theological or philosophical roots of the movement (Jewish wisdom or Platonic thought or both) are debated, but many scholars accept that these ideas began taking form as early as the first century AD and became widespread in urban centers such as Alexandria and Rome and in the cities of southern France and Asia Minor.

There is little or no doubt that various forms of Gnosticism were both internal and external challenges to early Christianity. We see internal challenges in 1 John and Colossians (Martin: 289-90), and various early church fathers, such as Irenaeus, Origen, and Tertullian, viewed it as a "deviant sectarian form of Christianity" (Perkins 2006: 581). However, the discovery of Gnostic texts in the twentieth century reveal that some Gnostic groups had little in common with Christianity and should be viewed as "external" religious movements that interacted with the early Christians. The best-known discovery (in 1945-46) of Gnostic texts is the Nag Hammadi library, consisting of thirteen codices written in Coptic. *The Gospel of Thomas* (in Codex II) and *The Gospel of Truth* (in Codex XII) appear in these Gnostic texts. The latter has similarities to John's Gospel and epistles in its emphasis on *revealing* and *truth*. But the differences are vast (see "Gnosticism" in Swartley, forthcoming).

As challenging as it is to describe the history of Gnosticism and its relationship to Christianity, it is even more difficult to identify core Gnostic beliefs. There is wide diversity in Gnostic mythology, cultic practices, ethics, and symbolism, yet there are common elements as well (Perkins 1990:

1351). The core feature is a negative view of the material world. Most groups accepted that there was a transcendent and good divine being far removed from the physical world. Thus most Gnostics would have a real sense of tension between the physical and spiritual realms, with the spiritual being viewed positively. We see evidence of an alternative viewpoint in 1 John 5:6-12, where the author argues that Jesus Christ *came by water and blood*. Many Gnostics believed a "divine spark" or essence was trapped in the human body. A special knowledge was needed to free this spark. Additionally, their disdain for the body was expressed in one of two extreme ways. Some Gnostic groups were moral libertines; however, most seemed to follow a rigorous asceticism, rejecting both sexuality and marriage (Yamauchi: 98).

THE JOHANNINE COMMA The so-called Johannine Comma (the longer reading in 1 John 5:7-8) first appears in a Greek text in the twelfth century and then only as a marginal gloss or comment. Nor does it appear in the most ancient versions of the Latin Vulgate. By the sixteenth century, however, when the Vulgate had become *the* church's Bible, these words are regularly included. The great debate over their originality begins when Erasmus, a Dutch Catholic scholar, created a reliable NT based on the Greek texts. Because the words do not appear in the early Greek texts, he refused to include them in his 1516 and 1519 editions of the Greek NT. Not surprisingly, he faced pressure to do so from church authorities; however, Erasmus still refused unless the authorities showed him a Greek text containing the Comma. He was shown manuscript 61, probably copied in 1520, and Erasmus then included the words in his 1522 third edition, protesting all the while. Subsequently, however, he refused to include the words in future editions. But Erasmus's third edition became the Textus Receptus for the early English versions and thus entered into the KJV translation, dominant for the next four centuries.

In 1897 the Roman Catholic Church published *Enchiridion biblicum #135*, which required that the Comma be accepted as authentic (Schnackenburg 1992: 44). This ruling was overturned by the Holy Office on June 6, 1927, which recognized the Comma as a late addition to the text (44). Contemporary translators, not being committed to the Vulgate text, have regularly omitted the comma. Even the NKJV has a translation similar to the NIV or NRSV. For further discussion see Brown 1982: 775-87, "Appendix IV: The Johannine Comma."

JOHN'S CROSS CHRONOLOGY The Gospel of John's chronology of Jesus' last days differs from that found in the synoptic Gospels. In the Synoptics the meal Jesus celebrates with his disciples is on the evening of Nisan 14 or Passover. He is arrested later that night, tried, and executed on the day after Passover. John 19:14, however, presents a differing chronology. In John 19:13-16 Pilate is depicted as passing sentence on Jesus, and 19:14 offers a very specific time when this occurred: "Now it was the day of Preparation for the Passover; and it was about noon." In other words, according to John's Gospel, Jesus was tried and executed before the celebration of the

Passover meal, which took place that evening. John's detailed reference to the day of Preparation and noon indicate that Jesus died when the Passover lambs were being slaughtered in preparation for the Passover meal. For further exploration of this, see Barrett: 48-51; Kysar 1986b: 326-28; Morris: 774-86; Schnackenburg 1987: 264-65.

LETTERS IN THE ANCIENT WORLD One fact that we can confidently assert about ancient people is that they wrote letters. Despite being written primarily on biodegradable materials, tens of thousands of letters have come down to us from antiquity. People in all levels of society, from slaves (see Richards 2004: 13-14) to well-known philosophers, such as Cicero and Seneca, wrote letters. These letters were written on treated animal skins, pottery shards, papyrus, and clay, wooden, lead, or bronze tablets (1 Macc 14:16-19) or even engraved on stone. Both the Persian (sixth century BC) and Roman Empires had organized services to deliver government correspondence. Private citizens entrusted their mail to either their slaves, employees, passing merchants, or traveling friends.

Early twentieth-century German NT scholar Adolf Deissmann placed these ancient letters into one of two categories. They were either "letters" intended for private use, with an unpolished form written by the lower classes; or "epistles" that tended to follow specific forms and clearly reflected a polished form. We know that the ancients took letter writing seriously because several handbooks on the subject remain (Richards 2004: 85-87). Contemporary scholars review the letters of the ancient world as being much more complex than Deissmann did. William Doty (5-8) identifies five general categories: business letters, official government letters, public letters designed as "open letters seeking to influence public opinion" (6), nonreal (or pseudonymous) letters, and discursive letters, which were essentially "essay like writings" (7). Stanley Stowers offers a different set of categories, including letters of friendship, family letters, letters of exhortation and advice (with seven subcategories), letters of meditation, and accusatory, apologetic, and accounting letters. While these ancient letters, regardless of category, have unique elements, they also tend to follow general patterns. They begin with a salutation identifying both the sender and the recipient(s) and a health wish or prayer for the recipient(s). Often there is a formulaic transition to the letter's body. They often close with final words of admonition and/or well-wishes (see Richards 2008: 639; cf. Sumney: 801-2).

The early Christians, like their peers, were letter writers. Twenty or twenty-one of the twenty-seven NT books are letters, and several "missing" letters are referred to in the NT (see Acts 18:27; 1 Cor 5:9; 7:1; 16:3; 2 Cor 2:3-4; Col 4:16; 2 Thess 2:2). All but one of these letters were designed to be read to a corporate body. The exception is 3 John, which is truly a private letter. Even Philemon, which deals with a private matter, seems to be intended for public reading, as verses 1-2 indicate. The public nature of these letters probably revolves around worship services, and so the standard health wish near the beginning is replaced by words of thanksgiving or a blessing (Richards 2008: 639). Richards also argues that Christian letters do not easily fit within established ancient forms. Among other things, they are considerably longer than most private ancient letters, which "averaged eighty-seven words in length." Cicero's letters averaged 295 words and Seneca's averaged 995. On the other hand, the average word count of Paul's letters is 2,495. However, an alternative view has been proposed by M. Luther Stirewalt Jr., who argues that Paul's letter writing was influenced by the official governmental letters of his day.

SIN AND PERFECTIONISM An attentive reading of 1 John quickly reveals that the author is working with a complex understanding of sin. At places he seems to say that believers can or must avoid sinning (3:6, 9; 5:18). At other points he firmly confronts anyone who would suggest they do not or have not sinned (1:8, 10). And at still other places he holds out the possibility of avoiding sin, but reassures his readers of divine grace if they do sin (2:1-2; 5:16-17). Apparently John's answer to the question, "Do believers sin?" is "Yes, no, and maybe." Though we may never totally resolve this dilemma, we certainly can make significant strides. In order to do this we need to recall the larger context for this letter, which included a schism and John's firm commitment to the Johannine tradition. In particular, the tradition about Jesus' teaching on love helps resolve this situation.

The first observation to be made has to do with the notion of "perfectionism," or sinlessness. Though the modern reader may look at various translations of biblical passages that talk about "being perfect" or "perfection" in one's behavior, we need to be very careful. As Jeffrey Lamp notes, the biblical words translated "perfect" usually refer to moral or ethical maturity, completion, or having reached a goal (443-44; cf. the comments on 1 John 2:4-6, above). Twenty-six times this concept is applied to OT figures who lead a "blameless" lifestyle (443). In this sense they are people of "integrity, honor, or truthfulness" (443; cf. Josh 24:14; Judg 9:16, 19; Prov 28:18) and not "perfect" as such. In the NT, God is identified as perfect, and God is the standard for Jesus' followers (Matt 5:48). However, this is not some vague ethical or moral abstraction; rather, Christians are to "exercise love" (Lamp: 443; cf. Matt 5:43-47).

Not surprisingly this theme of love, especially for members of the Johannine community, is a recurring theme in the first letter (1 John 2:7-11; 3:11-24; 4:7-21; 5:2-3), and it occurs also in the Gospel of John (13:34-35; 15:12-14; 17:26). It would not be an overstatement to say that love is the central moral or ethical concern within the Johannine tradition. The reason love is central is the fact that Jesus, the incarnate Word (John 1:1-5, 14-18), has both embodied divine love (15:13; 17:26) and commanded his followers to love (13:34-35; 15:12). When the author of 1 John refers to avoiding sin, he is possibly thinking quite "narrowly" in terms of "loving one another" within the community of faith, and doing so with specific tangible acts as evidence of this love. Thus the secessionists reveal their true nature as child[ren] of the devil (3:8) because they do not love tangibly in the face of other believers' needs (3:11-24, esp. 3:17-18). Yet despite their failure to adhere to the Johannine tradition of love, they still claim to be sinless.

If we were to think about sin within the narrow context of this tradition, letter, and social situation, this focus on love makes sense of John's understanding of sin. The ultimate issue is integrity or maturity in the way we love or view our behavior as it expresses or fails to express love. Within the Johannine community, anyone who has truly been *born of him* [*God*] (2:29) understands the importance of finding ways to display the love they have been called to embody. Only someone who does not understand this basic point can fail to express love in the face of needy brothers and sisters (3:11-17). Despite their failure to love, they may claim to be sinless, but they do so quite erroneously (1:8, 10). On the other hand, the mature ("perfect") believer knows the goal is to find tangible ways to live faithfully in light of Jesus' command to love (2:7-12; 3:11, 23-24; 4:7-21, esp. 12, 17-18; 5:2-3). Therefore, no one who *abides in him sins* (3:6, 9), that is, refuses to love other believers as the secessionists refuse to do. John is aware that no one, not even the most devout or mature believer, flawlessly embodies the commandment to love others. Therefore, at some level we do sin and need to accept the advocacy provided by Jesus Christ (2:1-2). Finally, we must recognize that John is not unaware of other types of sin, as 1 John 5:16-17 shows. However, these verses are almost like an addendum to his main argument about the commandment to love or the sin of failing to love.

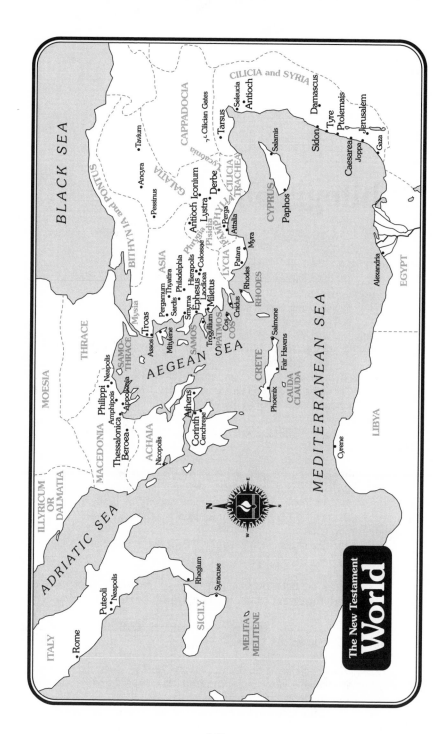

The New Testament World

313

Bibliography

Barrett, C. K.
    1978   *The Gospel According to St. John*. 2nd ed. Philadelphia: Westminster.
Bass, Christopher D.
    2008   *That You May Know: Assurance of Salvation in 1 John*. Nashville, TN: B&H Academic.
Bauckham, Richard, ed.
    1998   *The Gospels for All Christians: Rethinking the Gospel Audiences*. Grand Rapids: Eerdmans.
Bauckham, Richard, and Carl Mosser, eds.
    2008   *The Gospel of John and Christian Theology*. Grand Rapids: Eerdmans.
Becker, Ulrich, and Hans-Georg Link
    1976   "Liar." In *The New International Dictionary of New Testament Theology*, edited by Colin Brown, 2:470-74. Exeter, U.K.: Paternoster.
Bender, Harold S.
    1950   *The Anabaptist Vision*. Scottdale, PA: Herald Press.
Bogart, John
    1977   *Orthodox and Heretical Perfectionism in the Johannine Community as Evident in the First Epistle of John*. Society of Biblical Literature Dissertation Series 33. Missoula, MT: Scholars Press.
Bonhoeffer, Dietrich
    1959   *The Cost of Discipleship*. London: SCM Press. Original German ed., 1937.
Bray, Gerald, ed.
    2000   *James, 1-2 Peter, 1-3 John, Jude*. Ancient Christian Commentary on Scripture: New Testament 11. Downers Grove, IL: InterVarsity.
Brooke, A. E.
    1912   *The Johannine Epistles*. International Critical Commentary. Edinburgh: T&T Clark.
Brown, Raymond E.
    1979   *The Community of the Beloved Disciple: The Life, Loves, and Hates of an Individual Church in New Testament Times*. London: Geoffrey Chapman.
    1982   *The Epistles of John*. Anchor Bible 30. New York: Doubleday.

Bibliography 315

Bruce, F. F.
1970 *The Epistles of John.* London: Pickering & Inglis.
Bultmann, Rudolf
1927 "Analyse des ersten Johannesbriefes." In *Exegetica: Aufsätze zur Erforschung des Neuen Testaments,* by Rudolf Bultmann et al., 138-58. Festgabe für Adolf Jülicher zum 70. Geburtstag. Tübingen: Mohr-Siebeck. Reprint, edited by Erich Dinkler, 1967.
1973 *The Johannine Epistles.* Translated by R. Phillip O'Hara, Lane C. McGaughy, and Robert W. Funk. Hermeneia. Philadelphia: Fortress.
Burge, Gary M.
1996 *The Letters of John.* The NIV Application Commentary. Grand Rapids: Zondervan.
Calvin, John
1993 *Commentaries on the Epistles of Paul the Apostle to the Hebrews.* Calvin's Commentaries, vol. 22. Grand Rapids: Baker Book House.
Calvin, John, and Matthew Henry
1998 *1, 2, 3 John. 1 John* by John Calvin; *2-3 John* by Matthew Henry. Edited by Alister McGrath and J. I. Packer. Crossway Classic Commentaries. Wheaton, IL; Nottingham, U.K.: Crossway Books.
Carson, D. A.
1996 "Johannine Perspectives on the Doctrine of Assurance." *Explorations* 10:59-97.
Charlesworth, James H., ed.
1983-85 *The Old Testament Pseudepigrapha.* 2 vols. Garden City, NY: Doubleday.
Church of England
2000 *Common Worship: Services and Prayers for the Church of England.* London: Church House Publishing.
Collins, John J., ed.
1998 *The Encyclopedia of Apocalypticism.* Vol. 1, *The Origins of Apocalypticism in Judaism and Christianity.* New York: Continuum.
Cook, Stephen L.
2007 "Eschatology of the OT." In *The New Interpreter's Dictionary of the Bible,* 2: 299-308. Nashville: Abingdon.
Cosby, Michael R.
2009 *Apostle on the Edge.* Louisville: Westminster John Knox.
Cullmann, Oscar
1976 *The Johannine Circle.* Translated by John Bowden. Philadelphia: Westminster.
Culpepper, R. A.
1975 *The Johannine School.* Society of Biblical Literature Dissertation Series 26. Missoula, MT: Scholars Press.
1985 *1, 2, 3 John.* Knox Preaching Guides. Atlanta: John Knox.
2006 "Children of God." In *The New Interpreter's Dictionary of the Bible,* 1:590-93. Nashville: Abingdon.
Davis, Kenneth R.
1974 *Anabaptism and Asceticism: A Study in Intellectual Origins.* Studies in Anabaptist and Mennonite History 16. Scottdale, PA: Herald Press.

Delling, Gerhard
    1968   "*Plērophoria.*" In *The Theological Dictionary of the New Testament,* edited by Gerhard Friedrich, translated and edited by Geoffrey W. Bromiley, 6:310-11. Grand Rapids: Eerdmans.
Dodd, C. H.
    1946   *The Johannine Epistles.* London: Hodder & Stoughton.
Doty, William G.
    1973   *Letters in Primitive Christianity.* Guide to Biblical Scholarship: New Testament Series. Philadelphia: Fortress.
Dowley, Tim, ed.
    1977   *Eerdman's Handbook to the History of Christianity.* Grand Rapids: Eerdmans.
Dunn, James D. G.
    1980   *Christology in the Making.* Philadelphia: Westminster.
    1985   *The Evidence for Jesus.* Philadelphia: Westminster.
Dyck, Cornelius J., William E. Keeney, and Alvin J. Beachy, eds.
    1992   *The Writings of Dirk Philips.* Classics of the Radical Reformation 6. Scottdale, PA: Herald Press.
Eby, John
    2010   Personal correspondence via email, March 30.
Elias, Jacob W.
    1995   *1 and 2 Thessalonians.* Believers Church Bible Commentary. Scottdale, PA: Herald Press.
    2006   *Remember the Future: The Pastoral Theology of Paul the Apostle.* Scottdale, PA: Herald Press.
Erb, Peter C., ed.
    1983   *Pietists: Selected Writings.* New York: Paulist Press.
Fee, Gordon D., and Douglas Stuart
    1993   *How to Read the Bible for All It's Worth.* 2nd ed. Grand Rapids: Zondervan.
Foster, Richard J.
    1998   *Streams of Living Water.* San Francisco: HarperSanFrancisco.
Friedmann, Robert
    1961   *Hutterite Studies.* Edited by H. S. Bender. Festschrift. Scottdale, PA: Herald Press.
Furcha, E. J.
    1989   *The Selected Writings of Hans Denck (1500-1527).* Lewiston, NY: Edwin Mellen.
Fürst, Dieter
    1975   "Confess." In *The New International Dictionary of New Testament Theology,* edited by Colin Brown, 1:344-48. Exeter, U.K.: Paternoster.
Grayston, Kenneth
    1984   *The Johannine Epistles.* New Century Bible. Grand Rapids: Eerdmans.
Green, Joel B., and Mark D. Baker
    2000   *Recovering the Scandal of the Cross.* Downers Grove, IL: InterVarsity.

Grounds, Vernon
 1960 "Atonement." In *Baker Dictionary of Theology*, edited by Everett F. Harrison, 71-78. Grand Rapids: Baker Book House.
Gundry, Robert H.
 2002 *Jesus the Word According to John the Sectarian: A Paleofundamentalist Manifesto for Contemporary Evangelicalism, Especially Its Elites, in North America*. Grand Rapids: Eerdmans.
Haas, C., M. de Jonge, and J. L. Swellengrebel
 1972 *A Handbook on the Letters of John*. UBS Handbook Series. New York: United Bible Societies.
Hengel, Martin
 1977 *Crucifixion*. Translated by John Bowden. Philadelphia: Fortress.
Houlden, J. L.
 1973 *A Commentary on the Johannine Epistles*. Harper's New Testament Commentaries. New York: Harper & Row.
House, Adrian
 2000 *Francis of Assisi: A Revolutionary Life*. Mahwah, NJ: HiddenSpring.
Jackman, David
 1988 *The Message of John's Letters*. The Bible Speaks Today. Downers Grove, IL: InterVarsity.
Job, Rueben P., and Norman Shawchuck
 1983 *A Guide to Prayer*. Nashville, TN: The Upper Room.
Johns, Loren L., and James R. Krabill, eds.
 2006 *Even the Demons Submit: Continuing Jesus' Ministry of Deliverance*. Scottdale, PA: Herald Press.
Johnson, Thomas F.
 1993 *1, 2, and 3 John*. New International Biblical Commentary. Peabody, MA: Hendrickson.
Kanagy, Conrad
 2007 *Roadsigns for the Journey*. Scottdale, PA: Herald Press.
Kauffman, J. Howard, and Leo Driedger
 1991 *The Mennonite Mosaic: Identity and Modernization*. Scottdale, PA: Herald Press.
Kavanagh, Denis J., trans.
 1951 *Commentary on the Lord's Sermon on the Mount, with Seventeen Related Sermons*, by Augustine of Hippo. Fathers of the Church 3. Washington, DC: Catholic University Press.
Kearsley, Roy
 1990 "Faith and Philosophy in the Early Church." *Themelios* 15:81-86.
Kenney, Garret C.
 2000 *The Relation of Christology to Ethics in the First Epistle of John*. Lanham, MD: University Press of America.
Klaassen, Walter, ed.
 1981 *Anabaptism in Outline: Selected Primary Sources*. Classics of the Radical Reformation 3. Scottdale, PA: Herald Press.
Klassen, William, and Walter Klaassen, trans. & eds.
 1978 *The Writings of Pilgram Marpeck*. Classics of the Radical Reformation 2. Scottdale, PA: Herald Press.

Klauck, Hans-Josef
1988   "Internal Opponents: The Treatment of the Secessionists in the
        First Epistle of John." Translated by Robert Nowell. *Concilium*
        200:55-65.
Kruse, Colin
2000   *The Letters of John.* The Pillar New Testament Commentary. Grand
        Rapids: Eerdmans.
Kysar, Robert
1986a   *I, II, III John.* Augsburg Commentary on the New Testament.
        Minneapolis: Augsburg.
1986b   *John.* Augsburg Commentary on the New Testament. Minneapolis:
        Augsburg.
Lake, Kirsopp, trans.
1912   *The Apostolic Fathers.* Vol. 1. Loeb Classical Library. London:
        William Heinemann.
1926   *The Apostolic Fathers.* Vol. 2. Loeb Classical Library. London:
        William Heinemann.
Lamp, Jeffrey S.
2009   "Perfection." In *The New Interpreter's Dictionary of the Bible*, 4:443-
        44. Nashville: Abingdon.
Law, Robert
1909   *The Tests of Life: A Study of the First Epistle of St. John.* Edinburgh:
        T&T Clark.
Liechty, Joseph
1994   "Why Did Dirk Willems Turn Back?" *Anabaptism Today* 6 (June):
        7-12.
Lieu, Judith
1991   *The Theology of the Johannine Epistles.* New Testament Theology.
        Cambridge: Cambridge University Press.
2008   *I, II, and III John.* New Testament Library. Louisville: Westminster
        John Knox.
Link, Hans-Georg, and Erich Tiedtke
1975   "Deny." In *The New International Dictionary of New Testament
        Theology*, edited by Colin Brown, 1:454-56. Exeter, U.K.:
        Paternoster.
Malatesta, Edward
1978   *Interiority and Covenant: A Study of "einai en" and "menein en" in the
        First Letter of Saint John.* Analecta Biblica 69. Rome: Biblical
        Institute Press.
Malina, Bruce
1986   "The Received View and What It Cannot Do: III John and
        Hospitality." *Semeia* 35:181-83.
Marshall, I. Howard
1978   *The Epistles of John.* The New International Commentary on the
        New Testament. Grand Rapids: Eerdmans.
Martin, Ernest D.
1993   *Colossians, Philemon.* Believers Church Bible Commentary.
        Scottdale, PA: Herald Press.

Martínez, Florentino García
  1996   *The Dead Sea Scrolls Translated: The Qumran Texts in English.* Second
          Ed. Trans. Wilfred G.E.Watson. Leiden/New York: E.J. Brill and
          Grand Rapids: Eerdmans.
McLaren, Brian D.
  2005   *The Last Word and the Word After That.* San Francisco: Jossey-Bass.
Metzger, Bruce
  1971   *A Textual Commentary on the Greek New Testament.* London/New
          York: United Bible Societies. Second edition: 1994.
Morris, Leon
  1971   *The Gospel According to John.* Grand Rapids: Eerdmans.
Moule, C. F. D.
  1959   *An Idiom-Book of New Testament Greek.* 2nd ed. Cambridge:
          Cambridge University Press.
Neufeld, Dietmar
  1994   *Reconceiving Texts as Speech Acts: An Analysis of 1 John.* Biblical
          Interpretation Series 7. Leiden: E. J. Brill.
Noack, Bent
  1959/1960 "On I John II.12-14." *New Testament Studies* 6:236-41.
O'Neill, J. C.
  1966   *The Puzzle of 1 John.* London: SPCK.
Painter, John
  2002   *1, 2, and 3 John.* Collegeville, Minn.: Liturgical Press.
Perkins, Pheme
  1990   "Gnosticism." In *The New Jerome Bible Commentary*, 1350-53.
          Englewood Cliffs, NJ: Prentice Hall.
  2006   "Gnosticism." In *The New Interpreter's Dictionary of the Bible*, 2:581-
          84. Nashville: Abingdon.
Pine-Coffin, R.S., trans.
  1961   *Confessions*, by Augustine of Hippo. New York: Penguin Books.
Pipkin, H. Wayne, and John H. Yoder
  1989   *Balthasar Hubmaier: Theologian of Anabaptism.* Classics of the
          Radical Reformation 5. Scottdale, PA: Herald Press.
Pohl, Christine D.
  1999   *Making Room: Recovering Hospitality as a Christian Tradition.* Grand
          Rapids: Eerdmans.
Porter, Stanley E.
  1995   *Idioms of the Greek New Testament.* 2nd ed. Sheffield, U.K.: Sheffield
          Academic Press.
Rensberger, David
  1997   *1 John, 2 John, 3 John.* Abingdon New Testament Commentaries.
          Nashville: Abingdon.
Richards, E. Randolph
  2004   *Paul and First-Century Letter Writing: Secretaries, Composition and
          Collection.* Downers Grove, IL: InterVarsity.
  2008   "Letter." In *The New Interpreter's Dictionary of the Bible*, 3:638-41.
          Nashville: Abingdon.

Roten, Gertrude Wiebe
2004   "Commentary on Epistles of 1, 2, 3 John." Spiral notebook for
        AMBS alumni and family. Available in the Mennonite Historical
        Library, Goshen College, Goshen, IN, and in the Associated
        Mennonite Biblical Seminary Library, Elkhart, IN.
Roth, John D.
1998   "Mutual Aid Among the Swiss Brethren, 1550-1750." In *Building
        Communities of Compassion*, edited by Donald B. Kraybill and
        Willard M. Swartley, 119-43. Scottdale, PA: Herald Press.
Rowland, Christopher
2005   "Apocalyptic." In *Dictionary for Theological Interpretation of the
        Bible*, 51-53. Grand Rapids: Baker Academic.
2006   "Apocalypticism." In *The New Interpreter's Dictionary of the Bible*,
        1:190-95. Nashville: Abingdon.
Schnackenburg, Rudolf
1987   *The Gospel of John*. Vol. 3. Translated by David Smith and G. A.
        Kon. New York: Crossroad.
1992   *The Johannine Epistles*. Translated by Reginald and Ilse Fuller.
        New York: Crossroad.
Schönweiss, H.
1975   "Desire, Lust, Pleasure." In *The New International Dictionary of New
        Testament Theology*, 1:456-57. Edited by Colin Brown. Exeter, U.K.:
        Paternoster.
Sider, E. Morris, and Paul Hostetter, eds.
1980   *Lantern in the Dawn*. Nappanee, IN: Evangel Press.
Sider, Ronald J.
1999   *Just Generosity*. Grand Rapids: Baker Books.
2005   *The Scandal of the Evangelical Conscience: Why Are Christians Living
        Just Like the Rest of the World?* Grand Rapids: Baker Books.
Smalley, Stephen S.
1984   *1, 2, 3 John*. Word Biblical Commentary 51. Waco: Word Books.
Smith, D. Moody
1991   *First, Second, and Third John*. Interpretation: A Bible Commentary
        for Teaching and Preaching. Louisville: John Knox.
Sprunger, Mary S.
1998   "Mutual Aid Among Dutch Waterlander, 1605-1668. In *Building
        Communities of Compassion*, edited by Donald B. Kraybill and
        Willard M. Swartley, 144-67. Scottdale, PA: Herald Press.
Stirewalt, M. Luther, Jr.
2003   *Paul the Letter Writer*. Grand Rapids: Eerdmans.
Stott, John R. W.
1964   *The Epistles of John*. Tyndale New Testament Commentaries.
        Grand Rapids: Eerdmans.
Stowers, Stanley
1986   *Letter Writing in Greco-Roman Antiquity*. Philadelphia: Westminster
        Press.
Strecker, Georg
1996   *The Johannine Letters*. Translated by Linda M. Maloney. Hermeneia.
        Minneapolis: Fortress.

Sumney, Jerry L.
2000   "Letter." In *Eerdmans Dictionary of the Bible*, 801-2. Grand Rapids: Eerdmans.

Swartley, Willard M., ed.
1988   *Essays on Spiritual Bondage and Deliverance*. Occasional Papers No. 11. Elkhart, IN: Institute of Mennonite Studies.
1998   "Mutual Aid Based in Jesus and Early Christianity." In *Building Communities of Compassion*, edited by Donald B. Kraybill and Willard M. Swartley, 21-39. Scottdale, PA: Herald Press.
2006   *Covenant of Peace: The Missing Peace in New Testament Theology and Ethics*. Grand Rapids: Eerdmans.

Talbert, Charles H.
1992   *Reading John: A Literary and Theological Commentary on the Fourth Gospel and the Johannine Epistles*. Reading the New Testament Series. New York: Crossroad.

Thompson, Marianne Meye
1992   *1-3 John*. The IVP New Testament Commentary Series. Downers Grove, IL: InterVarsity.

Thompson, Michael B.
1998   "The Holy Internet: Communication Between Churches in the First Christian Generation." 49-70 in Bauckham, ed.

Umble, Jeni Heitt
1998   "Mutual Aid Among Augsburg Anabaptists, 1526-1528." In *Building Communities of Compassion*, edited by Donald B. Kraybill and Willard M. Swartley, 103-18. Scottdale, PA: Herald Press.

Vermès, Géza, ed. and trans.
1997   *The Complete Dead Sea Scrolls in English*. Fourth Ed. pb. London: Allen Lane / Penguin Press.
1995   *The Complete Dead Sea Scrolls in English*. Revised and Extended Fourth Ed. hb. Sheffield: Sheffield Academic Press.

Von Dobschütz, Ernst
1907   "Johanneische Studien I." *Zeitschrift für neutestamentliche Wissenschaft* 8:1-8.

Von Wahlde, Urban C.
1990   *The Johannine Commandments: 1 John and the Struggle for the Johannine Tradition*. New York: Paulist Press.

Watson, Duane F.
1989   "1 John 2.12-14 as *Distributio, Conduplicatio*, and *Expolitio*: A Rhetorical Understanding." *Journal for the Study of the New Testament* 35:97-110.
1993   "Amplification Techniques in 1 John: The Interaction of Rhetorical Style and Invention." *Journal for the Study of the New Testament* 51:100-118.

Wenger, J. C., ed.
1956   *The Complete Writings of Menno Simons*. Translated by Leonard Verduin. Scottdale, PA: Herald Press.

Wesley, John
1952   *A Plain Account of Christian Perfection*. London: Epworth.

Whitacre, Rodney A.
  1980   *Johannine Polemic: The Role of Tradition and Theology.* Society of
          Biblical Literature Dissertation Series 67. Chico, CA: Scholars
          Press.
Wise, Michael, Martin Abegg Jr., and Edward Cook
  2005   *The Dead Sea Scrolls: A New Translation.* San Francisco: Harper-
          SanFrancisco.
Witherington, Ben
  1990   *The Christology of Jesus.* Minneapolis: Fortress.
Wolterstorff, Nicholas
  2010   "The Light of God's Love." *Fuller Theology, News & Notes* 57, no.
          1:9-10, 26.
Wright, N. T.
  1999   *The Challenge of Jesus: Rediscovering Who Jesus Was and Is.* Downers
          Grove, IL: IVP Academic.
  2008   *Surprised by Hope: Rethinking Heaven, the Resurrection, and the
          Mission of the Church.* New York: HarperOne.
Yamauchi, Edwin M.
  1977   "The Gnostics." In *Eerdman's Handbook of the History of Christianity,*
          98-100. Grand Rapids: Eerdmans.
Yates, Roy
  1974   "The Antichrist." *Evangelical Quarterly* 46:42-50.
Yeatts, John R.
  2003   *Revelation.* Believers Church Bible Commentary. Scottdale, PA:
          Herald Press.
Yoder, John H.
  1973   *The Legacy of Michael Sattler.* Translated by John H. Yoder.
          Scottdale, PA: Herald Press.
Yoder Neufeld, Thomas R.
  2002   *Ephesians.* Believers Church Bible Commentary. Scottdale, PA:
          Herald Press.

Selected Resources

Brown, Raymond E. *The Epistles of John.* The Anchor Bible 30. New York: Doubleday & Company, 1982. This 812-page commentary by a moderate Roman Catholic scholar and priest is the exhaustive volume on the Johannine Letters. Brown's work is both detailed and complex in its exegesis of the letters.

Burge, Gary M. *The Letters of John.* The NIV Application Commentary. Grand Rapids, MI: Zondervan, 1996. This series sets similar goals as the BCBC series. The examination of each biblical unit is divided into three focal areas: "Original Meaning," "Bridging Contexts," and "Contemporary Significance." Burge teaches at Wheaton College in Illinois.

Kenney, Garrett C. *The Relation of Christology to Ethics in the First Epistle of John.* Lanham, MD: University Press of America, 2000. Kenney's revised and carefully argued master's thesis (Gonzaga University, 1986) proposes at the heart of 1 John is the biblical author's conviction that Christian ethics are determined by Christology.

Kruse, Colin G. *The Letters of John.* The Pillar New Testament Commentary. Grand Rapids, MI: Eerdmans, 2000. Kruse, an Australian biblical scholar, has written this detailed volume for the conservative evangelical series edited by D. A. Carson. It is recommended to readers who have some working knowledge of Greek.

Kysar, Robert. *I, II, III John.* Augsburg Commentary on the New Testament. Minneapolis, MN: Augsburg Publishing House, 1986. This small, readable text by a Lutheran pastor and biblical scholar is recommended for both pastors and lay people.

Lieu, Judith M. *The Theology of the Johannine Epistles.* New Testament Theology. Cambridge, U.K.: Cambridge University Press, 1991.

Lieu, Lady Margaret's Professor of Divinity at the University of Cambridge, explores the letters' theology for this series, attempting to provide an avenue for greater detail than is allowed by standard commentary introductions.

———. *I, II, III John*. The New Testament Library. Louisville, KY: Westminster/John Knox, 2008. Lieu's commentary is a contribution to a series designed to offer new translations of the Greek text while drawing upon ancient literary works, thus setting the biblical text in the ancient world. This volume is written primarily for biblical scholars.

Marshall, I. Howard. *The Epistles of John*. The New International Commentary on the New Testament. Grand Rapids, MI: Eerdmans, 1978. Although somewhat dated, this commentary by a British Methodist scholar, is part of a critical series attempting to provide readable and critical works on the New Testament. The series was "cutting edge" when it began employing both rhetorical and sociological methodology for reading the biblical text.

Painter, John. *1, 2, and 3 John*. Sacra Pagina. Collegeville, MN: The Liturgical Press, 2002. This Roman Catholic series is designed with biblical professionals and clergy as the target audience. Painter, who teaches in Australia, has produced a useful and readable text.

Rensberger, David. *I John 2 John 3 John*. Abingdon New Testament Commentaries. Nashville, TN: Abingdon Press, 1997. Rensberger, a Mennonite scholar, has written a very engaging and readable commentary that would be well received by both pastors and college students. Rensberger is professor of New Testament at Interdenominational Theological Center in Georgia.

Schnackenburg, Rudolf. *The Johannine Epistles*. Trans. by Reginald and Ilse Fuller. New York: Crossroad, 1992. Schnackenburg, a German Catholic scholar and priest, has produced a very detailed and critical volume for advanced scholars.

Smalley, Stephen S. *1, 2, 3 John*. Word Biblical Commentary 51. Waco, TX: Word Books, 1984. This volume, written by an Anglican priest, is included in a series gathering "the best in evangelical critical scholarship for a new generation."

Smith, D. Moody. *First, Second, and Third John*. Interpretation: a Bible Commentary for Teaching and Preaching. Louisville, KY: John Knox Press, 1991. Smith's commentary is quite readable with a practical theology bent, as the series title suggests. Smith taught at Duke Divinity School.

Thompson, Marianne Meye. *1-3 John*. The IVP New Testament Commentary Series. Downers Grove, IL.: InterVarsity Press, 1992. This series provides readable evagelical scholarship on the New Testament. Thompson is professor of New Testament at Fuller Theological Seminary in California.

Index of Ancient Sources

OLD TESTAMENT

Genesis
1:1 39
1:2 215
1:4 134
1:10 134
1:12 134
1:18 134
1:21 134
1:22 134
1:25 134
1:28 134
1:31 134
3 74
3–11 74
3:1-24 135
3:6 131
3:8 176
4 .... 74, 186
4:23-24 74
5:21-24 176
6 74
6:5 74
6:5-7 74
6:8-9 74
6:18 102
8:21 .... 69, 74
9 74

11 74
12:1-3 74
15:1-21 .... 102, 278
15:7-21 74
15:13 278
17:1 .... 61, 74
17:1-27 102
18:1-15 279
18:23-33 264
18:24 264
19 279
19:1-29 279
19:4 115
20:7 264
22:10 186
27:12 40
31:30 137

Exodus
3 176
3:1-17 196
3:7-8 198
3:7-12 236
3:12 236
3:18 236
4:22 302
4:31 236
5:1 236
5:3 236

6:5-7 198
10:9 .... 112, 115
12:22 245
12:43-49 278
19:3-6 196
20 196
20:2 236
20:22-26 236
20:22–23:19 75
20:1-17 75
20:2-17 86
20:1-21 102
20:2 278
20:2-3 .... 102, 196
20:4-6 135
20:5 135
20:17 137
21:1-11 237
21:2 237
21:3 237
21:8 237
21:9 237
22:21-24 198
22:21-27 278
23:9 198
24 196
31:3 215
32:1-24 135
32:11-34 264

32:32 264
34 196
34:6-7.............122
34:9 264
35:31 215
19–20 176

Leviticus
4–7 76
4:1-2................262
4:1-12..............64
4:13 262
4:22 262
4:27 262
5:5 67
11:44 196
15:15-18...........262
16 64
16:21 67
19:1-35.............64
19:2 196
19:18 94
19:33-34...........198
20:7 196
25 198
25:9 72
25:39-55............198
26:9 102

Numbers
9:12 245
9:14 278
11 215
11:4 137
11:17 215
11:34 137
12:8 277
14:16 186
14:18-19............123
14:19 264
15:27 262
15:27-31...........262

15:30 262
15:39 131
25:12 102

Deuteronomy
4:31 102
4:40 102
5:1-3................42
7:9 .... 67, 102, 123
8:6 103
10:12 278
10:12-20...........198
10:12-22...........278
10:15 278
10:18-19...........278
12:20-27...........137
13 156
13:1-5........... 156, 208
13:2 .... 156, 208
13:4 .... 103, 208
14:1-2..............302
14:28-29...........198
15 198
15:13-14...........237
17:6 246
17:12 262
18:20 156
18:20-22...........208
19:15 246
22:22-29...........262
24:14-15...........278
26 42
29:9 102
29:10-14...........278
32:4-6..............302
32:15-17...........176
34 176
34:9 215

Joshua
6:21 .... 112, 115
7:16-26............79

7:19 67
24:7 42
24:14 311

Judges
2:6–3:6 75
2:13 176
3:10 215
6:34 215
9:16 311
9:19 311
9:22-57.............214
10:6 176
10:10 176
11:29 215
12:6 186
13:25 215
14:6 215
14:19 215
15:14 215
15:19 215

1 Samuel
2:12 87
2:22-25............262
3:1-18..............176
10:1 148
10:9-13............215
12:10 176
16:1 148
16:13 .... 148, 215
16:14-23...........214
16:15 214
18:10 214

2 Samuel
7:14 49

1 Kings
1:39 148
2:4 61
8:22-53............75

8:33 79
8:35 79
8:46 69
16:29–22:40 176
17:1-24 279
18 .... 156, 176
18:18 176
18:40 186
19:9-13 176

2 Kings
20:3 61

1 Chronicles
21:1 173

2 Chronicles
6:2 300
6:24, 26 79
15:1 215
24:20-22 215

Ezra
9 264
10:1-44 79

Nehemiah
9:17 76
9 264

Job
...............175
1:6 173
32:6 115
36:12 .... 87, 100

Psalms
1:1 61
2:7 49
3:8 76
9:7 300
11 123

11:7 176
14:3 69
16 123
17:15 176
19:13 262
22:29 307
23 123
26 75
27 123
27:1 60
32 75
32:5 .... 67, 79
34:11 70
36:5 .... 67, 123
36:9 60
37:25 115
42:1-5 176
43 75
46:1-3 123
50 75
51 75
53:2 69
56:13 60
58:3 151
62–63 123
78 75
82 302
89:1-4 67
89:1-8 67
90:1-2 300
91 123
94 75
99:1 300
102:12 300
103 75
103:3 75
103:10 75
103:12 75
103:13 302
104:2 60
105:6-8 123
106:36-38 176

108:4 123
109 173
116:11 151
121 123
125 123
131 123
137:7 306

Proverbs
3:12 302
4:1 70
8:20 61
14:31 198
19:17 198
20:9 69
28:13 .... 67, 79
28:18 311

Isaiah
1:1-4 176
1:2 302
1:3 .... 87, 100
1:4 302
1:18 75
1:18-19 103
2:5 61
2:5-8 176
2:12 306
3:14-25 198
5:13 .... 87, 100
5:15 131
6:1-13 176
7:14 49
8:8-15 49
9:1-17 49
9:2 60
9:8–10:4 176
9:15-16 156
10:1-3 198
13:6 306
13:9 306
20:4 .... 112, 115

22:12-14................262
25:9 306
26:19 307
30:1 302
34:8 307
42:1-9.................215
54:1-8.................272
56:1 196
57:5 186
58:2 137
61:1-2.................216
61:1-11................215
64:6-7.................74

Jeremiah
2 196
2:1-3:5.................176
2:2-3...................75
3:12-13................103
5:25-29................198
7:8-15..................176
7:16-20................262
9:3 62
9:6 .... 87, 100
9:23-24........... 87, 100
11 196
11:9-17................176
14:7-12................262
22:22-29...............198
23:32 156
26:13 103
31:31-34...............101
31:33 86
31:34 .... 75, 87
34:8-21................196
36:3 75
46:10 307

Lamentations
3:22-23................123

Ezekiel
2:2–3:12 215
3:14 215
3:24 215
9:6 112
11:5-12................215
13:5 307
30:3 307
36:26-27......... 86, 100
36:27 215
37 307
37:23 75
48:35 300

Daniel
.... 134, 156, 302
6:26 300
7–12 306
9 .... 79, 264
9:20 67
11:36 156
12:2 307

Hosea
1:1–2:1 302
1:2-9...................103
4:1 .... 87, 100
4:6 100
4:1-3...................196
6:1-3.............. 87, 100
11:1 302
11:1-7.................176

Joel
2:1 307
2:28-29................115
2:12-14................123
2:28 144
2:28-29................215
3:14 307

Amos
2:10 42
3:1-15..................196
5:11-12................198
5:18 307
5:18-20................306
8:1-3...................306
8:11-14................306

Micah
2:1-3...................198
5:2 300
6:1-8...................196
6:4 103
6:8 .... 103, 196
7:18 75
7:18-19.................76
7:18-20................123

Habakkuk
1:12 300
2:14 .... 87, 100

Zephaniah
1:4-9...................196
1:7-8...................307
1:14-18................306
2:2-3...................307
3:1-2...................196

Zechariah
2:10-11................300

Malachi
4:5 307

NEW TESTAMENT

Synoptics
.............................309

Matthew

1:1 49
3:6 79
3:13-17 216
4:1-11 .... 135, 216
4:8-10 135
4:19 196
5:9 303
5:14 60
5:19 103
5:21-24 188
5:21-26 76
5:22 230
5:27 230
5:27-29 131
5:27-30 76
5:28 137
5:43-47 311
5:44 266
5:45 303
5:48 .... 293, 303, 311
6:9 303
6:19 197
6:19-24 139
6:22-23 131
6:23 60
6:24 130
6:33 252
7:7-8 192-93
7:7-11 192
7:15-23 .... 101, 207
7:21 103
8:5-13 76
8:22 196
9:9 196
9:9-13 77
10:22 113
10:27 60
10:32 79
12:31-32 262
13:14 225
13:17 137

13:24-30 160
14:33 303
15:9-10 230
15:21-28 76
15:22 49
18:15-20 .... 14, 161,
                263, 296
18:16 246
18:19-20 192
19:17 .... 86, 103
19:21 197
20:30-31 49
21:22 192
22 279
22:9 279
22:19 136
22:34-40 232
23:23 103
24 145
24:3 170
24:3-14 175
24:4-5 157
24:9 113
24:9-14 175
24:12 172
24:27 170
24:30-31 307
25:1-46 230
25:34-36 279
25:34-40 197
25:41 175
26:26-28 77

Mark

1:5 79
1:9-11 .... 216, 304
1:11 .... 49, 303
1:12-13 216
1:15 77
1:21-28 216
1:24 148
2:14 196

3:11 303
3:19-30 262
3:28-29 262
4:19 137
6:7-13 278
8–10 196
8:31–9:1 77
8:33 173
8:34-38 196
8:38 171
9:7 303
9:14-29 216
9:30-32 77
9:33-37 197
9:47 131
10:21 197
10:32-34 77
10:35-45 197
10:44-45 197
10:45 ....77, 249-50
12:18-27 307
12:28-34 232
12:44 132
13 .... 145, 305, 307
13:5-6 157
13:13 113
13:22 207
14:22-24 77
15:39 303

Luke

.... 197, 229
1:11 177
1:26 177
2:25-26 216
2:25-35 177
2:27 216
2:36-38 177
3:7-9 77
3:21-22 216
3:22 49

4:1-13.....................135
4:16-21...................77
4:18........................148
4:36........................216
5:27........................196
6:18........................216
6:35-36..................303
7:21........................216
8:1-3.......................216
8:12..........................61
10:25-28................232
11:2.........................303
12:8...........................79
12:10......................262
13:27......................172
15:1-32....................76
15:11-32................303
15:16......................137
18:9-14....................76
18:22......................197
21:8........................157
21:17......................113
22:3........................173
22:15......................130
22:19-20..................77
24:39........................41

John
........62, 66, 73, 92, 98,
     104, 184, 300, 308

1:1................. 158, 260
1:1-2......................234
1:1-5......................311
1:1-18....33, 47-48, 53,
                         145
1:2.........................158
1:3.................. 53, 304
1:4.........................234
1:4-9........................60
1:9.................. 96, 129
1:10......... 53, 129, 234

1:12 ...51, 158, 193-94,
                  256, 303
1:12-13....120, 226, 234
1:14....... 158, 234, 301
1:14-18......... 304, 311
1:17........................235
1:18....... 158, 235, 260
1:27........................234
1:29...... 52, 65, 69, 72,
          77, 129, 234
1:29-34....177, 215-16,
                   244-45
1:29-36..................244
1:34........................303
1:35..........................72
1:35-51..................177
1:36........................234
1:49........................194
2:4..........................244
2:11........................193
2:12-23......... 193, 235
3................ 226, 303
3:1-21......................121
3:3............... 226, 234
3:5............... 226, 303
3:6..........................226
3:7..........................187
3:13-16......................77
3:14-15..................303
3:14-16..................104
3:15-16......... 188, 193
3:16.....53, 72-73, 129,
          134, 163, 184
3:16-18..................303
3:17................. 53, 69
3:17-18......... 158, 303
3:18.........193-94, 256
3:19................. 73, 96
3:27-30..................234
3:29..........................47
3:36............... 188, 193
4:9-10.....................235

4:24........................245
4:39........................193
4:42 ...53, 129, 158-59,
               184, 229
5:17-18....................86
5:20........................194
5:21........................257
5:23........................194
5:24 ... 44, 70, 187, 307
5:25.............. 194, 303
5:25-29..................307
5:28........................187
5:28-29..................153
5:31-47..................247
5:33........................234
5:36........................247
5:38........................152
6:1-14....................235
6:4-14....................235
6:29........................193
6:33........................257
6:35.............. 193, 235
6:39-40..................144
6:44........................144
6:51-58..................235
6:54........................144
6:55..........................95
6:56........... 86, 93, 301
6:58........................186
6:63........................257
6:70........................175
7:2-24....................235
7:7................... 52, 129
7:13..........................49
7:17........................104
7:18..........................68
7:30........................244
7:37........................104
7:37-38..................235
7:37-39..................303
8:12 .... 60, 63, 96, 129,
               133, 235

8:17 246
8:19 101
8:20 244
8:21-30 .... 52, 69, 77
8:24 .... 77, 263
8:31-38 77
8:37-47 185-86
8:39-47 .... 121, 175
8:44 .... 69, 130, 173,
                    186, 206
8:48-59 235
8:51 70
8:51-52 86
8:54-55 101
9:5 .... 96, 129, 133
9:22 .... 26, 49, 79
9:35-41 77
9:39 136
9:39-41 .... 99, 263
9:41 66
10:1-18 185
10:9-10 188
10:11-18 188
10:15 288
10:16 159
10:17-18 288
10:22-39 .... 86, 235
10:25 86
10:28 257
10:30 .... 86, 260
10:36 .... 194, 303
10:37-38 260
10:38 .... 86, 301
10:40-41 234
11:4 .... 194, 303
11:22 192
11:24 144
11:25 .... 235, 260
11:25-26 188
11:27 .... 158, 194
11:50 158
11:52 303

12:12-19 235
12:20-26 159
12:23 244
12:25 153
12:27 244
12:31 ....52-53, 136,
                    206, 259
12:31-32 307
12:32 104
12:35 61
12:35-36 ...... 60, 63, 96
12:42 .... 26, 49
12:44-50 188
12:45-46 60
12:46 .... 96, 133
13 73
13-17 .... 216, 235
13-21 73
13:1 244
13:1-17 235
13:2 .... 173, 175
13:10 171
13:14 41
13:27 .... 173, 206
13:34 ....33, 94-95,
                    184-85, 232
13:34-35 .... 30, 104,
              184, 235, 239, 274,
                    301, 311
14 149
14-17 177
14:6 ...... 151, 188, 190,
                    260
14:7 .... 36, 101
14:7-11 260
14:10 230
14:10-11 301
14:13 256
14:13-14 192
14:15 .... 86, 103, 232
14:15-17 121
14:15-31 29

14:16 .... 145, 148-49
14:16-17 212
14:16-31 235
14:17 ..53, 212-13, 245
14:18 121
14:21 86
14:23-24 .... 70, 86
14:25-31 216
14:26 ..29, 145, 148-49
14:27 186
14:30 .... 53, 206, 259
15 .... 50, 85, 301
15:1-10 47
15:1-11 86
15:1-17 185
15:3 .... 70, 171
15:4 301
15:4-5 93
15:4-7 .... 93, 301
15:7 .... 152, 192, 256
15:9-17 187
15:10 85-86
15:11 47
15:12 ....85, 184-85,
              232, 239, 301, 311
15:12-13 ...188-89, 274
15:12-14 .... 30, 311
15:12-17 235
15:13 .... 95, 188, 311
15:16 192
15:17 ....184-85, 232,
                    274, 301
15:18 .... 53, 129
15:18-25 187
15:18-27 77
15:18-16:4 129
15:19 225
15:19-23 260
15:20 86
15:21 113
15:22 66
15:22-24 69

15:23-25 129
15:24 66
15:26 ..... 213, 216, 245
15:26-27 212
16 149
16:2 .... 26, 49
16:4-15 29
16:5-15 235
16:7 .... 145, 149
16:7-11 216
16:8 53
16:8-9 .... 69, 77
16:11 .... 53, 206, 259
16:12-13 152
16:12-14 216
16:13 .... 29, 149,
     212-13, 245
16:20-22 47
16:23 192
16:23-24 .... 192, 256
16:24 47
16:27 76
17 51
17:1 244
17:2 257
17:3 .... 101, 153
17:6 86
17:6-25 235
17:11 230
17:11-15 259
17:13 47
17:14 129
17:15-16 230
17:21 121
17:21-23 230
17:25-26 101
17:26 311
18-19 239
18:2 78
18:5 78
18:11 239
18:36 239

19:11 .... 66, 78
19:13-16 309
19:14 309
19:28-37 235
19:33 245
19:34..30, 235, 245, 303
19:35 41
20:18 159
20:30-31 ..... 48-49, 104
20:31 .... 33, 151, 188
     241, 247, 253
20:28 ..... 158, 177, 260
20:30 194
20:30-31 248
20:31 .... 33, 151
21:24 41

Acts
..............................197
1:8 216
2:1 216
2:4 216
2:17 144-45
2:17-21 .... 112, 115
2:42 .... 36, 50
2:43-47 197
2:45 198
4:12 289
4:17 289
4:27 148
4:30 .... 113, 289
4:32-37 197
4:34 198
5:1-11 263
5:42 159
5:9 217
6:1-8:1 216
8:4-40 216
8:12 289
8:29-39 216
9 235
9:3-9 177

9:20 303
9:21 289
9:22 159
9:28 289
10:1-11:18 216
10:9-16 177
10:19 216
10:38 148
10:43 289
11:12 216
11:27-30 198
11:29-30 198
12:9 95
13-28 235
13:1 207
13:33 49
13:52 47
14:21 103
14:23 271
15:2-6 271
15:3 289
15:22-23 271
16:4-15 277
16:6-10 216
16:18 289
18:24-28 159
18:27 310
19:18 79
19:29 287
20:4 287
20:17 271
20:35 198
20:38 289
21:1-6 216
21:5 289
22:16 289
26:9 289

Romans
..............................271
1:1 .... 137, 197
1:3 49

1:4 303
1:7 273
1:8-15 273
1:21 78
1:24 137
2:6-8 103
2:19 60
2:26 86
3:9 78
3:23 78
3:24-25 78
3:25 65
4:25 78
5:6-9 159
5:21 78
6 125
6:4 61
6:17 137
6:19 78
6:20 137
7:15 78
7:25 78
8 217
8:1 121
8:1-2 303
8:1-17 303
8:9 .... 121, 303
8:9-10 78
8:11 303
8:14 ....121, 302-3
8:15 121
8:16 302
8:17 303
8:18-21 250
8:19 302
8:21 302
8:34 71
8:38 206
9:8 302
9:26 302
10:9-10 79
12:2 .... 78, 136

12:5 51
12:9-21 279
12:10 301
12:13 277
12:21 291
13:8 301
13:8-10 103
13:12 .... 60, 130
14:15 61
14:17 106
15:23-24 277
15:24 289
15:25-29 198
15:26 50
16:5 277
16:23 287

1 Corinthians
.... 235, 271
1:3 273
1:4-5 101
1:8-9 121
1:9 67
1:10-17 20
1:10–4:21 235
1:14 287
1:18-20 135-36
1:22-23 50
1:30 235
2:4-5 235
2:6-16 217
2:10-16 235
2:12 135
3:1-23 20
3:11 52
3:16 235
4:16 293
5 164
5:1-5 263
5:1-13 20
5:1–7:40 235
5:5 307

5:7 65
5:9 310
5:11 118
6:1-20 20
6:11 235
6:19 235
7:1 310
7:15 97
7:19 103
7:26 307
7:31 .... 133, 136
8:1 101
8:10 101
10:1-13 291
10:11 144
10:13 67
11:1 293
11:1–14:40 236
11:17-22 236
11:32 136
12 .... 217, 236
12:1-11 236
12:3 .... 207, 217
12:12-13 236
12:12-31 51
12:28 207
13 236
13:12 101
13:13 .... 50, 236
15 .... 147, 236, 307
15:3 159
15:7 236
15:11 236
15:17 236
15:20 307
15:23 307
15:24 236
15:34 236
15:50-57 236
15:58 236
16:1-4 198
16:3 310

16:6 289
16:19 277

2 Corinthians
1:1 97
1:2 273
1:14 307
1:16 289
1:19 303
1:20-22 121
2:3-4 310
2:5-11 263
2:13 97
5:17 .... 78, 307
5:17-19 159
5:21 78
6:14 .... 60, 172
6:14–7:1 174
8–9 198
8:5 186
8:18 97
8:22-23 97
9:1-15 198
9:13 50
11:3-4 217
13:1 246

Galatians
.... 147, 235
1:3 273
1:3-4 .... 159, 250
1:6-10 19
2:10 198
2:20 .... 78, 159, 303
3:1-5 .... 19, 217
3:26 302
3:29 302
4:3 135
4:7 303
4:8-20 20
4:25 272
4:28 302

5:14 103
5:15-21 103
5:16-21 .... 131, 137
5:16-26 217
5:22 47
6:1-2 263
6:11 250
6:13 86
6:14 250
6:15 307

Ephesians
1:15-16 265
1:19-20 49
1:21 .... 206, 217
1:23 51
2:2 61
3:10 .... 206, 217
3:20 192
4:13 303
4:14 157
4:22 137
4:27 175
5:1 293
5:2 61
5:6 157
5:8-14 96
6:10 119
6:10-11 175
6:12 .... 206, 217
6:22 118
6:23 292

Philippians
..........................47
1:1 .... 137, 197
1:2 273
1:5 50
1:23 130
1:27–2:18 20
2:1 50
2:1-8 197

2:5-8 49
2:15 302
2:28 118
4:7 86

Colossians
..........................308
1:9-10 265
1:15-20 51
1:16 .... 206, 217
1:19 49
2:2 121
2:6-7 122
2:8 .... 135, 250
2:10 250
2:12 250
2:15 .... 206, 217, 250
2:20 135
3:7 61
4:5 61
4:8 118
4:15 277
4:16 310

1 Thessalonians
.... 133, 271
1:6 293
2:14 293
2:17 137
2:19 307
3:13 170
5:2 307
5:4-8 96
5:9-10 159
5:19-22 206
5:23 170
5:24 67

2 Thessalonians
.... 133, 271, 292
1:11 265
2 145

2:1 307
2:2 310
2:3 207
2:3-4 172
2:3-12 174
2:4 157
2:7-8 172
2:8-9 157
2:9 307
3:3 .... 67, 86
3:6-13 291
3:7 292
3:9 292
3:14-15 263

1 Timothy
1:2 273
1:10 263
1:19-20 263
3:2 279
3:6-7 175
3:15 277
4:1 214
4:1-2 .... 157, 217
4:2 263
5:1-2 112
5:17-19 271
5:19 246
6:3 152
6:9-10 137
6:14 .... 86, 103

2 Timothy
1:2 273
1:13 152
2:8 49
2:26 175
3:1 144
3:12-15 157
4:3-5 152
4:15 86

Titus
.... 97
1:1 197
1:4 36
1:8 279
1:9 152
2:1-8 .... 112, 115
3:7 303
3:13 .... 277, 289

Philemon
.... 271, 310
12 118
2 277
3 273

Hebrews
1:2 145
1:3 .... 49, 78
1:4 206
1:5 49
1:9 148
1:14 206
2:17 78
3:12-14 122
4:14 303
4:15-5:2 78
5:5 49
6:4-6 264
6:9-12 122
6:11 137
6:12 293
7:25 78
8:8-12 101
9:12-14 65
9:23-10:18 78
9:26 144
9:28 78
10:16-17 101
10:19-22 65
10:22 122
10:23 67

10:28 246
10:28-29 263-64
12:16-17 264
13:2 .... 279, 281
13:7 292-93
13:16 50
13:18 265

James
.... 271
1:1 197
1:5-8 192
1:17 60
1:22 103
1:27 136
2:14-15 198
2:14-18 103
2:15 97
2:19 86
4:4 .... 136, 138
4:7 175
4:16 132
5:3 144
5:7-8 .... 170, 307
5:13 265
5:13-20 263
5:14 271
5:15-16 265
5:16 .... 79, 263
5:19-20 263

1 Peter
.... 271
1:2 272
1:4 137
1:13-16 196
1:14 137
1:20 144-45
1:22 301
2:9 .... 60, 196
2:10 137
2:11 137

2:12 293
2:15-16 293
2:16 197
3:9-14 291
3:13 293
3:17 293
4:2 137
4:7-19 307
4:9 279
5:1-5 ..... 112, 115
5:1-9 175
5:2 175
5:6 175
5:6-11 122
5:8 175
5:12 95
5:13 272
5:14 292

2 Peter
1:1 197
1:2 272
1:4 136
1:16 ...... 170, 307
1:18 42
2:1 207
2:9 230
2:10 137
2:18 137
2:20 136
3:2 152
3:3 144
3:4 170
3:10 307
3:12 170

Jude
.................97
2 272
17 152
20 152

Revelation
...... 119, 134, 302, 305
1:5 65
2:2 .... 41, 207
2:3 113
2:18 194
2:20 157
3:7 .... 49, 148
4:1-11 177
5:1 177
5:2 249
5:5 49
5:6 .... 186, 249
5:9 186
5:9-10 249
5:12 186
6:4 186
6:9 186
6:15-17 171
7:14 307
12-13 145
12:9 .... 157, 213
12:17 ...... 86, 272
13:3 186
13:8 186
16:13 ...... 157, 207
18:11-14 137
18:14 130
18:20 41
19:20 ...... 207, 157
20:2-3 157
20:4-5 307
20:8 157
20:10 ...... 157, 207
20:11-15 307
21-22 307
21:1-4 177
21:5 177
21:14 41
22:16 49

APOCRYPHA

2 Esdras (4 Ezra)
.................302

1 Maccabees
1:54 156
1:59 156
14:16-19 310

2 Maccabees
1:11 273
6:3-5 156
6:18-21 156
7:15-26 156

Sirach
2:1 70
3:1 70
24:3 300
24:8 300

Wisdom
7:25 300
7:27 300

PSEUDEPIGRAPHA

Apocalypse of Abraham
.................302
24:3-5 186

Apocalypse of Moses
15-20 173

Apocalypse of Zephaniah
4:2-7 173
10:1-5 173

Ascension of Isaiah
..............................302

1 Enoch.................302
40:7 173

2 Enoch.................302

3 Enoch.................302

Jubilees
1:17 300
1:20 173
1:26 300
11:5 173
48:15 173
48:18 173

Life of Adam and Eve
9-17 173

Testament of Benjamin
7:1-5 186

Testament of Dan
5:4-6 172
6:1-6 172

Testament of Judah
20:1-2 206

QUMRAN
CD 5.21–6.2 62
CD 8.13 151
CD 13.11-13...........115
1QH 12 [4].10 62
1QH 12 [4].16 62
1QH 12 [4].7-12 157
1QH 15 [7].7 61
1QH 18 [10].29 60
1QpHab 2.1-2. 62, 151

1QpHab 5.11 62
1QpHab 12.4-5 115
1QS 1.9-10 60
1QS 3.13-14 207
1QS 3.13-15 206
1QS 3.17-19 61
1QS 3.20 60
1QS 3.20-24 172
1QS 3.24–4.26 60
1QS 4.9 172
1QS 4.9-10 157
1QS 4.17 172
1QS 4.19 172
1QS 5.2 172
1QS 5.4-5 131
1QS 5.20-21 207
1QS 5.25 61
1QS 6.13-24 115
1QS 7.18 61
1QS 8.15 61
1QSa 1.6-19 115

CHRISTIAN TEXTS

Athanasius 251

Augustine ...138, 190,
    218, 251, 266-67

Biblical Manuscripts
Codex Vaticanus
..................................275
Latin Vulgate 210,
    246, 309
LXX (Septuagint)
...... 40, 72, 112, 128,
    137, 148, 170, 173,
    186, 290, 300
Mount Athos Codex
1739 210

Chalcedonian Creed
..................................218

Clement of Alexandria..........251
About the Pasch 210

Didache
10.6 136
11.1-12 207
11.3-12 207
11.4-12 207
12 277
12.1 207
16.3-4 172

Epistle of Barnabas
4.1-4 172
14.5 172
15.7 172
18.2 172

Eusebius
Ecclesiastical History
3.39.3-4 33

Gregory of Nyssa
..................................251

Ignatius of Antioch
To the Ephesians
7.2 52
17.1 206
To the Magnesians
5.2 136
To the Philadelphians
6.2 206
To the Romans
7.1-2 136
To the Smyrnaeans
1-3 304
1-7 31

5.2 52
10.1 289
12.2 292
To the Trallians
9–10 .... 31, 304

Irenaeus 52, 308
Against Heresies
1.26.1 31
3 .... 31, 210
3.18.7 251
5.1.1 42

Montanus 220

Nicene Creed 218

Origen..........251, 308
Commentary on
Romans
8 210

Polycarp
To the Philippians
7.1 52
9.1 42

Prisca and
Maximilla 220

Shepherd of
Hermas
Mandates
4.31.1-6 266
11.1-4 207
11.7 207
11.7-16 207

Tertullian 52, 220,
251, 308

OTHER SOURCES

Cerinthus 31, 32,
304
Cicero 310-11

Demosthenes
Orations
3.3-4 192

Gnostic texts.........60

Greco-Roman
rhetoric...............112

Greek literature...24

Hermetic texts 60

Mani.....................218

Nag Hammadi.....308
Gospel of Thomas ...308
Gospel of Truth.......308

Papyri.......... 270, 310

Plato... 22, 50, 52, 308

Seneca 310-11

Tacitus
Agricola
45 42

Zoroastrian texts
..................................60

The Author

J. E. (Jay) McDermond was born and raised in rural Central Pennsylvania. At age 18 he was converted at a Dave Wilkerson Rally in Harrisburg, Pennsylvania, and the following year he enrolled at Messiah College, Grantham, Pennsylvania. He first learned of Anabaptism there, and was surprised to learn that other Christians also held to a "peace position." He is quick to note, however, that he is a "pacifist by choice, not nature." He came to this conviction through reading the Sermon on the Mount.

Upon graduating from Messiah College (1976), Jay attended Mennonite Biblical Seminary, Elkhart, Indiana, and earned his M. Div. in 1979. After serving as the pastor of the Nappanee Brethren in Christ Church, Nappanee, Indiana (1979-1982), he studied at the University of Durham (England) and was awarded a M.Litt. in 1989. He received his D.Min. degree from Pittsburgh Theological Seminary, Pittsburgh, Pennsylvania (1998).

In addition to serving at the Nappanee BIC Church, Jay had a "lay pastoral" role at the Roseglen Brethren in Christ Church (Duncannon, PA, 1975-1976) and was the youth pastor at the Pine Street Presbyterian Church (Harrisburg, PA, 1974-1975). He also served as the pastor of the Clydebank Central Church, Clydebank, Scotland (2001-2002). Ordained as a Brethren in Christ minister with special assignment at Messiah College, he has taught there since 1987. He is the professor of Christian Ministry and Spirituality. He has also taught in England (Sunderland Polytechnic, 1984-1985) and Kenya (Daystar University College, 1992-1993).

Jay and his wife, Wanda Thuma-McDermond, are members of the Grantham Brethren in Christ Church. In 1981-82 he served as a board member of Mennonite Central Committee, Great Lakes. He has also provided pulpit supply for a number of congregations fac-

341

ing senior pastor interims. McDermond has written many essays, articles, and book reviews for both scholarly and popular publications. This commentary is his first book.

Jay and Wanda have two children, Malcolm and Duncan. Both sons are competitive swimmers, and so he spends considerable amounts of his time around swimming pools. He also enjoys reading novels and crime fiction by British writers and watching English Premier League Football (soccer): "H'way, Newcastle!"

1, 2, 3 JOHN

"McDermond weaves the Gospel of John throughout his analysis of the Epistles of John, providing an additional degree of comprehensiveness and cohesion; after reading this commentary, one feels one knows Johannine thought more thoroughly overall."—*Lynn H. Cohick, Associate Professor of New Testament, Wheaton College*

"McDermond's treatment is extremely thorough, providing the reader with a wealth of information. At the same time, the lively interplay between the text in its biblical context and the text in the life of the church reveals his concern for relating this material to the needs and issues facing the 21st-century church."—*Robert Smith, Pastor, First Mennonite Church, Iowa City, Iowa*

"This commentary promises to be a helpful resource for pastors and anyone else who seeks to better understand the Epistles of John and untangle its complexities. The author's liberal use of visual diagrams brings greater clarity to what could be some confusing sections."—*Pauline C. Allison Peifer, Executive Pastor, Grantham Brethren in Christ Church, Grantham, Pennsylvania*

"McDermond provides new and intriguing insights into these epistles. With careful attention to the authenticity of the text, he offers a commentary characterized by clarity, relevance, and wisdom. Serious students and dedicated teachers of the Scriptures should enthusiastically embrace McDermond's contribution." —*Kim S. Phipps, President, Messiah College*